Attachment Across the Life Cycle

It has long been suspected that many of the common psychiatric and social problems of adult life have their roots in the early relationship between the child and its mother. Out of the infant's first experiences of attachment stem expectations and assumptions which will colour all subsequent relationships – for good or ill. To explain this simple observation, and to examine the part which these patterns of attachment play in the causation of psychiatric and social problems, a body of knowledge has sprung up which owes much to the pioneering work of the late John Bowlby.

This volume draws together recent theoretical contributions, research findings, and clinical data from seventeen psychiatrists, psychologists, sociologists, and ethologists from four countries. Their work has confirmed the importance of the earlier work and extended it to look at attachment throughout the life cycle. New findings add to our understanding of topics as diverse as agoraphobia, pathological grief, disorders of 'holding', family dynamics, depression, and the special vulnerability of people who grow up in an 'enterprise culture'.

Attachment Across the Life Cycle contains a postscript by John Bowlby and will be of interest to all those fascinated by the psychology of human relationships and concerned with solving the problems to which they give rise.

Colin Murray Parkes is Senior Lecturer in Psychiatry at the London Hospital Medical College, University of London. Joan Stevenson-Hinde is, at present, with the Medical Research Council Unit on the Development and Integration of Behaviour, University of Cambridge. Peter Marris is Professor of Social Planning at the Graduate School of Architecture and Urban Planning, University of California.

D0075270

Attachment Across the Life Cycle

Edited by

Colin Murray Parkes,

Joan Stevenson-Hinde

and

Peter Marris

Tavistock/Routledge

London and New York

First published in 1991
by Routledge
11 New Fetter Lane, London EC4P 4EE

Simultaneously published in the USA and Canada
by Routledge
a division of Routledge, Chapman and Hall Inc.
29 West 35th Street, New York, NY 10001

© 1991 The Tavistock Institute of Medical Psychology

Typeset in Times Roman by Leaper & Gard Ltd, Bristol
Printed and bound in Great Britain by
Mackays of Chatham PLC, Chatham, Kent

British Library Cataloguing in Publication Data
Attachment across the life cycle.
    1. Children. Interpersonal relationships. Psychological
aspects
I. Parkes, Colin Murray   II. Stevenson-Hinde, Joan
III. Marris, Peter
155.418

Library of Congress Cataloging in Publication Data
Attachment across the life cycle / editors, Colin Murray Parkes, Joan
    Stevenson-Hinde, Peter Marris.
    p.   cm.
    Includes bibliographical references and index.
    1. Attachment behavior. 2. Developmental psychology.
    3. Psychology, Pathological. 4. Parent and child. I. Parkes,
    Colin Murray.   II. Stevenson-Hinde, J. (Joan)   III. Marris,
    Peter.
    BF575.A86A77   1991
    155.9'24–dc20

ISBN 0-415-05650-0

Contents

Contributors

Ainsworth, Prof. M.D. Salter, Professor Emeritus of Psychology and Behavioral Medicine and Psychiatry, University of Virginia, USA.

Bifulco, Dr A., Sociologist, Dept of Social Policy & Social Sciences, Royal Holloway and Bedford New College, University of London, UK.

Bowlby, Dr J., was Honorary Consultant Psychiatrist, Child & Family Dept, The Tavistock Clinic, London, UK.

Bretherton, Prof. I., Professor of Child & Family Studies, University of Wisconsin–Madison, USA.

Byng-Hall, Dr J., Consultant Psychiatrist, Child & Family Dept, The Tavistock Clinic, London, UK.

Eichberg, Dr C.G., Columbia Associates in Psychiatry, USA.

Grossmann, Prof. Dr K.E., Professor of Psychology, University of Regensburg, FRG.

Grossmann, Dr Karin, Psychologist, University of Regensburg, FRG.

Harris, Mrs T., Sociologist, Dept of Social Policy & Social Sciences, Royal Holloway and Bedford New College, University of London, UK.

Hinde, Prof. R.A., Royal Society Research Professor & Honorary Director, Medical Research Council Unit on the Development and Integration of Behaviour, University of Cambridge, UK.

Hopkins, Mrs J., Psychotherapist, Child & Family Dept, The Tavistock Clinic, London, UK.

Liotti, Dr G., Psychiatrist, Association for Research on the Psychopathology of the Attachment System (ARPAS), Rome, Italy.

Main, Prof. M., Professor of Psychology, Dept of Psychology, University of California at Berkeley, USA.

Marris, Prof. P., Professor of Social Planning, Graduate School of Architecture & Urban Planning, University of California at Los Angeles, USA.

Parkes, Dr C.M., Senior Lecturer in Psychiatry, the London Hospital Medical College, University of London, UK.

Radke-Yarrow, Dr M., Chief of Laboratory of Developmental Psychology, National Institute of Mental Health, Bethesda, Md., USA.

Stevenson-Hinde, Dr J., Senior Scientific Officer, Medical Research Council Unit on the Development and Integration of Behaviour, University of Cambridge, UK.

Weiss, Prof. R.S., Professor of Sociology, Work & Family Research Unit, University of Massachusetts, Boston, USA.

Introduction

The human infant's attachment to its mother (or other primary caregiver) is a prerequisite for survival and a test-bed for all the other attachments he or she will make. Out of this first relationship stems a set of expectations and assumptions which will influence subsequent relationships – and which will not easily be changed – or so attachment theory and the research which spawned it implies. If this theory is correct then we can expect it to shed light not only on the interpersonal problems which can bedevil individual and family life, but also the very essence of the large scale societies to which we belong.

In recent years two researchers have done more than anyone else to bring these issues to our attention and to provide us with the ideas and tools that we need; they are John Bowlby and Mary Ainsworth. The publication of the three volumes of Bowlby's impressive work *Attachment and Loss* (in 1969, 1973, and 1980) and of Ainsworth's reports of her 'strange situation' (Ainsworth and Wittig 1969; Ainsworth *et al.* 1978) established a new frame of reference for future work in this field.

Since then other researchers in many parts of the world and from many disciplines have been encouraged to follow up and develop their approaches. The result has been an accumulation of knowledge about a range of phenomena which had not previously been linked. The field enlightens our thinking about animal behaviour, child development, dynamic psychiatry, interpersonal psychology, sociology, and other areas.

Several attempts have been made to draw these researchers together, including two workshops which were hosted by the King Edward VII Memorial Fund in London during 1981 and 1988. The aims of these workshops were twofold: to facilitate the interchange of ideas between researchers and to produce a book which would represent and update the state of attachment theory and the practice which had arisen out of it. Thus they are both very much more than a routine report of a conference.

The first volume was entitled *The Place of Attachment in Human Behaviour* (eds Parkes and Stevenson-Hinde 1982). It demonstrated clearly the impressive body of knowledge which had grown out of the earlier work and it stimulated the interest of other researchers. Consequently, the second workshop and the much larger conference which followed it drew together a new and much augmented group. They had been carefully chosen and brought from all parts of the world with the help of the royalties from the first volume. The publication of this second volume comes shortly after the sad news of John Bowlby's death. It constitutes a fitting memorial to his genius.

In recent years, follow-up of the children whose attachment behaviour was systematically observed in infancy many years ago has made it possible to examine the effects of secure and insecure attachments. At the same time an increasing number of retrospective studies have highlighted the importance of attachments arising and continuing at later stages across the life cycle.

The most significant research falls into three categories: studies which throw light on the *nature* of attachment, studies which elucidate various *patterns* of attachment, and studies which show how our understanding of attachments can enlighten our *clinical* management of psychiatric problems. The book has been divided into three parts to cover these types of study. We start with a review of the history of attachment theory as seen through the eyes of Inge Bretherton. Her concise summary will provide readers who are not well versed in the field with an introduction to its basic concepts. This chapter is followed by a contribution from one of the pioneers, Mary Ainsworth. She anatomizes love, defining and clarifying the distinctions between 'attachments', 'bonds', 'socializing', and other terms used in characterizing relationships. This is not pedantry, but the beginning of a process of dissection and analysis which is essential if we are to think clearly about attachment and its consequences.

The process of analysis is continued by Robert Hinde and Joan Stevenson-Hinde, who distinguish three desiderata which influence and are influenced by attachments: biological fitness, cultural norms (and values), and psychological well-being. Any of these may conflict with any or both of the others. All three need to be taken into account in explaining the findings of recent research in different parts of the world.

In Chapter 4 Robert Weiss shows how the bonds which arise in adolescence and adult life develop out of the attachments of childhood. In normal circumstances, the waning of attachment to parents in adolescence is associated with the development of new bonds to partners first and then to children. But the way is strewn with pitfalls.

Concluding Part I, Peter Marris elucidates the central part which attachment plays at the interface between sociology and psychology. He examines how, in their attempt to achieve security for themselves and for those who are attached to them, the more powerful members of society consistently seek to control the uncertainty in the behaviour of others, without constraining their own freedom. This inequality of control tends to displace the burden of uncertainty onto the weakest, and profoundly influences the circumstances of attachment, leaving the most vulnerable at most risk of depression, helplessness, and other pathological griefs. At the same time, attachment plays a crucial part in shaping our sense of what constitutes good relationship between members of society. Contemporary British and American culture is caught between a general commitment to social welfare and a competitive pattern of managing uncertainty which can be deeply destructive.

The next four chapters examine the qualities of parenting which may contribute to different patterns of attachment as revealed in the Ainsworth 'strange situation' (Ainsworth *et al.* 1978). Such patterns may predict aspects of later development, including the quality of relationships made with others.

The Grossmanns have demonstrated the temporal stability of patterns of attachment in German samples, by following up children from infancy to middle childhood. Their work includes fathers, and suggests how fathers may mitigate negative influences within the family. Patterns of attachment to mother are strong predictors of the quality of peer relationships as well as the existence of behaviour problems. Their careful research warns us not to expect to find simple solutions to complex problems.

Marian Radke-Yarrow focuses on a group of mothers who are very likely to have problems in relating to their children – mothers with clinical depression. It comes as no surprise to find that these mothers do often have insecurely attached children. She then looks beyond this statistical association to ask, what are the particular features of this heterogeneous group which foster insecure attachments? The answers that emerge move us towards an understanding of the roots of vulnerability.

So too does Mary Main in her chapter on the consequences of secure and insecure patterns of attachment on the developing thought processes of the child. In particular she examines how they influence the growing child's ability to recall early memories and to comprehend the privacy of thoughts. Turning to the thought process of the parents she demonstrates how incoherent, multiple models of experience and implausible ideation are associated with insecure attachments.

Clinicians are very familiar with the idea that problems can be passed from generation to generation, but we need to know a great deal more about this cycle if we are to help people to break it. In Chapter 9 Mary Ainsworth and Carolyn Eichberg reveal a close association between a particularly problematic pattern of attachment and a history of unresolved mourning in the parent. The histories which they report indicate that the failure to resolve mourning may itself be a reflection of the insecure attachments which had preceded the loss. It remains to be seen whether or not support given to people at the time of loss can reduce this risk.

The remaining chapters of the book look at the psychiatric problems which are now thought to result from problems in attachment and the implications of attachment theory for the treatment of these problems.

In Chapter 10 Juliet Hopkins looks at a very special type of problem which can arise among parents who cannot bear to hold their children. Her sensitive and logical case studies demonstrate how a therapist can accustom children who have been deprived of holding to being held. In doing so the children are enabled to break out of a pattern which, once established, can be self-perpetuating.

Moving to a wider perspective John Byng-Hall shows how an understanding of attachment can enlighten the practice of family therapy. Acting as a 'secure base' for each family member, Byng-Hall explores attachment-related issues. His chapter illustrates well the practical implications of attachment theory.

The two most frequent problems to present in a psychiatric setting are pathological anxiety and depression. The first of these often presents as agoraphobia which is redefined by Giovanni Liotti as a fear of separation from sources of security. In Chapter 12 Liotti shows how certain types of insecure attachment in childhood can predispose to agoraphobia later in life. He then spells out the implications of this understanding for the treatment of the problem.

Our understanding of depression has been greatly advanced by the work of Brown and Harris, whose book *Social Origins of Depression* (1978) showed that vulnerable women often develop clinical levels of depression after experiencing losses or other major life events. Yet their work left many questions unanswered – how does loss of a mother in childhood increase vulnerability, what are the crucial aspects of parenting which influence later depression, and can these be comprehended by means of a particular theory? In Chapter 13 Tirril Harris and Antonia Bifulco re-analyse the data from the earlier study to test out the extent to which a theory model derived from John Bowlby fits the findings obtained. They conclude that these data do in fact fit the theory remarkably well.

A life event which has particular relevance to attachment is bereavement, the loss by death of a loved person. In Chapter 14 Colin Murray Parkes analyses how a series of people who had sought psychiatric help after bereavement perceived their childhood relationship with their parents. These retrospective data confirm the importance of attachment theory and the related theories of learned helplessness and learned fear as explanatory hypotheses for later problems. He suggests that a desirable consequence of secure parenting is the development in the child of a reasonable degree of trust in oneself and others. Lack of either or both of these types of trust can have lasting effects on the relationships which then develop in adult life and contribute to the type of grief which results from the loss of such relationships.

The book ends with a postscript from the father of attachment theory,

John Bowlby. This was written shortly before his death. In summing up the findings reported in preceding chapters he drew attention to the misunderstandings which have bedevilled our thinking about love relationships in the past. He concluded that

> The urge to keep proximity is to be respected, valued, and nurtured as making for potential strength, instead of being looked down upon, as so often hitherto, as a sign of inherent weakness. This radical shift in valuation, with its far-reaching influence on how we perceive and treat other people, especially those whose attachment needs have been and still are unmet, is, I believe, the single most important consequence of the change of conceptual framework.

ACKNOWLEDGEMENTS

The editors wish to thank all of those whose critical comments and suggestions helped to make this book more than just a 'report of a conference'. In particular they appreciate the help of those who took part in the 1987 workshop, whether or not they contributed a chapter to the book, and the members of John Bowlby's Research Seminar who have inspired and helped to develop many of the ideas and research projects in this field.

The workshop and this book could not have been undertaken without the support of the King Edward VII Fund.

We thank the American Psychological Association for permission to reprint in Chapter 2 the substance of a paper by Mary Ainsworth which was published in *American Psychologist* for April 1989, also the *Journal of Child Psychotherapy* for permission to reprint in Chapter 10 a shortened version of a paper by Juliet Hopkins which was first published in Volume 13 (1987) Number 1 of that journal. Finally we thank the US National Institute of Mental Health for permission to publish, in Chapter 7, the results of research by Marian Radke-Yarrow which was carried out under their auspices.

REFERENCES

Ainsworth, M.D.S. and Wittig, B.A. (1969) 'Attachment and the exploratory behaviour of one-year-olds in a strange situation', in B.M. Foss (ed.) *Determinants of Infant Behaviour*, vol. 4, London: Methuen.

Ainsworth, M.D., Blehar, M.C., Waters, E., and Wall, S. (1978) *Patterns of Attachment*, Hillsdale, N.J.: Erlbaum.

Bowlby, J. (1969, 2nd edn 1982) *Attachment and Loss*, vol. 1: *Attachment*, London: Hogarth and New York: Basic Books.

Bowlby, J. (1973) *Attachment and Loss*, vol. 2: *Separation: Anxiety and Anger*, London: Hogarth and New York: Basic Books.

Bowlby, J. (1980) *Attachment and Loss*, vol. 3: *Loss: Sadness and Depression*, London: Hogarth and New York: Basic Books.

Brown, G.W. and Harris, T. (1978) *Social Origins of Depression: A Study of Psychiatric Disorder in Women*, London: Tavistock.
Parkes, C. Murray and Stevenson-Hinde, J. (eds) (1982) *The Place of Attachment in Human Behaviour*, London: Tavistock, and New York: Basic Books.

Part I

The Nature of Attachment

Chapter 1

The roots and growing points of attachment theory[1]

Inge Bretherton

Attachment theory in its current form is the joint work of John Bowlby and Mary Ainsworth. John Bowlby, using concepts from ethology, cybernetics, and psychoanalysis, formulated the basic outlines of the theory. We owe to him a new way of thinking about the infant's tie to the mother, and its disruption through separation and deprivation. Mary Ainsworth not only translated the basic tenets of attachment theory into empirical findings, but also helped us to expand the theory itself. Her two major theoretical contributions were the explanation of individual differences in attachment relations and the concept of the caregiver as secure base.

This paper delineates the historical development of attachment theory. It is divided into four parts. First, I show that the basic ideas guiding both protagonists' later contributions have roots in their early professional career. I then go on to discuss the development of the theory, laying out the sequence in which Bowlby proposed its basic postulates at the same time as Mary Ainsworth began to test and expand them in her empirical studies. The third part of the paper is devoted to a brief review of work on the validation and consolidation of attachment theory. Finally, I discuss future directions of attachment theory and research.

ROOTS

John Bowlby

John Bowlby was born in 1907. I am sure that experiences in his childhood must have played a role in directing his interest toward the study of attachment. However, Bowlby himself begins his intellectual autobiography with studies at the University of Cambridge where he read medicine, upon the advice of his surgeon father (see interviews with Senn (1977a) and Smuts (1977)). In his third year of study, John Bowlby became drawn to what would later be known as developmental psychology, and he temporarily gave up plans for a medical career.

After graduation he pursued his newfound interest through volunteer work at two progressive schools, the second a small analytically oriented residential institution that served about 24 maladjusted children, aged 4–18 years. Bowlby is modest about his actual work at the school: 'I don't think I would like to describe what I did – I did my best'. Two children there had an enormous impact on him. One was a very isolated, remote, and affectionless teenager with no experience of a stable mother figure. This child had been expelled from his previous school for stealing. The second child was an anxious boy of 7 or 8 who trailed Bowlby around, and was known as his shadow (Ainsworth 1974). An additional major influence on Bowlby's development was John Alford, one of the other volunteer staff at the school (later a professor of art at Toronto). It was with him that Bowlby spent many hours discussing the effect of early family experience, or lack of it, upon character development (see Senn (1977a)).

By the time Bowlby's volunteer service came to an end, John Alford had successfully persuaded him to resume his medical studies in order to pursue training in child psychiatry and psychotherapy so that he might further pursue his ideas about family influences upon children's development. Bowlby had accepted Alford's advice reluctantly because he did not look forward to the medical training which was required as the passport to psychiatry. A saving grace was his immediate acceptance into the British Psychoanalytic Society as a student-candidate. His analyst there was Joan Riviere who was a friend of and much influenced by Melanie Klein.

Interestingly, training in psychiatry and psychoanalysis provided Bowlby with a reasonably tolerant environment in which to develop his own ideas, but the direct impact on his thinking was relatively small. Much more influential than the analysts and psychiatrists who had been his teachers were two social workers whom he encountered during his stint as a fellow at the London Child Guidance Clinic upon completion of his training. These two individuals shared his ideas about the importance for healthy development of a child's early family experience.

Throughout this period, Bowlby felt very strongly that psychoanalysis was putting far too much emphasis on the child's fantasy world and far too little on actual events. He expressed this view in an interesting paper which already contains many of the ideas which were later to become central to attachment theory (Bowlby 1940). In emphasizing the influence of early family environment on the development of neurosis, he claims (p. 2) that 'psychoanalysts like the nurseryman should study intensively, rigorously, and at first hand (1) the nature of the organism, (2) the properties of the soil and (3) the interaction of the two'. Bowlby dwells on the adverse effects of early separation, advising mothers to visit their young children in hospitals. He suggests that for mothers with parenting difficulties

a weekly interview in which their problems are approached analytically and traced back to childhood has sometimes been remarkably effective. Having once been helped to recognize and recapture the feelings which she herself had as a child and to find that they are accepted tolerantly and understandingly, a mother will become increasingly sympathetic and tolerant toward the same things in her child.

(Bowlby 1940: 23)

This quotation demonstrates that Bowlby's interest in the intergenerational transmission of attachment relations dates from the very beginning of his professional career. The psychoanalytic object relations theories that were later put forth by Fairbairn (1952) and Winnicott (1965) were congenial to Bowlby in a number of ways, but his thinking about parent–child relationships developed independently of them.

Following his own injunction for more rigorous studies, Bowlby used case-notes from his work at the child guidance clinic to prepare the classic paper on 'Forty-four juvenile thieves, their characters and home lives' (published in revised form in 1944). A significant minority of the children turned out to have affectionless characters, a phenomenon Bowlby linked to their histories of maternal deprivation and separation.

During these early years in child psychiatry, Bowlby was also strongly influenced by two economists with whom he shared a house. These academic friends engaged him in frequent debates about the scientific status of psychoanalysis. Bowlby feels that he owes his academic orientation to their searching questions. With one of these friends, Evan Durbin, he wrote a book entitled *Personal Aggressiveness and War* which interestingly (in light of later attachment theory) contains a long section on aggression and social bonds in nonhuman primates (Durbin and Bowlby 1939). Moreover, in seeking corroboration for his ideas from outside psychoanalysis, Bowlby was already using an approach which stood him in good stead when he began to formulate attachment theory.

World War II led to an interruption in Bowlby's budding career as a child psychiatrist, but his development as a scientist continued. The army brought him in contact with several people who later formed the core of the post-war Tavistock Clinic and Institute of Human Relations. The group included psychiatrists, analysts, and psychologists, among them Henry Dicks, Ronald Hargreaves, Wilfred Bion, Adrian Stephen, Jock Sutherland, John Rickman, and Eric Trist. Some of them worked on officer selection procedures. Bowlby's special responsibility was the validation of these procedures, using large-scale survey techniques. As he put it, this experience was 'like doing a Ph.D. thesis in psychology under the guidance of Eric Trist and Jock Sutherland'. In response to their influence he began to rewrite the paper on the 44 juvenile thieves 'in a good deal better form than it had been before' (Senn 1977a). Indeed, the revised paper is noticeably different from Bowlby's earlier work: all the evidence on which his conclusions are based is presented in detail and statistically, not just intuitively, evaluated. Bowlby summarizes the findings thus:

The result has been that certain specifically adverse circumstances have been identified and their significance demonstrated both statistically in the whole group and clinically in a few individual cases. The conclusion has been drawn that, had it not been for certain factors inimical to the healthy development of the capacity for object-love, certain children would not have become offenders.... These findings thus not only confirm the general psychoanalytic thesis that it is the early years which count in character development, but demonstrate beyond doubt that the elucidation of the problem of juvenile delinquency is dependent upon psychoanalytic investigation.

(Bowlby 1944: 53)

Upon returning from army service in 1945, Bowlby became head of the Children's Department at the Tavistock Clinic. In order to highlight the importance of the parent–child relationship, he promptly renamed it the Department for Children and Parents. Unlike most psychoanalysts of his time, Bowlby was deeply interested in finding out the actual patterns of *family* interaction involved in both healthy and pathological development.

Directing the Department for Children and Parents meant running a clinic, undertaking training, and doing research. To Bowlby's chagrin, much of the clinical work in the Department was done by people with a Kleinian orientation who regarded his emphasis on actual family inter-action patterns as not very relevant. Because of this theoretical rift, Bowlby could not use the Department's clinical cases for the research he wanted to pursue. This led him to found his own research unit, not connected to the clinical work going on at the Tavistock.

Mary Ainsworth

Let us now turn to Mary Ainsworth, née Salter. She was born in 1913 in Ohio, but her family soon moved to Toronto where she later attended the University, specializing in psychology. In the course of her early graduate studies, she came under the influence of William Blatz who had developed security theory (Blatz 1940). Blatz subsequently asked her to pursue her doctoral studies with him, helping to further extend Blatz's theory. The resulting dissertation was entitled: 'An Evaluation of Adjustment Based on the Concept of Security'. Mary Salter obtained her Ph.D. in 1939 (the published version appeared in 1940). The collaboration with Blatz was to have a major impact on her future contribution to attachment theory.

Although security theory owed much to Freud, Blatz did not openly acknowledge this link, because of the strong anti-psychoanalytic bias that prevailed at the University of Toronto during this time (Ainsworth 1983). One of the major tenets of security theory is that infants and young children need to develop a secure dependence on parents before launching out into unfamiliar situations where they must cope on their own. Secure dependence provides a basis for learning the skills and developing the knowledge that make it possible to depend confidently on self and gain secure emancipation from parents. Indeed, secure dependence on parents should gradually become supplanted by mature secure dependence on peers, and eventually on a heterosexual partner. Blatz felt that secure independence is an impossibility. In her dissertation, Mary Salter states it this way:

> Familial security in the early stages is of a dependent type and forms a basis from which the individual can work out gradually, forming new skills and interests in other fields. Where familial security is lacking, the individual is handicapped by the lack of what might be called a *secure base* from which to work.

> (Salter 1940: 45; italics mine)

Her dissertation research involved the construction of two self-report paper and pencil scales to assess college students' familial and extrafamilial security, validated against the same students' autobiographical narratives. A classification procedure was used on these scales and related to the narratives, already foreshadowing procedures later used in attachment research.

Upon completion of her dissertation in 1939, Mary Salter became a lecturer at the University of Toronto. The war began shortly thereafter, causing her colleague Blatz to leave Toronto to set up war-time nurseries in Britain. Three years later she decided to join the Canadian Women's Army Corps where, for a short period of time, her work as an army examiner included counseling, testing, interviewing, and history-taking which gave her a taste for clinical work. However, all too soon she was 'dragged to Headquarters for an administrative job' (personal communication, 1989). After post-war work with rehabilitation services, she returned to the University of Toronto where she was asked to teach a course on personality assessment. To prepare for this assignment she volunteered her services in the Veterans Hospital and took workshops with Bruno Klopfer. This training with Klopfer ultimately led to a book on the Rorschach Test with Klopfer (Klopfer *et al.* 1954) which is still in print. In addition, she renewed her collaboration with Bill Blatz to refine the security scales originally devised for her dissertation. Her extensive experience in diagnostics and instrument development was to be important later in the development of attachment classifications.

In 1950 Mary Salter married Leonard Ainsworth, a World War II veteran and graduate student in psychology at Toronto. The Ainsworths decided that Leonard would continue his Ph.D. studies in London rather than Toronto where his wife was on the faculty. Upon arriving in London Mary Ainsworth was without an appointment, but a friend from her army days drew her attention to an advertisement in the London *Times*

Educational Supplement for a position at the Tavistock Clinic. The position happened to involve research, under the direction of John Bowlby, into the effect on personality development of separation from the mother in early childhood. Joining Bowlby's research unit reset the whole direction of Mary Ainsworth's professional career (Ainsworth 1983).

THE DEVELOPMENT OF ATTACHMENT THEORY

Phase 1

Bowlby had chosen to focus the efforts of his research team on a well-circumscribed area: mother–child separation. He did so because separation is a clearcut event that either happens or does not happen. He felt that it would have been too difficult to demonstrate environmental influences on the parent–child relationship by studying its subtler aspects (a task later tackled by Mary Ainsworth).

In 1948, after obtaining his first research funds, Bowlby hired James Robertson to do observations of young children who were hospitalized, institutionalized, or otherwise separated from their parents. During the war years Robertson, a conscientious objector, had been employed in Anna Freud's Hampstead residential nursery as a boilerman. In a moving interview with Milton Senn (1977b), Robertson explained that everyone on the staff at the nursery, regardless of the nature of their work and background, was required by Anna Freud to write up observations about the nursery children on cards that were then used in weekly teaching sessions. As a result of these sessions, Robertson came out of the Hampstead Nurseries with a much more thorough training in child observation than many people get in academic settings. After the war, he became a psychiatric social worker and began psychoanalysis.

At this point I would like to digress for a moment to discuss Bowlby's views regarding the sometimes incompatible attitudes held by researchers and clinical workers (Smuts 1977). Clinicians, says Bowlby, feel that researchers are remote from everyday life, whilst researchers believe that clinicians are fuzzy-headed, inclined to engage in leaps in the dark, hunches, and guesswork. The underlying cause for this difference in attitude is that clinicians have to take action, whereas researchers are able to reflect on a narrow area of study to unravel 'do-able' problems. Clinicians apply a theory, whereas researchers try to test it. Not many people find it congenial to work in both worlds, because doing so requires an often uncomfortable switch in frame of reference. Bowlby did live in both worlds, but solved the problem by performing the different functions in separate buildings.

Robertson found this division of interests difficult. He describes his dilemma as a researcher thus:

My task was to go out from the Tavistock Clinic to places where young children were separated from the mother and to bring back to Dr Bowlby and his colleagues in the Tavistock Clinic my first-hand observations on their behavior.... When on that first morning I walked into the pediatric ward of our parent hospital, I got the most enormous blow of my life ... I was hit by the enormity of it ... but I quickly recognized that this was not witting cruelty. The young children who shouted and screamed were regarded as atypical until they became settled, and uncomplaining.

(Senn 1977b)

After 2 years of collecting data in hospitals, Robertson could not continue as an uninvolved scientist. He felt compelled to do something for the children he had been observing. On a shoestring budget, with a hand-held cinecamera and without artificial light he made the deeply moving film 'A two-year-old goes to hospital' (Robertson and Bowlby 1952; Robertson 1953).

In collaboration with Bowlby, the filming was carefully planned to ensure that no one could later be able to claim that it was biased. Bowlby and Robertson decided to use time sampling, documented by the clock which was always in the picture, to prove that the filmed segments were not specially selected. The film, Bowlby says, was dynamite, even though the child who had been randomly picked for filming was a very self-contained little girl, and not at all like some of the other highly distressed children Robertson had previously observed on his research visits. Not only did this film play a crucial role in the development of attachment theory, but it also helped improve the fate of children in hospitals in Britain and many other parts of the world.

Others working in Bowlby's research team when Mary Ainsworth arrived were (besides James Robertson) Mary Boston and Dina Rosenbluth. Rudolph Schaffer joined the group somewhat later, as did Christoph Heinicke, and Tony Ambrose. Mary Ainsworth (1983) gives credit to Robertson (whom she considered too modest about his data) for teaching her about the value of naturalistic observations. She decided then that she would emulate his method were she ever to undertake a study of her own.

Aside from the work on young children's responses to separation from the mother, a further push for the development of attachment theory came from Geneva. In light of the research on separation then going on at the Tavistock Centre, and Bowlby's earlier article about the 44 affectionless thieves, it is perhaps not surprising that he received and accepted a request by Ronald Hargreaves of the World Health Organization to write a report on the fate of homeless children in post-war Europe. The report was subsequently published (Bowlby 1951) as *Maternal Care and Mental Health* by the World Health Organization. An abridged version complemented (in the second edition) by an extensive review chapter authored by

Mary Ainsworth soon appeared as a Penguin paperback: *Child Care and the Growth of Love* (Bowlby 1953; 2nd edn 1963).

The task of writing the WHO report gave Bowlby an opportunity to talk to many other professionals interested in the adverse effects of maternal separation and deprivation, to read the available literature on these topics, and – most importantly – to organize his ideas on paper. He soon realized that the material he was gathering cried out for a theory that could explain the profound effects of separation and deprivation experiences on young children. Psychoanalytic thinkers had long been interested in these topics, but as Bowlby says 'the theory was a mess. I wanted to contribute to the scientific role of psychoanalysis'.

Inspiration came from unexpected quarters. In 1951 a friend drew Bowlby's attention to Konrad Lorenz's work on imprinting. This had first been published in 1935, but had only now become available in translation. Not quite certain of the scientific respectability of ethology, Bowlby consulted Julian Huxley who was tremendously enthusiastic and lent Bowlby a pre-publication copy of Lorenz's book *King Solomon's Ring* (Lorenz 1957b). 'The more I read of this stuff, the more fascinating I found it', Bowlby remarked (Senn 1977a). He was especially drawn to imprinting as a process underlying the formation of strong social bonds, but not linked to feeding. He also favored the ethological approach in general, because much of the work was based on field observations of animals going about their daily business, an approach that was very compatible with the methods already developed by Robertson. In 1953, he published the first theoretical paper incorporating ideas from ethology.

At this point Bowlby was fortunate to meet Robert Hinde, under whose 'generous and stern guidance' (see Bowlby 1980b: 650) he set about trying to master the principles of ethology in the hope that they might help him gain a deeper understanding of the nature of the child's tie to the mother. In 1954 Robert Hinde began to attend regular seminars at the Tavistock Centre, and later drew Bowlby's attention to Harlow's work with rhesus monkeys (though this came too late to be incorporated in the first paper on attachment theory). The influence was not unidirectional, however. The contact with Bowlby was instrumental in Hinde's decision to study mother–infant interaction and separation in rhesus monkeys that were reared in social groups (Hinde and Spencer-Booth 1967), a fact of which Bowlby is very proud.

Surprisingly, the various empirical papers that Bowlby published with his research team during the same period show no trace of his new thinking, because he was unable to convince them that ethology was relevant to the mother–child relationship (Bowlby, personal communication, September 1989). Mary Ainsworth, though impressed by John Bowlby's nondoctrinaire approach to theory, was somewhat wary of the direction Bowlby's theorizing had begun to take. One paper on which

Bowlby and Ainsworth collaborated (Bowlby *et al.* 1956) and which deals with the effect on later development of early sanatorium experiences does not mention ethology at all. In historical terms, this paper is important because it prefigures later work by Mary Ainsworth. It is here that we find descriptions of three interaction patterns shown by children with early prolonged separations, and the *classification of their different patterns of behavior during reunion with parents* to which Robertson had drawn her attention.

In addition to analyzing the data from the sanatorium follow-up study, Mary Ainsworth worked on a second observational data set also collected by Robertson. This concerned the pre-separation, separation, and post-separation experiences of children in three settings: a fever hospital, a sanatorium, and a residential nursery. The findings, though never published, provided much fuel for Bowlby's theorizing as well as inspiration for Mary Ainsworth's subsequent observational studies of individual differences in attachment patterns.

Bowlby's first formal statement of attachment theory, drawing heavily on ethological concepts, was presented in London in three now classic papers read to the British Psychoanalytic Society. The first, 'The nature of the child's tie to his mother', was presented to the Society in 1957 (published 1958). It reviews the then current psychoanalytic explanations for the child's libidinal tie to the mother (in short the theories of Secondary Drive, Primary Object Sucking, Primary Object Clinging, and Primary Return-to-the-Womb Craving). Bowlby considered his new formulations to be closest to theories of primary object sucking and clinging, but in proposing that the human infant is ready to enter into social relations from the beginning he went far beyond these theories. To support his views he used research findings and personal observations. (Here it is important to point out that, for 20 years, Bowlby was involved in running a weekly mothers' group at a local well-baby clinic where he made informal observations of a random sample of babies and young children interacting with their mothers, and where he learned much about the mothers' day-to-day experiences with their children.)

Bowlby proposed that several instinctual responses that mature in the course of the first year, namely sucking, clinging, crying, following, and smiling, become organized into attachment behavior focused on a specific mother-figure during the second half of the first year. Of these, he believed clinging and following to be possibly more important than sucking and crying:

> During the final synthesis of these many behaviors into attachment behavior directed toward a single mother-figure it may well be that some components play a more central part than others.... Clinging and following seem more likely candidates for this role.... The association

which constantly impresses itself upon me is that between form and degree of disturbance and the extent to which the mother has permitted clinging and following and all the responses associated with them, or has refused them.

(Bowlby 1958: 21)

To buttress his arguments, Bowlby reviewed data from academic studies describing infants' cognitive and social development, including those of Piaget (e.g. 1954). Having laid this groundwork, Bowlby introduced ethological concepts, such as sign-stimuli or social releasers that 'cause' specific responses to be activated and shut off or terminated (see Tinbergen 1951). He emphasized that the origin of such stimuli can be internal as well as external, and that instinctual responses are often organized into complex chains, or chain hierarchies that can be altered by learning. Lorenz's (1935/1957a) work on imprinting is mentioned, but (as noted above) during the writing of this first paper, Bowlby was not yet aware of Harlow's studies regarding rhesus monkeys' preference for a cloth surrogate over a bottle-equipped wire surrogate mother. Harlow's work (Harlow and Zimmermann 1958) is first cited in Bowlby's subsequent theoretical paper on separation. Because the initial formulation of attachment theory focuses so strongly on attachment behavior, it has sometimes been overlooked that Bowlby also attended closely to the psychological experiences that accompany the activation, termination, and nontermination of instinctual responses (the latter leading to tension and anxiety).

The paper concludes by drawing a clear distinction between dependency and attachment, noting that psychological attachment and detachment are functions in their own right. Rather than being indicative of regression, attachment behaviors are said to perform a natural, healthy function even in adult life.

The paper on the child's tie to his mother raised quite a storm at the Psychoanalytic Society. Even Bowlby's own analyst, Joan Riviere, protested, and Donald Winnicott wrote to thank her: 'It was certainly a difficult paper to appreciate without giving away everything that has been fought for by Freud'. Anna Freud, who missed the meeting but read the paper, wrote: 'Dr. Bowlby is too valuable a person to get lost to psychoanalysis' (Grosskurth 1987).

The next paper in the series, 'Separation anxiety', was presented in 1959 (published in 1960). It built on relevant observations collected by James Robertson (1953) and Chris Heinicke (Heinicke and Westheimer 1965) as well as on informal maternal reports. In this paper Bowlby pointed out that traditional theory fails to explain both the intense attachment of infants to a mother-figure, and young children's dramatic responses to separation. In the course of his observations, Robertson (Robertson and Bowlby 1952) had identified three phases of separation response: protest (related to separation anxiety), despair (related to grief and mourning), and denial or detachment (related to defense). Bowlby emphasized that these responses were not confined to children whose relationship with their mother was already impaired, as some had claimed. After reviewing six psychoanalytic approaches to the problem of separation anxiety, he submitted his own hypothesis: separation anxiety is experienced when attachment behavior is activated but cannot be shut off or terminated. He distinguished anxiety from fright (fear of some external condition which sets off escape behavior), pointing out that young humans escape *to a haven of safety*, not just *from a frightening stimulus.* Later, the child is able to experience expectant anxiety in circumstances where there is a likelihood of disagreeable or noxious stimulation or where his or her haven of safety is not likely to be available. The following quote must have sounded strange at the time, in fact it still does because it mixes experiential with explanatory language:

> for to have a deep attachment for a person is to have taken them as the terminating object of our instinctual responses.
>
> (Robertson and Bowlby 1952: 13)

Bowlby held that reactions to separation from loved ones will remain a closed book unless we understand why only a very specific 'object' can terminate the response systems mediating attachment and escape behavior. He also touched on the link between frustrated attachment behavior and hostility toward the loved object. Rejection by the mother, separation from the mother, or mother's attention to someone else may all give rise to hostility and call primitive defenses into play. Bowlby argued that Freud was misled into thinking that a baby could have too much love because he had mistaken maternal pseudo-affection and overprotection without realizing that they represented a mother's overcompensation for unconscious hostility.

Unlike other psychoanalysts, Bowlby advanced the view that *excessive* separation anxiety is usually caused by adverse family experiences, such as repeated threats of abandonment or rejection by parents, or to a parent's or sibling's illness or death for which the child feels responsible. He also emphasized, however, that separation anxiety can be excessively low or be altogether absent. Such cases give an erroneous impression of maturity, but what looks like independence actually arises from defensive processes. A well-loved child, claims Bowlby, is quite likely to protest separation from parents but will later develop more self-reliance. Those familiar with attachment research will note that some of these ideas were further elaborated in Mary Ainsworth's classifications of secure, avoidant, and ambivalent patterns of infant–mother attachment.

In the third major theoretical paper, 'Grief and mourning in infancy and early childhood' read to the Psychoanalytic Society in 1959 (published in 1960), Bowlby questioned the then prevailing view that infantile narcissism is an obstacle to the experience of grief upon loss of a love object. He disputed Anna Freud's contention that infants cannot mourn, because of insufficient ego development, and hence experience nothing more than brief bouts of separation anxiety provided a satisfactory substitute is available. He also questioned Melanie Klein's claim that loss of the breast at weaning is the greatest loss in infancy. Instead he advanced the view that grief and mourning appear whenever attachment behaviors are activated but the mother figure continues to be unavailable.

Five topics related to adult mourning were discussed: thoughts and behavior directed to the lost person, hostility, appeals for help, despair, and reorganization. Bowlby underscored the fact that all of these processes had been documented in children as well. Indeed, Robertson's observations had demonstrated that in addition to longing (e.g. cries of 'I want to see my mummy'), infants or toddlers frequently engage in violent aggressiveness and rejection of caregiving by others before they begin to seek and accept new relationships. There may be a propitious outcome if the child can become attached to a new mother figure, but an overly frequent succession of figures may result in inability to form deep relationships.

As with the first paper, many members of the British Psychoanalytic Society voiced strong disagreement. Donald Winnicott wrote to Anna Freud 'I can't quite make out why it is that Bowlby's papers are building up in me a kind of revulsion although in fact he has been scrupulously fair to me in my writings'. Another analyst is said to have exclaimed: 'Bowlby? Give me Barabbas' (Grosskurth 1987).

By 1962 Bowlby had completed two further papers (Bowlby 1962a, b), never published, on defensive processes related to attachment. With them the basic blueprint of attachment theory was almost completely worked out, although it took until 1969 for the first paper to be expanded into *Attachment*, until 1973 for the second to be expanded into *Separation*, and until 1980 for the third (including material from the two unpublished papers on defensive processes) to be expanded into *Loss*. The original plan had been for a single book.

During this period, Colin Murray Parkes, well known for his research on bereavement, realized the relevance of Bowlby's and Robertson's work for gaining a deeper understanding of grief in adult life. While working with bereaved psychiatric patients, Parkes had come to realize how little was known about normal grief. After joining Bowlby's research unit at the Tavistock in 1962 he was able to visit unselected widows in their homes in order to help chart the course of normal grief. The resulting findings led to a joint paper with John Bowlby (Bowlby and Parkes 1970) in which the phases of separation delineated by James Robertson for young children were elaborated into four phases of grief during adult life: (1) numbness, (2) yearning and protest, (3) disorganization and despair, and (4) reorganization. Before the publication of this paper, Parkes had visited

Elizabeth Kubler-Ross in Chicago who was then gathering data for her influential book *On Death and Dying* (1970). The phases of dying described in her book (denial, anger, bargaining, depression, and acceptance) owe much to Bowlby's and Robertson's thinking. The founder of the modern hospice movement, Cicely Saunders, and Parkes used attachment theory and research in developing programs for the emotional care of the dying and bereaved. What they found particularly helpful in countering negative attitudes to the dying and bereaved was the concept of grief as a process toward attaining a new identity rather than as a state (Parkes, personal communication, 1989).

Let us now return to the research career of Mary Ainsworth. In late 1953, she had left the Tavistock Clinic, obviously familiar with Bowlby's thinking about ethology but not convinced of its value for understanding infant–mother attachment. The Ainsworths were headed for Uganda where Leonard had obtained a position. With the help of the East African Institute of Social Research at Kampala, Mary Ainsworth scraped together enough money to do an observational study on mother–infant separation during weaning. At this point she was still sufficiently uneasy about Bowlby's ethological notions to warn him, in a long letter, that his newfangled ethological ideas could ruin his reputation (Ainsworth, personal communication, October 1989). Although she experienced a change of heart once she began her observations, she did not inform Bowlby of this until several years later.

Thus it came about that the first study of infant–mother attachment from an ethological perspective was undertaken long before the publication of the seminal papers in which Bowlby laid out the ethological basis of attachment theory. Following in Robertson's footsteps, Mary Ainsworth based her Ganda project on naturalistic observations and interviews, carried out in the family home. The study had been planned as an investigation of separation responses during weaning, but it soon became obvious that the old tradition of sending the child away 'to forget the breast' had broken down. Mary Ainsworth therefore decided to switch gears and study the process of infant–mother attachment.

At the beginning of the study, the babies ranged from 15 weeks to 2 years of age. All were observed longitudinally, for two hours per visit and, if possible, every two weeks, over a period of 9 months. Visits (with the aid of an interpreter) took place in the family living-room where Ganda women generally entertain in the afternoon. Observations were coded in terms of the occurrence and onset of specific attachment-related behaviors.

Refining attachment theory: Bowlby and Ainsworth (phase 2)

Upon leaving Kampala, the Ainsworths moved to Baltimore, Maryland, where Mary began work as a diagnostician and part-time clinician at the

Sheppard and Enoch Pratt Hospital. Hence the data from the Ganda project lay fallow for several years. In 1958 Mary Ainsworth began to teach clinical psychology (with a later shift to developmental psychology) at the Johns Hopkins University. It was at this point that she received a reprint of 'The nature of the child's tie to his mother' from John Bowlby. When Bowlby visited her in Baltimore in 1960, she was able to give him an in-depth account of the Ganda study. As a result, her subsequent analysis of the data from that project was deeply influenced by the renewed contact and collaboration with Bowlby. Conversely, Bowlby drew on many of Ainsworth's ideas and findings as he elaborated and refined volume 1 of the future attachment trilogy (Bowlby 1969).

In examining data from the Ganda project, Ainsworth (1967) was particularly interested in individual differences. To tap into these, she devised a variety of ratings scales. Most important, in terms of her future work, was a scale evaluating maternal sensitivity to infant signals from interview data. The top rating of 7 was given to mothers who were identified as excellent informants and provided much spontaneous detail whereas low ratings were given to mothers who seemed imperceptive of the nuances of infant behavior. Individual differences in the babies were assessed by classification into three groups: securely attached infants who cried less, insecurely attached infants who cried more, and not yet attached infants who did not show differential behavior to the mother. Statistical analyses revealed that the three infant classifications were significantly correlated with the interview-based maternal sensitivity ratings and the amount of holding provided by the mother.

Mary Ainsworth first presented her findings from the Ganda project at the meetings of the Tavistock Study Group organized by Bowlby during the 1960s (Ainsworth 1963). Participants invited to these influential gatherings included infant researchers of diverse theoretical backgrounds (in addition to Mary Ainsworth, there were Genevieve Appell, Miriam David, Jack Gewirtz, Hanus Papousek, Heinz Prechtl, Harriet Rheingold, Henry Ricciuti, Louis Sander, and Peter Wolff) as well as animal researchers such as Harry Harlow, Robert Hinde, Charles Kaufmann, Jay Rosenblatt, and Thelma Rowell. Their lively discussions contributed much to the developing field of infant social development in general, but empirical studies reported and generated by these meetings also came to play a vital role in the elaboration of attachment theory. These papers were published in four volumes entitled *Determinants of Infant Behavior* edited by Brian Foss (Foss 1961, 1963, 1965, 1969).

It was in the early sixties that Mary Ainsworth embarked on the Baltimore Study. As in the Ganda project, she opted for direct observation, but interviews played a lesser role. Visits were made at 3- or 4-week intervals beginning in the first month and ending at 12 months. Each visit lasted 3–4 hours. During such prolonged visits the mother could more easily be induced to follow her normal routine and behave naturally. All visits for each quarter of the first year of life were grouped together for purposes of analysis. For each child there were altogether 72 hours of data collection. Raw data for the project took the form of narrative reports, jotted down in shorthand during the observations and later dictated into a tape-recorder for transcription.

Even more than in the Ganda study (Ainsworth 1967), methods of data gathering and analysis used in the Baltimore study were informed by attachment theory. In addition, Ainsworth became aware of the striking congruence between her old interest in Blatz's security theory and Bowlby's new approach. The Blatzian concept of the secure base was hence revitalized in the context of attachment theory. Ainsworth and her colleagues also elaborated and perfected the technique classifying infant and maternal behaviors in terms of behavioral patterns, rather than following the more traditional procedure of engaging in frequency counts of discrete behaviors. This methodology had roots both in Ainsworth's dissertation work where she had identified patterns of familial and extra-familial security, but was also influenced by her collaboration with Bowlby and Robertson.

Most of the findings from the Baltimore project were published during the years following the appearance of Bowlby's first volume on attachment in 1969. This volume contained elaborate, heavily documented theoretical chapters on ethology (especially on imprinting), on the appraisal function of emotion, on control systems theory, and of course, on the development of the infant's tie to the mother, both in terms of normative changes and individual differences. Much of the theorizing on individual differences in infant–mother attachment relationships drew on pre-publication results of the Baltimore study.

At the same time, analysis of the data from the Baltimore study was deeply influenced by Bowlby's ideas. There are papers on feeding (Ainsworth and Bell 1969), on mother–infant face-to-face play (Blehar et al. 1977), on crying (Bell and Ainsworth 1972), on infant greeting and following (Stayton and Ainsworth 1973), on obedience (Stayton, Hogan, and Ainsworth 1973), and an unpublished study on close bodily contact (Ainsworth et al. 1971). All of them describe striking individual differences in how sensitively or not the mother responded to infant signals throughout the first year of life.

At this point I need to discuss the Strange Situation, a laboratory observation procedure devised by Ainsworth and Wittig (1969) with a view to studying the interplay of the attachment and exploratory behavioral systems under conditions of low and high stress, a topic in which Harlow (1961) had aroused their interest. Believing that the balance between attachment and exploratory behavior could more easily be observed in an unfamiliar environment, Ainsworth and Wittig devised a laboratory procedure in which the Baltimore infants and their mothers participated when the infants were one year old. The Strange Situation is a miniature drama with eight episodes in which mother, infant, and a stranger participate. Ainsworth and Wittig were interested in the infant's exploratory behavior in the presence and absence of the mother.

Group data from the Strange Situation observations bore out Ainsworth's expectations about attachment and exploration: babies did indeed explore the playroom and toys more vigorously in the presence of their mother than after a stranger entered or while the mother was absent. Though these results were theoretically interesting, Ainsworth became especially intrigued with the unexpected variety of the infants' reunion behaviors. Some of the behavior patterns she observed reminded her of reunion responses Robertson had documented in children who had suffered prolonged separations. A few of the Baltimore infants observed in the Strange Situation were surprisingly angry when mother returned after a 3-minute (or shorter) separation. They cried and wanted contact, but could not simply cuddle or 'sink in' when picked up by the returning mother. Instead, they showed their ambivalence by kicking or swiping at her. Another group of children seemed to snub or avoid the mother upon reunion, even though they had often searched for her while she was gone. Analyses of home observation data revealed that those infants who had been ambivalent or avoidant of the mother on reunion during the Strange Situation had had a less optimal relationship with her at home than those (a majority) who sought proximity, interaction, or contact with the returning mother (Ainsworth *et al.* 1974). Thus originated the now renowned Strange Situation classification system (Ainsworth *et al.* 1978; p. 140, this volume).

Initially, many investigators disagreed with Ainsworth's inferences regarding the meaning of Strange Situation behavior, most often because they overlooked that the reunion patterns had been validated against home observations. Frequently, the avoidant infants' behavior was interpreted as independence. This situation began to change after the publication of Ainsworth's book (Ainsworth *et al.* 1978) which drew together all findings from the Baltimore project and presented findings from subsequent studies showing links between attachment classifications and development in toddlerhood and early childhood (Main 1973; Matas *et al.* 1978). Now researchers not closely connected with Ainsworth or her collaborators began to take her classification procedure more seriously.

During this period, I attended the Johns Hopkins University as a graduate student. There we were fortunate to have hands-on experience of analyzing the narrative data from the Baltimore study and to read the second volume of the attachment trilogy, *Separation*, in manuscript form during our research seminar with Mary Ainsworth. Personally, I felt especially lucky to have access to Bowlby's second volume because I had become intrigued with his concept of 'internal working models', e.g. mental representations which an infant builds of self and caregiver and with whose help he or she predicts, interprets, and plans attachment behavior. This concept, closely related to ideas proposed by Fairbairn (1952) and other object relations theorists, is briefly mentioned in the first volume (Bowlby 1969), but greatly elaborated in the second and third volumes of the attachment trilogy.

As professor at the Johns Hopkins University, Mary Ainsworth attracted many graduate students (amongst them Sylvia Bell, Mary Main, Mary Blehar, Michael Lamb, and Alicia Lieberman), but she also inspired many undergraduates whose first research training ground was the analysis of data from the Baltimore project. A number of these students subsequently wrote dissertations on attachment-related topics at their respective graduate institutions (amongst them Robert Marvin, Milton Kotelchuck, Mark Greenberg, Mark Cummings, and Everett Waters). When Everett Waters became a graduate student at the University of Minnesota in 1973, he introduced Alan Sroufe to the Strange Situation procedure. Until then Sroufe had only been vaguely familiar with attachment theory. Although he had read Mary Ainsworth's theoretical article about object relations and dependency (Ainsworth 1968) he was not yet cognizant of Bowlby's theoretical formulations (Sroufe, personal communication, 1988). Sroufe and Waters (1977) subsequently wrote an influential paper that made attachment as an organizational construct accessible to a much larger audience. Sroufe was also inspired to undertake a large-scale longitudinal study of attachment with an at-risk population (disadvantaged mothers). The Minnesota study, summarized in Sroufe (1983) but still ongoing, stands as the second major longitudinal study supporting the view that quality of caregiving is related to individual differences in attachment quality. The third and fourth large-scale longitudinal studies were conducted by Klaus and Karin Grossmann in Germany (Grossmann *et al.* 1985 and ongoing). The Grossmann studies also form part of an increasing body of cross-cultural attachment studies (for reviews see Bretherton and Waters (1985) and Van Ijzendoorn and Kroonenberg (1988)).

In other laboratories across the United States, much time was spent testing out Mary Ainsworth's propositions regarding the meaning of the Strange Situation reunion classifications. Many researchers came to train with Mary Ainsworth or her former students to learn the procedure and classification system. Hundreds of studies using the Strange Situation appeared in print. Often it almost seemed as if attachment and the Strange Situation had become synonymous.

GROWING POINTS

Now the gears are shifting again. Attachment theory and research are moving forward along three major fronts, as follows.

1. As a result of Mary Main's Berkeley Study (Main *et al.* 1985) and, I think, the publication of the SRCD Monograph 'Growing Points of Attachment Theory and Research' (Bretherton and Waters 1985) we are now beginning to explore the psychological, internal, or representational aspects of attachment, including the intergenerational transmission of attachment patterns which had been at the center of Bowlby's interests since his beginnings in psychiatry. At last, Volume III of the attachment trilogy (Bowlby 1980a), in which Bowlby elaborated his earlier (1962a, b) ideas of defense and representation, is coming into its own.

Interestingly, the inspiration for studies of individual difference in attachment at the representational level has come in large part from the translation of Ainsworth's infant attachment patterns into corresponding adult patterns. In the Adult Attachment Interview devised by Main and her colleagues (Main and Goldwyn in press) parents were asked questions about their attachment relations in childhood, as well as about the influence that these early relations had had upon their own development. Close examination of the interview text as a whole revealed three patterns of responding: autonomous–secure individuals were able to give a clear and coherent account of early attachments (whether these had been satisfying or not); preoccupied individuals produced many conflicted childhood memories about attachment, but could not draw these together into an organized, consistent picture; finally, dismissing individuals often claimed that they could not remember much about relations with parents in childhood. They tended to idealize their parents on a general level, but to disclaim any influence of attachment experiences on their own development, or to report memories of rejection when they did manage to remember specific episodes. Not only did the Adult Attachment Interview classifications correspond to Ainsworth's secure, ambivalent, and avoidant infant patterns at a conceptual level, they were also empirically correlated with them – e.g. a dismissing parent tended to have an avoidant infant, and so forth (Main *et al.* 1985; Main in this volume).

In addition, several representational measures of attachment were devised for use with children. A separation anxiety test for adolescents had been developed by Hansburg in 1972. In 1976 it was adopted for younger children by Klagsbrun and Bowlby (1976), and has now been revised and successfully validated against observed attachment patterns by Kaplan (1984) and Slough and Greenberg (in press). Attachment-based story completion tasks for 3- to 5-year-olds were validated against behavioral measures by Bretherton *et al.* (in press) and Oppenheim (1989). In these tests, emotional openness of responding tends to be related to secure attachment classifications.

Finally, several authors have created interviews that examine attachment from the parental as opposed to the filial perspective (e.g. Bretherton *et al.* 1989; George and Solomon 1989). In addition, Waters and Deane (1985) developed a Q-sort that can be used to assess a mother's internal working models of her child's attachment to her.

2. A related topic, the study of attachment relationships between adults, is also generating considerable research activity. It began in the early 1970s with studies of adult bereavement (Bowlby and Parkes 1970; Parkes 1972) and marital separation (Weiss 1973, 1977). More recently, however, interest in adult attachments has broadened to encompass mature attachment relations in marriage and similar relationships (Weiss 1982 and this volume). More recently, Shaver and Hazan (1988) have translated Ainsworth's infant patterns of attachment into adult styles of interpersonal relating and compared these styles with childhood antecedents. Much of this research has been masterfully summarized by Mary Ainsworth (1989 and this volume) in a wide-ranging theoretical analysis of attachment across the life cycle. The topic has been further extended by examining attachment with respect to family interaction (Belsky, Rovine, and Fish in press; Howes and Markman 1989; Byng-Hall 1985 and this volume; Marvin and Stewart in press). Finally, Marris, whose work on widows (1958) influenced Bowlby's early thinking about bereavement, has cast his net even wider by considering the implications of attachment for societal organization and vice versa (Marris 1982 and this volume).

3. Attachment theory and research are also making a considerable impact on the emerging field of developmental psychopathology (Sroufe 1988). There have been longitudinal attachment-based studies of families with depression (Radke-Yarrow et al. 1985; Radke-Yarrow in this volume), of families with maltreatment (e.g. Schneider-Rosen et al. 1985; Crittenden 1983), and families with low social support (Lieberman and Pawl 1988; Spieker and Booth 1988). Much of this work is represented in a volume on clinical implications of attachment (Belsky and Nezworski 1988). These topics hark back to some of Bowlby's seminal ideas from the 1930s, but have been greatly enriched by Mary Ainsworth's notions on the origins of individual differences of attachment patterns.

CONCLUDING REMARKS

In 1980 Bowlby published a paper about attachment theory entitled, tongue in cheek, 'By ethology out of psychoanalysis: an experiment in interbreeding'. The time has come when the psychoanalytical origins of attachment theory are coming into sharper focus. Thus attachment theory can now more clearly be seen as a theory of interpersonal relationships in the lineage of object relations theory (Bretherton 1987), incorporating much from ethology, but also shedding new light on and reworking from a new and more rigorous perspective the issues in which Klein (1932), Fairbairn (1952), and Winnicott (1965) had also been wrestling. Bowlby's remarks in the epilogue to the volume published in honor of his 75th birthday (Parkes and Stevenson-Hinde 1982: 313) continue to apply eight years later: 'Attachment theory is still growing. Its potential and its limitations remain unknown'.

ACKNOWLEDGEMENT

I would like to thank John Bowlby, Mary Ainsworth and Colin Parkes for helpful comments.

NOTE

1   This chapter was presented as a paper at a meeting organized by the Tavistock Clinic in honor of John Bowlby's eightieth birthday, June 1987.

REFERENCES

Ainsworth, M.D.S. (1963) 'The development of infant–mother interaction among the Ganda', in B.M. Foss (ed.) Determinants of Infant Behavior (pp. 67–104), New York: Wiley.
—— (1967) Infancy in Uganda: Infant Care and the Growth of Love, Baltimore: The Johns Hopkins University Press.
—— (1968) 'Object relations, dependency, and attachment: a theoretical review of the infant–mother relationship', Child Development 40: 969–1025.
—— (1974) 'Citation for the G. Stanley Hall award to John Bowlby', Unpublished manuscript.
—— (1983) 'A sketch of a career', in A.N. O'Connoll and N.F. Russo (eds) Models of Achievement: Reflections of Eminent Women in Psychology.
—— (1989) 'Attachments beyond infancy', American Psychologist 44: 709–16.
Ainsworth, M.D.S. and Bell, S.M. (1969) 'Some contemporary patterns in the feeding situation', in A. Ambrose (ed.) Stimulation in Early Infancy (pp. 133–70), London: Academic Press.
Ainsworth, M.D.S., Bell, S.M., Blehar, M.C., and Main, M. (1971, April) 'Physical contact: A study of infant responsiveness and its relation to maternal handling', Paper presented at the biennial meeting of the Society for Research in Child Development, Minneapolis, Minnesota.
Ainsworth, M.D.S., Bell, S.M., and Stayton, D. (1974) 'Infant–mother attachment and social development', in M.P. Richards (ed.) The Introduction of the Child into a Social World (pp. 99–135), London: Cambridge University Press.
Ainsworth, M.D.S., Blehar, M.C., Waters, E., and Wall, S. (1978) Patterns of Attachment: A Psychological Study of the Strange Situation. Hillsdale, N.J.: Erlbaum Associates.
Ainsworth, M.D.S. and Wittig, B.A. (1969) 'Attachment and the exploratory behaviour of one-year-olds in a strange situation', in B.M. Foss (ed.) Determinants of Infant Behavior (vol. 4, pp. 113–36), London: Methuen.

Bell, S.M. and Ainsworth, M.D.S. (1972) 'Infant crying and maternal responsiveness', *Child Development* 43: 1171–90.
Belsky, J. and Nezworski, T. (1988) *Clinical Implications of Attachment,* Hillsdale, N.J.: Erlbaum.
Belsky, J., Rovine, M., and Fish, M. (in press) 'The developing family system', in M. Gunnar (ed.) *Systems and Development: Minnesota Symposia on Child Development* (vol. 22), Hillsdale, N.J.: Erlbaum.
Blatz, W. (1940) *Hostages to Peace: Parents and the Children of Democracy,* New York: Morrow.
Blehar, M.C., Lieberman, A.F., and Ainsworth, M.D.S. (1977) 'Early face-to-face interaction and its relation to later infant–mother attachment', *Child Development* 48: 182–94.
Bowlby, J. (1940) 'The influence of early environment in the development of neurosis and neurotic character', *International Journal of Psycho-Analysis* XXI: 1–25.
—— (1944) 'Forty-four juvenile thieves: their characters and home life', *International Journal of Psycho-Analysis* XXV: 19–52.
—— (1951) *Maternal Care and Mental Health,* Geneva: World Health Organization Monograph Series, No. 2.
—— (1953) *Child Care and the Growth of Love* (2nd edn, 1963), Harmondsworth, Mx: Penguin.
—— (1953) 'Critical phases in the development of social responses in man and other animals', in J.M. Tanner (ed.) *Prospects of Psychiatric Research* (Proceedings of the First Conference of the Mental Health Research Fund), Oxford: Blackwell Scientific Publications.
—— (1958) 'The nature of the child's tie to his mother', *International Journal of Psycho-analysis* XXXIX: 1–23.
—— (1960a) 'Separation anxiety', *International Journal of Psycho-Analysis* XLI: 1–25.
—— (1960b) 'Grief and mourning in infancy and early childhood', *The Psychoanalytic Study of the Child* XV: 3–39.
—— (1962a) 'Loss, detachment and defence', Unpublished manuscript, Tavistock Child Development Research Unit, London.
—— (1962b) 'Defences that follow loss: Causation and function', Unpublished manuscript, Tavistock Child Development Research Unit, London.
—— (1969) *Attachment and Loss,* vol. 1: *Attachment,* New York: Basic Books, and London: Hogarth (2nd revised edn, 1982).
—— (1973) *Attachment and Loss,* vol. 2: *Separation: Anxiety and Anger,* New York: Basic Books, and London: Hogarth.
—— (1980a) *Attachment and Loss,* vol. 3: *Loss: Sadness and Depression,* New York: Basic Books, and London: Hogarth.
—— (1980b) 'By ethology out of psycho-analysis: an experiment in interbreeding', *Animal Behavior* 28: 649–56.
Bowlby, J., Ainsworth, M., Boston, M., and Rosenbluth, D. (1956) 'The effects of mother–child separation: a follow-up study', *British Journal of Medical Psychology* 29: 211–47.
Bowlby, J. and Parkes, C.M. (1970) 'Separation and loss within the family', in E.J. Anthony and C. Koupernik (eds) The child in his family, *International Yearbook of Child Psychiatry and Allied Professions,* New York: John Wiley.
Bretherton, I. (1987) 'New perspectives on attachment relations: security, communication, and internal working models', in J. Osofsky (ed.) *Handbook of Infant Development* (pp. 1061–100), New York: Wiley.

Bretherton, I. (in press) 'Open communication and internal working models: their role in attachment relationships', in R. Thompson (ed.) *Socioemotional Development (Nebraska Symposium 1987)*, Lincoln, Nebr.: University of Nebraska Press.

Bretherton, I., Biringen, Z., Ridgeway, D., Maslin, M., and Sherman, M. (1989) 'Attachment: the parental perspective', *Infant Mental Health Journal* (Special Issue) 10: 203–20

Bretherton, I., Ridgeway, D., and Cassidy, J. (in press) 'The role of internal working models in the attachment relationship: can it be assessed in 3-year-olds?', in M. Greenberg, D. Cicchetti, and E.M. Cummings (eds) *Attachment during the Preschool Years*, Chicago: University of Chicago Press.

Bretherton, I. and Waters, E. (eds) (1985) 'Growing points of attachment theory and research', *Monographs of the Society for Research in Child Development* 50 (1–2), Serial no. 209.

Byng-Hall, J. (1985) 'The family script: a useful bridge between theory and practice', *Journal of Family Therapy* 7: 301–5.

Crittenden, P.M. (1983) 'The effect of mandatory protective daycare on mutual attachment in maltreating mother–infant dyads', *Child Abuse and Neglect* 7: 297–300.

Durbin, E.F. and Bowlby, J. (1939) *Personal Aggressiveness and War*, London: Routledge and Kegan Paul.

Fairbairn, W.R.D. (1952) *An Object-Relations Theory of the Personality*, New York: Basic Books.

Foss, B.M. (ed. (1961, 1963, 1965, 1969) *Determinants of Infant Behavior* (vols 1–4), New York: Wiley.

George, C. and Solomon, J. (1989) 'Internal working models of caregiving and security of attachment at age six', *Infant Mental Health Journal* (Special Issue) 10: 222–37.

Grosskurth, P. (1987) *Melanie Klein: Her World and Her Work*, Cambridge, Mass.: Harvard University Press.

Grossmann, K., Grossmann, K.E., Spangler, G., Suess, G., and Unzner, L. (1985) 'Maternal sensitivity and newborns' orientation responses as related to quality of attachment in Northern Germany', in I. Bretherton and E. Waters (eds) Growing Points of Attachment Theory and Research, *Monographs of the Society for Research in Child Development* 50, Serial No. 209 (1–2).

Hansburg, H.G. (1972) *Adolescent Separation Anxiety: A Method for the Study of Adolescent Separation Problems*, Springfield, Ill.: C.C. Thomas.

Harlow, H.F. and Zimmermann, R.R. (1958) 'The development of affective responsiveness in infant monkeys', *Proceedings of the American Philosophical Society* 102: 501–9.

Harlow, H.F. (1961) 'The development of affectional patterns in infant monkeys', in B.M. Foss (ed.) *Determinants of Infant Behavior* (pp. 75–97), New York: Wiley.

Heinicke, C.M. and Westheimer, I. (1965) *Brief Separations*, New York: International Universities Press.

Hinde, R.A. and Spencer-Booth, Y. (1967) 'The effect of social companions on mother–infant relations in rhesus monkeys', in D. Morris (ed.) *Primate Ethology*, London: Weidenfeld and Nicolson.

Howes, P. and Markman, H.J. (1989) 'Marital quality and child functioning: a longitudinal investigation', *Child Development* 60: 1044–51.

Kaplan, N. (1984) 'Internal representations of separation experiences in six year olds: related to actual experiences of separation', Unpublished master's thesis, University of California, Berkeley.

Klagsbrun, M. and Bowlby, J. (1976) 'Responses to separation from parents: a clinical test for young children', *British Journal of Projective Psychology* 21: 7–21.

Klein, M. (1932) *The Psycho-Analysis of Children*, London: Hogarth Press.

Klopfer, B., Ainsworth, M.D., Klopfer, W.F., and Holt, R.R. (1954) *Developments in the Rorschach Technique* (vol. 1), Yonkers-on-Hudson, N.Y.: World Books.

Kubler-Ross, E. (1970) *On Death and Dying*, London: Tavistock.

Lieberman, A.F. and Pawl, J.H. (1988) 'Clinical applications of attachment theory', in J. Belsky and T. Nezworski (eds) *Clinical Applications of Attachment*, Hilldale, N.J.: Erlbaum.

Lorenz, K.Z. (1957a) 'The companion in the bird's world', in C.H. Schiller (ed.) *Instinctive Behavior* (pp. 83–128), New York: International Universities Press. Translated from Lorenz, K.Z. (1935) 'Der Kumpan in der Umwelt des Vogels', *Journal für Ornithologie* 83: 137–213.

—— (1957b) *King Solomon's Ring*, New York: Thomas Y. Crowell.

Main, M. (1973) 'Exploration, play and cognitive functioning as related to child–mother attachment', Unpublished doctoral dissertation, The Johns Hopkins University, Baltimore, Md.

Main, M. and Goldwyn, R. (in press) 'Interview-based adult attachment classifications: related to infant–mother and infant–father attachment', *Developmental Psychology*.

Main, M., Kaplan, K., and Cassidy, J. (1985) 'Security in infancy, childhood and adulthood: a move to the level of representation', in I. Bretherton and E. Waters (eds) Growing Points of Attachment Theory and Research, *Monographs of the Society for Research in Child Development*, 50, Serial No. 209 (1–2): 66–104.

Marris, P. (1958) *Widows and their Families*, London: Routledge & Kegan Paul.

—— (1982) 'Attachment and society', in C.M. Parkes and J. Stevenson-Hinde (eds) *The Place of Attachment in Human Behavior* (pp. 185–201, New York: Basic Books.

Marvin, R.S. and Stewart, R.B. (in press) 'A family system framework for the study of attachment', in M. Greenberg, D. Cicchetti, and M. Cummings (eds) *Attachment beyond the Preschool Years*, Chicago: University of Chicago Press.

Matas, L., Arend, R.A., and Sroufe, L.A. (1978) 'Continuity and adaptation in the second year: the relationship between quality of attachment and later competence', *Child Development* 49: 547–56.

Oppenheim, D. (1989) 'Assessing the validity of a doll play interview for measuring attachment in preschoolers', Unpublished doctoral dissertation, University of Utah, Salt Lake City, Utah.

Parkes, C.M. (1972) *Bereavement: Studies of Grief in Adult Life*, New York: International Universities Press.

Parkes, C.M. and Stevenson-Hinde, J. (eds) (1982) *The Place of Attachment in Human Behavior*, New York: Basic Books.

Piaget, J. (1954) *The Child's Construction of Reality*, New York: Basic Books.

Radke-Yarrow, M., Cummings, E.M., Kuczinsky, L., and Chapman, M. (1985) 'Patterns of attachment in two- and three-year-olds in normal families and families with parental depression', *Child Development* 56: 884–93.

Robertson, J. (1953) 'Some responses of young children to loss of maternal care', *Nursing Care* 49: 382–6.

Robertson, J. and Bowlby, J. (1952) 'Responses of young children to separation from their mothers', *Courier of the International Children's Centre, Paris* II: 131–40.

Salter, M.D. (1940) 'An evaluation of adjustment based upon the concept of security', *Child Development Series*, The University of Toronto Press.

Schneider-Rosen, K., Braunwald, K.G., Carlson, V., and Cicchetti, D. (1985) 'Current perspectives in attachment theory: illustration from the study of maltreated infants', in I. Bretherton and E. Waters (eds) Growing Points of Attachment Theory and Research, *Monographs of the Society for Research in Child Development*, 50, Serial No. 209 (1–2).

Senn, M.J.E. (1977a) 'Interview with John Bowlby', Unpublished manuscript, National Library of Medicine, Washington D.C.

—— (1977b) 'Interview with James Robertson', Unpublished manuscript, National Library of Medicine, Washington D.C.

Shaver, P.R. and Hazan, C. (1988) 'A biased overview of the study of love', *Journal of Social and Personality Relationships* 5: 473–501.

Slough, N. and Greenberg, M. (in press) '5-year-olds representations of separation from parents: responses for self and a hypothetical child', in I. Bretherton and M. Watson (eds) *Children's Perspectives on the Family* (New Directions for Child Development, W. Damon, Series Editor), San Francisco: Jossey-Bass.

Smuts, A. (1977) 'Interview with Dr. John Bowlby', Unpublished manuscript.

Spieker, S. and Booth, C. (1988) 'Maternal antecedents of attachment quality', in J. Belsky and T. Nezworski (eds) *Clinical Implications of Attachment* (pp. 95–135), Hillsdale, N.J.: Erlbaum.

Sroufe, L.A. (1983) 'Infant–caregiver attachment and patterns of adaptation in pre-school: the roots of maladaptation and competence', in M. Perlmutter (ed.) *Minnesota Symposium in Child Psychology* (vol. 16, pp. 41–81), Hillsdale, N.J.: Erlbaum.

—— (1988) 'The role of infant–caregiver attachment in adult development', in J. Belsky and T. Nezworski (eds) *Clinical Implications of Attachment* (pp. 18–38), Hillsdale, N.J.: Erlbaum.

Sroufe, L.A. and Waters, E. (1977) 'Attachment as an organizational construct', *Child Development* 49: 1184–99.

Stayton, D. and Ainsworth, M.D.S. (1973) 'Development of separation behavior in the first year of life', *Development Psychology* 9: 226–35.

Stayton, D., Hogan, R., and Ainsworth, M.D.S. (1973) 'Infant obedience and maternal behavior: The origins of socialization reconsidered', *Child Development* 42: 1057–70.

Tinbergen, N. (1951) *The Study of Instinct*, London: Clarendon Press.

Van Ijzendoorn, M.H. and Kroonenberg, P.M. (1988) 'Cross-cultural patterns of attachment: a meta-analysis of the Strange Situation', *Child Development* 59: 147–56.

Waters, E. and Deane, K.E. (1985) 'Defining and assessing individual differences in attachment relationships: Q-methodology and the organization of behavior in infancy and early childhood', in I. Bretherton and E. Waters (eds) Growing Points of Attachment Theory and Research, *Monographs of the Society for Research in Child Development* 50, Serial No. 209 (1–2).

Weiss, R.S. (1973) *Loneliness: The Experience of Emotional and Social Isolation*, Cambridge, Mass.: MIT Press.

—— (1977) *Marital Separation*, New York: Basic Books.

—— (1982) 'Attachment in adult life', in C.M. Parkes and J. Stevenson-Hinde (eds) *The Place of Attachment in Human Behavior* (pp. 171–84), New York: Wiley.

Winnicott, D.W. (1965) *The Maturational Process and the Facilitating Environment*, New York: International Universities Press.

Chapter 2

Attachments and other affectional bonds across the life cycle

Mary D. Salter Ainsworth

> ... attachment behaviour is held to characterize human beings from the cradle to the grave.
>
> (Bowlby 1979: 129)

The great strength of attachment theory in guiding research is that it focuses on a basic system of behavior – the attachment system – that is biologically rooted and thus species-characteristic. This implies a search for basic processes of functioning universal in human nature, despite differences attributable to genetic constitution, cultural influences, and individual experience. Substantial progress has been made toward understanding what are the basic developmental processes relevant to attachment in infancy; now research is needed to find out what they are throughout later phases of development. That is the first major concern of this chapter.

The second major consideration is the issue of long-lasting interpersonal relationships that may involve affectional bonds. These include the attachments of child to parents, the bonds of parents to child, bonds with other kin, sexual partnerships, and the bonds that may occur between friends. These classes of bond differ from one another in regard to the role played by the attachment system and its interplay with other basic behavioral systems.

ATTACHMENT OF CHILD TO PARENTS BEYOND INFANCY

Here we are concerned with normative shifts in the nature of a child's attachment to parent figures beyond infancy. At some time between a child's third and fourth birthdays he becomes capable of what Bowlby (1969/1982) termed a 'goal-corrected partnership'. He suggested that this developmental phase was triggered by certain cognitive advances, which Marvin (1972, 1977; Marvin and Greenberg 1982) promptly began to investigate and elaborate. The onset of simple cognitive perspective-taking enables the child to begin to grasp something of his parent's motivation and plans, and thus he becomes more able than before to induce the parent to change plans so that they more closely agree with his own. Although language began to develop in the previous phase, now the further improvement of the child's language skills helps both child and parent better to communicate their plans and wishes to each other and thus to facilitate their negotiation of a mutually acceptable plan. Confidence in the stability of this mutual understanding becomes built into the child's working model of his relationship with his mother figure, and enables him to tolerate separation from her for longer periods and with less distress. Meanwhile there has occurred a qualitative advance in locomotion, from uncertain toddling to assured walking and running – presumably contingent on neurological development. This enables him to venture farther away from his secure base to explore his expanded world, and to connect with a wider variety of people, including strangers – and especially with age peers. Although age peers are attractive to children in Phase 3 of the development of attachment, now in Phase 4 they play an increasingly significant role in a child's life.

Attachment researchers have begun to explore individual differences in patterns of attachment in the sixth year of life (e.g. Main *et al.* 1985; Cassidy 1988). Although it has been demonstrated that significant changes take place in the ways in which patterns of attachment are manifested, attachment researchers have not yet turned their attention to the nature of the processes that underlie these manifestations. However, it is reasonable to suppose that a major shift in functioning may take place at about this phase of the life cycle, when children are expected to begin in earnest to assume some of the responsibilities of adulthood – be these attending school in order to learn the knowledge and skills needed to function eventually as successful adults or, in non-literate societies, acquiring appropriate knowledge and skills through apprenticeship.

It seems certain that another major shift takes place with the onset of adolescence, ushered in by hormonal changes. This shift is universally recognized as marking the onset of physical maturity – at least the achievement of reproductive capacity – and in this sense the coming of adulthood. The young person becomes increasingly concerned with a search for a partnership with an age peer, usually of the opposite sex – a relationship in which the reproductive system as well as the caregiving and attachment systems are likely to be involved. However, it seems likely that adolescence also brings changes in cognitive ability that likewise herald the onset of more mature functioning. Thus, for example, Piaget noted the advent of 'formal operations' that enable logical thought, and cognitive psychologists have observed the onset of 'meta-cognition', the ability to reflect about one's own cognitive processes.

Yet another shift with clear biological underpinnings takes place in the case of women in the course of pregnancy, childbirth, and the period during which infants and young children are being reared. The need to rely on an attachment figure or figures for increased care is intensified – whether this be the partner in a sexual pair bond or, in the case of the unavailability of such a partner, the woman's mother (or another available attachment figure), or both. The implications of this shift are indeed important, and raise two major issues.

One issue is the biological underpinnings of the human sexual partnership itself – which is discussed in a later section. The other issue relates to the proposition that there is a genetic bias for females throughout the course of development to be somehow more predisposed toward becoming attached and relying more on attachment figures than do males. The evolutionary argument would point out first that females are less strong physically than males, and not capable of the same speed in running. Therefore, in the environment of evolutionary adaptedness they were less able to protect themselves from environmental threats that are likely to occur. When the time came for pregnancy, childbirth, and the rearing of young children, they were even more vulnerable to danger, especially because they had their offspring as well as themselves to protect. Thus, the implication is that they were less able than males to vest their security in themselves and their own capabilities, and thus more obviously reliant on others for support and protection. This implies that the female is genetically biased to be both more attachment-oriented and more predisposed toward caregiving than males, even though the utility of such biases in our contemporary environment may not become apparent until pregnancy occurs and its sequelae. At this juncture even the most capable of women would be likely to concede that support and cooperation in a shared enterprise would be helpful and welcome.

It seems fairly certain that a genetic bias for females to be more attachment-oriented than males is not evident in infancy. Although male infants may tend to differ from females in such temperamental characteristics as activity level, and strength and vigor of movement, there is no evidence that they lag behind females in becoming attached to their principal caregiver(s) or that attachment is less significant to them. Indeed this makes sense biologically, for in infancy males and females are equally in need of nurturance and protection. If then there is indeed such a genetic bias, when and how does it begin to manifest itself?

Much more research is required before we have a good understanding of the normative changes that take place throughout the life cycle. In this we must be alert to the fact that key changes in the nature of attachment may be occasioned by hormonal, neurophysiological, and cognitive changes and not merely by socio-emotional experience.

Child–parent attachment during adulthood

There is reason to believe that a sense of autonomy from parents is normally achieved early in adulthood, presumably as a result of processes that operate gradually from infancy onward through adolescence, although research into such developmental processes is as yet sadly lacking. On the other hand, even an optimum degree of autonomy may not imply cessation of attachments to parent figures. Even though the individual is likely to have found a new principal attachment figure when a sexual partnership is eventually established, this does not mean that attachment to parents has disappeared. Most adults continue a meaningful association with their parents, regardless of the fact that parents penetrate fewer aspects of their lives than they did before. Moreover, response to the death of a parent usually demonstrates that the attachment bond has endured. Even if living quite independently of the parent, there is usually a deep sense of loss, and after mourning has been resolved, internal models of the lost figure continue to be an influence. However, there is little systematic knowledge of the nature of these continuing attachments to parents.

Thus, for example, we do not know to what extent a parent and a child grown to adulthood can enter into a reciprocal relationship in which each in some ways and at some times views the other as stronger and wiser, so that each can gain security in the relationship and each give care to the other. Or do the old dispositions persist for the parents to feel themselves stronger and wiser than their children and/or to be so viewed by them? It is generally believed to be malfunctional for the parent of a young child to reverse roles and to seek care, support, and security from the child. But it seems likely that some such role reversal might be healthy should a parent become impaired through illness or old age, as indeed Minuchin (1988) suggests. More research into such issues is needed.

Parent surrogates

There is a dearth of systematic investigation of children's relationships with parent surrogates to whom they may become attached, and who may play an important role in their lives, especially in the case of children who find in them the security they could not attain with their own parents. These might include an older sibling, another relative such as a grandparent, an especially perceptive and understanding teacher or athletic coach, and so on. Ainsworth and Eichberg (this volume) report that the death of a surrogate figure to whom the person is attached is mourned and, in some cases, the mourning may be prolonged and difficult to resolve. As potential attachment figures such parent surrogates deserve research attention.

In the case of adults, attachment figures cast in the parental mold might include mentors, priests or pastors, or therapists. Bowlby (e.g. 1988b) holds that in psychotherapy the therapist should assume the role of an attachment figure, who by inspiring trust can provide a secure base from which the patient may confidently explore and reassess his working models of attachment figures and of himself.

These secondary or supplementary attachments may differ from primary attachments in their continuing pervasiveness in the life of a person. The therapeutic relationship is a case in point. It may be very influential for a limited period in a person's life, but when therapy has been terminated the active relationship usually ceases. To be sure, the therapist and his or her influence may continue to be valued, and the representational model of the relationship may persist. However, may the attachment to a surrogate figure be said to continue, even though the active connection has ceased, and all that remains is the representational model? To be sure, death of such surrogate may be mourned, even in cases where neither help nor proximity has been sought for some time. Furthermore, later circumstances might lead a person again to seek support or otherwise renew an active relationship with a former surrogate figure. What, then, is the status of the bond during an inactive period, or indeed when all that remains is a grateful or fond recollection of an attachment figure who once was very important in one's life?

OTHER AFFECTIONAL BONDS THROUGHOUT THE LIFE SPAN

Now let us consider affectional bonds other than attachments to parents and surrogate parent figures. Affectional bonds are not synonymous with relationships; relationships differ from them in three ways. First, relationships are dyadic, whereas affectional bonds are characteristic of the individual but not the dyad; although they develop in the context of the dyad, they come to entail representation in the internal organization of the individual person. Second, relationships may be either long-lived or fleeting, whereas affectional bonds are by definition long-lasting. Third, as Hinde (e.g. 1979) has pointed out, the nature of a relationship between two individuals grows out of the total history of their interactions. These interactions are likely to be varied, involving a number of categories of content. Thus a relationship is likely to have a number of components, some of which may be irrelevant to what makes for an attachment or indeed any kind of affectional bond. For example, a mother may interact with her infant as caregiver, as playmate, and/or as teacher. All these facets characterize that particular relationship, but perhaps only one of them – the caregiving component – is directly related to the protective function believed to have been responsible for attachment having evolved.

Weiss (1974) suggested that different classes of relationship offer different 'provisions'. He identified six categories of relational provisions. (1) Attachment relationships provide a sense of security and place; in their absence we feel restless and lonely. (2) Other relationships in a social network provide a shared interpretation of experience and a source of companionship. (3) Caregiving relationships offer a sense of being needed, an opportunity for giving nurturance. (4) Other relationships provide the individual with a sense of worth and/or competence, for example, colleagues for some, families for others. (5) Kin especially give a sense of reliable alliance and the possibility of continuing assistance if needed. (6) Still other relationships are important, especially in a stressful situation, because they provide guidance – as in a relationship with a mentor. Of the relationships offering one or more of these provisions, some but not all are likely to be identified as entailing an affectional bond.

Let me define an 'affectional bond' as a relatively long-enduring tie in which the partner is important as a unique individual, interchangeable with none other. In an affectional bond there is a desire to maintain closeness to the partner. In older children and adults that closeness may to some extent be sustained over time and distance and during absences, but nevertheless there is at least an intermittent desire to re-establish proximity and interaction, and usually pleasure – often joy – upon reunion. Inexplicable separation tends to cause distress, and permanent loss would cause grief.

An 'attachment' is an affectional bond, and hence an attachment figure is never wholly interchangeable with or replaceable by another, even though there be others to whom one is also attached. In attachments as in other affectional bonds there is a need to maintain proximity, distress upon inexplicable separation, pleasure or joy upon reunion, and grief at loss. There is, however, one criterion of attachment that is not necessarily present in other affectional bonds, as both Hinde (1982) and Weiss (1982) agree. This is a seeking to obtain an experience of security and comfort in the relationship with the partner. If and when such security and comfort is available, the individual is able to move off from the secure base provided by the partner, with confidence to engage in other activities.

A relationship or a class of relationships may be important to a person without implying either an affectional bond in general or an attachment in particular. Nevertheless, relationships characterized by affectional bonds are likely to be the most important in a person's social network, even though others may undeniably play a significant part. Thus Weiss (1982) compares the loneliness experienced when an attachment figure is absent but yearned for (as in persons who have recently ended marriages and have not yet found a new partner) with the isolation experienced, for example, by one who moves into a new community away from kin, friends, and colleagues. When one is lonely, friends do not fill the gap, even though they may make loneliness easier to bear. When one is isolated, even the presence of a beloved spouse does not altogether make up for feeling without a sense of belonging in a community.

It is reasonable to focus on affectional bonds that seem to be species-characteristic because they seem to occur universally among all cultures, and are likely to have evolved because they forwarded some vital survival function. Bowlby (1969/1982) implied that affectional bonds involving the reproductive, caregiving, and/or attachment systems deserved particular attention. We have already considered the bond of child to parent which involves the attachment system. I will continue by examining the bonds of parents to child, that involve the caregiving system, then sexual-pair bonds that involve the reproductive system, and then proceed to consider other kinds of bonds whose biological basis is perhaps less readily apparent.

The bond of mother to infant

It is obvious that the core component of this bond is the caregiving system. Klaus and Kennell (e.g. 1982; Klaus, Trause, and Kennell 1975) and their associates have highlighted the phenomenon of delight and intimacy manifested by a mother who has an opportunity immediately postpartum to hold her baby in close bodily contact and to interact with him. They have amassed evidence that suggests that mothers who had this sort of experience turned out to have better maternal care practices than those who had the usual hospital delivery experience, and that their children developed better and tended to have fewer later indications of difficulty. At first, extrapolating from the ethological literature, they proposed that there was a critical period immediately after birth during which contact with the baby effected the bonding of mother to child. Thus they inadvertently implied that the caregiving system could only be activated by such immediate postpartum experience and that in its absence bonding could not take place. The impact of these studies has been great indeed, having led to a revolution in obstetric ward practices that was perhaps long overdue. On the other hand, there was a well-grounded protest that many mothers do indeed become bonded to their babies in the absence of immediate postpartum contact – a fact that Klaus and Kennell readily acknowledged.

Nevertheless there is much in the animal research literature that could support their original proposition of a sensitive period. There are species in which a mother, if separated from her infant for a brief period immediately postpartum, subsequently rejects it. But if she has even a short period with the infant following delivery she bonds to it rapidly, and later separation does not lead to rejection. Rosenblatt's research with rat mothers (e.g. Rosenblatt, Siegel, and Meyer 1979) suggests that the most potent factor in evoking and sustaining maternal behavior is the presence, appearance, and behavior of the young themselves, and that the capacity for caregiving wanes rapidly if the young are removed, and cannot be fully restored even though they are returned after brief separation. Such evidence is not to be shrugged off. Anecdotal and clinical evidence suggest that some human mothers who are separated from their babies soon after birth and not reunited with them until substantially later do indeed have difficulty in experiencing the same tenderness and commitment that others feel who have not been separated. Thus, although Robson and Kumar (1980) reported that it might take as long as a week before primiparae delivered in hospital feel bonded to the baby – and usually after they had returned home – Peterson and Mehl (1978) in a longitudinal study found that the most significant variable predicting differences in maternal bonding was the amount of time a mother had been separated from her baby during the hours and days after his birth.

However, in humans we must also reckon with representational models. Some women undoubtedly have formed a model of themselves in relation to an infant perhaps even long before the infant is conceived, maybe on the basis of their experience with their younger siblings or other infants. (And from animal studies there is reason to believe that previous experience with infants tends to make for better mothering.) Such women may be primed to bond to their infants even under difficult circumstances.

We talk of the *bond* of a mother to her child. This usage is tacitly in agreement with those who hold that this is not an attachment because a mother does not normally base her security on her relationship with her child, however eager she may be to give care and nurturance. However, despite recent research into mother–infant bonding we still know remarkably little about the processes involved in the formation and maintenance of the bond, or even of the criteria that mark its establishment. Klaus and Kennell (1982) suggested criteria, but these emerge as essentially the same as those characteristic of a responsive and accessible mother who is likely to foster secure attachment in her baby (e.g. Ainsworth *et al.* 1978). But not all babies become securely attached to their mothers, and certainly not all mothers who become bonded to their babies approximate the suggested criteria. As Crittenden (1983) makes clear, mothers who maltreat their children want desperately to keep them from being removed to foster homes. They are bonded in their own ways – ways that we do not yet know how to identify before the threat of separation intrudes. Clearly, more research is needed.

The bond of father to child

Despite the rich testimony from history and literature that fathers can have strong commitment to their offspring, the tendency has been to consider the bond of father to child as somehow less deeply rooted than the bond of mother to child. During the past ten years or so, however, there has been active research into father–infant interaction that suggests that fathers can and sometimes do perform a caregiving role and presumably become bonded to their infants.

Does paternal behavior have the same kind of biological underpinning as maternal behavior? Consideration of other species is instructive. In a number of species of birds and mammals paternal sharing in the care of offspring is clearly built in, and the same holds for a few nonhuman primate species with sexual pair bonding. But with other primate species, such as baboons, macaque monkeys, and chimpanzees, mating has been thought to be promiscuous, and males appear at best to play an indirect role in protecting the young, namely through fending off predators that generally threaten the troop.

However, in a longitudinal field study of olive baboons, Smuts (1983a, b) observed special long-term male–female relationships, in which the partners seek to be together, and indeed nest together at night, and in which the male is active in protecting the female and her offspring when they are threatened by danger. The male himself is likely to improve his chances of reproductive success through such a relationship, either because he had indeed sired the infant whom he now protects, or because the female is more likely to mate with him when she comes into oestrus.

Even in the rat – a species conspicuous for the absence of caregiving by the male – caregiving behavior may be induced under special conditions. Thus Rosenblatt *et al.* (1979) demonstrated that a male rat will manifest caregiving behavior if he is confined in the company of newborn rat pups for long enough. This suggests that caregiving behavior is built into even the male of this species but is less readily evoked than in the female. Although it is unjustified to make a direct extrapolation from one species to another, it nevertheless seems likely that when circumstances ensure that a human male has sufficient exposure to a young child, he will become a caregiver.

In our society individual differences in male and female roles and commitments are indeed great. In some families the father may spend so little time with his young children that he scarcely has a chance to become bonded to them or they to him. In other families, as Parke and Sawin (1976) have shown for example, fathers are capable of effective caregiving when they undertake it.

So far, research into father–infant interaction has been conducted on samples in which fathers were particularly interested in such interaction. We need much more representative samples of families before we can achieve a clearer picture of the range of paternal involvement even in our own society.

Sexual partnerships

Sexual pair bonds are not characteristic of all species, and there are wide differences between species in which they do occur (Rowley 1983; Wickler and Siebt 1983). There is evidence that in the environment of evolutionary adaptedness of the human species, bonds were formed between a male and one or more females and that the presence of the male enhanced the survival chances of the young (Hinde 1987). It is likely that three basic behavioral systems were involved and may still be characteristic of present-day human sexual pair bonds: the reproductive, attachment, and caregiving systems. Let us consider each of these in turn.

The reproductive system may achieve its functional outcome without an enduring bond being involved. In the human case it is obvious that mating can occur without a bond forming, but when pair bonding does occur, the caregiving system is likely to be involved, with the male concerned with the care and protection of children either directly, or indirectly through care and protection of his mate, or both. Furthermore, various societies tend to foster enduring bonds through marriage customs, whether monogamous or polygynous, thus backing up biological predispositions to ensure that young are cared for and not merely produced. In the course of a long-term sexual relationship, whether in customary marriage or not, attachment of each partner to the other tends also to be built up, the attachment and caregiving components interacting to make for a reciprocal give-and-take relationship. Typically, at least in Western societies, each partner at some times and in some ways looks to the other as stronger, wiser, and/or more competent, and the other reciprocates by providing care, comfort, reassurance, and thus feelings of security.

As mentioned earlier, an evolutionary perspective suggests that the female partner in a sexual pair bond is especially in need of caregiving during pregnancy and childbirth, and continuing while the child or children still are unable to survive without parental care. In providing care to his partner, the male helps her to care for her infant or young child, even in cases in which he gives little or no direct care to the child, only protection when needed. This might well make for a less reciprocal relationship during the early years of child-rearing, during which the female's caregiving is chiefly directed toward the child, with the male's role the seemingly more demanding one of giving care and/or protection to both. However, it makes sense to suppose that the female may also strive to give care to her partner in appropriate ways, if only in acknowledgement of the care she needs from him.

The evolutionary view makes it easy to see how culturally-ingrained sex role differences could have arisen. Nowadays in Western societies these traditional roles are being challenged, and many couples are experimenting with alternative ways of providing adequate care to their infants and young children. The more successful solutions seem to involve the male taking more responsibility for direct caregiving to the children, and the female sharing the male's responsibility for providing sustenance to the family as a whole. The less successful solutions are well-known to us. Single parents struggle to take on double responsibility, without support from a partner.

Even though parents share responsibility, the caregiving arrangements may be such that infants and young children receive inadequate care. Women may well be overburdened by responsibilities both as parents and as wage-earners, and indeed the same may hold for her male partner. Perhaps no solution can be wholly successful that does not ensure that during the period spanning pregnancies, childbirths, and the early years of child-rearing the woman somehow receives the help that she requires in order that she can fulfil her reproductive function without undue strain. (For a discussion pertinent to these issues see Bowlby (1988a).)

Although in many cultures sexual attraction may be the most important component at the start of a relationship, those that depend entirely on the sexual component are likely to be short-lived. As the relationship persists, the caregiving and attachment components are likely to become important also and tend to sustain the bond even in cases in which sexual interest has waned. Much of the research into human sexual pair bonds has focused on the break-up of the relationship – with separation or divorce and adjust-ment afterwards. It is clear that the attachment component is long lasting, tending to persist long after the pair has been parted, and even when the parting was much desired. There is a tendency to miss the partner and to feel lonely (e.g. Weiss 1979).

In many marriages there are components other than the three funda-mental components that I have emphasized so far. For example, spouses may be professional or business partners, or they may spend more than the usual time together because they enjoy sharing the same leisure time interests and activities. These and other components of the relationship with the partner in a marriage or quasi-marriage are not essential, however, and may or may not contribute to its persistence over time.

It is assumed that bonds similar to heterosexual pair bonds may be formed with same-sex partners, despite the fact that the sexual component cannot fulfill its biological function of reproduction. Such bonds may be more difficult to sustain, however, for the partners may well experience social custom as a divisive influence rather than as, in the case of marriage, a force supporting continuation of the bond.

Friends, companions, and intimates

Harlow and Harlow (1965) identified a number of affectional systems characteristic of rhesus monkeys, including a peer–peer affectional system, that led infant monkeys to approach and to interact with their age-peers. They reported evidence that experience in relations with peers played an essential role in normal development.

In all social species that have been observed in their natural environ-ment, it is clear that the group itself possesses a protective function for the individuals that comprise it. Studies of predators and their prey suggest that those who stray from the group are most likely to become victims of predation. Thus it is advantageous for individuals to keep company with other members of the group. Furthermore, in many social species it is apparent that in some activities, such as hunting, cooperative enterprise is more likely to be successful than individual efforts.

It is thus reasonable to believe that there is some behavioral system that has evolved in social species that leads individuals to seek to maintain proximity to conspecifics, even to those to whom they are not attached or otherwise bonded, and despite the fact that wariness is likely to be evoked by those who are initially unfamiliar. Some have suggested the term 'affiliative' for such a system, despite the fact that it suggests a child–parent relationship. It seems better to use another term; Greenberg and Marvin (1982) have suggested that it be called the 'sociable' system. That such a system exists in humans and may conflict with fear/wariness is suggested by the work of Bretherton and Ainsworth (1984) with 1-year-olds encountering a stranger in the strange situation. Most infants they observed showed a mixture of wary and sociable behavior upon first encountering an adult stranger when the mother was present; very few showed only wariness or only sociability. There is also evidence to suggest that infants and young children are much more likely to be sociable than wary when encountering unfamiliar age peers, and that wariness aroused by friendly adult strangers may disappear rapidly as they become more familiar.

If the sociable system leads to the establishment of a more or less enduring relationship with conspecifics that has survival function, is this a relationship to a group as a whole, or is it a matter of dyadic relationships with other individuals, or both? We can think of instances in which coherence to a group is valued by an individual, perhaps especially in the case of males – for example, the teenager who belongs to a gang of age-peers. He may or may not have a special relationship with one or more members of the group, but it is the group as a whole that is most important. However, I submit that one should not say that he is attached to the group, or even that he has an affectional bond to it, for by definition affectional bonds, including attachments, pertain to the individual in a dyadic relation-ship with another specific person. Important though identification with a group may be, let us here confine the discussion to dyadic relationships.

Friendship can connote a wide range of dyadic relationships, including relationships with acquaintances with whom one has occasional pleasant interactions, relationships with congenial companions with whom one spends quite a lot of time in activities of mutual concern or interest, and close, intimate relationships with one or a few particularly valued persons whose company one seeks intermittently. It seems likely that some of these relationships are sufficiently close and enduring to be characterized as affectional bonds, in which the partner is felt to be a uniquely valued person, not interchangeable with anyone else who might play a similar role.

Weiss (1982) described how such bonds often exist between army buddies, and that they may be identified as attachments. Indeed, there seem to be both attachment and caregiving components in such bonds. The partners seek proximity to each other; they give care and protection to each other; each feels more secure when with the other; separation or threat of separation occasions anxiety, and loss would certainly cause grief.

That such a relationship is likely to be fostered under hazardous conditions is indeed common knowledge. It is known that people who have been through a disaster together, and have protected each other, feel differently about each other thereafter – and that these feelings of closeness tend to persist. Camaraderie between strangers in wartime London became famous, as they shared danger and helped, comforted, and protected each other. That affectional bonds are especially likely to be formed under conditions of danger is only to be expected since the attachment and caregiving systems are concerned with needing and providing of protection.

However, in present-day Western societies, many friendships are formed in other than adventurous or hazardous contexts. Many are short-lived or entirely context-specific, whereas others endure despite conditions that make proximity-keeping difficult. We may attribute this enduring quality to people's capacity to form representational models of another and of themselves in relation to the other and thus to be able to sustain a bond over time and distance. But this does not help us to understand how it is that some relationships achieve this transcendent quality whereas others do not.

There are many studies of children's relations with age peers, of which relatively few deal specifically with friendships. Of these I should like to mention one by Youniss (1980), who interviewed children of three different age levels about their view of friendship. The youngest group (aged 6 to 8) emphasized playmate relations and sharing. The middle group (aged 9 to 11) tended to give more attention to the kind of reciprocity implicit in mutual attachment relationships – the kind of help that friends could give to each other, and being able to depend on that help, including companionship when lonely. The oldest group (aged 12 to 14) thought of close friendship as a relationship characterized by co-operation, reciprocity, and trust, in which one can reveal one's feelings, negotiate differences, and feel understood. However, they also stressed that recognition of congeniality of interests and activities was important in beginning and in maintaining a friendship – a feature that enhances any relationship but which is not essential to an attachment

In view of the fact that most 4-year-olds have developed enough capacity for cognitive perspective-taking and communication to establish goal-corrected partnerships with attachment figures (Marvin 1977), it is interesting that 6- to 8-year-olds seem not to have done so with friends. However, such a capacity may be obscured by the fact that metacognitive ability is not sufficiently developed in children under approximately 12 years of age to enable them in interview to reflect about relationships and actually to put into words subtle feelings and attitudes that have been implicit since a much younger age.

There is reason to believe that some close friendships have an attachment component, and some, but not all, constitute enduring affectional bonds. On the other hand, Youniss's child subjects did indicate that friendships were likely to come to an end when diverging interests drew the partners apart and/or when one partner found a new friend whose interests were more congenial than the previous best friend's continued to be. But regardless of such evidence of childhood fickleness, some early friendships do persist over many years, and are valued despite circumstances that preclude literal proximity-keeping. Indeed, close friendships formed at any age may be lasting, with the partners able again to pick up the threads after long and untroubled absences, with both still feeling they can depend on each other for understanding, reassurance, and help when needed.

Bonds with siblings and other kin

Older siblings may on occasion and to some extent play a paternal, caregiving role with one or more of their younger siblings, and thus may become supplementary attachment figures for them. When two or more siblings are separated from their principal attachment figure and cared for in the same setting, the distress of each may be somewhat diminished by interaction with the other (e.g. Heinicke and Westheimer 1965). When a child's parent dies, his feelings of grief and abandonment may be alleviated by the care he receives from an older sibling who plays a protective, caregiving role. Indeed this role may actually help the older sibling to feel more secure himself, whether because caregiving makes him feel less helpless, or because it diverts him from his own feelings of distress or grief.

Ainsworth and Eichberg (this volume) found evidence that both feelings of responsibility in caring for others in the family and/or a sense of family solidarity were important factors in successful resolution of mourning the loss of a family member. Further, in many societies (and in some families in our own society) it is common for older siblings to be expected to assume some responsibility as caregivers for their younger brothers or sisters, even when there has been no loss or major separation (e.g. Konner 1976). However, there has been little systematic research into siblings as attachment figures.

Among the few studies that have been done is one by Stewart (1983), who reported that approximately half of his sample of 3- and 4-year-old children acted to provide reassurance, comfort, and care to their younger siblings when their mothers left them alone together in a waiting room setting. He later confirmed this finding in a study (Stewart and Marvin

1984), in which the separation from the mother took place in a modified 'strange situation'. Whether the older sibling displayed caregiving behavior to the younger was found to be strongly related to his conceptual perspective-taking ability, and this in turn was related to the younger's use of the older as a secure base from which to explore the unfamiliar situation. Thus even a child of preschool age may serve as an attachment figure to a younger sibling.

Siblings close in age may also be playmates, especially when both are beyond infancy, and some of these may become friends, perhaps best friends, with the same sort of cooperative, reciprocal, mutually trusting relationship earlier described as characteristic of close friendships. This implies a secure attachment component to such sibling friendships.

On the other hand, many sibling relationships are characterized by ambivalent feelings rather than mutual cooperation and trust, and yet are likely to constitute enduring affectional bonds. Whereas friends who had once been close may drift apart as their interests shift and they become less congenial, bonds with kin tend to be much more persistent, even though they may be more ambivalent. One may account for the longevity of kinship bonds in various ways – sociological, biological, and psychological.

Cultural practices tend to regulate relations among kin in such a way as to foster in the individual a sense that he can rely on kin as allies or for substantial help when needed – as Weiss (1974) implied. Indeed, many people feel that they can ask material help from kin that they would hesitate to seek from friends, however close and congenial. In turn, they feel morally obliged to provide such help to kin when it is demanded. Such attitudes make kin especially important in a person's social network.

The biological explanation is based on the principle that the key dynamic of evolution is neither individual survival nor even species survival, but gene survival. Thus an individual organism, who shares on average half of its rare genes with each of its offspring, promotes the survival of its genes by promoting the welfare of its offspring, and in this regard stands to gain more than by supporting the welfare of others who are more distantly related or not related at all. Siblings, who also share on average half of their rare genes, tend to promote the survival of their genes by promoting each other's welfare (and thus survival) and so on, to a lesser extent, with kin less closely related.

A psychological explanation of kinship bonds rests on a shared background of experience within the family or other kinship group. Thus, despite current differences in activities and interests, and despite rivalries or other causes of ambivalence, siblings have a background of shared experience over a relatively long period of time, which not only promotes similarities in their perception of situations and in value systems that influence their decisions, but also promotes mutual understanding, without necessarily requiring explicit communication – and by extension this may also hold with other kin less closely related.

Indeed the sharing of experience over a long period of time is important not only in kinship bonds but also may well play a role in all affectional bonds that are especially lasting. In enduring marriages, surely, shared experiences are pleasant to talk about and connote a basis of mutual understanding, that in turn contributes to security and mutual trust. Even after a husband and wife have agreed to divorce, they may still find themselves tied by a long history of shared experience in which they find pleasure, despite mutual hostility, divergent aims, disparate interests, and new bonds that compete with the old. Like congeniality of interests and activities, shared experience with friends contributes to the feelings of understanding and being understood that are so focal to close friendships.

CONCLUSION

This has been a largely theoretical paper sketching how attachment theory, which initially was directed toward understanding the attachment of infant to mother (Bowlby 1969/82), can be useful in understanding attachments and other kinds of affectional bonds beyond infancy. However, the major function of attachment theory is to guide further research, which in turn will extend and refine our theoretical understanding. Throughout this chapter the need for further research has been stressed. We need further research into: (1) how attachments to parents and surrogate figures develop throughout the life cycle; (2) the caregiving system, the nature of the affectional bonds of parents to child, and their interaction with the attachments of child to parents; (3) sexual partnerships and their complex components; (4) the behavioral systems underlying friendships, how they develop from childhood onward, under what circumstances they become enduring bonds, and how such bonds resemble and differ from other affectional bonds; (5) kinship bonds, and how it is that, although often ambivalent, they are likely to be especially long-lasting.

Observational research outside the laboratory is essential in the study of attachments and other affectional bonds beyond infancy – as it was essential as a first step in the study of attachments in infancy. Indeed from it individual differences in overt behavior, both at home and in the laboratory, could be viewed as signifying different patterns of internal organization. So far, the significance of individual differences at various ages beyond infancy has rested on inferences from infant patterns of attachment, despite obvious differences in their behavioral manifestations in older children and adults.

Increasingly, across the years of childhood verbal behavior rivals non-verbal behavior as a basis for inferences about inner organization. Linguists know that there is more information to be gained from verbal behavior than the manifest content of what is conveyed in words. The latent content of what is conveyed in the form and context of discourse is important also – often more important than manifest content. This is pertinent to studies of adolescents and adults, in which interview may be a useful adjunct to naturalistic observation especially if it be considered as discourse between the interviewer and interviewee. Both researchers and funding agencies are strongly urged to turn their attention both to naturalistic observations and to the latent content of verbal behavior in discourse and interview in studies of the various kinds of affectional bonds beyond infancy.

© 1991 Mary D. Salter Ainsworth

REFERENCES

Ainsworth, M.D.S., Blehar, M.C., Waters, E., and Wall, S. (1978) *Patterns of Attachment: A Psychological Study of the Strange Situation*, Hillsdale, N.J.: Erlbaum.

Ainsworth, M.D.S. and Eichberg, C.G. (this volume) 'Effects on infant–mother attachment of mother's unresolved loss of an attachment figure, or other traumatic experience'.

Bowlby, J. (1969) *Attachment and Loss*, vol. 1: *Attachment* (2nd edn, 1982), New York: Basic Books.

—— (1979) 'The making and breaking of affectional bonds', in J. Bowlby *The Making and Breaking of Affectional Bonds* (pp. 126–60), London: Tavistock Publications.

—— (1988a) 'Caring for Children', in J. Bowlby *A Secure Base: Clinical Applications of Attachment Theory* (pp. 1–19), London: Tavistock Publications.

—— (1988b) 'Attachment, communication, and the therapeutic process', in J. Bowlby *A Secure Base: Clinical Applications of Attachment Theory* (pp. 137–57), London: Routledge, and New York: Basic Books.

Bretherton, I. and Ainsworth, M.D.S. (1984) 'Responses of one-year-olds to a stranger in a strange situation', in M. Lewis and L.A. Rosenblum (eds) *The Origin of Fear* (pp. 134–64), New York: Wiley.

Cassidy, J. (1988) 'Child–mother attachment and the self in six-year-olds', *Child Development* 59: 121–34.

Crittenden, P.M. (1983) 'The effect of mandatory protective daycare on mutual attachment in maltreating mother–infant dyads', *Child Abuse and Neglect* 7: 297–300.

Greenberg, M.T. and Marvin, R.S. (1982) 'Reactions of pre-school children to an adult stranger: a behavioral systems approach', *Child Development* 53: 481–90.

Harlow, H.F. and Harlow, M.K. (1965), in A.M. Schrier, H.F. Harlow, and F. Stollnitz (eds) *Behavior of Non-human Primates*, New York: Academic Press.

Heinicke, C.M. and Westheimer, I. (1965) *Brief Separations*, New York: International Universities Press.

Hinde, R.A. (1979) *Towards Understanding Relationships*, London: Academic Press.

—— (1982) 'Attachment: some conceptual and biological issues', in C.M. Parkes and J. Stevenson-Hinde *The Place of Attachment in Human Behavior* (pp. 60–76), New York: Basic Books.

——— (1987) *Individuals, Relationships, and Culture*, Cambridge: Cambridge University Press.

Klaus, M.H. and Kennell, J.H. (1982) *Maternal–Infant Bonding* (2nd edn), Saint Louis: Mosby.

Klaus, M.H., Trause, M.A., and Kennell, J.H. (1975) 'Does human maternal behavior after delivery show a characteristic pattern?' in *Parent–Infant Interaction*, Ciba Foundation Symposium 33 (new series) (69–78), Amsterdam: Elsevier.

Konner, M.J. (1976) 'Maternal care, infant behavior, and development among the !Kung', in R.B. Lee and I. De Vore (eds) *Kalahari Hunter Gatherers: Studies of the !Kung San and their Neighbors* (pp. 218–45), Cambridge, Mass.: Harvard University Press.

Main, M., Kaplan, N., and Cassidy, J. (1985) 'Security in infancy, childhood, and adulthood: a move to the level of representation', in I. Bretherton and E. Waters (eds) Growing Points of Attachment Theory and Research, *Monographs of the Society of Research in Child Development* 209 (1–2, Serial No. 209), pp. 66–104.

Marvin, R.S. (1972) 'Attachment-, exploratory-, and communicative behavior in 2, 3, & 4 year-old children', Unpublished doctoral dissertation, University of Chicago.

——— (1977) 'An ethological–cognitive model for the attenuation of mother–child attachment behavior', in T. Alloway, P. Pliner, and L. Krames (eds) *Advances in the Study of Communication and Affect*, vol. 3 (pp. 25–68), New York: Plenum.

Marvin, R.S. and Greenberg, M.T. (1982) 'Preschoolers changing conceptions of their mothers: a social-cognitive study of mother–child attachment', in D. Forbes and M.T. Greenberg (eds) *New Directions in Child Development, vol. 14: Developing Plans for Behavior* (pp. 47–60), San Francisco: Jossey-Bass.

Minuchin, P. (1988) 'Relationships within the family: a systems perspective on development', in R.A. Hinde and J. Stevenson-Hinde (eds) *Relationships within Families: Mutual Influences* (pp. 7–26), Oxford: Clarendon.

Parke, R.D. and Sawin, D.B. (1976) 'The father's role in infancy: a re-evaluation', *Family Coordinator* 25: 365–77.

Peterson, G.H. and Mehl, L.E. (1978) 'Some determinants of maternal attachment', *American Journal of Psychiatry* 135: 1168–73.

Robson, K.M. and Kumar, R. (1980) 'Delayed onset of maternal affection after childbirth', *British Journal of Psychiatry* 136: 347–53.

Rosenblatt, J.S., Siegel, H.I., and Meyer, A.D. (1979) 'Progress in the study of maternal behavior in the rat: hormonal, non-hormonal, sensory, and developmental aspects', in J.S. Rosenblatt, R.A. Hinde, C. Beer, and M.C. Busnel (eds) *Advances in the Study of Behavior*, vol. 10 (pp. 225–311), New York: Academic Press.

Rowley, I. (1983) 'Re-mating in birds', in P. Bateson (ed.) *Mate Choice* (pp. 331–60), Cambridge: Cambridge University Press.

Smuts, B.B. (1983a) 'Dynamics of "special relationships" between adult male and female olive baboons', in R.A. Hinde (ed.) *Primate Social Relationships* (pp. 112–16), Oxford: Blackwell.

——— (1983b) 'Special relationships between adult male and female olive baboons: selective advantages', in R.A. Hinde (ed.) *Primate Social Relationships* (pp. 262–6), Oxford: Blackwell.

Stewart, R.B. (1983) 'Sibling attachment relationship: child–infant interactions in the strange situation', *Developmental Psychology* 19: 192–9.

Stewart, R.B. and Marvin, R.S. (1984) 'Sibling relations: the role of conceptual perspective-taking in the ontogeny of sibling caregiving', *Child Development* 55: 1322–32.

Weiss, R.S. (1974) 'The provisions of social relationships', in Z. Rubin (ed.) *Doing unto Others* (pp. 17–26), Englewood Cliffs, N.J.: Prentice-Hall

—— (1979) *Going it Alone*, New York: Basic Books.

—— (1982) 'Attachment in adult life', in C.M. Parkes and J. Stevenson-Hinde *The Place of Attachment in Human Behavior* (pp. 171–84), New York: Basic Books.

Wickler, W. and Seibt, U. (1983) 'Monogamy: an ambiguous concept', in P. Bateson (ed.) *Mate Choice* (pp. 33–50), Cambridge: Cambridge University Press.

Youniss, J. (1980) *Parents and Peers in Social Development: A Sullivan–Piaget Perspective*, Chicago: University of Chicago Press.

Chapter 3

Perspectives on attachment[1]

Robert A. Hinde and Joan Stevenson-Hinde

INTRODUCTION

The success of attachment theory is due in large measure to John Bowlby's eclecticism. In his trilogy (Bowlby 1969 (revised 1982), 1973, 1980), Bowlby integrated ideas from psychoanalysis, ethology, experimental psychology, learning theory, and other sources to produce a theory that is having a major impact on studies of child development and has implications for many areas of psychology and psychiatry. For example, early on, attachment theory contributed to the abandonment of the view that food reinforcement is critically important for the development and maintenance of the mother–infant relationship. More recently, attachment theorists have contributed to the demise of the view that the child develops autonomously, with the social environment playing a merely supportive role.

Bowlby's ideas were given an observational/experimental basis by Mary Ainsworth's insight in identifying different 'patterns of attachment' and developing a reliable method of assessment in a laboratory 'strange situation' (e.g. Ainsworth *et al.* 1978). This permitted investigations concerning the antecedents and consequences of different types of attachment relationships. This period was not so much a time of testing of Bowlby's theory, but rather a filling out of the framework which he provided. Therefore, this period may be regarded as one of gestation, during which the theory was largely protected from new outside influences by its own amnion. Now that attachment theory is fully fledged, its continued development will depend upon its relations with other theories, approaches and conceptual schemes. Currently, attachment theorists are coming to terms with temperament theorists, recognizing that children differ from birth but insisting that their individual characteristics are influenced by social experience: the mother–child relationship both affects, and is affected by, characteristics of both participants (e.g. Belsky and Rovine 1987; Stevenson-Hinde 1988). Bowlby's concept of an internal working model, too easily elaborated as a catch-all that will explain anything (Hinde 1988), is being integrated with data and theories about cognitive development with quite other roots (Bretherton 1985, 1987) and the time is certainly ripe for an integration of attachment concepts with a Vygotskyan approach to cognitive development (e.g. Wertsch and Sammarco 1985).

In this chapter, we focus on the particular issue of the relations between aspects of attachment theory that stem from its biological origins, and the current view of the importance of cultural forces in influencing child development. Although attachment theory received an early cross-cultural input from Ainsworth's study of infancy in Uganda (Ainsworth 1967), the emphasis has been primarily on presumed pan-cultural aspects of the development of the child and the mother–child relationship. Indeed, Bowlby used evidence from non-human species, and explanations in terms of function in our 'environment of evolutionary adaptedness'. For instance, he suggested that, in our evolutionary past, behaviour that maintained proximity to the mother must have been adaptive for an infant, and it was for that reason that natural selection promoted the elaboration of an attachment behavioural system. Thus, much of classical attachment theory refers to aspects of human behaviour that were regarded as *pre*-cultural.

Yet anthropological studies demonstrate the importance of cultural differences in child development (e.g. Whiting and Whiting 1975), an issue by no means limited to pre-industrial societies (e.g. Bronfenbrenner 1979). Even within one culture, parental values about behaviour appropriate for males and females may have profound effects on personality development (Hinde and Stevenson-Hinde 1987). And it is only a few decades since cultural forces in the UK decreed that babies should be fed on a rigid Truby King schedule, and parents were restricted from visiting their children in hospital; now, thanks largely to Bowlby, all that has changed.

For attachment theorists, the possible importance of cultural influences was raised by the finding of a marked difference between the proportion of securely attached infants in a North German sample and that previously found in the USA (Grossmann *et al.* 1985). Subsequent results have confirmed the existence of marked differences between samples, though differences must not be regarded as primarily national ones (Grossmann and Grossmann in press). How far does this affect the bases of attachment theory? Does attachment theory deal with issues in human development so fundamental that cultural considerations are irrelevant? Or must attachment theory somehow come to terms with the issue of cultural diversity?

BACKGROUND ISSUES

Before addressing that question, some background issues must be mentioned briefly.

(a) First, biological considerations do not imply that behaviour is *determined* by genetic factors which are or were selected in evolution, but rather by a continuous interplay between those factors and experiential ones. In animals, natural selection has operated to produce individuals who can develop, and select between, alternative courses of action to suit the vicissitudes of their environments. In humans, the diversity of circumstances that an individual may encounter is even greater than in animals. What implications does this have for attachment theory?

(b) Second, natural selection acts through behaviour or its consequences to affect the mechanisms or propensities on which behaviour depends. Since a given behavioural propensity may affect diverse types of behaviour, and since the extent to which it affects any one depends on experiential and environmental factors, natural selection has shaped propensities that gave rise to behaviour that was *in general* biologically adaptive in our environment of evolutionary adaptedness but may be so no longer, and/or that was adaptive in some circumstances but not in others. To take an example, birds of the genus *Parus* have a repertoire of responses that enable them to obtain food, such as tearing bark to get organisms underneath, opening seeds, and so on. It is coincidental that this repertoire also enables them to get food provided by a new artefact in their environment – milk bottles (Hinde and Fisher 1951). Propensities evolved under the influence of natural selection in one context proved also to be advantageous in another. But similar propensities sometimes lead tits to enter houses and tear wallpaper, peck at lampshades, and so on. This fails to provide them with food, and may even lead to an untimely death. Here the biological propensities lead to disadvantageous consequences.

(c) Third, as we have seen, human development occurs in diverse cultural environments, and for every child the processes of development, socialization, and acculturation proceed hand-in-hand within the child's own social and physical environments. In matters relevant to personality development, modern environments may or may not be within the range of our environments of evolutionary adaptedness. This has several implications:

(i) Behaviour that was biologically essential then may be less so now. For example, 'fear of strangers', which most children show by about nine months of age (e.g. Bretherton and Ainsworth 1974; Schaffer 1966), might have been more appropriate in our environment of evolutionary adaptedness than it is now, when it may sometimes actually hinder desirable social interactions. However, some 'wariness of strangers' may be appropriate even now, in view of the prevalence of sexual assaults and kidnappings for various reasons (Ainsworth, personal communication, 3 March 1988).

(ii) The relations between the behavioural potentials of the newborn and adult personality may not be the same now as they were then. Forces impinging on the individual in the intervening years and affecting personality development may be different, when close family ties are not maintained throughout the life span. For example, in our environment of evolutionary adaptedness, it is likely that families remained in close proximity throughout an individual's life. Close and long-lasting family bonds were probably essential for survival then. Although close families are still advantageous – for routine caretaking of either the very young or very old, in times of illness and stress, etc. – they are no longer essential to survival, and are increasingly less common as people spread over the globe in our present Western culture.

(iii) Indeed, since natural selection acted only within a restricted range of environments, different principles of development may operate outside that range. This is analogous to the possibility that the principles operating in families experiencing severe deprivation may differ from those operating in more normal populations (see Rutter 1988).

For such reasons, any suggestion that a particular type of relationship is to be preferred over another because it is *natural* is suspect.

(d) Fourth, the forces of natural selection are concerned solely with an individual's *inclusive fitness* – that is, the eventual reproductive success of the individual and that of his/her close relatives devalued by their degree of relatedness. Whilst considerations of biological adaptation throw considerable light on the nature of human behavioural propensities, those propensities may be used to serve goals that are only remotely influenced by, or are even at variance with, considerations of biological fitness. For instance, cultural considerations may decree *Dulce et decorum est, pro patria mori*, but self-sacrifice in war rarely increases an individual's inclusive fitness.

Thus, cultural imperatives may coincide with, or run counter to, biological ones. However, culture is not to be seen as something imposed on biological man from the outside. Rather the propensities that give rise to culture – to learn from particular others, to conform, to teach, and so on – must themselves be seen as products of natural selection. As Boyd and Richerson (1986) have shown, in many circumstances it may pay individuals (in biological terms) to be guided by tradition rather than to experiment on their own. Individuals, shaped by an interplay between biological and environmental (including cultural) factors, themselves play a part in determining the nature of the cultural climate in which they live. Indeed the successive levels of social complexity (interactions, relationships, families and other groups) are to be seen as continually influencing and influenced by each other and by the sociocultural structure – that is, the institutions with their constituent roles, norms, values, beliefs, etc., and the relations between them. To understand development we must come to terms with the ways in which individuals, in developing their own self-concepts and participating in social relationships, both shape and are shaped by their social and cultural environment (Hinde 1987).

The mutual influences between the biological propensities selected to maximize inclusive fitness, and motivations directed towards cultural goals, are complex. In the remainder of this paper we consider relations between the desiderata of biology, culture, and individual 'mental health' or 'psychological well-being' (see Table 3.1), and their relevance to attachment theory.

BIOLOGICAL DESIDERATA

Bowlby's discussion of biological adaptations was concerned with species characteristics. The so-called fears of childhood were seen as biologically valuable to all individuals in our environment of evolutionary adaptedness. Now proof of biological adaptedness depends on the study of differences. It is necessary to show that one type of behaviour is more likely to lead to reproductive success than another. In so far as the behaviour in question is ubiquitous, this is impossible. Nevertheless there is often strong circumstantial and comparative evidence that many universal human characteristics are or have been adaptive, and it is reasonable to presume that the underlying propensities have been shaped by natural selection. The fears of childhood and separation anxiety are obvious examples.

However, where behavioural propensities are universal but vary in strength, it can be meaningful to ask whether the capacity to vary behaviour in particular ways in the particular circumstances that occur for a range of individuals produces adaptive outcomes. For instance, the fact that individuals are more likely to show prosocial behaviour to individuals who are related to them than to those who are not, and to individuals who are likely to reciprocate than to those who are not, are in line with predictions of evolutionary theory (Essock-Vitale and McGuire 1985).

This approach poses questions that have hitherto been asked too seldom. For instance, attachment theorists suggest that sensitively responsive mothering will produce a securely attached child, who will in turn be socially competent. (Sensitivity must of course be defined independently

Table 3.1 Desiderata that are relevant to attachment theory

Biological
  to maximize an individual's *inclusive fitness*

Cultural
  to strive after the *norms and values* of society

Psychological
  to achieve *psychological well-being*

of the outcomes, and implies responsiveness 'appropriate' to the child's needs.) However, attachment theorists seldom ask *why* this should be so – that is, why human beings are built in such a way that receiving that sort of mothering should favour the subsequent appearance of those particular adult characteristics. After all, it could be the other way round, with sensitive mothering 'spoiling' the child, and/or making the child overly dependent on one person and unlikely to form new relationships. It is usually implied that the relation between secure attachment and later social competence is part of human nature. The answer to *why* humans are like that must be given in functional/evolutionary terms. Evolutionary theory would predict that natural selection would have affected the response to childhood experiences in such a way that the sequelae would augment the survival and reproductive potential of the individual in the environments likely to be experienced. But the only predictor of later environments available to the young individual is the current environment. One would therefore expect natural selection to have shaped young individuals to use the quality of their early environment as an index of what life would be like when they grew up, and to develop personalities suitable for such an 'anticipated' environment.

In general, the data seem to be in agreement with this view: experiences of sensitive, warm, loving care are recalled by those mothers or fathers who in turn are sensitive and loving to their own children and to others (Grossmann *et al* 1988; Main *et al.* 1985; Sroufe and Fleeson 1988), whilst authoritarian parenting and a stressful environment tends to be associated with aggressive and assertive children (e.g. Baumrind and Black 1967; Maccoby and Martin 1983). Indeed, 'a reinforcing dynamic between problem behaviour and unstable ties in the family' (Caspi and Elder 1988: 237) was found across four generations of women in the Berkeley Guidance Study. Caspi and Elder suggest

> that relational styles that are learned in one situation are likely to be evoked in other situations of similar structure, especially in relatively ambiguous situations that can be structured to permit the pattern to be expressed. Moreover, when relational patterns are carried into new situations they typically elicit responses from others that support and validate that pattern.
>
> (Caspi and Elder 1988: 237)

Such continuity across generations is not incompatible with an expectation of flexibility. One would expect that individuals should show some readjustment of personality if conditions change. This also is in harmony with the studies of both attachment theorists and psychiatric epidemiologists, which show that the consequences of adverse early experiences can be ameliorated by subsequent supportive relationships (Grossmann *et al.* 1988; Main *et al.* 1985; Rutter 1988).

A further point concerning the biological desiderata of survival and reproductive success is that the interests of mother and child may differ. As the child develops, it may be in the child's biological interests to demand more maternal resources than it is in the mother's long-term interests to provide, if she is to care adequately for her next infant (Trivers 1974). There are always diverse considerations that affect this balance and thus the degree of conflict of interests between mother and infant, but the principle that mothers promote independence earlier than infants demand it holds in a wide range of animal species. It is also in harmony with the observation that, at least in Western societies, mothers tend to push their children on from one stage to the next before the children themselves, if left to their own devices, would make the move. The balance of interests will of course depend on circumstances, and weaning conflict could be much reduced in societies where it is in the mothers' interests to space births.

It is of course important to be clear about the nature of the argument here. There can be no *proof* that such properties of human behaviour and development are the products of natural selection operating in our environment of evolutionary adaptedness. All that can be said is that, in such cases, a wide range of otherwise apparently independent facts are integrated better by the theory of natural selection than by any other (e.g. Hinde 1987).

CULTURAL DESIDERATA

As we have seen, whilst natural selection acted to shape human propensities in the remote past, and may still so act today, much behaviour is aimed towards goals other than the maximization of inclusive fitness, goals determined in large part by the cultural norms and values of the society in which individuals live. In non-industrialized societies, cultural desiderata may still be such as to enhance the reproductive success of the individuals who pursue them. Amongst the Turkmen of Persia those men who acquire most money, amongst the Kipsigis of Kenya those who acquire most cows, and amongst the inhabitants of Haluk in Melanesia those who acquire most wealth, tend to leave the most offspring (Betzig *et al.* 1988). It is reasonable to presume that the ability to acquire the desideratum in each case depends on general propensities evolved under the influence of natural selection. The cultural differentiation of the desiderata depends on similarly adapted abilities of human minds to select their goals in accordance with considerations of inclusive fitness (Irons 1979). However, in modern industrialized societies wealth is not related to numbers of offspring (Vining 1986), and people pursue goals that are quite unrelated to reproductive success. The roles that individuals occupy in institutions within the society, and the norms and values that influence their behaviour, depend on diverse behavioural propensities and are often far removed, and even directly contradictory to, the biological desiderata. This poses a number of questions with which attachment researchers must now be concerned, as follows.

(a) Can we identify local forces that impose the norms of child care? This task might be more difficult in our own present, complex society than in small social groups where conformity is essential to the viability of the group. Maccoby and Martin (1983) suggest that in tightly structured societies with explicit social constraints, 'child-rearing practices of individual parents may account for less of the variance among individuals' (p. 84) than in our own society.

(b) Are the child-rearing practices in each culture in fact such as to produce adult personalities that conform to the desiderata of that culture, such as obedience, compliance, or self-assertiveness? In some cases, anthropological evidence indicates this to be the case (e.g. Mead 1935; Whiting and Whiting 1975). For example, the Whitings found cross-cultural differences in the socialization training that children received, which were related to differences in children's characteristics, such as sharing and helping.

However, as learned from the different distributions of A, B, and C patterns of attachment between a sample from North Germany (where A was predominant) and South Germany (where B was predominant), it may be misleading to make national generalizations (see also Van Ijzendoorn and Kroonenberg in press).

(c) Are child-rearing practices compatible with producing other desiderata, such as the biological one of reproductive success or the individual ones of psychological well-being in the child or a feeling of fulfilment in the mother?

(d) Given cultural differences in patterns of child rearing, are the methods of assessment used equally suitable in every case? This question concerns the *meaning* of a particular method of assessment when it is used in different cultures, and may be thought of in at least three ways:

(i) *Concurrent meaning.* For instance, does temporary separation from the mother, as employed in the Ainsworth strange situation (Ainsworth *et al.* 1978), mean the same thing to children from different sociocultural groups? In stressing the importance of meaning within relationships, Emde (1988) gives as one example the unusually high proportion of infants (compared with the USA and both North and South Germany) classified as showing the resistant, C pattern of behaviour upon reunion with mother, when the Ainsworth strange situation was used in Hokkaido, Japan (Miyake *et al.* 1985). The authors interpret this finding as arising from 'the combined influence in Japanese infants of greater temperamental proneness to inhibition and crying, more proximal interactions, infrequent separation from the mother, and less experience with situations approximating the Strange Situation paradigm' (p. 282). The latter three variables, and possibly the first as well (see Stevenson-Hinde 1988), reflect a pattern of child-rearing that is different from Western cultures.

With a Japanese style of rearing, even a 'brief' period of separation may be highly stressful. However, this need not imply that the strange situation should not be used in different cultures, but rather that it should be modified appropriately for each culture. For example, in the Japanese study, if the infants were distressed during an episode involving maternal separation, the episode was shortened from 3 minutes to 2 minutes. However, that was still a longer period than that used by most researchers in the USA, where, as argued above, separation is probably less stressful. Instead of allowing distress to occur for a fixed interval, it might be preferable to curtail a separation episode *as soon as* a particular level of distress is reached, and smoothly move into the next episode. Such a flexible rule, rather than a fixed one, would permit calibration across cultures (and indeed across individuals within a culture).

(ii) *Antecedent meaning.* Assuming modification of a method to fit a particular culture, will the antecedents of the patterns that are found be the same across cultures? For example, is the caregiver's psychological availability and sensitive responsiveness to signals inevitably an antecedent of a B pattern, as found in Ainsworth's original study (Ainsworth *et al.* 1978). This appears to be so in the USA (Belsky *et al.* 1984; Maslin 1983) and in Germany (Grossmann *et al.* 1985), and Bretherton (1985) suggests it may be true in all cultures.

Thus, at a general level, sensitive responsiveness is likely to be a precursor to security of attachment across cultures. However, at a more specific level, in terms of descriptions of the precise patterns of mothering involved, antecedents of secure attachment may well *differ* between cultures. If the means by which sensitivity is shown may vary across cultures, we need to specify which patterns should map onto the general level and which should not.

(iii) *Predictive meaning.* Will the sequelae for A, B, and C patterns be similar across cultures? In a number of studies in the USA, children who were securely attached to mother as infants were later found to have relatively long attention spans, persistence, positive affect, empathy, compliance, ego resilience, and social competence (reviewed in Bretherton 1985). As argued in (ii), at a general level, one may infer that such 'positive' outcomes may be associated with security of attachment across cultures. However, at a more specific level, what is 'positive' in one culture may well *differ* between cultures. We therefore need to clarify exactly what desiderata are involved in each culture.

This implies a need for a greater liaison between developmental psychology on the one hand and social psychology and sociology on the other, and an understanding of the dialectical relations between the levels of social complexity and the sociocultural structure (see above). The challenge here is the greater just because of the liability of these cultural norms.

PSYCHOLOGICAL DESIDERATA

Following Bowlby's lead, attachment theorists lay considerable emphasis on the desirability of 'psychological well-being'. For them, the term has an *absolute* meaning, not unlike physical well-being.

> A young child's experience of an encouraging, supportive and co-operative mother, and a little later father, gives him a sense of worth, a belief in the helpfulness of others, and a favourable model on which to build future relationships. Furthermore, by enabling him to explore his environment with confidence and to deal with it effectively, such experience also promotes his sense of competence. Thenceforward, provided family relationships continue favourably, not only do these early patterns of thought, feeling and behaviour persist, but personality becomes increasingly structured to operate in moderately controlled and resilient ways, and increasingly capable of continuing so despite adverse circumstances. Other types of early childhood and later experience have effects of other kinds, leading usually to personality structures of lowered resilience and defective control, vulnerable structures which also are apt to persist.
>
> (Bowlby 1982: 378)

The Grossmanns (in press) focus on the last point here, emphasizing resilience in adverse, attachment-related circumstances, rather than general competence in all circumstances. This involves the ability to appraise and express emotions, and to rely on close social relationships for support in times of stress. Such a restricted use of well-being is compatible with Bowlby's view that attachment reflects only one aspect (but probably the most important one) of the mother–child relationship, namely the child's use of mother as a secure base in times of need.

Thus, most attachment theorists regard the B (secure) pattern of attachment as producing the *best* outcome, leading to behavioural flexibility and the capacity to cope with a wide range of environments. Insecure patterns lead to lowered resilience and vulnerability, as implied in the preceding paragraph. For example, an insensitive or somewhat rejecting mother may require the child to adopt a style of 'avoidant' behaviour that may lead in later life to escaping into defences when stressed. In other words, an A (insecure, avoidant) pattern is forced on the child by circumstances, and its sequelae are unfortunate consequences of those circumstances (e.g. Main and Weston 1982).

An adaptationist's view also would be that behaviour is shaped by circumstances. However, the adaptationist would adopt what Bretherton (1985) has called a *relative* position: what is (or was) best, at least in terms of biological desiderata, is relative to circumstances. With this view, children may be so constituted that they adopt an A pattern, and develop a corresponding personality structure, when the latter offers the best hope for reproductive success in the circumstances prevailing (or would have done so in our environment of evolutionary adaptedness, see *Biological desiderata*, above). It then remains possible for an attachment theorist to argue that the personality best suited for reproductive success may be incompatible with psychological well-being. In other words, our biological heritage cannot prevent a course of development that may lead to less than optimal mental health.

Thus, attachment studies within the USA have shown that secure attachment leads to outcomes that may reflect an inner psychological well-being in Bowlby's sense. The assumption that security of attachment may promote psychological well-being in all cultures seems reasonable, especially if limited to the issues of emotional appraisal and expression, and resilience in attachment-related circumstances. However, one is left with the question of whether psychological well-being *necessarily* implies a fit with cultural, or with biological, desiderata. Relations among the three desiderata need to be clarified.

CONCLUSION

In considering the biological bases of attachment, we must remember that natural selection is concerned solely with an individual's eventual reproductive success and that of his/her close relatives devalued by their degree of relatedness. We may therefore think of such *inclusive fitness* as the desired long-term consequence of mother/child relationships only from a biological point of view. From a cultural point of view, behaviour and attitudes are shaped by the norms and values of the society in which an individual lives. Finally, a mental health point of view suggests that 'psychological well-being' is the desired outcome.

The greatest overlap among the three desiderata – biological, cultural, and psychological – is most likely to be found in non-industrialized societies. Modern industrialized societies are unusual in the extent to which the three desiderata have diverged, and may even be in conflict. Biological desiderata may be incompatible with a cultural desideratum to control population growth. The Western cultural desideratum of 'achievement' may require a singleness of purpose that is incompatible with psychological well-being, or indeed that is incompatible with other cultural desiderata, such as being a 'good' mother. Nevertheless, these desiderata must be seen as influencing each other. As we have seen, biological propensities, shaped by natural selection acting through the biological desideratum of inclusive fitness, affect the cultural desiderata. These in turn may influence how far behaviour is directed towards reproductive or other goals, and the circumstances in which individuals develop psychological well-being.

In conclusion, although we have done little more than pose questions, we hope that recognizing different types of desiderata will clarify thinking and lead to exploration of the relations among them.

© 1991 Robert A. Hinde and Joan Stevenson-Hinde

ACKNOWLEDGEMENTS

We would like to thank Mary Ainsworth and Klaus and Karin Grossmann for their helpful comments on the manuscript.

NOTE

1   This chapter is based on a talk first given in a symposium at the Society for Research in Child Development, Baltimore, 1987. It overlaps with the version of that talk published in *Human Development*, in press.

REFERENCES

Ainsworth, M.D. Salter (1967) *Infancy in Uganda: Infant Care and the Growth of Love*, Baltimore: Johns Hopkins University Press.
Ainsworth, M.D., Blehar, M.C., Waters, E., and Wall, S. (1978) *Patterns of Attachment*, Hillsdale, N.J.: Erlbaum.
Baumrind, D. and Black, A.E. (1967) 'Socialization practices associated with dimensions of competence in preschool boys and girls', *Child Development* 38: 291–327.
Belsky, J. and Rovine, M. (1987) 'Temperament and attachment security in the strange situation: an empirical rapprochement', *Child Development* 58: 787–95.
Belsky, J., Rovine, M., and Taylor, D.G. (1984) 'The Pennsylvania infant and family development project, 3: The origins of individual differences in infant/mother attachment: Maternal and infant contributions', *Child Development* 55: 718–28.
Betzig, L.L., Borgerhoff Mulder, M., and Turke, P.M. (1988) 'Human reproductive behavior: introduction and a review', in *Human Reproductive Behaviour: a Darwinian Perspective*, Cambridge: Cambridge University Press.
Bowlby, J. (1951) *Maternal Care and Mental Health*, Geneva: WHO, London: HMSO, and New York: Columbia University Press. Abridged version, *Child Care and the Growth of Love*, Harmondsworth: Penguin Books, 2nd edn, 1965.
—— (1969/1982) *Attachment and Loss*, vol. 1: *Attachment*, London: Hogarth.
—— (1973) *Attachment and Loss*, vol. 2: *Separation: Anxiety and Anger*, London: Hogarth.
—— (1980) *Attachment and Loss*, vol. 3: *Loss: Sadness and Depression*, London: Hogarth.

Boyd, R. and Richerson, P.J. (1986) *Culture and the Evolutionary Process*, Chicago: Chicago University Press.

Bretherton, I. (1985) 'Attachment theory: retrospect and prospect', in I. Bretherton and E. Waters (eds) Growing Points of Attachment Theory and Research, *Monographs of the Society for Research in Child Development*, No. 209, 50 (1–2).

—— (1987) 'New perspectives on attachment relations: security, communication and internal working models', in J.D. Osofsky (ed.) *Handbook of Infant Development*, 2nd edn, New York: Wiley.

Bretherton, I. and Ainsworth, M.D.S. (1974) 'Responses of one-year olds to a stranger in a strange situation', in M. Lewis and L.A. Rosenblum (eds) *The Origins of Fear*, New York: Wiley.

Bronfenbrenner, U. (1979) *The Ecology of Human Development*, Cambridge: Harvard University Press.

Caspi, A. and Elder, G.H. (1988) 'Emergent family patterns: the intergenerational construction of problem behaviour and relationships', in R.A. Hinde and J. Stevenson-Hinde (eds) *Relationships within Families: Mutual Influences*, Oxford: Oxford University Press.

Emde, R.N. (1988) 'The effect of relationships on relationships: a developmental approach to clinical intervention', in R.A. Hinde and J. Stevenson-Hinde (eds) *Relationships within Families: Mutual Influences*, Oxford: Oxford University Press.

Essock-Vitale, S.M. and McGuire, M.T. (1985) 'Women's lives viewed from an evolutionary perspective. 2. Patterns of helping', *Ethology and Sociobiology* 6: 155–73.

Grossmann, K.E. and Grossmann, K. (in press) 'The wider concept of attachment in cross-cultural research', *Human Development*.

Grossmann, K., Fremmer-Bombik, E., Rudolph, J., and Grossmann, K.E. (1988) 'Maternal attachment representations as related to patterns of infant/mother attachment and maternal care during the first year', in R.A. Hinde and J. Stevenson-Hinde (eds) *Relationships within Families: Mutual Influences*, Oxford: Oxford University Press.

Grossmann, K., Grossmann, K.E., Spangler, G., Suess, J., and Unzer, L. (1985) 'Maternal sensitivity and newborn's orientation responses as related to quality of attachment in northern Germany', in I. Bretherton and E. Waters (eds) Growing Points of Attachment Theory and Research, *Monographs of the Society for Research in Child Development*, No. 209, 50 (1–2).

Hinde, R.A. (1987) *Individuals, Relationships and Culture: Links between Ethology and the Social Sciences*, Cambridge: Cambridge University Press.

—— (1988) 'Continuities and discontinuities: conceptual issues and methodological considerations', in M. Rutter (ed.) *The Power of Longitudinal Data: Studies of Risk and Protective Factors for Psychosocial Disorders*, Cambridge: Cambridge University Press.

Hinde, R.A. and Fisher, J. (1951) 'Further observations on the opening of milk bottles by birds', *British Birds* 46: 393–6.

Hinde, R.A. and Stevenson-Hinde, J. (1987) 'Implications of a relationships approach for the study of gender differences', *Infant Mental Health Journal* 8: 221–36.

Irons, W. (1979) 'Cultural and biological success', in N. Chagnon and W. Irons (eds) *Evolutionary Biology and Human Social Behaviour*, N. Scituate, Mass.: Duxbury.

Van Ijzendoorn, M.H. and Kroonenberg, P.M. (in press) 'Cross-cultural patterns of attachment: a meta-analysis of the strange situation', *Child Development.*

Maccoby, E.E. and Martin, J.A. (1983) 'Socialization in the context of the family: parent child interaction,', in P.H. Mussen (ed.) *Handbook of Child Psychology,* vol. IV, New York: Wiley.

Main, M. and Weston, D.R. (1982) 'Avoidance of the attachment figure in infancy', in C.M. Parkes and J. Stevenson-Hinde (eds) *The Place of Attachment in Human Behaviour,* London: Tavistock.

Main, M., Kaplan, N., and Cassidy, J. (1985) 'Security in infancy, childhood, and adulthood: a move to the level of representation', in I. Bretherton and E. Waters (eds) Growing Points of Attachment Theory and Research, *Monographs of the Society for Research in Child Development,* No. 209, 50 (1–2).

Maslin, C.A. (1983) 'Anxious and secure attachment: antecedents and consequences in the mother–infant system', unpublished doctoral dissertation, Indiana University.

Mead, M. (1935) *Sex and Temperament in Three Primitive Societies,* New York: Morrow.

Miyake, K., Chen, S., and Campos, J. (1985) 'Infant temperament, mother's mode of interaction, and attachment in Japan: an interim report', in I. Bretherton and E. Waters (eds) Growing Points of Attachment Theory and Research, *Monographs of the Society for Research in Child Development,* No. 209, 50 (1–2).

Rutter, M. (1988) 'Functions and consequences of relationships: some psychopathological considerations', in R.A. Hinde and J. Stevenson-Hinde (eds) *Relationships within Families: Mutual Influences,* Oxford: Oxford University Press.

Schaffer, H. (1966) 'The onset of fear of strangers and the incongruity hypothesis', *Journal of Child Psychology and Psychiatry* 7: 95–106.

Sroufe, L.A. and Fleeson, J. (1988) 'The coherence of family relationships', in R.A. Hinde and J. Stevenson-Hinde (eds) *Relationships within Families: Mutual Influences,* Oxford: Oxford University Press.

Stevenson-Hinde, J. (1988) 'Individuals in relationships', in R.A. Hinde and J. Stevenson-Hinde (eds) *Relationships within Families: Mutual Influences,* Oxford: Oxford University Press.

Trivers, R.L. (1974) 'Parents–offspring conflict', *Amer. Zool.* 24: 249–64.

Vining, D.R. (1986) 'Social vs. reproductive success', *Behavioral and Brain Sciences* 9: 167–216.

Wertsch, J.V. and Sammarco, J.G. (1985) 'Social precursors to individual cognitive functioning: the problem of units of analysis', in R.A. Hinde, A-N. Perret-Clermont, and J. Stevenson-Hinde (eds) *Social Relationships and Cognitive Development,* Oxford: Oxford University Press.

Whiting, B.B. and Whiting, J.W.M. (1975) *Children of Six Cultures,* Cambridge: Harvard University Press.

Chapter 4

The attachment bond in childhood and adulthood

Robert S. Weiss

Bowlby has demonstrated that the accessibility of parental figures is uniquely capable of sustaining children's feelings of security and has used the term, 'attachment', to refer to the responsible relational bond (Bowlby 1969, 1973, 1977). Three characteristics have been proposed as distinguishing attachment from other relational bonds: (1) proximity seeking, (2) secure base effect, and (3) separation protest (West *et al.* 1987, following Rutter 1981; Weiss 1982).

1   *Proximity seeking.* The child will attempt to remain within protective range of his parents. The protective range is reduced in strange or threatening situations.
2   *Secure base effect.* The presence of an attachment figure fosters security in the child. This results in inattention to attachment considerations and in confident exploration and play.
3   *Separation protest.* Threat to the continued accessibility of the attachment figure gives rise to protest and to active attempts to ward off the separation.

Still other properties of childhood attachment can be identified. These include:

4   *Elicitation by threat.* Children become directed toward the parents as a source of security when they feel under threat. In a situation of security parents may be treated as friendly playfellows or may be ignored. When children are made anxious, attachment feelings and behaviors are displayed.
5   *Specificity of attachment figure.* Once attachment to a particular figure has formed, only that figure is an object of attachment in the sense that proximity to the figure provides a secure base and separation from the figure gives rise to protest. Whereas other figures may provide companionship, the attachment system seems to require the particular figure it has already incorporated. Attempts to substitute other figures fail, no matter how solicitous or caring the other figures may be.

6   *Inaccessibility to conscious control.* Attachment feelings persist despite recognition that there can be no rejoining, as after the death of the attachment figure. Separation protest continues even when an attachment figure has become inaccessible and adequate alternative figures are available.

7   *Persistence.* Attachment does not wane through habituation. Attachment in long-lasting relationships seems as reliable as in newly established relationships; if anything, conditions of threat elicit attachment more reliably to long-established attachment figures. Furthermore, attachment seems to persist in absence of reinforcement. Continuing separation from an attachment figure produces pining which abates only slowly and imperfectly. Should inaccessibility of the attachment figure be fully accepted, the result, for an extended interval at least, is not cessation of pining but rather the incorporation of pining in an outlook of despair.

8   *Insensitivity to experience with the attachment figure.* Attachment seems to persist even when the attachment figure is neglecting or abusive. Feelings of anger or misuse may then be associated with attachment feelings, and attachment feelings may consequently give rise to conflict, but, under conditions of threat, security nevertheless remains linked to proximity to the attachment figure.

Certain relationships maintained by adults appear to possess the properties of childhood attachment. Studies of individuals whose marriages are ending in divorce, for example, show that even though each of the partners is apt to feel misused by the other, each continues to feel linked emotionally to the other (Weiss 1975). In other ways, too, the pair-bonds of adults display the properties of childhood attachment. So too do parents' emotional investments in their immature children, the relationships with parents maintained by some adults in which the parents continue to be seen as guarantors of security, and the relationships of patients with counselors or therapists.

Not all pair bonds, relationships of adults and their parents, relationships of patients to therapists, and parental relationships are attachments, nor is it impossible for friendships, work relationships, or kin ties to be attachments. However, some of these relationships are likely to be attachments, others unlikely. The question is whether the relationship displays attachment properties.

Pair bonds and parents' emotional investments in immature children seem regularly to display the eight properties of childhood attachment. But most adults do not display continued child-like relationships with their own parents. Rather, most of the time at least, they treat their parents as close kin for whom they feel affection, about whom they may worry, but whose presence does not enhance their feelings of security. It is an unusual relationship of adult and parent in which the adult continues to view the parent as an attachment figure. Relationships with therapists and counselors seem sometimes to display attachment, perhaps as a 'positive transference', sometimes not.

Friendships, relationships among adult kin no longer living together, and close relationships in the workplace, although unlikely to be attachments, can be. Only rarely will loss of any of these relationships give rise to persisting grief and only rarely does a sense of emotional linkage persist in these relationships when the relationships have been troubling or injurious. Most often, none of the properties of childhood attachment are fully in evidence in these relationships.

Because they possess the properties of childhood attachment, pair-bond relationships, parental investments in immature children, some relationships with therapists and counselors, and continued childlike linkage to parents may reasonably be referred to as adult attachments. The other relationships, because they link individuals to networks of fellow workers, friends or kin, may be characterized as relationships of community.

That particular relationships should be attachments – that, for example, the pair bond should quite regularly be an attachment relationship – may be true only in societies whose social arrangements are like ours. In societies of different social arrangements the adult relationships that regularly display properties of childhood attachment might be different. Furthermore, the evidence of attachment – for example, the way separation distress is experienced and expressed – might be more muted or more strident. But it seems likely that no matter the nature of social arrangements, some relationships of adults will display properties of childhood attachment.

Social psychology traditionally divides relationships into those that are 'primary', in which the other is important as a person, and those that are more nearly instrumental (such as a relationship with a shop clerk), in which it is not the person but the service that matters. A better division would seem to be between relationships that have the properties of childhood attachment and relationships that have different properties.

The relationships that most often display the properties of childhood attachment in our society – the pair bond, parental relationships with children, some adult relationships with parents, the relationships of some parents with their therapists – differ markedly in certain respects. Especially, they differ in the extent to which the attachment figure is seen as wiser and stronger and therefore able to be protective at times when the self seems inadequate. In childhood attachment the attachment figure is, of course, seen as wiser and stronger. One aspect of the process by which adolescents relinquish attachment may be to attempt to combat their own continued tendency to see the parents as wiser and stronger. In the pair bond neither self nor attachment figure seems established as wiser and stronger, although each may now and again be seen in this way. In relation to their immature children, parents, of course, understand themselves to be the wiser and stronger. Only in persisting childhood attachment to parents and in relationships with counselors and therapists do adults view the attachment figure as children view their parents, as wiser and stronger.

There are differences, too, among these relationships, in the nature of the threat that elicits attachment behaviors and feelings. In all relationships that have attachment properties, contact with the attachment figure may be sought if there is threat to the self, threat to the attachment figure, or threat to the relationship. In childhood attachment and in adult relationships with therapists and counselors, it is threat to the self that seems most often to elicit attachment feelings and behaviors; in parents' relationships with their immature children, it is threat to the other. In the pair bond it can be any of the three, but often enough it is threat to continuation of the relationship that elicits attachment feelings and behaviors.

Are the bonds of adult attachment developments of the childhood attachment bond? This is an important question because continuity between adult attachment and childhood attachment would provide an explanation for the continued expression in adulthood of both behavior styles and behavior pathologies that have their roots in childhood experience.

Several arguments may be advanced in support of this supposition, of which three would seem to be of special weight.

1   *Similarity of emotional characteristics.* It appears that aside from choice of attachment figure, relationship to attachment figure, and nature of triggering threat, the properties of childhood attachment and adult attachment are the same. They are, in general, alike in the feelings associated with their arousal. They are also alike motivationally, in their ability to command attention and energy under conditions of threat. Only in their perceptual aspects are they different. So, they differ in the image of the attachment figure and the target of the triggering threat. This is consistent with the idea that we are dealing with the same emotional system, but one whose perceptual elements have been modified.

Loss of the attachment figure, in attachment relationships of adult life as in childhood attachment, produces grief. Separation protest as a component of grief in adults is similar to the separation protest of childhood attachment in behavioral expression. In each case a syndrome can be observed that includes calling and crying, determined and sometimes frantic search, persisting perceptual recall of the lost figure, restlessness, and eventual despair. The indefinite persistence of grief in adult attachments is also similar to the persistence of childhood distress on loss of the attachment figure.

2   *Generalization of experience.* It appears that emotional elements which
    have become associated with childhood attachment are expressed in
    adult attachments. In particular, evidence is mounting that children
    who lose confidence in their parents as attachment figures – perhaps
    because of parental divorce – are likely later to have difficulties in pair
    bonding because of distrust of their parents. No such effects are seen in
    their work relationships (Wallerstein and Blakeslee 1989).
3   *Temporal linkage.* Adult attachments in the form of pair bonding and
    parental attachment appear only after parents have largely faded as
    attachment figures. This is consistent with the surmise that adult
    attachment is a later stage of the childhood attachment system.

There are still other arguments in favor of the idea that the attachment
system in adults is a development of that in children. A later system with
the same emotional properties as an earlier one would seem likely to have
evolved as a persistence of the earlier one beyond the point in life at which
the earlier one would once have atrophied. And if an emotional system
which fostered bonding *were* to develop in adulthood independently of the
childhood system, it would be most unlikely that it would have exactly the
same properties.

Of course, it may be held that there is no special attachment system in
adults to be found in the four relationships I named, but only a tendency to
form relationships which is exhibited in any relationship. Relationships
might vary in closeness, in trustworthiness, in the extent to which they elicit
feelings of protectiveness, and in still other ways, but there is no special set
of 'attachment' relationships distinct from other relationships. This alternative theory of relationships would affirm that there are quantitative
differences among relationships but deny that there is anything quali-
tatively different about relationships of attachment.

Against this alternative theory is evidence that independent contributions to well-being are made by adult attachment relationships that are
different from those made by, to give examples, relationships of work
colleagues and friendships and kinship ties. And the converse is also true:
relationships of community, such as relationships with work colleagues,
make contributions to well-being different from the contributions made by
attachment relationships. Henderson and his colleagues have found that
individuals experiencing stress are benefited both by adequacy of attachments and by adequacy of relationships to community (Henderson *et al.*
1981).

Also, work on loneliness suggests that there exist two distinct forms of
loneliness: one produced by absence of an attachment figure, the other
produced by absence of relationships of community (Weiss 1973). Here
too it appears that attachment relationships and relationships of
community make distinct contributions to well-being.

The weight of evidence would seem to support the belief that the emotional system of childhood attachment is the parent system for the emotional systems of adult attachment. This raises the question of what might be the processes through which the emotional system of attachment in children gives rise to the emotional systems of adult attachment?

The course of development of attachment in children seems to move from overwhelming dependence on the presence of the attachment figure to relative autonomy of the attachment figure. Mary Ainsworth and her students have demonstrated that small children in strange surroundings require a parent's presence for security. The latency-age child, however, can make do with periodic assurance that the parent is accessible: for example, if a parent is at home when the child returns from school, it's off to do something else. Adolescents are still less needful of a parental presence. Although they may well dislike returning from school to an empty home, the experience is less likely to produce in them overwhelming anxiety. The progression of attachment feelings in childhood is from the 2-year-old who is dependent on parental presence to the 17-year-old who, while uncomfortable in the parent's absence, can nevertheless manage.

The relinquishing of the parents as attachment figures seems to proceed in fits and starts. Beginning in early adolescence, perhaps before, young people experience intervals in which their parents are not seen as attachment figures and the young people therefore feel themselves emotionally isolated. We can only guess at what initiates this process: it may be sexual and social maturation; it may be increased capacity to recognize the limitations of the parents or displays by the parents of frailty; it may be the young person's increasing self-confidence or increasing desire for independence; it may be distancing and rejection initiated by the parent.

The intervals of withdrawal of attachment feeling appear at first to be infrequent and short-lived; as the child matures they occur more frequently and are longer lasting. In these intervals of withdrawal of attachment feeling, the young people are likely to see their parents as they will when they are themselves fully adult: people whom they love as kin, to whom they feel emotionally linked, and in relation to whom they have obligations, but not guarantors of security nor people with whom they maintain an emotional partnership. In these intervals they no longer regulate their inner states primarily through interchange with their parents; and they may, indeed, make some effort not to do so.

By the end of the summer following high school most adolescents seem fairly far along in this process of relinquishing parents as attachment figures. Some have a boyfriend or girlfriend or best friend who fosters feelings of security just as might a parent; or, to put the matter another way, who contributes to the maintenance of an inner state of well-being. Those who do not, but who nevertheless are in process of relinquishing their parents as attachment figures, may be lonely much of the time.

Studies of loneliness across the life span (see Perlman 1988) suggest that it is in the developmental phase from late adolescence to early adulthood that loneliness occurs most frequently and, when it does occur, is most painful.

The final phase of the transformation of the attachment system of childhood is one in which an adult attachment figure is chosen. There has been a great deal of work and a great deal of speculation on the determinants of mate selection. Three types of theory dominate discussion.

The first is a theory of choice in a situation of competition for attractive partners. This type of theory has it that attractiveness, however judged, is agreed on throughout the mating pool, and that the most attractive men and most attractive women choose each other, and drop out of the pool. Then the next most attractive choose each other, and so on. The process works equally well if the most attractive do not actually choose each other sooner than others but only hold themselves aloof, waiting for each other. Attachment plays no role in this theory of mating choice – only desirability.

The second type of theory has people being attracted by a sense of adequate commonality in some important respect: values, interests, ideals, goals, or underlying dynamics. The commonality that those who hold this theory emphasize is likely to be dependent on the data they have available; sociologists who work with census data are likely to emphasize demographic similarity. Again, attachment plays no role.

The third type of theory is of complementarity: people choose others who, while they may share backgrounds or values, also provide some sort of need satisfaction. If he needs to be nurturant, she needs to be nurtured; and so on. And, again, attachment plays no role.

There may well be truth in all these theories. And they may be correct in their indifference to attachment formation. On the other hand, it may be that early attachment experience decides the kinds of partners with whom new attachments are formed most easily and also the developmental course of such new attachments. Study of the further course of arranged marriages suggests that the basis for mate selection is of secondary importance so far as eventual attachment is concerned.

But in many parts of the world the choice of mate is made with very little contribution from the young people themselves; the marriages are instead arranged by their kin. In Blood's (1967) study of arranged marriages among the Japanese, some among his respondents spoke of the wonderful experience of falling in love with the person, recently a stranger, to whom they were now married.

It appears that, however mates are chosen, attachment can be expected. Gay Kitson, in a study of separating couples – surely a worst case – found only 16 per cent of her sample to display no indication of persisting attachment (Kitson 1982). Very likely the development of attachment in marriage is fostered by proximity and sexual accessibility. It may well be further promoted by the very stressfulness of the transition to married life, which might foster uncertainty regarding the adequacy of the self. Further, marriage effectively limits the pool of potential attachment figures to the marital partner.

In many couples, in our society, attachment is already on its way to being established before marriage occurs. Indeed, courtship behaviors can best be understood as expressions of attachment in formation. That a couple seen in a restaurant are in process of forming attachment can be recognized by their behaviors. They look deeply into each other's eyes, they listen raptly to each other's speech, their hands seek to touch. We know from our own experience that such touch would be charged, electric.

In this interaction each member of the couple appears engaged in a process of incorporating visual, auditory, and kinesthetic images of the other. Accompanying and fostering this process of incorporation would be the sense each experiences of well-being: of being understood and admired; of feeling thoroughly secure; of being, almost, fulfilled. Also fostering this process would be the uncertainties of a developing relationship.

Attachment to new figures seems to proceed in fits and starts, just as does the relinquishing of attachment figures. During courtship the other person may at times be seen as a stranger, without emotional significance. This can lead to panic that commitment to this relationship will mean not being available to someone who would more reliably provide a sense of security and augmentation. In courtship there can be intervals of distress as well as heightened well-being.

Sometimes courtships end here; the gratifications in the relationship are insufficient; the questions too great. But should courtship continue, a perceptual model of the other, of the way the other person looks, sounds, and feels, is incorporated within the individual's security-fostering system. Then, as the attachment to the other person becomes reliable – and the ceremony of marriage may help this happen – less energy need be given to assuring the continuation of the attachment relationship. Instead, the secure base of the attachment relationship can be taken for granted, and attention and energy given to efforts to achieve goals in the world outside the self.

Just as children display secure attachment by an absence of attention to the attachment figure, so do adults. A couple whose attachment to each other is of long standing might be identified in a restaurant by a mutual comfort devoid of the intense mutual attention characteristic of courtship. Such a couple would no longer gaze deeply into each other's eyes. Instead they might talk in a friendly, perhaps desultory, fashion, sometimes glancing at each other, often looking elsewhere. Instead of listening to each other with rapt attention, they would permit themselves to be distracted. They would no longer seek opportunities to touch. Should they nevertheless touch, the touch would no longer be charged. They would, in short, look like any married couple. This is attachment in place, functioning as a stable base.

Few among the married give much attention to the critical role of the attachment system in their emotional lives. Their attachment to their husbands or wives is, instead, taken for granted. Relatively brief separations may, however, produce – much to their surprise – separation distress. Here is a comment made by a businessman interviewed in the course of a study of stress and support among occupationally successful men. The man is a successful production engineer. His wife is herself a capable woman, head of their neighborhood association. The man said that he liked to get off by himself after dinner so that he could quietly read. He said:

> I believe in togetherness, but not total togetherness. In the evenings, of course, we have dinner together and then Doris goes off and does her association work and I do my reading and fall asleep. It's always been like this. I like to have some time to myself by myself. I need it. Always did. Provided I know she's in the next room.
>
> About eleven years ago I sent Doris and all the children to visit her sister for Christmas vacation, and while we were planning it I was looking forward to it. And when it happened, I couldn't stand it. I did it again about two years ago, for a shorter period, and I didn't like that either.
>
> I don't like an empty house. I like to be by myself, provided I know Doris is in the next room. I don't like it when she goes out at night. It is strange. I'm perfectly happy to be in one room by myself as long as I know she's in the next one.

Attachment in marriage (or other adult pair-bonding) seems potentially lifelong. Even in conflict-filled marriages attachment usually remains in place and, despite the marriages' other problems, provides a stable base for goal-directed activity (Weiss 1975). The death of the marital partner ordinarily is responded to with deep and persisting grief, in which separation protest is a principal component.

The development of parental attachment to immature children seems to occur suddenly and to persist strongly. Unsystematic observation and interview suggest that adults who may have had no sensed need for a relationship with children for many years may, in a very brief time, develop very strong investment in newly born children, in children still in gestation, or in only the idea of having children. Loss of a child seems regularly to give rise to a state of grief in which separation protest is intermeshed with protective drives. This state is remarkable for its persistence. Although in time the intensity of pain seems often to abate, the sense of continued connection to the child seems to persist indefinitely, and grief seems easily elicited even many years after loss (Lehman *et al.* 1987). Discussions with members of The Compassionate Friends organization corroborate this.

Little more can be said about parental investment in children as an attachment phenomenon, except that parents seem to display diminished attachment to children who have matured. Under ordinary circumstances parents seem content with only occasional contact with mature children. However, risk to mature children may again elicit attachment feelings, and the death of mature children produces in their parents the same persisting grief that is displayed by parents whose immature children have died.

There is much to be learned about the attachments of parents to children, immature and mature. We know little about what triggers attachment to children, about its modification with time, and about how it ordinarily expresses itself in day-to-day life. Nor do we understand fully why parental grieving so regularly persists indefinitely.

The development of the third attachment bond of adult life, persisting attachments to parents, appears to be a failure to follow the more usual developmental course. In this more usual course parents are largely relinquished as attachment figures by the time the individual enters adulthood. Why this happens in some individuals has not been studied.

The development of an attachment bond in client relationships with therapists or counselors has been characterized as transference of child-hood feelings toward parents to figures in a similar relational position. Very likely this is correct. It seems likely that such transference would most often occur when individuals feel themselves inadequate to the challenges confronting them and seek a strengthening alliance. The definition of the therapist or counselor as wiser and more knowledgeable may also play a role.

Attachment relationships appear to be of special importance for the maintenance of feelings of security, just as relationships of community appear to be of special importance for goal attainment. The loss of any attachment relationship would seem to lead to separation protest, one aspect of which is a sense of helplessness and fear. The presence of attachment, on the other hand, buffers what could otherwise be devastating events (Brown and Harris 1978). In adults as well as in children, attachments appear to be relationships critical to continuing security and so to the maintenance of emotional stability.

© 1991 Robert S. Weiss

REFERENCES

Blood, R. (1967) *Love Match and Arranged Marriage*, New York: The Free Press.
Bowlby, J. (1969) *Attachment and Loss*, vol. 1: *Attachment*, New York: Basic Books.
—— (1973) *Attachment and Loss*, vol. 2: *Separation: Anxiety and Anger*, New York: Basic Books.

—— (1977) *Attachment and Loss*, vol. 3: *Loss: Sadness and Depression*, New York: Basic Books.
Brown, G. and Harris, T. (1978) *The Social Origins of Depression: A Study of Psychiatric Disorder in Women*, New York: The Free Press.
Henderson, A. Scott, Byrne, D.G., and Duncan-Jones, P. (1981) *Neurosis and the Social Environment*, New York: Academic Press.
Kitson, G. (1982) 'Attachment to the spouse in divorce: a scale and its application', *Journal of Marriage and the Family* 44: 379–93.
Lehman, D.R., Wortman, C.B., and Williams, A.F. (1987) 'Long-term effects of losing a spouse or a child in a motor vehicle crash', *Journal of Personality and Social Psychology* 52: 218–31.
Perlman, D. (1988) 'Loneliness: a life span, family perspective', in R.M. Milardo (ed.) *Families and Social Networks*, Beverly Hills, Calif.: Sage.
Rutter, M. (1981) 'Attachment and the development of social relationships', in M. Rutter (ed.) *Scientific Foundations of Developmental Psychiatry* (pp. 267–79), Baltimore: University Park.
Wallerstein, J.S. and Blakeslee, S. (1989) *Second Chances: Men, Women, and Children a Decade After Divorce*, New York: Ticknor and Fields.
Weiss, R.S. (1973) *Loneliness: The Experience of Emotional and Social Isolation*, Cambridge, Mass.: MIT Press.
—— (1975) *Marital Separation*, New York: Basic Books.
—— (1982) 'Attachment in adult life', in C.M. Parkes and J. Stevenson-Hinde (eds) *The Place of Attachment in Human Behavior*, New York: Basic Books.
West, M., Sheldon, A., and Reiffer, L. (1987) 'An approach to the delineation of adult attachment: scale development and reliability', *The Journal of Nervous and Mental Disease* 175 (12): 738–41.

Chapter 5

The social construction of uncertainty[1]

Peter Marris

Our theories of human behavior split into largely independent systems of thought: psychology and social science. When we think psychologically, we mostly take the institutional relationships, the economy and culture of society for granted, and attend to the way people manage, successfully or not, the circumstances of life. When we think as sociologists or economists, we treat human beings as if they could be reduced to a definable role in a system of relationships – the rationally self-interested economic actor; the bureaucrat; the mother's brother – and go on to explore the implications of that system. We rarely explore the interaction between each unique human actor and the social systems of which she or he is part. Yet, surely this interaction ought to be at the foundation of any theory of human behavior. How can we begin to understand ourselves except as creatures of the societies from which we learned the language itself to think about ourselves? And how can we understand society except as a network of patterns of relationship which each of us is constantly engaged in creating, reproducing, and changing? For lack of this crucial theoretical link, we have never developed within psychology a strong tradition of social criticism, while our sociology and economics have often been psychologically naive and insensitive. We need a way of thinking about the interaction between unique human beings and the social relationships they form, not only because our theories are crippled without it, but because without it we cannot articulate clearly many of the gravest causes of social distress.

I want to present the argument that attachment theory powerfully links the social and psychological aspects of human behavior. John Bowlby's contribution will, I believe, be seen to be as central to the development of sociology as it has been to psychology. Talcott Parsons, the outstanding American social theorist of the 1940s and 1950s, recognized this many years ago. In a paper first published in 1958 he noted: 'In this connection [the interaction between personality and culture] I am particularly indebted to a paper by John Bowlby, "The Nature of the Child's Tie to its Mother" ... and to personal discussions with Bowlby' (Parsons 1967: 83). Parsons, however, continued to work with Freudian concepts and did not fully realize the significance of attachment. I will try to set out my own understanding of the part attachment plays in the construction of social relationships and of ourselves as social beings. My argument relies on three key terms: meaning, attachment, and uncertainty.

MEANING

A meaning is an organization of experience which enables us to identify those events which matter to us, relate them to previous experiences, and determine how we should respond to them. It involves classifying events, ordering purposes, and recognizing feelings associated with events and purposes. Like all living organizations, it evolves constantly and reiteratively, as events provoke emotions which influence purposes which in turn influence the events which follow and how we feel about them.

We would not be able to survive for any length of time without these meanings. Unless experience can be perceived as patterns which recognizably repeat, we cannot learn or predict anything. The process of growing up is, then, as much as anything, the maturing of organizations of meaning.

But meanings are organized as social institutions as well as personal understandings – as science, religion, ideology, law, art, and most fundamentally in the structure of a language. And these institutionalized meanings, too, have a life of their own, evolving as they are reiterated. As much as our personal understandings, which incorporate them, they create the predictability of human interaction.

ATTACHMENT

Attachment is the first and most crucial relationship through which human beings learn to organize meaning. Since our well-being depends on securing the protection of our attachment figures, that relationship is our central concern throughout childhood, and its unresolved insecurities linger into adult life. As John Bowlby has emphasized, attachment evolves as an interaction between a unique child and its unique parents, through which each learns a set of strategies by which to manage the relationship. Even within the first few months an infant's strategies begin to be informed by learning, so that long before a boy or girl can express meanings in words, each has already established a powerful organization of emotions, desires, and patterns of experience centered upon the two essential tasks of childhood: to secure the attention of attachment figures and to learn to use growing abilities. A young child has to figure out, above all, how to get what's needed from attachment figures – including the need not to be interfered with when trying to learn some new skill, without ever being abandoned to the consequences of failure. To succeed in this, a child has two resources – making a fuss and working the system – and so have the parents. By making a fuss, I mean all those behaviors by which we express our want of attention or frustration at attentions which do not satisfy us – such as crying or an outburst of temper. By working the system, I mean understanding how to comply with the requirements of a relationship to achieve a desired result. These strategies merge in practice: by demands for attention, a child helps to create the patterns of an attachment relationship with which he or she may then comply. And expressions of anger may become part of a pattern of interaction which the child learns to be effective. But the balance between assertion and compliance in a child's experience of attachment represents a fundamental learning about the nature of order and security. Both compliance and assertion imply a trust that attachment figures will respond predictably to behavior, but they imply different strategies of coping when that trust breaks down: one seeks to understand better, the other intensifies assertion. I want to suggest that as we grow up, our bias towards one or the other represents a fundamental aspect of our attitude towards the problem of securing relationships, and even of securing social order at large.

Learning to manage the attachment relationship therefore is learning to understand order and control. Since this relationship is the source of virtually all security, comfort, and nourishment in early life, the management of attachment is the starting point and model for understanding every other kind of order. As John Bowlby wrote in the second volume of *Attachment and Loss*:

> no variables ... have more far-reaching effects on personality development than have a child's experiences within his family: for, starting during his first months in his relation with both parents, he builds up working models of how attachment figures are likely to behave towards him in any of a variety of situations, and on those models are based all his expectations, and therefore all his plans, for the rest of his life.
>
> (Bowlby 1973: 369)

I think this is why, when as grown men and women we are under stress, we revert to treating even the physical world like a parent – we lose our temper with recalcitrant machinery, pray for the dangerous storm to pass, make promises to heaven. Throughout our lives, asserting our will and seeking knowledge remain the two often competing means by which we create order, predictability, and meaning. Whether we tend to see order as natural and secure, something to learn about and respond to, or as the fragile imposition of human will on chaos and destructive impulses will be determined, I believe, largely by our childhood experience of attachment. And that experience will be influenced in turn by the child-rearing practices of a culture. This is the first crucial link between sociological and psychological understanding: the experience of attachment, which so profoundly influences the growth of personality, is itself both the product of a culture, and a determinant of how that culture will be reproduced in the next generation – not only the culture of attachment itself, but all our ideas of order, authority, security, and control.

Meanings tend to be self-confirming. We create relationships which embody them and avoid, repudiate, or deny situations which buffer or contradict them. Scientists, as Thomas Kuhn has argued, abandon their paradigms of theory as reluctantly as all of us give up our self-conceptions (Kuhn 1962). For the most part, this conservative impulse to protect the predictable order we have learned to perceive and reproduce serves us well, both in our private lives and our cultural institutions. Yet that ordering of experience also constantly breaks down, not only because we encounter events which we cannot understand, but because the purposes which inform that ordering become disrupted. We cannot, in the long run, prevent relationships from changing and becoming contradictory, if only because the act of reproducing a relationship changes it. It becomes more familiar and commands less attention, latent inconsistencies and incompatibilities become manifest with development, anomalies accumulate, meanings break down as their embodied forms disintegrate and are contradicted by experience. This vulnerability constitutes uncertainty.

UNCERTAINTY

Uncertainty, in these terms, is distinct from risk. Risks are characteristically intelligible and predictable: a gambler knows what the odds are and why; an entrepreneur can calculate what it would take to make a profit, and guess at the chances of success. Win or lose, they can readily make sense of their situation. Uncertainty arises when we can no longer make sense.

The uncertainties we face are essentially of three kinds: first, events which we do not understand enough to make them predictable – including the seemingly arbitrary or random acts of others; second, events which, although they are intelligible, disrupt the purposes which make actions and attention meaningful, such as the loss of an attachment or a natural disaster; and third, the breakdown of organization through internal contradictions, as when the latent inconsistencies in a theory can no longer be ignored, or the ambivalence of our purposes becomes unmanageable, or the disparity between normative understanding and experience is overwhelming.

We handle such uncertainties constantly in everyday life. If we cannot succeed in understanding an event, we may ignore it, pretend it never happened, or remember it differently. When our purposes are disrupted, we retreat to more essential purposes, and learn how to convince ourselves that we can live without what we cannot have. We reformulate ideas and purposes to extricate ourselves from their inherent contradictions. The strategies by which we reintegrate the organization of meaning are subtle, complex, often devious, sometimes enlightening and empowering, some-times impoverishing and perverting. The measure of their failure is anxiety, defensiveness, depression, and grief.

Each person's vulnerability to uncertainty depends partly on how well the culture and institutions of his or her society can impose meaning on events, discovering predictable patterns to guide his or her actions. But it also depends largely on that person's place in society because, as I shall discuss later, the social control of uncertainty is competitive, often protecting the more powerful at the cost of greater uncertainties for the less powerful. People who have experienced, or fear they will experience, more unexpected and disruptive events will develop different coping strategies than the more fortunate. The distribution of uncertainty, therefore, affects both vulnerability and the response to it, affecting vulnerability in the future. In this paper, I want to raise two questions about these complex interactions. First, in what conditions is a person's ability to cope with uncertainty most likely to break down and recovery to be most difficult? Second, how does the social organization of control over uncertainty affect the likelihood that someone will be exposed to these conditions?

GRIEF

When is the ability to make sense most likely to break down? That is, under what circumstances does our difficulty in understanding what is happening, in retrieving a sense of purpose, or in coping with contradic-tions overwhelm us with anxiety, despair, or grief? Research on bereave-ment, depression, and the effects of unemployment suggest that childhood experience of attachment, the nature of events themselves, and the social context in which they occur all affect our resilience.

Any loss which fundamentally disrupts the central purposes of our lives will normally provoke severe and long-lasting grief. To reintegrate those purposes, so that they can once again inform life, the bereaved have at once to retrieve and consolidate the meaning of what they have lost, detach that meaning from the irretrievable past, and reformulate the meaning so that it becomes relevant to the present. It is a painful, ambivalent process, but within a year or two, most people recover a sense of worthwhile activity.

A study of widowed people in Boston (Parkes and Weiss 1983) shows that three circumstances especially affect the difficulty of recovering from bereavement: the suddenness and unexpectedness of the loss, ambivalence towards the lost relationship, and an over-dependence on that relationship which seems to reflect an underlying insecurity about attachments. A recent study of people bereaved by automobile accidents confirms how extraordinarily difficult it is to recover from grief when there is no time to prepare (Lehman and Wortman in press).

Brown and Harris's (1978) study of depression amongst women in the Camberwell district of London reveals a corresponding set of causes. Women who had lost a parent in childhood were more vulnerable to depression, as were those whose marriages were not emotionally supportive or who had the stress of coping with three or more children under fourteen. But episodes of depression were precipitated by some unforeseen misfortune – a bereavement, losing a job, eviction from a home. Studies of men and women laid off after years of steady employment – as has happened frequently to employees in the older established manufacturing industries in Britain and America in recent years – have noted the prevalence of stress and stress-related symptoms, such as alcoholism, impotence, marital breakdown, and increasing death rates from heart disease (Ferman and Gordus 1979; Buss and Redburn 1983). Even though unemployment clearly results from economic circumstances beyond the worker's control, the unemployed are increasingly inclined to blame themselves as their search for comparable re-employment fails, and their self-esteem falters. But men whose marriages are less gender-stereotyped survive the experience of unemployment better because their sense of themselves is less uniquely invested in their role as provider.

From these, and many other studies – including studies of collective disasters (see, for example, Miller (1974); Erikson (1979); preface to Marris (1986)) – we can begin to put together a general description of the circumstance which affect our ability to cope with uncertainty.

First, because meaning is organized by purposes, any event which thwarts our crucial motives for action is likely to cause bewilderment and a sense of futility. Since these motives are intimately associated with attachments, the loss of a crucial attachment is characteristically the most severely disruptive of such events. But the loss of a self-conception, especially if it affects attachments or other relationships, can be traumatic too: as when a man, shamed by loss of status, feels he cannot face his wife, his children, or his friends.

Second, all unintelligible events are disturbing, but unintelligible events which also disrupt our purposes and attachments are doubly threatening. Intelligibility is not only a matter of whether the event itself is identifiable, but whether what happens makes sense in the context of someone's life. The reasons for a plant closure can be explained, for instance, but it still often does not make sense to the workers, who saw themselves working harder and more productively than ever, making something worthwhile. We know about cancer, but we still cannot easily understand why someone young and healthy whom we love should be struck down by it. Such events are hard to assimilate, I think, because they contradict the foundation of our security – the child's faith in the fundamental benevolence of the order its attachment figures present.

Third, disruptive events are much harder to deal with if they are both sudden and unexpected, because we cannot prepare for them. They are often unintelligible, too, in the sense that we cannot understand why this should have happened to us.

Fourth, people are less likely to be overwhelmed by disruptive events, and will recover from them more quickly, if they can be sustained by supportive relationships which continue. An intimate marriage, where the couple communicate their feelings to each, and treat their life together as a partnership, rather than a division of labor, appears as a protection against depression both in the Brown and Harris study, and in studies of the effects of unemployment. Continuity of friendship is valuable to the bereaved, as are services such as those run by Cruse.

All these conditions are at least partly independent of the personal history of the person who experiences them. That is, our vulnerability to grief and depression is as much a factor of the social and physical environment we inhabit as it is of personality. Anyone may suffer a traumatic loss, a bewildering change of fortune, and have to face it alone and unaided. But our childhood experience of attachment also profoundly influences our resilience, both because our fundamental sense of security or insecurity is formed by it, and because insecurity in childhood is likely to lead to more ambivalent attachments in adult life. Anyone, for instance, who has lost an attachment figure in childhood, whether by death or separation, is likely thereafter to mistrust attachment. Since our purposes arise most fundamentally out of attachments, the whole organization of life's meaning is then founded on ambivalence. The motives for living are confused by anxious impulses to test, conciliate, or defend oneself against attachment figures. Disruptive events impose upon an already fragile, conflicted structure of interpretation. At the same time, this underlying mistrust is likely to inhibit the relationships which could provide support in misfortune.

In general, then, the more likely our environment is to engender unintelligible, unexpected, and disruptive events, the less support we have, and the more our confidence in attachment has been undermined or distorted by the experiences of childhood, then the more likely it is that our vital organizations of meaning will be overwhelmed, or crippled in their development. Or to put this the other way about – a society that best protected its members from grief and depression would organize its relationships so that they were as stable, predictable, understandable, and careful of attachments as is humanly possible. And the qualities of behavior that would need to inform such relationships – sensitivity, responsiveness, mutual understanding, consistency, ability to negotiate – are very much the same as those which create secure attachment. I believe such a familial conception of social order is attractive to most of us: our need to nurture and to be nurtured, to make attachment secure, to see the meaning of our lives confirmed by the meaning of society at large all respond to it. Yet, at the same time, we have powerful impulses pulling us in the opposite direction, towards an unequal, unsupportive distribution of uncertainty.

THE DISTRIBUTION OF UNCERTAINTY

There is a fundamental asymmetry in the logic of control over uncertainty. Suppose you have a purpose which depends on factors beyond your control, such as the state of the market or the weather. Your chances of fulfilling that purpose are likely to be greater the more ways there are to carry it out. If, for instance, the purpose depends on a fine day, the more days you can hold open to accomplish that purpose, the more likely you will be free to choose a fine one. Or if you want to start a business, the more options you can exercise in putting together capital, suppliers, labor, markets, sites and buildings, the greater the chance of holding some possibilities open while negotiating others, until you are able to bring together the resources you need. But this freedom of action is only possible so long as other people make commitments in advance to go along with whichever line of action you choose. The seller is bound to honor the option to buy, whatever happens to the market, though the buyer is not bound to take it up. The more predictable other people's responses can be made to be, the more surely can the potential consequences of alternative action be traced out, and the more confidently can the most promising be chosen. But the advantage of this position depends upon not committing your own response in advance.

This asymmetry is not necessarily oppressive. Those who wait upon another's actions may exact a reward for their compliance which makes it worth their while. And there are many human endeavors which cannot be organized without people being willing, sometimes, to wait upon the decisions of others. Human as well as material resources may have to be held back, ready to be deployed or not, as a situation develops. We can accept this, patiently, as in the nature of what we want to achieve, even when it is personally frustrating, if the collective purpose means enough to each of us. But whether it is paid for, an agreed necessity of organization, given, or extorted, freedom of action in the face of uncertainty is a privileged freedom.

In an office, for instance, a secretary who has had nothing to do all afternoon is presented with a report to type ten minutes before she expected to leave. Or a husband calls from his office to say he won't be home for dinner after all. Or a candidate for a job is left to wait indefinitely for a decision. In each instance, someone's freedom of action requires that someone else is reliably there, that a meal is cooked, that a candidate is waiting to hear, whose own plans and purposes meanwhile take second place. A privilege of power is casually assumed in each of these exchanges. Such inequalities are embedded in more complex chains of manipulation.

The husband who does not come home to dinner may be responding, like the secretary, to the sudden demands of a boss who also faces an emergency. Within any hierarchy, the time and resources of those at the lower levels are geared to the rhythms and needs of their superiors, and so the scope to initiate purposes of one's own becomes more and more restricted.

But the capricious and unpredictable use of authority is constrained by the collective power of the various subordinate ranks to demand a reciprocal predictability from authority. The management of uncertainty becomes codified in rules of procedure. Who is to be laid off first when business is bad, which operative is to be sent home when a machine breaks down, who is to be promoted when someone leaves, are determined by principles which leave less and less freedom of action. Over time, the internal relationships of a mature organization tend to become mutually constrained; and this, as critics of bureaucratic management have often remarked, inhibits the ability of the organization as a whole to change.

In this stage of development, therefore, organizations tend to protect their own internal structure from external threats which would upset the established internal balance of control by interposing buffers. Large firms, for instance, protect themselves against fluctuations in the market by contracting out part of their production to smaller firms, which can then be forced to absorb most of the variation in demand. Or a company insulates its headquarters from its production – employing low-paid, unorganized women workers in factories in depressed areas, for instance, while the core of the organization operates in a much more protected environment. At the same time, trade union organizers may be indifferent to these women workers, because accepting their vulnerability enables the union to win a measure of security for the remains of its traditional constituency. The same principle of differentiation appears in the international dispersion of production or the importation of temporary workers: in each instance, the core of an organization – a company, a bureaucracy, even a nation – protects itself against uncertainty by interposing a set of relationships which it can control but does not internalize. These peripheral relationships absorb at least the initial disruptions of uncertainty.

The same pattern appears in governmental relationships. The most powerful departments and authorities maintain their balance by forcing the weaker to bear the burden of adjustment. National government in Britain, for instance, regulates economic policy partly by manipulating local government expenditure, now requiring cutbacks, now offering selective grants to stimulate employment, in a series of short-term maneuvers which tend to frustrate local planning. Correspondingly, some proposals by the Reagan administration, under the slogan of a 'new Federalism', can be seen as attempts, in practice, to insulate the Federal Government from the increasingly difficult and unstable environment of social service provision.

The exploitation of both subordination and marginality are universal tendencies of the management of uncertainty. The two processes are related. The attempt to secure one's freedom of action by imposing a predictable set of subordinate relationships will generate a reaction, setting limits to that freedom – limits which have to be accepted to prevent the system of relationships becoming too vulnerable to instability and disruption. But this reciprocity, because it tends to establish a balance of control with small margins of tolerated flexibility, then leads to a process of insulation from external threat by the interpolation of weaker organizations or groups who have to bear the largest burden of uncertainty.

For instance, as I found in interpreting the British Community Development Project (Marris 1987) the deprivation of many inner city neighborhoods is neither an accident of economic change nor a concentration of 'social pathology' in the least desirable housing. It represents the slack in the system: the reserve of labor, land, optional expenditures which can be taken up or laid aside, as circumstances change, protecting others from the threat of disruptive adjustments. The consequences for the least powerful of having to contend with so disproportionate a burden of cumulative uncertainties can be crushing; and the characteristic responses to it – resignation; withdrawal from long-term hopes, purposes, or commitments; feelings of depression and hopelessness – also decrease the likelihood of any collective organization of defense. If this burden of uncertainty cannot be redistributed more equally, there will continue to be a substantial minority in our societies, so hemmed in by the unpredictability of circumstances they cannot control, that the meaning of their lives is impoverished.

But these impulses of subordination and marginalization threaten more and more of us. As economic resources come to be organized under the control of great international corporations, we all become dependent on these corporations for the jobs, tax revenues, and expenditures that sustain our way of life. In return, because they are so powerful, they can demand our commitments while insisting upon their own freedom of action. Much that has happened in the last few years in Britain and America – the weakening of trade unions, the repudiation of tariffs and restrictive regulations, the commercialization of public resources and destruction of communities – has been justified as giving businesses the freedom to generate greater profit. But whatever this may do to promote the wealth of nations, it reinforces all those conditions which tend to make uncertainty overwhelming. Because multinational corporations can reorganize their resources on a vast scale very quickly, their freedom of action makes every community vulnerable to abrupt economic changes; and because these changes arise from organizational needs remote from the community, they are often locally unintelligible and hard to foresee or prepare for. As unemployment rises and whole communities lose the sense of their future, the accumulating stresses act upon families. More marriages break down, more wives and children are battered, more children are born to youngsters out of boredom and despair (Brenner 1973, 1976). Children's experience of attachment is less and less likely to be secure. Our society is tending sharply away from those qualities which I suggested earlier would best protect its members from grief and depression. Its relationships are becoming less stable, less predictable, less easy to understand, and less careful of attachment.

Such a society creates two sorts of people. Some command a wide range of knowledge and resources. They experience the world as understandable and manipulable, and their ambitions are enriched by their confidence. But others experience the world as governed by remote and largely unintelligible systems over which they have no control, and the meaning of their lives is correspondingly narrowed by their vulnerability. For some of them, the range of choices open to them is so narrow and so insecure that sustaining any worthwhile purpose is a constant anxiety. The children of these parents will learn the consequences of this anxiety in their own experience of attachment, and grow up in turn less trusting of the world. So insecurity becomes embedded and acquires a cultural history.

Yet there is something in this conception of society which appeals to us: not the anxiety and despair it provokes, but its celebration of assertiveness. If there is a side of our natures that seeks a secure and nurturing order, there is another side that sees order as guaranteed, above all, by the assertion of will over all the destructive impulses we contain. Both, I suggest, can be traced to our experience of attachment. For in any child-rearing culture, such as our own, where parents take the initiative in guiding and controlling their child's development, a struggle of wills between parent and child must sometimes develop. Children learn from this when it is that willfulness works, when it is punished and how frighteningly, and whether it is possible to avoid a struggle without sacrificing crucial needs. For fortunate children, the world will come to seem ordinarily nurturing and only punishing for good reason. For unlucky children, it will seem held in place only by an arbitrary parental will, at once resented and yet necessary to repress all the self-destructive impulses of revenge to which it gives rise. (I suppose, too, if parents refuse to exercise any control at all, that a child may see the order of the world as depending only on his or her own arbitrary will – and the burden of this responsibility is perhaps the most frightening of all.)

I do not mean to suggest by this that our political ideologies are merely an extension of childhood experience. They may be informed by a great deal of adult experience and rationally organized. But this sophistication is founded on the strategies of control and conceptions of order which, from our early years, have begun to shape our experience and how we interpret it. This, surely, is why people of the same knowledge, intelligence, interests, and culture may understand the nature of social order in profoundly different ways.

CONCLUSION

Let me now try to draw together the threads of my argument. I began by asking how we can link the social and psychological aspects of human behavior; and answered that attachment is the essential bridge, because it is at once the primary relationship through which personality develops, and the relationship through which we create our sense of order. Society, as I conceive it, is a structure of meanings embodied in patterns of relationship, and the attachment relationship is both a microcosm of those meanings – an expression of a culture as its child-rearing practices embody them – and the experience out of which each generation recreates a meaningful order. We do not, as some sociological accounts seem to suggest, passively absorb the values of society. We each create our own meaning out of a unique experience of attachment which is still also recognizably the product of a culture.

This ordering of meaning requires both predictability of behavior and continuity of purpose. Purposes arise out of, and remain closely associated with, attachment. From this, we can determine the conditions which are likely to reinforce or undermine our ability to sustain our organizations of meaning – the kinds of disruptive, unintelligible, or unexpected events which overwhelm us; the ambivalences and insecurities of childhood which inhibit our adult strategies for coping with uncertainty.

A good society, then, would seem to be one which, as far as is humanly possible, minimizes these disruptive events, protects each child's experience of attachment from harm, and supports us when we are grief stricken. Yet the logic of controlling uncertainty also tempts us, instead, to make our own command over circumstances more secure by imposing a greater burden of uncertainty on others. By exacting commitment without reciprocity, we enhance both our freedom of action and the predictability of our social environment. But those who must wait upon our decisions then have less freedom and more uncertainty. In so far as subordinates can control this uncertainty by collective sanctions, organizations become less adaptable. Organizations then protect themselves against disturbances in their environment by interposing buffer-organizations, which absorb the first impact. These principles of subordination and marginalization are, I suspect, universal temptations of the exercise of power.

So there is a fundamental tension between our impulse to create a secure, predictable social order; and the impulse to escape from our collective failure to eliminate all insecurity by maximizing our own advantage. How we handle this tension, both collectively and individually, is again profoundly influenced by the experience of attachment.

There are aspects of both personality and social order not accounted for in this framework of interactions. Personality, for instance, is influenced by variety of genetic endowment. Social systems have properties of behavior independent of the intentions and perceptions of human actors, and some sociologists would, I think, regard these as the essential subject matter of the discipline. But attachment theory provides an interconnected set of links between the social and psychological aspects of human behavior which seems to me very powerful, as an organization of meaning in its own right.

It seems to me also to imply a political message. The qualities of good social relationships and good experiences of attachment are essentially the same: predictability, responsiveness, intelligibility, supportiveness, reciprocity of commitment. To achieve this, we have to struggle constantly against the tendency of the powerful to subordinate and marginalize others in the interest of their own greater security. The worse we fail, the more widespread insecurity becomes, and the greater the temptation to rescue our own command of circumstances at the expense of others. To save ourselves from this declining spiral, those at most risk of subordination and marginalization need to organize themselves to apply all the sanctions at hand to demand reciprocity. But this in itself is not enough, because success often only displaces marginalization elsewhere. We need also to institute a style of governing our relationships with each other which takes as its first principles reciprocity of commitment, predictability, and respect for the unique structure of meaning and attachment which makes life worthwhile for each of us. It is a radically more collaborative and democratic style of government than any we have experienced. And it profoundly contradicts the political ideologies which have recently prevailed in Britain and America. Yet, if the argument I have presented today is right, such a style of creating and reproducing social relationships responds to our deepest and most universal need to create a world in which we dare become attached.

© 1991 Peter Marris

NOTE

1   This is the text of a talk given on 27 June 1987 to the Tavistock Clinic's Conference on 'Fruits of attachment theory: findings and applications across the life cycle' in honour of Dr John Bowlby's eightieth birthday.

REFERENCES

Bowlby, J. (1973) *Attachment and Loss*, vol. 2: *Separation: Anxiety and Anger*, New York: Basic Books.
Brenner, M.H. (1973) *Mental Illness and the Economy*, Cambridge, Mass.: Harvard University Press.
—— (1976) *Estimating the Social Cost of Economic Policy: Implications for*

Mental and Physical Health and Criminal Aggression, Washington: Government Printing Office.

Brown, G. and Harris, T. (1978) *The Social Origins of Depression*, London: Tavistock.

Buss, T.F. and Redburn, F.S. (1983) *Mass Unemployment: Plant Closings and Community Mental Health*, Beverley Hills: Sage.

Erikson, K. (1979) *In the Wake of the Flood*, London: Allen & Unwin.

Ferman, L. and Gordus, J. (eds) (1979) *Mental Health and the Economy*, Kalamazoo, Mich.: W.E. Upjohn Institute for Employment Research.

Kuhn, T. (1962) *The Structure of Scientific Revolutions*, Chicago: University of Chicago Press.

Lehman, D.R. and Wortman, C.B. (in press) 'Long term effects of losing a spouse or child in a motor vehicle crash', *Journal of Personality and Social Psychology*.

Marris, P. (1986) *Loss and Change*, London: Routledge & Kegan Paul.

—— (1987) *Meaning and Action*, London: Routledge & Kegan Paul.

Miller, J. (1974) *Aberfan: A Disaster and its Aftermath*, London: Constable.

Parkes, C.M. and Weiss, R.S. (1983) *Recovery from Bereavement*, New York: Basic Books.

Parsons, T. (1967) 'Social structure and the development of personality: Freud's contribution to the integration of psychology and sociology', in T. Parsons *Social Structure and Personality*, New York: Free Press.

Part II

Patterns of Attachment

Chapter 6

Attachment quality as an organizer of emotional and behavioral responses in a longitudinal perspective[1]

Klaus E. Grossmann and Karin Grossmann

INTRODUCTION

Attachment theory pulls together several lines of thought to create an integrated body of knowledge about human emotions. Although many aspects are different from traditional perspectives of developmental psychology, attachment theory is particularly concerned with emotional development from a life span perspective (Ainsworth 1985). Its main features are as follows.

1　Attachment theory accepts phylogenetic behavioral dispositions (Bowlby 1969) of infants and parents as a starting point for onto-genetic manifestation of an environmentally stable propensity to form close social bonds. Differences in ontogenetic quality of attachments by the end of the first year of an infant's life came as a surprise (Ainsworth and Wittig 1969).
2　Attachment research relies on observations in an ethological tradition, looking at the context and function of behaviors. Purely quantitative behavior counts are held to be counterproductive. The observations are designed to reveal the underlying adaptive strategies of infants, children, and adolescents, given their preprogrammed need for attachment and the caregiver's readiness to accept and respond to this need.
3　Earlier theories about the effect of early experiences on later development have suffered from lack of longitudinal data, or of empirical data altogether. Therefore, longitudinal studies are required to reveal the effects of different attachment qualities.
4　Attachment theory has a clinical basis, concentrating on individuals rather than on single variables. Sroufe and Waters (1977) talk about attachment as an organizational construct to integrate and understand a person's behavioral strategies.

Bowlby's notion of a person's working model of attachment relationships indicates that early attachment-related experiences become eventually transformed into inner representations (Bowlby 1973). Such inner representations, he proposes, have predictable implications for attachment-relevant situations throughout life, and for extremely stressful interpersonal experiences.

Present research in attachment is concerned with more or less effective behavior strategies of people in various attachment-related situations. This task requires expensive and time-consuming prospective and longitudinal developmental research designs with a clinical and psychodynamic orientation. It should try to assess personality differences in terms of coping with social–emotional needs in a life span perspective (Ainsworth 1985).

DEVELOPMENTAL PROCESSES

From a developmental perspective, attachment theory postulates four processes that have to be explained:

1   the development of attachment patterns between infants and caretakers, based on infants' need expressions, that eventually lead to individual differences in attachment quality by the end of the first year;
2   the process that transforms these relational differences into individual differences, i.e. the transition from dyadic attachment interactions to individual (inner) representations thereof;
3   the transition of specific behavior strategies from early childhood, through adolescence, into adulthood and into old age;
4   the transmission of caregiving qualities across generations, i.e. the way in which attachment behavior strategies are passed on from parents to children.

Ainsworth's empirical studies in Uganda (Ainsworth 1967) and in Baltimore (Ainsworth *et al.* 1974) provided the empirical bases utilizing Bowlby's theory. In fact, the 'strange situation', a laboratory situation assessing differences in attachment qualities at the end of the first year, became the motor for an increase in the popularity of attachment research. There was a certain danger (and still is) that the strange situation (Ainsworth *et al.* 1978) may eclipse the actual interactional processes responsible for the differences in attachment organization. The concept of maternal sensitivity, i.e. the caregiver's ability to perceive and to interpret the infant's signals correctly and to respond promptly and appropriately to them (Ainsworth *et al.* 1974, 1978), has opened a most fruitful research area within process 1 listed above. It is basic to the study of the transition from relational patterns to social–emotional strategies in infancy (see below).

Main *et al.* (1985) achieved a breakthrough in the study of processes 2 and 4 listed above. They derived from attachment theory various aspects relating to an individual's emotional tolerance of ambiguity. They presented differences in behavior strategies of 6-year-old children in attachment-related procedures, whom they had seen in the strange situation 5 years earlier. In line with the tradition of ethological observation, longitudinal design, and clinical orientation, they developed methods that enabled them to circumscribe the children's working models with five assessments: the children's reaction to a family photograph, their reactions to the Klagsburn–Bowlby adaptation of the separation-anxiety test, their behavior and their discourse with their mothers after 1 hour of separation, and the children's family drawings. Each assessment represented a different aspect of the working model of attachment relationships underlying the children's operations. Main's assessments are located on a continuum somewhere between the dyadic beginnings of the attachment process, e.g. the 6-year-olds' child–mother reunions, and its internal representations by the individual children, e.g. the rest of the assessment when the mother was outside the experimental room but the child was inside.

A first method for assessing differences in mental and psychodynamic representations of the present organization of attachment-related childhood memories is the adult attachment interview (Main *et al.* 1985) and the corresponding adult attachment classification system (Main and Goldwyn 1985). This refers to process 4 above. The adult attachment interview may elucidate the process by which inner working models of self and attachment figures are transmitted to the next generation.

Process 3 above, the transition across the life span, needs

> the development of psychological methods for assessing patterns of attachment and their derivations at each phase of the life cycles.... To cast light on problems of continuity and discontinuity of both patterns of attachment and also of different degrees of resilience and vulnerability, prospective studies following personality development through different phases of the life cycle and in different environments are plainly indispensable, despite their being very costly.
>
> (Bowlby 1988:9)

This challenge has been taken seriously by ongoing studies, including our own.

RESEARCH INTENTIONS

In our interpretation of attachment theory and research we first concentrated (in part) on replication. Replication of the correlation between maternal sensitivity and strange situation classification was necessary for two reasons. In 1975, when we started the Bielefeld longitudinal study (Grossmann, K.E. *et al.* 1981) no data other than Ainsworth's were available, and the strange situation had not been validated in different cultural and lingual contexts. We have continued this line of research because it provided a good basis for finding out what, in cross-cultural comparison, is conceptually equivalent, and what methodological adjustments have to be made in order to gain insights about the working models of the individual children regardless of certain conspicuous cultural differences (Grossmann, K.E. and Grossmann in press).

As well as capitalizing directly on Ainsworth's and Main's research, we focused on the communicative aspect of attachment formation and quality. During the first year, in addition to observations of maternal sensitivity we analyzed audio-recordings of mothers' and infants' vocalizations. We also reviewed all 196 of our strange situations in terms of changes in the infants' communication patterns with increasing separation stress, and, of course, in relation to quality of attachment. We found open communications of emotions in secure dyads. The avoidant pattern in the strange situation, in contrast, reflected a strategy on the part of the infant to deny negative feelings elicited by maternal separation. There were clear qualitative differences in dyadic communication styles which paralleled the different attachment patterns in the strange situation (see below). We suppose that verbal and nonverbal expressions, signals, and communications are indications of attachment-related differences at different phases of the life cycle in the individuals' organization of emotional and behavioral responses (Grossmann, K.E. 1988).

We also paid close attention to possible constitutional differences between newborns with predictive effects on attachment classifications of infant–mother and infant–father dyads in the strange situation (Grossmann, K. et al. 1985). It was our notion from the very beginning that 'heritable differences ... must be assumed to exist between different individuals in their capacity to deal with the various environmental hazards, especially inadequate parenting, which influence vulnerability' (Bowlby 1988: 9). By looking at infants who are independently characterized by hereditary features, perhaps as crudely as by 'temperament', and by assessing whether they are easy or difficult to care for, one may eventually be able to determine the infants' contribution to their quality of attachment to both parents (Grossmann, K. and Grossmann in prep.).

Attachment theory addresses the organization of behavior as an adaptive strategy of an individual to emotional and social experiences that tax his coping capacity. 'An evolutionary perspective is necessary [also] if we are to understand psychological stress and the environmental conditions that cause it' (Bowlby 1988: 3). In addition to traditional variables, such as communication, aggression, or retreat, attachment research focuses on individual behavior strategies, i.e. how the individual integrates his personal and social resources in various combinations to master the challenge and to keep his integrity. In fact, 'coherence' (Sroufe 1979; Main et al. 1985) is a term that captures the quality of integrating contradicting or conflicting emotions; it captures the individual's ability to make emotional information available through open communication, and use it for his emotional health.

This concept has proven empirically fruitful (see Bretherton and Waters 1985), and has also guided our research.

ATTACHMENT IN LONGITUDINAL PERSPECTIVE: RESULTS FROM TWO STUDIES

We started two longitudinal studies, one in northern Germany, at Bielefeld, in 1976 and one in southern Germany, at Regensburg, in 1980. The Bielefeld study started shortly before the infants were born. Forty-nine families from all classes participated, and sex of infant and sibling status were mixed (Grossmann, K. *et al.* 1985). The Regensburg study started when the infants were 11 months old. The families had a similar background and composition to that of the Bielefeld study (Escher-Gräub and Grossmann 1983).

Maternal sensitivity and infant behavior during the first year in the home

The key concept in Ainsworth's research is 'maternal sensitivity', defined as the mother's ability and willingness to perceive the infant's communications as reflected in his behavior, emotional expression, and vocalizations, see and interpret them from the infant's point of view, and respond to them promptly and appropriately according to the infant's developmental and emotional needs (Ainsworth *et al.* 1974). We applied the scale of maternal sensitivity to the narrative reports, made during the home visits, of mother–infant interaction when the infants were 2, 6, and 10 months old. We also coded a number of maternal and infant behaviors as well as mother–infant vocal exchanges. We confirmed many of Ainsworth's findings and gained additional information on the implications of maternal sensitivity for the infant's communicative competence. Infants of sensitive mothers responded more positively to body contact with the mother but were also less distressed when body contact was terminated. They followed the mother when she left the room, but cried less upon her departure. Generally, they cried less at 2, 6, and 10 months and vocalized happily more often at 6 and 10 months than infants of less sensitive mothers.

Behavioral sensitivity of the mothers was reflected in specific behaviors like affectionate holding which is not abrupt and less often motivated by mere caretaking routines, by acknowledging the baby upon return to the room, and especially in their prompt reactions to the baby's crying. Their voice quality was more often tender-warm and they responded to more infant vocalizations than insensitive mothers. (Preliminary data were reported in Grossmann, K.E. and Grossmann (1984). More detailed data were presented in Grossmann, K. *et al.* (1987).)

Thus a sensitive mother allows her infant to express his emotions freely and supports his communicative skills by responding to them promptly and appropriately. This fosters the development of a secure attachment. When the infants' attachment qualities were assessed at 12 months, the secure attachment patterns were significantly related to maternal sensitivity, especially at 2 and 6 months (Grossmann, K. *et al.* 1985).

Emotional communication, play interaction, and clown empathy as related to patterns of attachment at 12 and 18 months

Attachment correlates in the communication styles and various interactions of 12- and 18-month-old infants with their mothers and fathers in three different situations could be established. We explored the relation between security of attachment to either parent and the dyad's communicative and interactive quality in the strange situation, in an infant–parent play session, and in an emotional response session with a clown-play partner as devised by Main and Weston (1981).

The re-analysis of the strange situations of all infants of both samples with their mothers and fathers focused on the emotional communication of the infants and its consequence for parental behavior. The findings can be summarized as follows. The more infants with an avoidant attachment to the parent present were impaired in their mood and play behavior by the two separations, the less they communicated directly to the parent. As a consequence, there was less togetherness which could have relieved the infant's distress if the parents had been psychologically responsive. The opposite sequence was seen in the majority of infants with a secure attachment to the parent present: the more they were distressed, the stronger they addressed their communications directly to the parent and the sooner they gained help and comfort from the parent (Grossmann, K.E. and Grossmann 1986; Grossmann, K.E. *et al.* 1986; Grossmann, K.E., Grossmann, and Ernst in prep.).

Different attachment patterns of one infant to mother and father have been reported (Grossmann K.E. *et al.* 1981; Main and Weston 1981). The style of communication was found to be dependent on the quality of attachment to the parent present. Therefore, free affective exchanges were, at least at 12 and 18 months of age, not a function of the individual infant's communicative competence but a function of the infant–parent relationship.

Parent–infant interactions were also observed in a free play situation in relation to attachment quality, conducted 1 month before the strange situation with either parent in the Regensburg sample. One set of results show that infants in securely attached B-dyads communicate more subtly with soft vocalizations, whereas infants in insecure attached A-dyads initiate interaction more often with toy presentations and loud vocalizations. Another set of results addresses parental sensitivity in terms of reacting to the infant's emotional state and independent play activity. If infants in B-dyads, independent of sex of parent, played with high interest, the parent (statistically) stayed away from the infant, observing his activity. But if the infant played with low interest or was bored or distressed, the parent sought proximity and offered a toy or suggested a play activity. This latter intervention was usually followed by a more positive mood and higher interest in play by the infant. The reverse pattern was observed in parents of A-dyads. They rarely offered a toy, and stayed away from the infant when the infant was in a low interest state or in poor mood, but they initiated many play activities when the infant was already playing with high interest. These parental interferences usually resulted in abrupt cessation of the joint play activity and in many gestures and expressions of uncertainty in the infants (Grossmann, K.E. and Scheuerer-Englisch in prep.). There were too few cases of insecure–ambivalent relationships (C) to be considered here. The play analyses showed that both types of parents monitored the infant's play intensity closely, but took opposite actions as a consequence of their appraisal. The parents in A-dyads were more interfering, and the parents in B-dyads were more supportive of the infant's independent play.

In a third situation we addressed the infant's emotional response to various emotions of an adult play partner, a strange person dressed as a clown. This situation was originally devised by Main and Weston (1981) to assess infant's and parent's expressive behaviors. We added a microanalytic assessment. While the clown went through a series of activities, being happy, wanting play interaction with the infant, and finally crying, infants securely attached to the parent present reflected the clown's emotional states more accurately and promptly than infants with an avoidant attachment to the parent present. Not surprisingly, similar expressions were seen in the parents. Parents of insecurely attached infants showed a greater lack of affect than the others, and expressed a stronger aversion to bodily contact with the infant (Grossmann, K.E., Fremmer-Bombik, and Escher-Gräub in prep.). Again it was the quality of attachment to the parent present that was related to the infant's reactions to the clown. The same infant behaved differently in the two sessions if his quality of attachment to mother and father differed.

By the age of one year the effects of different attachment patterns that have been established during the first year of the infant's life by more or less sensitive interactions with the parent may be summarized as follows. In secure attachment relationships the infants experienced more support for their independent activity, communicated more openly with their parents, especially when distressed, and were more sympathetic with a new adult play partner's changing emotions. Before the emergence of spoken language the infants had learned different functions of social–emotional communication within a relationship, whether it serves as means to elicit support and comfort from the attachment figure, or whether communications of distress are discouraged or ignored by the parent. These very early established communication patterns should have consequences for the child's future relationships and his image of himself as worthy of love and support (see also Bretherton 1987).

Parents as playmates and as attachment figures

In a play-session at home with the 2-year-old Bielefeld children for each parent separately we could observe the different functioning of the parents as playmates and teachers in contrast to the same parents as attachment figures. During a lengthy home visit the mothers and later the fathers were asked to play with their child for 10 minutes with wooden mosaic pieces or play dough. Also during that visit the children's Mental Developmental Index (MDI) (Bayley 1969) was assessed. During the interactive play time the children's cognitive level of play was coded for each second. Each parent was also rated separately on 31 items for her/his interactive behavior with the child during play.

The interactive ratings of the parents were factor analyzed and three factors emerged that were almost identical for mothers and fathers: (1) the cheerful, supportive parent, (2) the explaining, teaching parent, and (3) the patient, accepting parent. These three factors were statistically independent of each other. If a mother or a father received high scores on the factor 'explaining teaching parent', they also had more education, belonged to a higher socio-economic level, and had a child with a higher MDI who played longer at a higher cognitive level. Most of these parents were married to each other. On the other hand, if a parent received high rating scores on the factor 'patient and accepting parent', this mother or father more likely had a securely attached child to her or him, and these parents were less likely to be married to each other (Grossmann, K. 1984).

These findings support Bowlby's notion of the different roles of attachment-figures and playmates (Bowlby 1982: 307) with the acknowledgement that parents can fulfill both roles. As we have argued (Grossmann, K.E. and Grossmann 1986) the systems of cognitive functioning and attachment may have evolved along different lines. As we see from this and other studies (see Scarr and Kidd (1983) for a review of influences on cognitive development, and Bretherton (1985) for a review of the influences on attachment quality) a child's cognitive competence and a child's attachment quality are associated with different parental behavior strategies.

Play quality and peer interactions in preschool at 5 years

When the children of the Regensburg sample were 5 years old they were observed with their peers in preschool (Suess 1987). Five dimensions of behavior were assessed in search of the possible influence of early attachment qualities on the functioning of a child 4 years later in a situation not affected by parental presence. Generally, the attachment quality to the mother proved to be more predictive in the various behavioral areas than the attachment quality to father. But when summing up all indices of competent behavioral functioning, the children who had a secure attachment to both parents were greatly overrepresented in the highest ranks, whereas the children with a double avoidant attachment were more likely to be in the lowest ranks.

More specifically, children with a secure rather than an avoidant attachment to mother played with more concentration and higher quality, and children securely attached to fathers initiated more play activities with other children. The children's conflict management with their peers was more self-reliant and satisfying for the conflicting partners when they had a secure attachment with either parent. Although severe behavior problems were rare in this normal sample, a child who had more than a minor problem had been more likely insecurely attached to his mother in infancy. In a projective picture test on interpersonal aggression (Dodge *et al.* 1986), children with a secure attachment to mother were more often accurate or well meaning in their social perception than children with an avoidant attachment to mother. In the judgement of the preschool teachers, the personality of children with a secure attachment to either parent was described more positively and more favourably along the dimensions of ego-control and ego-resiliency (Suess 1987).

The differences between children with the two types of attachment histories were not overwhelming in any single area or variable of competence, but they emerged in the overall evaluation of the individual children and in the sympathy of the preschool teacher for them. We might conclude that for most children the preschool experience has largely reinforced their patterns of interaction with their parents on a more sophisticated level as reflected in their play quality, communicative competence over conflict, social perception, and sympathy from their teacher (Suess and Grossmann in prep.).

Child–mother reunion patterns at 6 years and their predictability from infant attachment patterns

An assessment of the attachment quality of 6-year-olds was devised by Main and Cassidy (1988), adjusting a mother–child separation situation to the developmental and cognitive level as well as to the social skills of that age. Parent and child were separated for 1 hour in which child and parent did different things. Upon reunion a child who greeted the parent warmly, shared his recent experiences freely, seemed pleased by the parent's return, and who would eventually gravitate toward the parent slowly was considered to show a secure attachment pattern. An avoidant attachment pattern at 6 was highly compatible with avoidance in the strange situation at 1 year of age. These children ignored or greeted the returning parent coolly, maintained or increased the physical or emotional distance from the parent, did not initiate a conversation, and answered only minimally according to socially accepted standards. An insecure–ambivalent reunion pattern at 6 was characterized by mixed feelings of avoidance, responsiveness, sadness, or open hostility. Some of these children showed immature behaviors or they evidenced their ambivalence in close contact. A fourth pattern was found with the 6-year-olds: a set of behaviors aimed at controlling the parent in a positive or negative way.

This situation and the method of analysis were applied to the Regensburg sample. Predictability from infant attachment patterns to the 6-year-olds' reunion pattern was accurate for 35 of 40 cases, or 87 per cent for the traditional three classifications A, B, or C. Avoidance ratings on a 7-point scale in infancy were highly significantly related to avoidance ratings at 6 years (Wartner 1987; Wartner and Grossmann in prep.).

Given this continuity in attachment from 1 to 6 years, it is not surprising that the classifications at 6 years also related to the competencies in preschool at 5 years. Children with a secure reunion pattern at 6 years had scored higher in their play quality, had been more competent in their conflict management, and had been more skilled or well meaning in their social perception. Only the number of behavioral problems no longer differentiated significantly between the secure and the insecure patterns at 6 years, although twice as many children with an insecure pattern had some behavioral problems (Suess and Grossmann in prep.). It was surprising to find that attachment quality at 1 year predicted behavior problems at 5 years more accurately than attachment quality at 6 years could do so retrospectively.

The reunion patterns of the 6-year-olds were not readily observable by an uninformed observer, since the variations in greeting behavior, justifiable engrossment in play, and subtle ways of terminating a conversation are all within the boundaries of accepted, perhaps even polite social conduct. Only when the underlying function of the verbal or physical behavior of the child was recognized could the pattern of attachment and communication be detected. This pattern recognition strategy was crucial for unravelling the relational meaning of the child's verbalizations. There were patterns composed of many different individual elements that served the purpose of an open, appropriate, and responsive communication. On the other hand, there were verbal patterns intended to keep the mother puzzled, quiet, or even to embarrass her in front of the observers (Main *et al.* 1985). Thus, we see the effects of attachment experiences moving to a representational level with increasing cognitive skill of the growing child.

Representations of attachment qualities in 6-year-old children's family drawings and their responses to separation pictures

At the 6-year assessment and during the mother's absence the Regensburg children were asked to draw a picture of their family doing something. Kaplan and Main (1986) had developed a classification system for family drawings of 5–7-year-old children in terms of their representation of attachment. Our students B. Bundscherer (1988) and B. Pfäffl-Gerullis (1988) transformed the criteria for classification into a scoring system, giving points for various aspects of individualization of the figures, lack of repetitiveness, well grounded and complete figures, and various details marking the setting or the activity of the family figures.

The total score and especially the score for individualization of the figures differentiated significantly between the children with secure versus insecure attachment quality at 6 years and at 1 year. The highest scores on individualization were obtained by those children who had shown the secure attachment pattern to both parents in infancy. Children with high total scores had shown conspicuously little resistance to their mothers in the strange situation and their mothers had shown very little aversion to bodily contact during the clown session. In kindergarten these children were more skillful in conflict management than children with low total scores and they were less often seen to be isolated from their peers.

A realistic representation of an imagined situation was also the special feature of the responses of some Bielefeld children to separation pictures, the Klagsbrun–Bowlby adaptation of Hansburg's Separation Anxiety Text (Klagsbrun and Bowlby 1976). Children who had been classified securely attached to their mothers in infancy verbalized openly that the child in the picture would feel anxious, lonely, or sad, but at the same time they came up with ideas on how to cope constructively with the imagined separation, including requests for social support from others. Their nonverbal behavior was mostly relaxed during the conversation. Many of the children with an avoidant attachment history seemed strained and tense during the picture session. Some denied any feelings of vulnerability in the child, others were overly pessimistic for the pictured child, few included a statement that the parents might never come back. Their suggested coping behaviors were mostly unrelated to the reported feelings, or even plainly unrealistic (Friedl *et al.* 1988).

As Bowlby suggested in 1979, a child who is certain of his parent's acceptance and support is able not only to tolerate his ambiguous feelings toward his parents but also to be confident that he can control them without having to deny them. This we saw in the reactions of the securely attached 6-year-old children from the Bielefeld sample. They were not afraid to admit negative affects as a consequence of an imagined parental leave taking, because they could think of a positive, constructive solution.

Observed play interactions between the 6-year-olds and their parents in the home

During the home visits of the Bielefeld families, each parent was asked to play two types of games with the child. One was to construct a building with wooden blocks, the other was to stage a little play with hand-puppets. As expected, only emotional variables, not intellectual variables or successful construction, were related to earlier attachment classifications. In the block building game, self-confidence, self-assertiveness, involvement, but also open refusal to cooperate and personal aggression in the play context, were higher in children who had shown a secure attachment to their mothers in infancy. The father and child data have not been analyzed yet. By assigning each child to a group of engaged cooperative children, a group of engaged uncooperative ones, and a group of passively compliant children, it was found that former maternal sensitivity was lowest in the mothers of the last group. But most interactive behaviors that governed the progress of the block construction work were unrelated to attachment but were related to the socio-economic status of the family (Remmers 1987).

In the puppet game, a triadic situation in which most families relinquished control to father, the attachment quality of the child to the father was more readily observable than the attachment quality of the child to the mother. Father–child interactions were more harmonious and positive when they had been classified securely attached, but many interactive behaviors were unrelated to attachment. On the other hand the general rating of the emotional climate of the whole session was significantly related to the child–mother attachment quality, not to the child–father attachment quality (Berghammer 1987; Kempe 1987).

In reviewing these findings in interactive situations in the homes, we have the impression that either the attachment system of the children was not sufficiently aroused or the children would not reveal their working models of their parents in their parents' presence. It seems important to choose appropriately stressing situations in which the children are separated from their parents in order to make their attachment-related working models of themselves and their parents visible. A careful selection of life circumstances for observation in which emotional resources matter appears to be crucial for assessing 'patterns of attachment and their derivations at each phase of the life cycle' (Bowlby 1988: 9).

Relationship-interviews with 10-year-old children and their parents

The results of the study with the 6-year-old Bielefeld children stimulated another assessment of these children at 10 years. At this age more emphasis was put onto the children's reported perceptions of their parents' supportiveness and their emotional organization when interviewed alone. A team of young researchers visited 43 of the original 49 Bielefeld families (Stephan 1989; Scheuerer-Englisch 1989). The parents of the children were interviewed as well.

The interview with the children, on which we will concentrate here, spanned a wide variety of topics: school, hobbies, perceived relationship to each parent, friends, and personal strategies when problems of various kinds occur. The four major parameters for analysis were: perceived support from each parent, strategies for stressful situations and report of negative feelings, peer relations, and the child's response style to the interview (Scheuerer-Englisch 1989).

No longitudinal relation was found between early attachment quality to mother or father and perceived parental support for the child. However, parental support, as perceived by the children, was strongly related to parental support as reported by the parents themselves in the concurrent but separate interviews. Since perceived parental support was estimated from recent and actual episodes, which the children remembered and convincingly talked about, a recency effect may have overridden a more general mental representation.

Subsequently, the children's reported behaviors in stressful situations were analyzed in concrete everyday problem situations in school, with the parents when negative feelings occurred, in less specific situations when the children were afraid, angry, or sad. Only the latter strategies were related to early attachment quality. Children with an early secure attachment to their mother more readily admitted negative feelings and more often reported relationship-oriented strategies, like going to someone for help or comfort. Formerly avoidantly attached children, in contrast, reported staying by themselves and trying to work the problem out without anybody's help.

Peer integration reported by the children as well as by their parents was most highly related to early attachment quality, even to the point of a clear rank order from secure to avoidant to ambivalent. Early secure – with mother – children more often had one or a few good friends who were trustworthy and reliable. Early avoidant and, even more so, early ambivalent children had either no good friends or reported very many friends without being able to name one. They more often reported problems like being exploited, ridiculed, or excluded from group activities by their peers. The statements of the parents and of the children were highly concordant, supporting our interpretation of attachment-quality influencing friendship relations.

In terms of coherence (Main *et al.* 1985), early attachment quality was not very influential at this age. Short or no answers were more typical of insecure children, and strange, inappropriate answers were more typical of children with an early ambivalent attachment to mother. However, social behavior of the children toward the interviewer was significantly related to early attachment quality. Insecure children were more often either openly ignoring to the point of impoliteness or overly close, inappropriately intimate, even seeking close bodily contact to the visitor. Observable sibling rivalry, but not observable child–parent conflicts, were also significantly related to early attachment insecurity.

In summary, more than half of the selected variables were unrelated to early attachment quality, and the others only to the attachment quality to the mother. But those variables related to early attachment add to the picture of the child's emotional organization. Thinking about negative feelings in unspecific situations, a secure child suggested he would seek out others for help. A secure child was also successful in having a few good friends, again a source of help but also a chance of giving affection and support. And the secure children handled the interview as a social situation more appropriately, despite the intense and often unpleasant questions. Thus early security seems to be reflected at 10 years in a general confidence in oneself, one's friends, and in potential supporters. When asked about more recent and specific situations, all children reported what had happened, and the supportive quality of these episodes was unrelated to early attachment classification. They seemed rather to be anchored in the ups and downs of daily parent–child interactions, and asking about such recent happenings might not be a fruitful way to assess the children's mental representation of their parent's expected supportiveness.

Inquiry into the parents' attachment memories of their childhood

Almost all mothers and about three-quarters of the fathers agreed to an interview about their past and present relationship with their parents. This was done when the children of both samples were 6 years old. The interview was developed by George *et al.* (in prep.) from attachment theory and its clinical implications (Bowlby 1980). The responses of the mothers have been analyzed to date. Analyses of the fathers' interviews are in progress.

The Adult Attachment Interview probes for descriptions of close relationships in childhood, supportive memories, contradictory statements, and evaluations of the relationship to the parents who are now the grandparents of the observed children (Main *et al.* 1985). The rating and classification system (Main and Goldwyn 1985) was not readily transferable to the German interviews. Therefore our coworkers created another method of analysis based on Main *et al.*'s. (1985) system (Grossmann, K. *et al.* 1988; Fremmer-Bombik *et al.* 1989). In this method four parameters make up the core of the analysis: presentation of each parent or another attachment figure as supportive or unsupportive, ability to focus on the topic of attachment, reflections on their own attachment experiences, and defensiveness against the interview including the present emotional relationship with the grandparents.

Four patterns of maternal attachment representations were defined. Two patterns, a 'positive' one and a 'reflexive' one, corresponded closely to their infant's secure attachment to them 5 years earlier, and two patterns, a 'defensive' one and 'repressive' one, were typical for mothers of insecurely attached infants (concordance of 78 per cent for $n = 89$; see also Grossmann, K. *et al.* 1988).

For the mothers of the Bielefeld sample early maternal interaction data with the infant were compared with the parameters and single criteria of the Attachment Interview. Maternal sensitivity and cooperation with her infant during the first year correlated significantly with the amount of attachment-relevant information in the interview, with the mother's readiness to recall her childhood experiences, especially her feelings as a child, and with the mother's lack of defensiveness (Grossmann, K. *et al.* 1988).

In line with the thinking of Main *et al.* (1985) we propose the following interpretation for the detected relationship between attachment representations in the mother and her behavioral sensitivity as well as her emotional integrity and coherence. We observed and assume that an infant's cry or distress alarms a parent and elicits ambivalent feelings. If a parent lacks the experience and model of an attachment figure able to integrate negative feelings into emotional empathy and active assistance to the child, but has instead experienced more often rejection or unsupportiveness during distress, the parent might seek to exclude this present reminder of her own former misery from her perception by ignoring the infant's crying. This we observe as low sensitivity. The mother seems to turn from infant distress management to the management of her own emotional conflicts, i.e. from reality to the epiphenomenal appraisal system (Bowlby 1982: Ch. 7). As a consequence, the infant experiences more often than not an emotional unavailability of the mother when he actually needs her most and thus develops an avoidant attachment pattern.

The striking stability of these early formed attachment patterns shows that the emotional experience during the first year cannot be easily compensated by later cognitive skills such as reasoning or perspective taking.

CONSEQUENCES AND OUTLOOK

Attachment theory focuses on the very nature of human social–emotional development (Bowlby 1982). The need for attachment is as basic as the need for food and water. There is no survival without it. Responses to separation (Bowlby 1973) are pronounced and show definite patterns, modifiable but not basically changeable, in the universal appearance of emotional reactions. Secure attachment strategies in relation to significant others are designed to maintain and further develop the person's emotional coherence and integrity (Main *et al.* 1985). Insecure attachments involve alternative patterns of interaction: an avoidant, ambivalent, or disorganized strategy. These differences, even weak ones, seem to make a difference for the quality of a person's emotional life. Under pressure or stress, insecure attachment strategies may turn out to make a person more vulnerable in terms of psychological health. This vulnerability depends on the intricate interplay of the quality of the 'internal models, including models of self and other', social–emotional support and environmental stress which are important for mental health in any culture (Grossman, K.E. and Gross-mann 1989).

The task of attachment research, then, is to provide models and supporting data for the process whereby emotional coherence and con-fidence in the supportiveness of others are helpful to the individual in adverse life circumstances. Research has to be conducted on the func-tioning of working models and their adaptive value in unforeseen life situations during ontogenesis. This kind of research could replace 'a moun-tain of jargon' (Bowlby 1988: 2) by observable and testable behavior strategies.

Our own data come from normal families. A few of them experienced hardship and emotional difficulties, but most of them fared well. The data are not 'clinical' material, because the studies have not been designed as such. The findings, rather, concern growing healthy children and their parents. Early attachment experiences with mothers show at this point a stronger influence on the child's social competence and emotional co-herence than experiences with fathers. This does not exclude, by any means, fathers from the picture. The findings imply only that, for the domain of attachment and for the ages studied, mothers play a larger role under the prevailing life circumstances than fathers. For the child–mother pairs of these normal, fairly well adjusted families we found definite and, compared with most other data in developmental psychology, strong effects of early attachments. The stability, around 80 per cent over a 5- to 10-year period, is impressive.

The differences found in the 5-year-old children located in 33 different preschools came as a surprise to us. Sroufe (1983) showed compelling differences related to early attachments for the children in his poverty sample, but in our study we found differences in peer adaptation of children which are by no means 'extreme' or 'unusual'. Our data reveal the very subtle differences in emotional organization that develop as integral parts of personality development during childhood as a consequence of the external organization of emotions in infancy by the mother, and somewhat less by the father. Marvin Minsky, certainly not an attachment theoretician, contrasted ordinary learning – which goal to pursue in which circumstance – with attachment learning – what goals one should have:

> In the case of ordinary forms of failure or success signals, the learner modifies the methods used to reach the goal. In the case of fear-provoking disturbances, the learner may modify the description of the situation itself. In the case of attachment-related failure or reward signals, the learner modifies which goals are considered worthy of pursuit.
>
> (Minsky 1987: 175)

This may indeed be the very essence of attachment learning over the early years of life.

The complex concept of attachment yields, if sensibly translated into research designs, theoretically meaningful data. The powerful organizing effect of attachment theory is seen when complex data sets can be recognized as behavioral strategies. Secure behavior strategies are capable of integrating diverse emotional experiences into a coherent goal-corrected productive solution. Avoidant strategies negate negative emotions in order to maintain personal integrity at the expense of reality. This was termed by Main (1981) a 'second best strategy', effected in order to nevertheless ensure parental protection. Children with ambivalent–insecure strategies, which we have neglected here because of lack of sufficient data, seem to be caught up in their conflicts (Main *et al.* 1985).

If research resources continue to be available, we will try to observe the children of both samples through adolescence and into early adulthood. The 8-year-olds and their parents in Regensburg are presently being interviewed using attachment-related conceptualizations (Grossmann, K.E. and August in press). Some of the results of the 10-year-olds in Bielefeld have been reported here. Thus, we have embarked on exploring the process of transformation of individual behavior strategies in a life span perspective. It is an enterprise where adaptational changes appear to be greatly influenced by an impressive stability of the underlying internal working models of the attachment figures' availability in relation to the self.

The four main features of attachment theory mentioned in the introductory part constitute a rather demanding as well as challenging learning process on the part of researchers who are used to concentrating on combinations of single variables only. But it is the context and the history which reveals the motivation and function of a behavior, e.g. when a child shows aggression in a context of preserving one's sense of integrity or self-worth, or in a context of hurting others, without any noticeable eliciting event (Suess 1987).

The four developmental processes continue to be challenging domains of research; they open new perspectives. The first perspective aims at an understanding of the intricate interplay of an attachment figure's role in organizing emotional and behavioral responses in infants. The second perspective will be concerned with the nature of internal working models (see Bretherton 1985, 1987). The third perspective will focus on the way the internal working models are shown behaviorally at various ages, and the fourth meets the first perspective in exploring how and why it is transmitted onto the next generation. We suggested that the quality of social–emotional communication may serve as a link for these four processes or perspectives.

We have experienced shock and disbelief in students and colleagues to whom we reported our stability or concordance data. To date we have only tentative answers to the question why the stability exists. Bowlby suggested that the spiral of never-retested expectancies and the mechanisms of self-fulfilling prophecies serve to increase the stability of inner working models. We were reminded of Stanley Milgram's famous experiments, in which 2 out of 3 students under the authority of a scientist applied heavy electric shocks to (fictitious) learners who yelled with pain and cried for help. We then, as students, wanted to know what protected the 1 out of 3 students from obeying and complying with the experimentally suggested cruelty. Now, as researchers, we want to know what protects a human being from perpetuating the pattern of insecure attachment from infancy into adulthood. So, we may add a fifth process or perspective to the four already mentioned: the process of changing an insecure internal working model into a secure one. There are some suggestions in the parents' adult attachment interviews: psychotherapy, illness, supportive spouses, and emotionally significant others seem to be important (Fremmer-Bombik 1987). Sufficient data, however, will not come easily, because of the high stability, but the work needed will certainly be worth the effort.

NOTE

1   The empirical research has been funded by Stiftung Volkswagenwerk (1975–80) and repeatedly by Deutsche Forschungsgemeinschaft (Grants 299/9–13). Summing up several data sets longitudinally, and preparation of this article, has been greatly facilitated by an Akademiestipendium, Stiftung Volkswagenwerk (1986–7) to the first author.

REFERENCES

Ainsworth, M.D.S. (1967) *Infancy in Uganda: Infant Care and the Growth of Love*, Baltimore: Johns Hopkins University Press.

—— (1985) 'Attachment across the life span', *Bulletin of the New York Academy of Medicine* 61 (9): 792–812.

Ainsworth, M.D.S., Bell, S.M., and Stayton, D.J. (1974) 'Infant–mother attachment and social development: "socialization" as a product of reciprocal responsiveness to signals', in M.P.M. Richards (ed.) *The Integration of a Child into a Social World* (pp. 99–135), Cambridge: Cambridge University Press.

Ainsworth, M.D.S., Blehar, M.C., Waters, E., and Wall, S. (1978) *Patterns of Attachment*, Hillsdale, N.J.: Erlbaum.

Ainsworth, M.D.S. and Wittig, B.A. (1969) 'Attachment and the exploratory behavior of one-year-olds in a strange situation', in B.M. Foss (ed.) *Determinants of Infant Behavior*, vol. 4 (pp. 113–36), London: Methuen.

Bayley, N. (1969) *Bayley Scales of Infant Development*, New York: The Psychological Corporation.

Berghammer, E. (1987) 'Sechsjährige Kinder in einer unstrukturierten Familien-Spiel-Situation: Analyse der Vater–Kind-Interaktionen' (Six-year-olds in an unstructured family-play-situation: analysis of the father–child interaction), Diplom thesis, Universität Regensburg.

Bowlby, J. (1969) *Attachment and Loss*, vol. 1: *Attachment*, London: Hogarth Press and Institute of Psycho-Analysis.

—— (1973) *Attachment and Loss*, vol. 2: *Separation: Anxiety and Anger*, New York: Basic Books. Frankfurt: Fischer, 1983.

—— (1980) *Attachment and Loss*, vol. 3: *Loss: Sadness and Depression*, New York: Basic Books. Frankfurt: Fischer, 1983.

—— (1982) *Attachment and Loss*, vol. 1: *Attachment* (Orig. 1969), New York: Basic Books.

—— (1988) 'Developmental psychiatry comes of age', *American Journal of Psychiatry* 145: 1–10.

Bretherton, I. (1985) 'Attachment theory: retrospect and prospect', in I. Bretherton and E. Waters (eds) Growing points of Attachment Theory and Research, *Monographs of the Society for Research in Child Development* 50: 3–35.

—— (1987) 'New perspectives on attachment relations: security, communication, and internal working models', in J.D. Osofsky (ed.) *Handbook of Infant Development* (pp. 1061–1100), New York: Wiley

Bretherton, I. and Waters, E. (eds) (1985) Growing Points of Attachment Theory and Research, *Monographs of the Society for Research in Child Development* 50.

Bundscherer, B. (1988) 'Zusammenhänge zwischen Familienzeichnungen sechsjähriger Kinder und der Beziehungsqualität zu ihren Müttern' (Family drawings of six-year-olds as related to their attachment quality to their mother), Diplom thesis, Universität Regensburg.

Dodge, K.A., Pettit, G.S., McClaskey, C.L., and Brown, M.M. (1986) Social Competence in Children, *Monographs of the Society for Research in Child Development* 51 (2).

Escher-Gräub, D. and Grossmann, K.E. (1983) 'Bindungsunsicherheit im zweiten Lebensjahr – Die Regensburger Querschnittsuntersuchung' (Insecure attachments in the second year – the Regensburg cross-sectional study), Unpublished research report, Universität Regensburg.

Fremmer-Bombik, E. (1987) 'Beobachtungen zur Beziehungsqualität im zweiten Lebensjahr und ihre Bedeutung im Lichte mütterlicher Kindheitserinnerungen' (Observations of attachment quality in the second year of life and its meaning with respect to maternal memories of her childhood), Doctoral dissertation, Universität Regensburg.

Fremmer-Bombik, E., Rudolph, J., Veit, B., Schwarz, G., and Schwarzmeier, I.

(1989) 'The Regensburg method of analyzing the Adult Attachment Interview',
Unpublished manuscript.

Friedl, A., Kohlmeier, V., and Grossmann, K.E. (1988) 'Six-year old's responses to
imagined separations compared to early security of attachment', Paper presented at
the 3rd European Conference on Developmental Psychology, Budapest, 15–19 June.

George, C., Kaplan, N., and Main, M. (in prep.) 'The adult attachment interview',
in M. Main (ed.) *Behavior and the Development of Representational Models of
Attachment: Five Methods of Assessment.*

Grossmann, K. (1984) 'Zweijährige Kinder im Zusammenspiel mit ihren Müttern,
Vätern, einer fremden Erwachsensen und in einer Überraschungssituation:
Beobachtungen aus bindungs- und kompetenztheoretischer Sicht' (Two-year-
olds in interaction with their mothers, fathers, a stranger, and in a surprise
situation: Observations from an attachment and a competence point of view),
Doctoral dissertation, Universität Regensburg.

Grossmann, K., Fremmer-Bombik, E., Rudolph, J., and Grossmann, K.E. (1988)
'Maternal attachment representations as related to child–mother attachment
patterns and maternal sensitivity and acceptance of her infant', in R.A. Hinde and
J. Stevenson-Hinde (eds) *Relations within Families,* Oxford: Oxford University
Press.

Grossmann, K., Friedl, A., and Grossmann, K.E. (1987) 'Preverbal infant–mother
vocal interaction patterns and their relationship to attachment quality', Paper
presented at the 2nd International Symposium 'Prevention and Intervention in
Childhood and Youth: Conceptual and Methodological Issues', Bielefeld, 28–30
September.

Grossmann, K. and Grossmann, K.E. (in prep.) 'Newborn behavior, early parenting
quality and later toddler–parent relationships in a group of German infants', in
J.K. Nugent, B.M. Lester, and T.B. Brazleton (eds) *The Cultural Context of
Infancy,* vol. II, Norwood, N.J.: Ablex.

Grossmann, K., Grossmann, K.E., Spangler, G., Suess, G., and Unzner, L. (1985)
'Maternal sensitivity and newborns' orientation responses as related to quality of
attachment in northern Germany', in I. Bretherton and E. Waters (eds) Growing
Points in Attachment Theory and Research, *Monographs of the Society for
Research in Child Development* 50: 233–78.

Grossmann, K.E. (1988) 'Longitudinal and systemic approaches in the study of
biological high- and low-risk groups', in M. Rutter (ed.) *The Power of
Longitudinal Data: Studies of Risk and Protective Factors for Psychosocial
Disorders,* Cambridge: Cambridge University Press.

Grossmann, K.E. and August, P. (in press) 'Emotional development', in R.M.
Lerner, A.C. Peterson, and J. Brooks-Gun (eds) *Encyclopedia of Adolescence.*

Grossmann, K.E., Fremmer-Bombik, E., and Escher-Gräub, D. (in prep.) 'Toddlers' responses to display of sadness as related to the qualities of the relationships to their mothers and fathers: Cross-national implications'.

Grossmann, K.E. and Grossmann, K. (1984) 'Discovery and proof in attachment
research', Commentary to M. Lamb, R.M. Thompson, W. Garner, E.L.
Charnov, and D. Estes: 'Security of infantile attachment as assessed in the
Strange Situation – Its study and biological interpretation', *The Behavioral and
Brain Sciences* 7 (1): 154–5.

—— (1986) 'Phylogenetische und ontogenetische Aspekte der Entwicklung der
Eltern-Kind Bindung und der kindlichen Sachkompetenz', *Zeitschrift für
Entwicklungspsychologie und Pädagogische Psychologie* 18 (4): 287–315.

—— (1989) 'The wider concept of attachment in cross-cultural research', *Human
Development* 32.

Grossmann, K.E., Grossmann, K., and Ernst, R. (in prep.) 'Emotional communication in differently attached infant–parent dyads'.
Grossmann, K.E., Grossmann, K., Huber, F., and Wartner, U. (1981) 'German
children's behavior towards their mothers at 12 months and their fathers at 18
months in Ainsworth's Strange Situation', *International Journal of Behavioral
Development* 4: 157–81.
Grossmann, K.E., Grossmann, K., and Schwan, A. (1986) 'Capturing the wider
view of attachment: a reanalysis of Ainsworth's Strange Situation', in C.E. Izard
and P.B. Read (eds) *Measuring Emotions in Infants and Children* 2 (pp. 124–
71), New York: Cambridge University Press.
Grossmann, K.E. and Scheuerer-Englisch, H. (in prep.) 'Differences in relationship
during play between infants and parents as related to quality of attachment.'
Kaplan, N. and Main, M. (1986) 'Assessments of attachment organization through
children's family drawings', Unpublished manuscript, University of California,
Berkeley.
Kempe, B. (1987) 'Sechsjährige Kinder in einer unstrukturierten Familien-
Spielsituation: Analyse der Muter–Kind-Interaktionen (Six-year-olds in an
unstructured family play situation: Analysis of the mother–child interaction)',
Diplom thesis, Universität Regensburg.
Klagsbrun, M. and Bowlby, J. (1976) 'Responses to separation from parents: a
clinical test for young children', *British Journal of Projective Psychology* 21: 7–
21.
Main, M. (1981) 'Avoidance in the service of attachment: a working paper', in K.
Immelmann, G. Barlow, L. Petrinovich, and M. Main (eds) *Behavioral
Development: The Bielefeld Interdisciplinary Project* (pp. 651–93), New York:
Cambridge University Press.
Main, M. and Cassidy, J. (1988) 'Categories of response to reunion with the parent
at age six: predictable from infant attachment classification and stable over a one-
month period', *Developmental Psychology* 24: 415–26.
Main, M. and Goldwyn, R. (1985) 'Adult attachment classification and rating
system', Unpublished manuscript, University of California, Berkeley.
Main, M., Kaplan, N., and Cassidy, J. (1985) 'Security in infancy, childhood, and
adulthood: a move to the level of representation', in I. Bretherton and E. Waters
(eds) Growing points in Attachment Theory and Research, *Monographs of the
Society for Research in Child Development* 50: 66–106.
Main, M. and Weston, D.R. (1981) 'The quality of the toddler's relationship to
mother and to father: related to conflict behavior and the readiness to establish
new relationships', *Child Development* 52: 932–40.
Minsky, M. (1987) *The Society of Mind*, London: Heinemann (Pan Books, Picador
Edition, 1988).
Pfäffl-Gerullis, B. (1988) 'Familienzeichnungen sechsjähriger Kinder im Kontext
sozial-emotionaler Beziehungen zu den Eltern. Eine empirische Analyse' (Family
drawings of six-year-olds and their social–emotional relationship to their parents.
An empirical analysis), Diplom thesis, Universität Regensburg.
Remmers, G. (1987) 'Längsschnittliche Aspekte des Interaktionsverhaltens 6-
jähriger Kinder und ihrer Müter bei Bauklotzkonstruktionen nach Anweisung'
(Longitudinal aspects of the interaction between six-year-olds and their mothers
during a block building game), Diplom thesis, Universität Regensburg.
Scarr, S. and Kidd, K.K. (1983) 'Developmental behavior genetics', in P. H. Mussen
(ed.) *Handbook of Child Psychology*, 4th edn, vol. II: *Infancy and Developmental Psychobiology* (pp. 345–433), New York: Wiley.
Scheuerer-Englisch, H. (1989) 'Das Bild der Vertrauensbeziehung bei 10-jährigen

Kindern und ihren Eltern: Bindungsbeziehungen in Iängsschnittlicher und aktueller Sicht' (Representations of trust-relationships in ten-year-olds and their parents: Attachment relationships in longitudinal and present perspectives), Doctoral dissertation, Universität Regensburg.

Sroufe, L.A. (1979) 'The coherence of individual development: Early care attachment, and subsequent developmental issues', *American Psychologist* 34 (10): 834–41.

—— (1983) 'Infant–caregiver attachment and patterns of adaptation in preschool: The roots of maladaptation and competence', in M. Perlmutter (ed.) *Minnesota Symposium in Child Psychology* 16: 41–81, Hillsdale, N.J.: Erlbaum.

Sroufe, L.A. and Waters, E. (1977) 'Attachment as an organizational construct', *Child Development* 48: 1184–99.

Stephan, C. (1989) 'Die sachorientierte Beziehung und die Entwicklung von Interessensystemen. Beziehungsaspekte aus der Sicht 10-jähriger Kinder und ihrer Eltern' (Activity-oriented relationships and the development of interest-systems. Relationship aspects from the point of view of 10-year-olds and their parents), Doctoral dissertation, Universität Regensburg.

Suess, G. (1987) 'Auswirkungen frühkindlicher Bindungserfahrungen auf Kompetenz im Kindergarten' (Consequences of early attachment experiences on children's competence in kindergarten), Doctoral dissertation, Universität Regensburg.

Suess, G. and Grossmann, K. (in prep.) 'Effects of early attachment on competence in preschool: from dyadic to individual organization of self.'

Wartner, U. (1987) 'Attachment in infancy and at age six, and children's self-concept: A follow-up of a German longitudinal study', Doctoral dissertation, University of Virginia.

Wartner, U. and Grossmann, K. (in prep.) 'Stability of attachment patterns and their disorganizations from infancy to age six in south Germany.'

Chapter 7

Attachment patterns in children of depressed mothers[1]

Marian Radke-Yarrow

This study concerns the developing relationships between depressed mothers and their young children. When mothers are depressed, what kinds of affective environments do they create for their children? What are the psychosocial consequences for the children? There is a special significance in singling out depressed mothers in relation to mother–child attachment patterns and children's psychosocial functioning. In healthy mother–child relationships, one expects to see mothers who are available to their children, who are sensitive and responsive, and who are confident in themselves. Translation of the classic symptoms of depression into the role of mother suggests problems for the mother–child relationship: depression is characterized by feelings of hopelessness and lack of self-worth, low involvement and low energy, disordered interpersonal relationships, episodic emotional dysregulation, and psychological unavailability. Such impairments in the mother would seem to place the child in a perilous and uncertain caregiving environment.

Indeed, epidemiological studies of the offspring of affectively ill parents document a significantly higher occurrence of problems in these children than in children of well parents (see review by Beardslee *et al.* 1983). These studies have been mainly of offspring in their adolescence or adulthood. They have had little to say about the experiences of these offspring growing up in the care of depressed parents. When young children of depressed parents have been investigated (e.g. Zahn-Waxler *et al.* 1984; Hammen *et al.* 1987) impairments in mother–child relationships and in children's psychosocial development have been found.

How mothers' affective states influence their feelings toward, and inter-actions with, their children is not well understood. For some depressed mothers, their depressive symptoms may be very much entangled in their relationships with their children. Other mothers, perhaps less ill, may protect interactions with their children from their own depressive symp-toms. Because depressed mothers are not a homogeneous group in aetiology or in their symptomatology, one would not expect uniform effects on their children. However, when disturbed affect is a dominant part of the mothers' functioning, because children are finely tuned and sensitive to their human surroundings (Zahn-Waxler and Radke-Yarrow 1982), costs to children seem highly likely.

In the present study, mothers' affective behaviour is investigated in relation to attachment relationships and children's moods and emotions. Mothers' moods and emotions and their emotion regulation are the terms of maternal assessment. The feelings that young children have about themselves and their caregivers are assessed in terms of the mother–child attachment relationship and children's expressed moods and emotions.

THE SAMPLE

A longitudinal study (Radke-Yarrow 1989) designed to investigate the social and emotional development of the children is the source of the data. Families in which the mother has a diagnosis of unipolar depression ($N =$ 45) or bipolar depression ($N = 21$) and families in which the mother has no history of psychiatric disorder ($N = 45$) are the participants in the study. Maternal diagnoses are based on a standard psychiatric interview (SADS-L, RDC criteria) (Spitzer and Endicott 1977), conducted at the time of the family's entry into the study. Although all depressed mothers met criteria for a diagnosis of affective disorder, there is a range in severity of illness. The episodes of depression (and in the case of bipolar illness, the episodes also of mania) differ in length and frequency. Some mothers have been hospitalized and have been in therapy over long periods, while others have only occasionally been in treatment. All of the mothers are community-dwelling and have the major responsibility for the care of their children. The families are middle class, except for nine families from very economically disadvantaged circumstances. The middle-class families are intact; most of the lower-class families are single-parented. When the study began, the children ranged from 16 months to $3^{1}/_{2}$ years. The families are seen again when the children are between 5 and 6 years of age, and again when they are between 8 and 9 years. The present analyses are based on the first period of assessment.

PROCEDURE

The families are observed in an informal, comfortable research apartment (a home-like suite of rooms with kitchenette and bathroom). There are three half-day sessions spaced over a period of 2 weeks. The sessions are videotaped. Balancing experimental and naturalistic methods, time in the apartment is composed so as to provide reasonably natural sequences of situations and events that are representative of daily routines and rearing demands (eating, playing, separating, encountering problems, etc.) and that tap different potentials for behaviour (pleasurable, social, task-oriented, stressful, 'free time' interaction).

The family's time in the research apartment includes several mildly stressful events. The mother is asked to simulate sadness. Following standard procedure, mother and child look at a book of pictures of infants who are expressing various emotions. The mother is instructed to interest the child and to talk with the child about the babies. She is asked, after completing the series, to return to the picture of the crying baby and to show her own sadness and concern about this infant. This simulation is intended to draw out behaviour that is representative of mother's and child's history of interaction around depressive feelings – how the mother expresses sadness and how the child responds to her sadness. The usefulness of this procedure in bringing out individual differences in toddler's arousal and mobilization in response to mother's distressed feelings has been demonstrated in earlier normative research (Zahn-Waxler and Radke-Yarrow 1982).

Other kinds of stress that occur naturally during the observations over the three half-days are the many instances in which mothers attempt to influence or discipline their children. Mothers' fearfulness in confronting children's opposition is particularly relevant for depressed mothers (see Kochanska *et al.* 1987). This affective quality is an indication of the mother's helplessness, a characteristic linked with depression.

A comment is needed concerning the depressed mother's state at the time she is seen in the study. Depression is episodic in nature. Depressed mothers were not always in a depressive or manic episode when they were seen. One cannot, of course, manipulate research to coincide exactly with episodes. We have assumed, with research findings that are supportive of the assumption (Weissman *et al.* 1972), that underlying personality organization and behavioural dispositions are enduring, and that it is history or chronic experience of child and mother together that we are tapping.

Attachment measures. The Strange Situation (Ainsworth *et al.* 1978) was part of the sequence of events in the mother's and child's first visit to the apartment. The standard procedure was followed with two alterations: (a) lengthening the time for which mother, stranger, and child are together from 5 to 7 minutes (episode 3) and (b) having the mother return in the last episode with a small case of toys. These changes were made to fulfil objectives in the larger study. The attachment classifications are based on the criteria outlined by Ainsworth *et al.* (1978). The details of classification and adjustments made in the scoring to accommodate the higher ages of the children are provided in Radke-Yarrow *et al.* (1985).

Maternal and child variables. Maternal and child behaviour was measured in moods and emotions. Videotaped records of behaviour in the apartment were coded for a continuous record of visible affect. Each

minute was coded for the dominant affect expressed. Affect was characterized as (a) irritability or anger, (b) anxiety or sadness, (c) downcast
negative mood, (d) neutral to mild positive mood, (e) pleasure or happiness, and (f) affection. Two coders coded 20 per cent of the protocols.
Kappa values on minute-by-minute coding were 0.78 for mothers' affect
and 0.75 for children's affect. The mothers' and children's scores were the
number or percentage of minutes in which a given mood or emotion was
expressed. The scores are based on 8 to 9 hours of observations. Sometimes mother's emotions were directed to the child; at other times they
were expressed simply in the presence of the child. Similarly, the child's
emotions were in interactions with mother and in activity alone.

In summary, the relations among four sets of data are investigated:
mothers' diagnoses, mothers' moods and emotions, patterns of attachment,
and children's moods and emotions.

FINDINGS

Patterns of attachment and maternal diagnosis

The data reported here on attachment extend an earlier report by Radke-
Yarrow *et al.* (1985) by including the larger sample currently enrolled in the
longitudinal study. Children of bipolar depressed mothers are less likely to
have a secure attachment (24 per cent) than are children of well mothers
(62 per cent), $\chi^2(1) = 8.45$, $p < 0.005$, and less likely than children of
unipolar depressed mothers (53 per cent), $\chi^2(1) = 5.07$, $p < 0.05$. The
unipolar depressed dyads are directionally but not significantly less likely
than the well dyads (62 per cent) to have a secure attachment. To ascertain
possible age differences in attachment, the present sample was examined in
three approximately equal age groups between 16 and 42 months. No
significant age differences were found. The percentages of secure attachments, from youngest to oldest groups, in the well families are 75, 60, and
67 per cent respectively. The comparable figures for secure attachments in
the depressed families are 47, 50, and 40 per cent.

The relatively high frequency of secure attachment in unipolar mother–
child pairs raises interesting questions concerning the nature of these
relationships. The high rate of insecure attachments among the manic
depressive mother–child pairs also sharpens questions regarding the
processes involved. Does being securely attached to a depressed mother
hold the same kind of security and have the same consequences for the
child as being securely attached to a well mother? How does a secure
attachment develop with a depressed mother and how is it maintained?
How do the depressed mother–child dyads with secure and insecure
attachment relationships differ from one another? The analyses that follow
begin to identify differences in affect that characterize the interactions of

mothers and children in each of these groups, in secure and in insecure relationships.

Maternal affect and patterns of attachment

There was remarkable variation in the emotions and moods that were exhibited by mothers in the three sessions of childrearing observed in the apartment. In each of the specific categories of affect, the range in mothers' scores is from near zero occurrence to presence in fifty to sixty per cent of the minutes observed – with a few extreme outliers. Are these individual differences systematically related to mothers' psychiatric status (which one would expect) and, within these person-contexts, are maternal differences in affect reflected in the attachment relationship?

Profiles of each of the groups of mothers are represented in Table 7.1 in terms of the percentage of mothers who exhibit each of the emotions and moods with high frequency. A standard score of $+ 0.50$ based on the total sample was used as the criterion. Considering the patterns of affects that characterize each group of mothers, it is apparent that differences relating to mothers' diagnostic status are more pronounced in the insecure attachment relationships than in the secure relationships. In the secure attachments (rows 1–3 in Table 7.1), relatively few well mothers and unipolar

Table 7.1 Percentage of mothers showing high levels[a] of emotions and moods (by maternal diagnosis and attachment relationship)

	Negative emotions and mood			Positive emotions and neutral mood		
	Angry, irritable	Anxious, sad	Downcast	Affectionate	Happy	Neutral
Secure attachment						
Well mothers ($n = 28$)	25	11	7	25 (25)[b]	32	43
Unipolar depressed mothers ($n = 24$)	17	8	17	38 (54)	13	33
Bipolar depressed mothers ($n = 5$)	60	40	40	40 (40)	60	20
Insecure attachment						
Well mothers ($n = 17$)	6	6	6[c]	24 (60)	18	65[d]
Unipolar depressed mothers ($n = 21$)	24	38	43	29 (71)	19	19
Bipolar depressed mothers ($n = 16$)	19	43	13	25 (38)	38	13

Notes: [a] Percentage of mothers with standard score of ≥ 0.50.
[b] Percentage of mothers with scores above the total group mean.
[c] Significant differences in downcast mood between well mothers and unipolar mothers and between unipolar and bipolar depressed mothers, $p < 0.02$.
[d] Significant differences in neutral mood between well mothers and unipolar and bipolar depressed mothers, $p < 0.02$.

mothers express negative affects with high frequency. The well and the unipolar mothers are not very different from each other. In other words, children's secure attachments to unipolar mothers are in affective contexts in which manifestations of maternal depression are muted. (In the bipolar depressed group there are too few secure attachments to permit conclusions about maternal affect.)

On the other hand, within the groups of insecurely attached dyads (rows 4–6), well mothers and depressed mothers surround the child with quite different patterns of emotions. High frequencies of negative emotions and mood (anxiety and sadness and downcast mood) are found significantly more often among depressed mothers than well mothers.

Well mothers in insecure attachment relationships express very little affect, positive or negative. Sixty-five per cent of them are high in neutral mood. In addition to these contrasts there is a category that differentiates all of the insecurely attached group from the well, securely attached group, namely, affection. In absolute numbers, the instances of expressed affection are very low in all groups. Therefore, affection was re-examined using the more lenient criterion, above the mean of the total group, to compare groups. More frequent than average display of affection was found to be characteristic of mothers in insecure attachment relationships – well and depressed mothers, and also of depressed mothers in secure attachment relationships.

Mothers' affection requires further comment. In observing some of the more severely depressed unipolar mothers, coders became aware of affection at particular times and in particular forms that did not always appear to be entirely appropriate. We gain some perspective on the nature of this affection from another data set in the longitudinal study (Kuczynski and Radke-Yarrow 1984). Mothers were observed in a standard manipulation. A man in a white coat visited mother and child in the apartment to take a series of physical measurements of the child. In this situation, some mothers markedly increased behaviours such as hugging and stroking their child. This kind of signalling of stress through affection was most apparent in depressed mothers. It is perhaps a similar stress-related affection that is reflected in the group profiles of mothers in insecure attachment relationships and depressed mothers generally.

In the present study, there are two probes into maternal behaviour under stress (described on p. 117). The findings are compatible with an interpretation of stress-related affection. The first probe involves the mother's behaviour when her attempts to regulate her toddler are met with resistance from the child. We assume that some degree of stress is generated. It was reasoned (see Kochanska et al. 1987) that mothers who are fearful and unsure of themselves will have difficulty in enforcing their demands on the child. These authors found that depressed mothers were significantly more likely than well mothers to 'back-off' when the child resisted. In the context of the present analyses this kind of uncertain and ineffective response by the mother is seen as not providing the child with security and understanding of self and other. Such fearfulness on the part of the mother in confronting her child with limits was found to be significantly more frequent in mother–child pairs with insecure than with secure attachment relationships. The mean percentages of nonconfrontation in discipline encounters are 25 per cent in the insecure groups and 19 per cent in the secure groups ($F = (1,63)$ 5.72, $p < 0.02$). It is hypothesized that intense affect in response to stress, more frequent in insecure and depressed mothers, is a ready context for stressful affection.

The second probe of mothers' affective behaviour in circumstances of distress involved the mothers' simulation of sadness (relating to the photograph of a crying baby). The typical pattern of responding was for mothers to look sad, comment about the distress of the baby, and indicate that it made them feel sad to see a baby so unhappy. Mothers generally acknowledged the child's comments and concerns. Discussion was brief and the incident was concluded. Less appropriate kinds of maternal reactions also occurred in which mothers could not focus on the sadness of the baby and focused instead on their own feelings or on their child, making the child the cause of their own sadness (e.g 'You're not listening to me. It really makes me sad when you don't obey', or 'You're gonna help me feel better'). Some mothers could not resolve or close the episode, and continued for several minutes. Although these less appropriate responses occurred in all groups of mothers, they are rare among well mothers (3 cases) but appear in more than a third of the depressed mothers. It is especially the unipolar mothers who, by the processes just described, tend to pull their child into their own distress. Indeed, exchanges of sadness and concern between mother and child are significantly more prolonged in the unipolar mother–child dyads than in the well mother–child dyads (F $(1,68) = 10.83$, $p < 0.01$). This evidence, although indirect, fills out a picture of affectively stressful interaction in which affection is likely to occur, at least some of the times, in the depressed mother–child dyad.

Thus far the patterns of maternal affect have been described in terms of specific emotions. An additional code of affect was constructed to provide a summary index of the dysregulated quality of mother's total affective expression. Dysregulation is defined as mother's exhibiting elevated frequencies (above the mean) in two or more negative affects or scoring one or more standard deviations above the mean in one affect. (Theoretically, in the manic depressive mothers, extremes could also occur in positive affect. In this sample, mothers very high in positive expression also qualified for dysregulation on the negative emotions.) Eighteen per cent of the well mothers, 51 per cent of the unipolar mothers, and 71 per cent of the bipolar mothers were categorized as dysregulated ($\chi^2(2) = 16.98$, $p < 0.01$). Significantly more mothers in the insecure attachment groups (57 per cent) than in the secure attachment groups (26 per cent) scored as dysregulated in affect ($\chi^2(1) = 11.05$, $p < 0.001$). In Table 7.2 dysregulation of affect is summarized with consideration of maternal diagnosis and attachment. As in the succession of previous analyses, the less desired affect in the maternal role is associated with insecure attachment relationships, regardless of maternal diagnosis.

Children's emotions and moods

We have seen that mother's affective qualities (her affective illness and her expressed emotions and moods in the maternal role) are associated with the security and insecurity of her child's attachment. The other link in the picture is the child's affective qualities in relation to maternal affect and attachment.

Scoring of children's emotions and moods followed the form used for mothers' affect. The group profiles of the children's moods and emotions are presented in Table 7.3. The substantial manifestation of sadness and anxiety and downcast mood in many of the children of unipolar depressed mothers, securely as well as insecurely attached, convey the distress in these children. They are like their troubled mothers. Anxious–sad feelings are also frequent in insecurely attached children of bipolar depressed mothers and well mothers. It is the securely attached children of well mothers who, with a low frequency of sad and anxious behaviour, contrast with the children in all of the other groups.

Our analyses of children's and mothers' emotions have been in terms of group differences. The interrelations of maternal and child affect and attachment are more complex than can be identified in these comparisons. In an attempt to get a bit closer to the processes involved in the relationships within mother–child pairs, small homogeneous groups of mothers were selected for further qualitative analysis of their interaction with their children and their children's behaviour.

Two groups of 10 unipolar depressed mothers were identified as outliers or extremes in their affective behaviour, and as relatively 'pure types' of

Table 7.2 Percentage of mothers with profiles of dysregulated affect (by mothers' diagnosis and attachment relationship)

	Well mothers	Unipolar depressed mothers	Bipolar depressed mothers
Secure attachment	(4/28) 14	(9/24) 38	(2/5) 40
Insecure attachment	(4/17) 24	(14/21) 67	(13/16) 81

Note: Ns are in parentheses; e.g. of 28 well mothers in secure attachment relationships, 4 exhibited dysregulated emotion.

Table 7.3 Percentage of children showing high levels[a] of emotions and moods (by maternal diagnosis and attachment relationship)

	Negative emotions and mood			Positive emotions and neutral mood		
	Angry, irritable	Anxious, sad	Downcast	Affectionate	Happy	Neutral
Secure attachment Children of:						
Well mothers (*n* = 28)	25	21	18	7	21	17
Unipolar depressed mothers (*n* = 24)	13	67	13	38	29	25
Bipolar depressed mothers (*n* = 5)	20	60	0	40	40	40
Insecure attachment Children of:						
Well mothers (*n* = 17)	6	47	6	18	18	47
Unipolar depressed mothers (*n* = 21)	29	52	43	19	19	29
Bipolar depressed mothers (*n* = 16)	31	50	19	25	19	25

Note: [a] Percentage of children with standard score of ≥ 0.50.

affective patterns. These are mothers who are truly extreme either in expression of sadness and anxiety or in expression of anger and irritability. Because our approach is exploratory, findings from these groups are only suggestive.

The extremely sad and anxious mothers appear to be offering the least in a secure base for their children. These mothers expose their children to emotions that are not isolated incidents of sadness or anxiety, but rather a continuing flow of tension, either a helpless anxiety or a 'driven' quality of tension. Their behaviour appears to be independent of the child's behaviour, certainly not contingent on the child's actions. These mothers are unsure of themselves and ineffectual in regulating the child. They show little pleasure in the child, although they show affection blended with anxiety. These mothers present unrelieved distress to their children. Only 1 of the 10 children in this group is securely attached; 4 are avoidant, 4 are resistant, and 1 is unable to separate from mother. These children show high frequencies of anxious sadness, and sometimes anger. One child ('A' attachment) referred to the staff person as 'Mommy' and turned to her for help even though the mother was present. One child ('A' attachment) responded to her mother's chronic sadness by 'shutting down' her own emotions. The most troubled child in the group is a little girl who is completely engulfed, unable to separate from her mother. She and her mother are described by the staff as waifs, sad and fearful and affectionate, staying in close proximity to each other.

At this early age, some of these children appear to have taken into themselves the feeling states of the mother, and at the same time some of the children are distancing themselves from their mothers. Speculatively, one could anticipate that with mother's anxious sadness, communication leading to understanding of each other will suffer. A secure base in the mother figure is unlikely to develop or to be maintained. Good feelings about self may be hard to achieve. Mother's and child's abilities to relate positively and intimately with others seem endangered.

The angry, irritable mothers present a different stimulus to their children. These depressed mothers are often distressingly insensitive to the dignity of their children. Unlike the mothers for whom sadness and anxiety are the continuing, overwhelming dimension, mothers with high rates of anger cannot fill all, or even the majority, of the time with overt anger. Although irritability may be ongoing, anger tends to come in episodes.

In contrast to the totally sad and withdrawn mothers, these mothers respond to their children, sometimes contingently. Some mothers are able to set and maintain strict limits for the children – in this respect providing a predictable and, in some respects, secure structure to the environment, though not a very pleasant one. Even some of the very angry mothers have some redeeming moments of enjoyed interactions, which perhaps lessen the impact of the anger. For other angry mothers, sadness and anxiety fill in the time between anger outbursts. Here one would seem to have the worst of worlds.

Variable means of coping are evident in children subjected to angry mothers. Despite the unfavourable conditions that high frequency of maternal anger creates, 4 of the 10 children are securely attached; 3 others are avoidant and 3 are resistant. Several of these angry mothers are able to set limits for the child. They are also positively invested in the child. Nevertheless the emotional toll on the child is a high rate of anger and anxiety and sadness.

In these children we see virtually no expression of affection. With maternal affective qualities at the extreme, we see some children moving into their mothers' affective organizations, in part becoming like their mothers, others are attempting in different ways to protect themselves from their mothers' stressful affect. These extreme cases point up the fact that children develop attachments (secure and insecure) in very different affective contexts, thereby carrying forward with them quite different feelings about, and images of, themselves and their mothers.

SUMMARY COMMENTS

This research is focused on the affective qualities of mothers and children in relation to attachment patterns. The risks to attachment from maternal affective disturbance are evident in the findings. Generally, in the secure attachment relationships, regardless of mothers' psychiatric status, mothers' profiles of emotions and moods are without extremes of affect. On the other hand, dysregulated negative affect is characteristic of the majority of insecure relationships with depressed mothers.

Secure attachments develop in various contexts of maternal affect; sometimes when negative maternal affect is high. Children at the toddler age are developing varied means of coping with painful maternal emotions. We have seen, for example, that some children of unipolar depressed mothers are drawn into very close relationships with their mothers, with mixed consequences: having the security of the mother's closeness and affection carries with it the mother's anxious sadness. These feelings may become part of the child's self, and shape the child's mode and content of interaction with the mother. Other children of depressed mothers arrive at a different resolution: namely, one in which they are avoidant. They thereby sacrifice closeness, partly avoiding mother's sadness and anxiety, but still not avoiding their own anxious and sad feelings.

The findings reported here suggest issues for further study. The data raise questions concerning attachment relationships with psychologically impaired mothers. The extremely high rates of both 'C' and 'A' attachments in bipolar mother–child relationships are a specific challenge. With the present data, it has not been possible to come to a really good understanding of this group. In some respects, the problems of these children are like those of the children of unipolar mothers, but there is far less predictability and uniformity in the bipolar group. Judged by their attachment patterns, these children should be most 'badly off', but it is unclear in observing the children that they are. They present, instead, significant heterogeneity in their coping behaviour.

Findings from the present study also point up the importance of personality facets of mothers that have been overlooked in attachment and childrearing research generally. Mothers' emotional make-up is just one aspect of this domain.

Children have been dealt with in the present analyses as the recipients of influences. Their individualities in temperament and personality are contributions to mother–child relationships and child outcome that have just begun to be taken seriously in research.

NOTE

1   This work was supported by the National Institute of Mental Health, Bethesda, Maryland, and by the John D. and Catherine T. MacArthur Foundation, Research Network Award on the Transition from Infancy to Early Childhood, Chicago, Illinois.

REFERENCES

Achenbach, T.M. and Edelbrock, C. (1980) *Child Behavior Checklist – Teacher's Report Form*, Burlington, Vt: University of Vermont.

Ainsworth, M.D.S., Blehar, M.C., Waters, E., and Wall, S. (1978) *Patterns of Attachment: A Psychological Study of the Strange Situation*, Hillsdale, N.J.: Erlbaum.

Beardslee, W.R., Bemford, J., Keller, M., and Klerman, G. (1983) 'Children of parents with major affective disorder: a review', *American Journal of Psychiatry* 140 (7): 825–32.

Cummings, E.M., Zahn-Waxler, C., and Radke-Yarrow, M. (1984) 'Developmental changes in children's reactions to anger in the home', *Journal of Child Psychology and Psychiatry and Allied Disciplines* 25 (1) : 63–74.

Hammen, C., Adrian, C., Gordon, D., Burge, D., Jaenicke, C., and Hirogo, D. (1987) 'Children of depressed mothers: maternal strain and predictors of dysfunction', *Journal of Abnormal Psychology* 96: 190–8.

Kochanska, G., Kuczynski, L., Radke-Yarrow, M., and Welsh, J.D. (1987) 'Resolutions of control episodes between well and affectively ill mothers and their young children', *Journal of Abnormal Child Psychology* 15 (3): 441–56.

Kuczynski, L. and Radke-Yarrow, M. (1984) 'Regulation of children's affective distress', Unpublished manuscript.

Radke-Yarrow, M. (1989) 'Family environments of depressed and well parents and their children: issues of research methods', in G.R. Patterson and E. Blechman (eds) *Family Social Interactions: Content and Methodological Issues in the Study of Aggression and Depression*, Hillsdale, N.J.: Erlbaum.

Radke-Yarrow, M., Cummings, E.M., Kuczynski, L., and Chapman, M. (1985) 'Patterns of attachment in two- and three-year-olds in normal families and families with parental depression', *Child Development* 56: 884–93.

Radke-Yarrow, M., Kochanska, G., Kuczynski, L., Nottlemann, E., Wilson, W.E., Belmont, B., Mayfield, A., Polissar, A., and Stilwell, J. (1987) 'The affective rearing environment: a comparison of normal and depressed parents', Unpublished manuscript.

Spitzer, R.L. and Endicott, J. (1977) *Schedule for Affective Disorders and Schizophrenia: Lifetime Version*, New York: New York State Psychiatric Institute, Biometrics Research.

Weissman, M.M., Paykel, E.S., and Klerman, G.L. (1972) 'The depressed woman as mother', *Social Psychiatry* 7: 98–108.

Zahn-Waxler, C., Cummings, E.M., McKnew, D.H., and Radke-Yarrow, M. (1984) 'Affective arousal and social interactions in young children of manic-depressive parents', *Child Development* 55: 112–22.

Zahn-Waxler, C. and Radke-Yarrow, M. (1982) 'The development of altruism: alternative research strategies', in N. Eisenberg-Berg (ed.) *The Development of Prosocial Behavior* (pp. 109–317), New York: Academic Press.

Chapter 8

Metacognitive knowledge, metacognitive monitoring, and singular (coherent) vs. multiple (incoherent) model of attachment

Findings and directions for future research

Mary Main

This chapter concerns some potential relations between metacognitive knowledge, metacognitive functioning, and processes related to attachment. Following a review of recent work concerning metacognition, representation, and mental models, I suggest that difficulties with the 'appearance–reality' distinction and the dual coding of single entities will make a young child vulnerable to responding to unfavorable attachment experiences by developing 'multiple (conflicting or incompatible) models' of attachment. I next discuss individual differences in the narratives which adults produce during structured, hour-long interviews regarding their own attachment histories. When a parent presents a coherent singular model of her attachment history, the infant is typically judged 'secure' on the basis of its behavioral response to that parent in a structured separation-and-reunion observation. When a parent presents instead incoherent, multiple models of her experience and its influence, or implausible ideation, the infant is typically judged insecure in this observation. Our pilot studies are indicating relatively advanced metacognitive monitoring in secure children, difficulties with accessing early memories in insecure children, and, as expected, failure to comprehend the privacy of thought in 6-year-olds judged insecure–ambivalent with mother. Finally, I suggest some directions for further research.

In a series of recent studies, behaviour-based assessments of individual differences in the infant's response to separation from and reunion with the parent in the Ainsworth Strange Situation (Ainsworth *et al.* 1978) have been compared with individual differences in both the parent's represent-ations of his or her attachment history, and the child's later representations of attachment-related situations. These studies (e.g. Main *et al.* 1985) have shown significant relations between the quality of the infant's attachment to the parent (secure, insecure–avoidant, insecure–ambivalent, insecure–disorganized/disoriented) and (1) the adult's reconstruction of his or her attachment history, as well as (2) the child's later representation of self and others.

The connections between behavior-based infant attachment assessments and attachment-related representations seen in these studies are diverse, and can be considered in several ways. At one level, representational responses may simply echo or 'reflect' some component of the behavioral responses originally used to identify the category. Representations directly reflective of experience and/or the behaviors used to identify the category are demonstrated when a 3-year-old judged secure with mother on the basis of positive responses to reunion with her portrays similarly positive reunion responses in a doll-family (Bretherton *et al.* in press), or when a 6-year-old who was judged avoidant of proximity and contact with the mother in the Strange Situation later draws a family lacking in arms (Kaplan and Main 1989). At a more complex level, we can also see a reflective matching in the connection established between, e.g., a parent's propensities to be 'Dismissing of Attachment' during the Adult Attachment Interview, and the infant's tendency to 'dismiss' (avoid and ignore) the parent in the Ainsworth Strange Situation (Main and Goldwyn in press; Ainsworth and Eichberg in this volume).

Representational vs. metarepresentational processes can be roughly distinguished in terms of *thinking* vs. *thinking about thought*, or, at a deeper level, possessing a mental representation of an experience vs. being able to reflect on its validity, nature, and source. For individuals differing in attachment organization, I suggest that metarepresentational (metacognitive) processes may differ as strikingly as those representational processes which seem simply to reflect the infant behavior patterns originally identifying placement in a given attachment category. The mental processess of secure individuals may then be distinguished from those of insecure individuals not only in terms of their *content*, but also in terms of their *flexibility and readiness for examination*.

The essay opens with a discussion of representation, internal working models, and 'multiple' models of attachment figures and attachment-related situations, followed by a brief review of recent literature concerning early metacognition. I then examine the hypothesis that the young child's failure to have acquired certain aspects of the 'appearance–reality' distinction, and her difficulty with the dual-coding of single entities, may make her particularly vulnerable to developing 'multiple' (conflicting/incompatible) models in response to unfavorable attachment-related events.

The basis of this hypothesis is a relatively recent literature in metacognition, which suggests that children under the age of 3 do not understand the *merely* representational nature of their own (or other's) thinking, because they are as yet unable to operate upon (or 'metarepresent') it. Not having a metacognitive distinction between appearance and reality available, they are unable to imagine that some propositions are in fact without validity; that some individuals believe things which are not true; and that they themselves may have false beliefs at present or may have harbored false beliefs in the past. These aspects of metacognitive knowledge have important consequences for social–emotional development (Flavell *et al.* 1986), and have usually been mastered by age 6.

Following the above discussion of potential relations between metacognition and vulnerability to the creation of multiple models of attachment during childhood, I turn to the differing narratives produced by adults in response to the Adult Attachment Interview (George *et al.* 1985). The most striking feature of the narrative produced by a parent whose infant is judged secure with him or her in the Ainsworth Strange Situation is its *coherence.* This coherence appears both in an analysis based upon Grice's 'maxims' with respect to coherence of discourse (Grice 1975), and in terms of overall plausibility, and suggests that the adult is working with a singular model of his or her attachment-related experiences (cf. Johnson-Laird 1983). Parents of insecure infants, in contrast, present 'multiple' models of attachment-related experiences, and/or striking lapses in plausibility. These studies link the coherence of a one-hour narrative concerning an adult's attachment history to an external criterion – the infant's response to that adult as a parent in a stressful situation (Main and Goldwyn in press), and, relatedly, the parent's behavior towards the infant (Crowell and Feldman 1988).

In the fourth section of this essay I examine the proposal that children judged secure with the parent(s) are likely, on average, to be more advanced than insecure children with respect to metacognitive knowledge and metacognitive monitoring of attachment-related experiences. For young children, these experiences are expected not only to influence the development of certain first-order representations (in philosophical terms, propositional attitudes such as 'I believe that I am an unworthy person'), but may also influence the child's ability to create and manipulate second-order representations (metarepresentations) such as 'I find myself believing that I am an unworthy person – why?'. In other words, experiences with the parents may not only alter the *contents* of the young child's mind, but may also alter *her ability to operate upon those contents.* Pilot studies suggesting support for this hypothesis are reviewed, and the essay ends with some suggestions for future studies.

REPRESENTATION, INTERNAL WORKING MODELS, AND 'MULTIPLE' MODELS – AN OVERVIEW OF RECENT LITERATURE

Representation

The recent interest in the connections between attachment and attachment representation leads naturally to a concern with the nature of representation itself. The objective of this section is to review some recent work involving mental representation and metacognition, with a view to considering the concept of the 'internal working model' and differences observed in the coherence of that model across individuals.

A first distinction between representations is that between representational artifacts (such as drawings, or interview transcripts) and the internal processes which they are presumed to represent (Mandler 1983). Although we infer the nature of a child's or adult's internal representations of attachment from her representational artifacts, it is the internal representation itself which is of interest to attachment theorists. Two initial questions are: (1) What is the *form* (or forms) taken by internal representation, and, relatedly, (2) should we presume that thinking unfailingly follows the rules of formal logic?

The continuing dialogue among philosophers, computer scientists, and psychologists indicates that the form taken by internal representations remains unknown. Thus, it is at present undetermined whether thinking (and by implication, the 'internal working model') is entirely reducible to propositions (Fodor 1978; Pylyshyn 1984), or mental imagery (Kosslyn 1983), or whether thought of both or several kinds is possible (Paivo 1971; see also Anderson 1983).

One of the most interesting recent accounts of mental modeling has de-emphasized the role played by syllogistic logic in individual comprehensions of reality. Johnson-Laird (1983) proposes that there are at least three major kinds of representations, or 'options for encoding information': propositional representations, images, and mental models. Johnson-Laird's concept of the mental model is closely tied to Craik's 'working model' (1943), and emerged from his efforts to make sense of the kinds of explicit and implicit inferences people make in problem-solving tasks, e.g. in the manipulation of syllogisms. An examination of the patterning of subject errors convinced him that individuals ultimately develop an integrated set of 'pictures' of the premises which is then submitted to a Popperian-like test to determine whether there is any way of interpreting the premises that is consistent with a denial of the conclusion. This is not to say that reasoning does not sometimes take the form of propositional logic, but that reasoning can also take place without using formal logic, by using mental models. Although much of the research discussed by Johnson-Laird consists in the study of subjects' short-term responses to experimental situations, his more general discussion is frequently focused upon Craik's broader concept. Thinking utilizing 'mental models' with respect to attachment might therefore be expected to follow a similar path.

Two further issues concerning us are (1) limits on rationality and (2) the relation between performance on tests of logic and familiarity with the contents. As most psychologists are now aware, the majority of adult subjects make systematic reasoning errors under some conditions, or may engage in 'magical thinking' regarding materially impossible sympathetic contagions among objects (Wason and Johnson-Laird 1972; Kahneman and Tversky 1982; Rozin *et al.* 1986). In the discussion of the potential relations between reasoning and security status which might be uncovered in future experiments (below), we should remain aware that some errors in reasoning should be expected in even the most secure and intellectually sophisticated of subjects. In addition, if thinking about human relationships resembles other forms of thinking (which it probably does – see Case 1985), then some errors in reasoning regarding attachment-related issues should also be expected.

Finally, some recent investigations suggest that individuals perform more effectively on tests which presumably involve abstract logic *if they are familiar with the contents* (Johnson-Laird *et al.* 1972; Wason and Johnson-Laird 1972). Similarly, Piaget has frequently argued that formal operations are most likely to develop in areas for which an individual has considerable experience of concrete operations. This relation of goodness of reasoning to familarity of content is of special interest, since it bears upon the way in which adult reasoning regarding attachment-related issues may depend upon adequate comprehension of earlier experience.

Internal working models

Bowlby (1973), following Craik (1943; as see Bretherton 1985), has selected the term 'internal working model' to describe the individual's internal representation of the world, his attachment figures, himself, and the relations among them. Among other things, the internal working model is expected to contain a rough-and-ready sketch of the environment and the self which can be mentally manipulated prior to undertaking possible future action. The internal working model is conceived as an integral and necessary component of the attachment behavioral system (see Bretherton's diagrammatic sketch *re* placement of the internal working model in relation to the attachment behavioral system (Bretherton 1985: 10)). At a broader level, the internal working model must contain multiple representations which reference not only direct experiences regarding the attachment figure, but also concepts of the self which are derived from such experiences (Bowlby 1973: Bretherton 1985). With respect to attachment figures, for example, the model should contain information regarding who the attachment figure(s) are; where they are currently located; and how likely they are to respond to bids for access. As noted above, it is clear that some model of the world must exist in individuals capable of planning and representing action (Bowlby 1973; Craik 1943; see also Dennett 1978; Johnson-Laird 1983). The term stands for the fact that we have models of the world which enable us to act in new situations without rethinking each situation from the beginning; which may be mentally manipulated; which are in part the product of experience; and which may be in part unconscious.

It is when we attempt to assess an individual's 'internal working model' of someone or something on the basis of his or her representational artifacts, or describe systematic differences in the thinking of individuals, that we become most aware of difficulties with any literal interpretation of the concept. In contrast to the 'integration of information relevant to attachment' seen in secure children and adults (Main *et al.* 1985) is the incoherence and lack of integration of, or lack of access to, information seen in those who are insecure with respect to attachment. Pressed to describe and evaluate their attachment experiences and relations, insecure individuals frequently present a jumble of contradictory thoughts, feelings, and intentions which can only loosely be described as a 'model'. As used to characterize an insecure individual's conceptualizations regarding attachment, then, the term 'internal working model' is only a 'conceptual metaphor' (Bretherton 1985) and may be somewhat misleading.

Multiple models

To account for incoherence of ideation regarding attachment in troubled individuals and, in extreme cases, for some forms of psychopathology, Bowlby (1973) introduced the term 'multiple models', a term that suggests models which are contradictory or incompatible in that both or several could not be true at one time. An example of multiple models would be contradictory ideas regarding attachment figures and the self, or regarding the existence, nature, and interpretation of attachment-related events. According to Bowlby, 'the hypothesis of multiple models, one of which is highly influential but relatively or completely unconscious, is no more than a version, in different terms, of Freud's hypothesis of a dynamic unconscious' (Bowlby 1973: 205).

Bowlby's usage of the term 'multiple models' is not, of course, intended to reference the multiplicity, embedding, and hierarchy of mental models which inevitably characterizes normal mental life. That an adult mind may contain models of diverse aspects of reality, as well as models of itself and possible realities; that some models are contained within, or contain others; that hierarchies of models of increasing degrees of abstraction exist (Stern's RIGS – Representations of Interactions which are Generalized – may provide the basic level; see Stern 1985: 114); that context affects models, and levels of abstraction or embeddedness interact is taken for granted. Thus, Bowlby's concept of multiple models refers not to the diversity of models of differing parts or aspects of reality (including, of course, possibility) mentioned above, but rather to multiple and implicitly contradictory models of the *same* aspect of reality. It refers, in short, to multiple models of a thing which ought to have a singular model.

Because it is simpler to discuss contradictions between postulates than between mental images, for the remainder of this essay I shall discuss multiple (and singular) models of attachment in terms of *propositions*. This approach is taken for heuristic purposes only: it does not imply that thinking about relationships cannot take place in terms of mental imagining or mental models. Such propositions consist of two parts: a propositional attitude (believing, hoping, wanting, fearing, desiring) and a related content (that my attachment figure will respond positively to me when I approach her, that my attachment figure dislikes me, etc.). 'Multiple models' of attachment-related events would then be described as conflicting propositions such as, e.g., 'I believe that mother is unfailingly loving and has always acted in my best interest/I believe that mother is ridiculing and rejecting and does not consider my interests' (an example of conflicting *contents*), or, 'I fear that father will leave this family/I hope that father will leave this family' (an example of conflicting propositional *attitudes*). Note that propositional attitudes can be seen as instances of the recursive embedding of mental models within mental models (Johnson-Laird 1983).

As I will show shortly, however, while younger thinkers have beliefs, hopes, fears, and full propositional attitudes, they do not usually understand that representations are expected to be 'semantically evaluable' (Fodor 1987), i.e. that any given representation is presumed to have satisfaction conditions – conditions which may or may not be met in the world, but which are necessary to affirming the truth-value of the proposition. Even though the very young child recognizes the distinction between 'pretend' and 'real' entities (Bretherton 1984; Leslie 1987), then, it is only the older child who recognizes that our understanding of the 'real' world as well as the 'pretend' world is representational and can in fact be counter-factual. Thus, most young children fail to allow for a distinction between 'reality' (which can never be directly comprehended) and our limited and diverse representational grasp of that 'reality' as human beings (Kant's noumenal–phenomenal distinction). And, as I will discuss later, because the young child will not look for counter-factual conditions, she will be all the more vulnerable to the early development of multiple models.

METACOGNITION, THE APPEARANCE–REALITY DISTINCTION, AND EARLY DIFFICULTIES WITH THE 'DUAL-CODING' OF SINGLE ENTITIES

The term metacognition refers to cognition as a target of thought, whether declarative and stateable ('I know that false belief is possible') or, in a somewhat more mysterious sense (see Marshall and Morton 1978), procedural ('I am presently multiply accessing my multiple cognitions for contradictions and fallacies, which may lead to the significant if unstateable intuition that I am in error'). The consideration of multiple models of attachment leads directly to the topic of metacognition, since it is likely that where multiple contradictory models of the self or of experience exist, either metacognitive knowledge has yet to develop or there have been failures of corrective metacognitive monitoring.

Metacognition as a topic in its own right was drawn to the attention of developmentalists by Flavell (1979) in an article entitled 'Metacognition and cognitive monitoring: a new area of cognitive-developmental inquiry'. The term metacognition has been described by Brown and her colleagues (Brown *et al.* 1983) as referring to one's 'knowledge and control of the domain cognition' and more specifically to *knowledge about cognition* (e.g. the appearance–reality distinction) and the *regulation of cognition* (e.g. cross-checking for error).

The *regulation of cognition,* or *metacognitive monitoring,* includes planning activities, monitoring them, and checking outcomes. It necessarily includes the self-regulation of knowledge which should occur when the thinker becomes aware of contradictions between presently held ideas, a state which ideally ought to lead to cognitive reorganization (Inhelder *et al.* 1974; Karmiloff-Smith 1979). Brown points out that the notion, if not the term, has a long history, since Binet, fascinated by individual differences in his daughter's styles of self-regulation, selected *autocriticism* as a central component of intelligence (Binet 1909, cited in Brown *et al.* 1983: 117).

In contrast to the regulation of cognition, *knowledge about cognition* refers to second-order cognition – a theoretically stateable second-order or 'meta'-representation rather than the representation itself. Thus the simple proposition, 'I am an unworthy person' is not an example of metacognition, whereas the thought that 'I am a person who thinks that I am an unworthy person rather frequently' is a second-order representation and an example of metacognitive knowledge. Metacognitive knowledge is described by Brown *et al.* as 'relatively stable, statable, often fallible, and late-developing information that human thinkers have about their own cognitive processes and those of others'. It is, in fact, only when learners have acquired some appreciation of the fallible nature of knowledge that they can consider their own cognitive processes as objects of reflection.

Some critical aspects of the ability to step back and consider (one's own) cognitive processes as objects of thought and reflection is acquired by a minority of children by 3 years of age, and simple forms have been acquired by most (but not all) children by 6 years. The appearance–reality distinction is an example of knowledge about cognition which, as Brown notes (Brown *et al.* 1983), gradually becomes relatively stable and stateable, but which is fallible (one can be incorrect regarding which is which) and which is late-developing (not being understood by young thinkers – even in simple form – until typically around 4 years of age). Knowledge of the appearance–reality distinction is an instance of the more general knowledge that the same object or event can be represented (apprehended, experienced, etc.) in different ways by the same person at different times, and can be represented differently by different people (Flavell *et al.* 1986). For developmentalists, the appearance–reality distinction is the example of metacognition *par excellence*, since it is 'the distinction which probably provides the intellectual basis for the fundamental epistemological construct common to science, "folk" psychology, religion and myth, of a real world "underlying" and "explaining" the phenomenal one' (Braine and Shanks 1965: 241–2, cited in Flavell *et al.* 1986). Acquisition of this distinction is part of the acquisition of 'commonsense metaphysics' (Forguson and Gopnik 1988), which holds that 'there is a single world of objects, events, states of affairs, people and other sentient beings which I (and others) experience perceptually and think about, and that this world is independent of the thoughts and experiences I and others have of it'. It is on this basis that children come to understand *representational diversity* (what others know, I may not; what I know, others may not; what I or others think may be false) and *representational change* (what I thought Thursday, I do not think today, and may not think tomorrow (Gopnik and Astington 1988)). Most of these aspects of metacognitive knowledge are available to 6-year-olds (albeit in limited form – see Chandler (1988)), while most 3-year-olds have not acquired this understanding. If the results of these experiments can be appropriately extended from the laboratory, then we can posit that below 4 years of age the child is not usually equipped to query either her own representations of reality or those offered by attachment figures.

A related source of early vulnerability to multiple models is the possibility that young children have special difficulty with the 'dual-coding' of single entities. The dual-coding deficit hypothesis has been advanced with respect to the 'one-word' stage of language learning by Markman (1984; see also Clark 1987) and is discussed with respect to the appearance–reality distinction by Flavell (Flavell *et al.* 1986). The suggestion is that young children, working with an 'assumption of mutual exclusivity' (Markman 1984), are unable to fit the same item into two categories at once – a seeming disadvantage which may actually assist with early language learning, when learning that something is a 'dog' rules out that it could also be a 'cat'. Research on children's understanding of social roles would also seem to bear out the notion that children experience this type of difficulty, since according to one study 3-year-olds cannot see how the same person can be simultaneously a doctor and a father or both a father and a grandfather (Watson 1984).

The dual-coding hypothesis is closely related to the notion developed by neo-Piagetian theorists (Case 1985; Fischer 1980) that there is a limit to the number of propositions which the young child can manage simultaneously, and that propositions or representations involving conflicting or opposing emotions will be particularly difficult to hold in working memory. For example, Fischer (1980) reported that young children have difficulty comprehending that the same person can be both 'nice' and 'mean'. In a particularly elegant recent study, Harter and Buddin (1987) were able to demonstrate that the great majority of 4-year-olds used all-or-none thinking regarding emotions, and were unable to integrate sets of positive and negative emotions either in general or with respect to a particular target, these emotions being viewed as conceptually distinct and therefore incompatible.

THE APPEARANCE–REALITY DISTINCTION, DUAL-CODING, AND EARLY VULNERABILITY TO THE CONSTRUCTION OF 'MULTIPLE MODELS'

Young children have always been presumed more vulnerable than older children and adults to unfavorable attachment-related experiences. Some reasons mentioned to date include the young child's greater dependence upon others, her more easily activated and less easily modulated attachment behavior, her less fully developed understanding of the concepts of space and time, greater egocentricity, and increased vulnerability to engaging in magical thinking with respect to playing a causal role in malignant events (Bowlby 1980). However, difficulties with the appearance–reality distinction and with the dual-coding of single entities provide us with still other reasons to suspect vulnerabilities to the creation of multiple (incompatible) models in response to unfavorable events in early childhood.

Vulnerability to unfavorable interaction patterns

Bowlby (1973) has suggested that unfavorable interaction patterns with attachment figures may render the young child vulnerable to the development of multiple models of the attachment figure, and, relatedly, to the development of multiple models of the self. If we consider this early vulnerability in the light of the new literature concerning metacognition, we can see that the ability to operate upon propositions, to embed working models, or to recognize alternative worlds, is likely to lead to an advantage for the older as opposed to the younger child in similar circumstances.

Relatedly, although the working model of the self is probably endangered by unfavorable interactions with an attachment figure at any age ('I am a bad person, since my attachment figure rejects me'), an older child – who has attained understanding of the appearance–reality distinction and its corollary, representational diversity – will be advantaged. As opposed to a younger child, this child can 'operate upon' or meta-represent a proposition such as 'I am a bad person' as follows: 'I *may* be a bad person because my attachment figure seems to think so, but, on the other hand, she has been found with false beliefs in other circumstances'. Understanding that people may actually be experiencing a different emotion than the one they express (Harris *et al.* 1986), or that a speaker can deliberately lie (Wimmer *et al.* 1984) should also assist a 5-year-old in situations in which a 3-year-old remains vulnerable.

Both the 'dual-coding hypothesis' and children's newly reported difficulties with comprehending the possibility of representational change add to our understanding of the difficulties and vulnerabilities of the child whose parent is prone to strong and unpredictable changes in (good/bad) mood and/or responsiveness. If, for example, young children have difficulties with the dual-coding of single entities, then the experience of extended interactions with an attachment figure whose behavior is unpredictable and highly conflicting (such as the insecure–preoccupied parents of insecure–ambivalent children – see Ainsworth *et al.* 1978; Crowell and Feldman 1988) must make the development of an organized overview of that figure especially unlikely, and the development of multiple models concerning that figure correspondingly greater.

While, at a clinical level, the young child's vulnerability to the creation of multiple models of attachment-related experiences has long been recognized, the dual-coding hypothesis suggests more specifically (a) that *insecure–ambivalent* children will be especially vulnerable (b) given difficulties in the coding of experiences which are in fact contradictory. In addition, difficulties in holding personal representational changes in mind ('what I thought yesterday I do not think today' – Astington and Gopnik 1988; Gopnik and Astington 1988) will still further increase the likelihood of the development of multiple models for these children. A child who has highly contradictory experiences with the same attachment figure will be more likely to develop *and maintain* an insecure–ambivalent attachment organization if she is too young to remember prior feelings in the face of new and different experiences.

Vulnerability to trauma

A source of 'multiple models' of special interest to Bowlby is the parent's denial or distortion of traumatic interactions or events which have in fact been observed (Bowlby 1973). Here the child may be presented with at least two contradictory images or memories (both stored in long-term memory, one witnessed, one taken from the parent's perhaps frequently offered verbal account/distortion/denial of the event), while being enjoined to recognize and remember only one. In a recent article ('On knowing what you are not supposed to know, and feeling what you are not supposed to feel') Bowlby cites the work of Cain and Fast (1972) who studied 45 children between the ages of 4 and 14, all of whom had lost a parent by suicide and had become psychiatrically disturbed, many of them severely (Bowlby 1988). About one quarter had personally witnessed some aspect of a parent's death and had been subjected to pressure from the surviving parent to believe that they were mistaken in what they had seen or heard, and that the death had not been due to suicide but to illness or accident. Cases Bowlby cites include a girl who discovered her father's body hanging in a closet and was told he died in a car accident, and two brothers who found their mother with slit wrists, but were told she had died by drowning. Cain and Fast concluded that many of the children's psychiatric problems (including feelings of unreality) were directly traceable to experiences of these kinds.

In one set of studies of the appearance–reality distinction in young children, Flavell and his colleagues (Flavell *et al.* 1983) suggested that some difficulties experienced in making these distinctions might be due to 'a specific metacognitive limitation, namely, *a difficulty in analyzing the nature and source of their own mental representations*' (italics mine). A recent study by Gopnik and Graf (1988), focused specifically upon children's memory for source, suggested that memory for the *sources* of beliefs or information is acquired only between 3 and 5 years of age. Gopnik and Graf found that in recalling an event, most 3-year-olds were unable to distinguish whether their memory came from direct observation, inference, or from having been told about it by others, and their performance typically did not improve with training. Four-year-olds were often initially able to remember the source of an item of information, but after only a brief delay they forgot the source – while retaining the information itself.

While memory for personally important information may be less vulnerable than memory in brief laboratory experiments to such surprising omission of source-marking, this finding certainly suggests that children under 3 will be more likely than older children to develop multiple models in response to parental misconstructions, denials, and deceptions regarding events the child directly witnesses. If she is *not* able to mark the source of 'information' together with the information itself, a child under 3 years who directly observes one thing but is told something else will be *at the least* extremely vulnerable to 'multiple models' of the same event.[1] Note in addition that whereas an older child might not only remember the two divergent items together with accurate marking as to source, for the older child events witnessed are also likely to have a greater 'truth value' than those inferred or told. For a child who does not yet comprehend the possibly counter-factual nature of information, there is no evidence of a comparable hierarchy.

Given that the work in cognitive development reviewed here is so recent, it is not surprising that attachment theorists have tended to emphasize *mental suffering* as opposed to cognitive factors, as the primary explanation for the early 'defensive exclusion' of a given idea from further processing (as see Peterfreund 1971; Bowlby 1980). However, while the recent work reviewed here calls for increased attention to the role of cognitive factors in the development of multiple models of attachment, we should bear in mind that attempts to avoid mental suffering can probably lead to the same development as late as adulthood (when, presumably, neither dual-coding nor the various appearance–reality distinctions present difficulty). Particularly poignant examples of experiences of multiple models during adulthood involve loss of a child or spouse. Thus, for example, 12 of 20 widows in a Tokyo study reported difficulty believing that their husbands were dead 6 weeks following a road accident. One reported that she would go to the tramway stop at the hour her husband used to return home from work, and another would go to the door when she heard a motorbike, supposing it to be her husband's (Yanomoto *et al.* 1969, cited in Bowlby 1980: 135). Although individual differences in attachment organization may have played some role in the development of incompatible beliefs regarding the spouse's state as both alive and dead, the difficulty of fully accepting the mental suffering attendant upon a sudden loss is likely to have played the strongest part.

ATTACHMENT-RELATED NARRATIVES: COHERENCE VS. INCOHERENCE IN ADULT DISCOURSE PREDICTS SECURITY VS. INSECURITY OF INFANT ATTACHMENT

The Berkeley Adult Attachment Interview (George *et al.* 1985) is a structured interview regarding an individual's early attachment relationships and experiences, and evaluations of the effects of these experiences on present functioning. As noted earlier, the coherence of the resulting narrative has been found strongly linked to *external* criterion – namely, to the year-old infant's response to the structured separation and reunion episodes of the Ainsworth Strange Situation. Thus, strong correspondences between adult and infant attachment categories appear whether the adult interview is conducted 5 years following the Strange Situation (Main and Goldwyn in press); only a few months following the Strange Situation (Ainsworth and Eichberg in this volume); or before the first child is born (Ward *et al.* 1989). It appears therefore that when an interview focused upon an individual's history is approached (a) using not the individual's retrospective account as such, but rather *coherence, cohesiveness* and *plausibility* as the basic forms of analysis, (b) hypotheses can be constructed regarding the predicted relation between particular forms of interview response and infant–parent behavior patterns observed in other settings. These hypotheses are (c) susceptible to disconfirmation.

Here, I first describe the Ainsworth Strange Situation and the four major infant–parent attachment categories. I next describe the Adult Attachment Interview, the four major 'adult attachment categories', and the central forms of interview analysis.

The Strange Situation: infant–parent attachment categories

The Strange Situation is a structured laboratory procedure in which infants are observed responding to two brief separations from, and reunions with, the parent. The procedure was first utilized in conjunction with a year-long study of the interactions of a sample of 26 Baltimore infants and mothers (60–80 hours of observation per dyad). Strong relations were found between maternal behavior in the home and infant response to the laboratory procedure (Ainsworth *et al.* 1978). Infant responses to this situation are categorized as follows.

Secure (Group B). The infant shows signs of missing the parent on departure, seeks proximity upon reunion, and then returns to play. In the Baltimore study, this response was associated with maternal 'sensitivity to infant signals and communications' (Ainsworth *et al.* 1978; for a review of succeeding studies see Bretherton 1985).

Insecure–avoidant (Group A). The infant shows few or no signs of missing the parent, and actively ignores and avoids her upon reunion. This pattern was associated with maternal insensitivity to infant signals, and specifically with rejection of attachment behavior (Ainsworth *et al.* 1978; see also Main and Weston 1981).

Insecure–ambivalent (Group C). The infant is distressed and highly focused on the parent, but cannot be settled by the parent on reunion, often expressing anger and seeking contact in quick succession and generally failing to return to play. In Baltimore, this category was found associated with maternal insensitivity and unpredictability of maternal responsiveness.

Insecure–disorganized/disoriented (Group D). A recent review of video-tapes of Strange Situation behavior of many infants considered unclassifiable in the A, B, C system indicated that these infants in fact exhibited a diverse array of 'disorganized and/or disoriented behaviors' such as freezing of all movement, or stereotypies in the parent's presence (Main and Solomon in press). Parental behavior associated with the 'D' category is not yet known. Main and Hesse (in press) hypothesize that unresolved trauma may lead the parents to be frightened and/or frightening at times, which would place the infant in a momentarily irresolvable conflict situation and could lead to disorganized/disoriented ('conflict') behaviors as outcome.

To date, the continuing study of individual differences in infant attachment organization has shown independence of A, B, C, and D categories across parents and other caregivers. Therefore, by 'the parents of secure infants' I will mean only those *individual* parents with whom an infant has been judged secure.[2]

The Adult Attachment Interview

The Adult Attachment Interview is a structured, 15-question, semi-clinical interview focusing largely upon an individual's early attachment experiences and their effects and influences. Toward the beginning of the interview, the subject is asked to choose five adjectives which best describe the relationship with each parent during childhood. The subject is then asked for episodic memories illustrating each of these choices of adjective. Later, the subject is asked what she did when upset during childhood; to which parent she may have felt closer, and why; whether she ever felt rejected or (later) threatened by the parents in any way; why the parents may have behaved as they did; how the relationship with parents may have changed over time; and how these early experiences (including experiences of major loss up to the present time) may have affected adult functioning and personality. The technique has been described as one of attempting to 'surprise the unconscious' (George *et al.* 1985), and a quick review of the interview format shows that it provides ample opportunities for a speaker to contradict, or fail to support, earlier or succeeding statements.

Despite the fact that many adults have had disparate experiences with their differing attachment figures, a *single* classification for overall 'state of mind with respect to attachment' can be reliably assigned to each verbatim interview transcript (Main and Goldwyn in press). Judgements are made on the basis of an assessment of the coherence of the transcript and other aspects of present state of mind rather than retrospective reports. Adults categorized as Secure/autonomous with respect to attachment typically have infants judged secure with them in the Strange Situation; adults judged Dismissing of attachment have avoidant infants; adults judged Preoccupied by past attachments have ambivalent infants; and adults judged Unresolved with respect to traumatic attachment-related events have disorganized/disoriented infants. (Judgements are of course made blind: see Ainsworth and Eichberg (this volume) for a more complete description of the adult categories.)

Because infant Strange Situation behavior is presumed ultimately reliant upon parental behavior towards the infant in the home situation, the underlying association is between the adult's interview responses and the same adult's behavior towards the infant. Crowell and Feldman (1988) tested this association directly by comparing Secure, Dismissing, and Preoccupied mothers in interactions with their preschoolers during a tool-using task. Secure mothers were supportive and gave clear, helpful assistance. Dismissing mothers were less warm: they focused on task completion and often seemed cool and remote. Mothers in the Preoccupied category presented the task instructions in a confusing and dyssynchronous manner. In keeping with Ainsworth's original descriptions of the mothers of Group C infants, these mothers were unpredictable in their responsiveness: at times warm and gentle, they were at other times coercive, angry, and puzzled.

Interviews with the parents of secure infants: 'Singular' models of attachment-related events, and coherence of discourse

In the original Bay Area study, the strongest correlate of infant security of attachment to a given parent was the overall 'coherence' of the parent's presentation of (his or) her own attachment history. The parents of the 10 very secure (B3) infants in this study were highly coherent during the Adult Attachment Interview, receiving a modal score of 8 on the 9-point scale. These parents focused easily on the questions; showed few departures from usual forms of narrative or discourse; easily marked the principles or rationales behind their responses; and struck judges as both collaborative and truthful.

Both parents who seemed to have experienced insecure or even traumatic childhoods, and parents who enjoyed loving relationships and stable circumstances had secure infants so long as they were coherent in describing, discussing, and evaluating the effects of their experiences. The parents of secure infants also gave the impression of having unusually easy access to childhood memories: the modal score for the 10 parents of the 'very secure' B3 infants on *insistence on lack of recall for childhood* was 1 (9 is high).

In our first Bay Area study, we identified a coherent transcript as one in which the judge felt satisfied that her own assessment of the subject's experiences and their effects was very close to that which the subject herself provided. As a simple example, if the subject described her parents as accepting, the judge found no contradictory evidence within the transcript, and if the subject described herself as presently being relatively free of efforts to please the parent, the judge's internal analysis of the interview led to agreement. Our original definition of coherence as applied to the interview transcript was then close to that recently offered by Johnson-Laird (1983), who suggests that a necessary and sufficient condition for discourse to be coherent is that 'it is possible to construct a single mental model from it'. Coherent subjects seemed to be working with a singular model, whether of favorable or unfavorable experiences and their effects.

An interest in the Adult Attachment Interview as discourse has led me to increasing specification of the rules for identifying coherent transcripts in terms of Grice's maxims. Grice (1975) formulated a general, overriding principle of coherent conversation called the Cooperative Principle. Arranged beneath this superordinate principle are the four maxims of:

1   *Quality* – be truthful, and have evidence for what you say.
2   *Quantity* – be succinct, and yet complete.

3   *Relation* – be relevant.
4   *Manner* – be clear and orderly.

Of these, the maxim of quality is taken as the most important.

In the most recent edition of the Adult Attachment scoring system (Main and Goldwyn 1989) we have attended to the above maxims in providing specifications for rating '*coherence of transcript*'. We are, however, aware that a speaker can remain coherent while preferring not to answer our questions, and, following Mura (1983), we allow for legitimate 'licensing' in violation of these maxims. For example, speakers can 'license' refusals to answer by saying they find a question too personal or emotionally difficult without being considered to violate the maxim of quantity. Note that this licensing still appeals to the higher principle of 'being cooperative' (Mura 1983).

Interviews with the parents of avoidant and ambivalent infants: multiple models of attachment-related events, and incoherencies

In our original Bay Area study, we found that the parents of A and C infants were relatively incoherent in their interview transcripts, exhibiting logical and factual contradictions; inability to stay with the interview topic; contradictions between the general descriptors of their relationships with their parents and actual autobiographical episodes offered; apparent inability to access early memories; anomalous changes in wording or intrusions into topic; slips of the tongue; metaphor or rhetoric inappropriate to the discourse context; and inability to focus upon interview questions. In addition, from an internal examination of the transcript judges seldom agreed with the subjects' description of their histories and/or their present attitudes and evaluations, suggesting that in hour-long interview these adults were exhibiting (a) multiple models of their histories and attitudes while (b) seemingly intending to present a singular model.

Earlier, we summarized these transcript characteristics of the parents of A and C infants as evidencing difficulties in obtaining *access* to attachment-related information; in maintaining *organization* in attachment-related information; and in preventing attachment-related information from undergoing *distortion* (Main and Goldwyn 1984). The most interesting emerging (in-progress) findings appear, however, to be more specific: Parents of infants who have been judged insecure in differing ways (avoidant, ambivalent, or disorganized/disoriented) during the Strange Situation appear to feature differing types of incoherence of discourse.

Briefly, we find that the Dismissing parents of avoidant infants are usually distinguished for their insistence upon their inability to recall childhood. Violating the *maxim of quality* ('have evidence for what you say'), these adults often also seem to 'idealize' their parents as shown in the use of extremely favorable relationship descriptors which are unsupported, or activity contradicted, by autobiographical memories.[3] Excessively succinct and consequently incomplete in their responses, their transcripts often violate the *maxim of quantity*.

As opposed to parents of avoidant infants, the Preoccupied parents of ambivalent infants violate the maxim of quantity through failures to be succinct (often producing extremely long interview responses), and violate the maxim of quality in unexplained oscillations of viewpoint. Violations of the *maxim of relevance* appear frequently in the form of tangential or irrelevant responses, in which the speaker occasionally appears to lose track of the interview question. Finally, violations of *manner* occur in highly entangled, confusing, run-on sentences; failures to use past markers in quoting conversations with the parents; rapid oscillations of viewpoint within or between sentences; unfinished sentences; insertion of extremely general terms into sentence frames ('sort of thing', 'and this and that'), and use of nonsense words or trailers as sentence endings ('dada-dada-dada').

Failures in plausibility and slippages in metacognitive monitoring: the relation between thought processes regarding loss of attachment figures through death and infant disorganization

Philosophers have traditionally differentiated between two theories of truth:[4] a *coherence* theory of truth which relies upon consistent internal co-reference (as see Russell 1948), and a *correspondence* theory of truth which relies upon the plausibility of statements in terms of correspondence to the real state of affairs in the external world (see Bradley 1955; see also Wittgenstein 1961). For speakers to receive high ratings for 'coherence of transcript', they must be consistent or 'coherent' in terms of internal co-reference. However, in order to determine the overall *plausibility* of the subject's remarks – in other words, the likelihood of their corre-spondence to the state of affairs in the external world (Main and Goldwyn 1989) – the judge must be able to step outside of the internal boundaries of the interview. The recent development of a scale assessing plausibility was thought necessary because some speakers made statements which did not violate any internal coherence principle, but which seemed to violate our more usual or general understanding of causality and of physical laws. Otherwise cooperative speakers who make ill-founded statements are now assigned low scores for plausibility or, in our terms, for *coherence of mind* (Main and Goldwyn 1989).

The best illustration of the use of this new scale is its power to predict infant placement in the 'D' Strange Situation category. The parent of a disorganized/disoriented infant is not infrequently a moderately coherent speaker in terms of collaboration and co-reference, who nonetheless makes highly implausible statements regarding the causes or consequences of traumatic attachment-related events such as loss. In these statements, the adult may indicate beliefs in 'magical' causality surrounding a death or other trauma, or subtly indicate a belief that a deceased attachment figure is simultaneously dead and alive. Such failures in the *plausibility* of portions of the transcript (or, slippages in the 'metacognitive monitoring of reasoning', as see Main and Hesse in press and 1989) lead to assignment of the adult to the Unresolved adult attachment category, and to especially low scores for overall coherence of mind (see Ainsworth and Eichberg, this volume, for examination of the relation between adult Unresolved attachment status and infant Disorganized attachment status, and for especially poignant illustrations of such slippages in otherwise well-functioning adults).

METACOGNITIVE KNOWLEDGE, METACOGNITIVE MONITORING, AND INDIVIDUAL DIFFERENCES IN ATTACHMENT ORGANIZATION DURING CHILDHOOD

Earlier, we considered the ways in which difficulties with the dual-coding of single entities and with the appearance–reality distinction could make a young child more vulnerable than an older one to developing 'multiple models' out of unfavorable attachment-related experiences. Here we consider a second, related, proposal: because of the differing nature of their experiences, children who are securely vs. insecurely attached to primary attachment figures will differ with respect to both metacognitive knowledge and metacognitive monitoring.

In her original Baltimore study of infant–mother interaction, Ainsworth found that 9–12-month-old infants who would later be judged secure in the Strange Situation were distinguished for use of the mother as a 'secure base for exploration' in the home environment (Ainsworth *et al.* 1978). Similarly, Main (1973, 1983) suggested that secure children are more likely to be able to devote more attention to exploration (or, more generally, to 'epistemic activity' – see Case 1985) than insecure children, since less attentional monitoring need be devoted to the parent. This hypothesis received early support when children judged secure vs. insecure in relation to the mother at 12 months of age were observed in exploratory play 9 months later (Main 1973, 1983). Both the length of solitary play bouts, and the intensity (concentration or undistractability) of the child's attention to her play during these bouts were positively related to security of attachment to the mother. A recent German study comparing security of attachment to mother in infancy with preschool behavior at age $5^1/2$ in Germany yielded similar outcomes, with secure children tending to spend more time in solitary play (p. 101) and showing far more concentrated – i.e. undistracted or absorbed – play than insecure children (Suess *et al.* 1989).

The child who does not have to monitor the physical and psychological accessibility of primary attachment figures may indeed have a greater attentional (or working memory) capacity than other children (Main 1973). There are, however, other reasons to expect metacognitive functioning to favor secure over insecure children. The secure child may also have more epistemic 'space' in which to review her actions, situations, or thinking processes because her thinking processes are not compartmentalized. Thus, insecurity of attachment may lead to the development of defensive thinking processes – processes which are likely from the first to distort, disorganize, or limit access to memories, feelings, intentions, and recognition of options (Main *et al.* 1985; Main and Hesse in press). Metacognitive monitoring will almost certainly be more difficult when models are difficult to access, or when information is distorted or disorganized, and we should therefore expect more slippages. Indeed, since defensive and/or self-deceiving processes are compartmentalizing processes which act to separate feeling, attention, perception, and memory, they will inherently place limits on metacognitive monitoring.

Security of infant–mother[5] attachment related to self-directed speech in toddlerhood

Perhaps the first examination of the relation between security of attachment and an aspect of behavior ultimately related to metacognitive monitoring consisted in an examination of spontaneous 'self-directed' speech guiding exploratory play in the 21-month-old toddlers participating in the doctoral study described above (Main 1973, 1983). As predicted, self-directed speech appeared much more often in secure than in insecure toddlers (Main 1983), and was often used to guide the toddler to the correct means to achieving some end (see Vygotsky 1966). For example, while still seeking an object on the couch, one secure child said 'Where? Down there', then successfully changed her search strategy to one of looking under the couch rather than on top of it. Another said 'No go, try again' as she failed to fit a square shape through a round hole; another said 'Put it here' in similar circumstances; and a third advised herself 'Don't peek!', apparently trying to persuade herself not to get ahead of herself in turning the pages of her book too quickly.

Spontaneous 'metacognitive' remarks made by 6-year-old children during a Separation Anxiety interview

In conjunction with her doctoral thesis conducted at Berkeley, Kaplan (1987) presented 6-year-olds with pictured parent–child separations, enquiring what the pictured child would feel and do about the separation. One of the central findings of this study was the difference in the apparent sense of a child's behavioral options in such situations. Children who had been secure with mother in infancy were likely to offer constructive solutions to the pictured child's situation, while – even if they had given elaborate detail to their description of the separated child as feeling lonely or sad – insecure children tended to say that they didn't know what the child could do.

Although no formal examination of metacognitive functioning was undertaken in Kaplan's study, secure children more often spontaneously acknowledged experiencing more than one feeling at a time, and showed an awareness of how feelings might change depending on the situation, e.g. 'he might be sad if he is left alone, but happy if friends are there'. Secure children also sometimes acknowledged representational diversity, e.g. 'I was happy the first day at school, but this girl might be sad. All kids are different'. Finally, asked if the pictured child might feel that he 'didn't care', another secure child responded 'Well, well, um, if he says he doesn't care that means he *does* care', differentiating between 'what is meant and what is said' (Kaplan personal communication; cf. Robinson *et al.* 1983).

Failure to comprehend the privacy of thought in insecure–ambivalent children at age 6

In a recently completed pilot study, we interviewed a group of 6-year-olds regarding their understanding of both the nature and privacy of thought. The interview began with the question, 'What is a thought?'. The interviewer then asked where thoughts are located; whether the child had a thought she often thought, and, if so, what was the nature of that thought; whether anyone knew what she was thinking when they could not see or hear her; whether she knew what anyone else was thinking in the same circumstances; and what thoughts look like. Interview responses were compared with the child's attachment classification with mother at 6 years of age, using the Main and Cassidy classification system (1988).

Our specific hypothesis was that insecure–ambivalent children would have difficulty in understanding the privacy of thought. This hypothesis was derived from already established connections between the insecure–ambivalent infant attachment classification and the parent's Preoccupation with her family of origin; slips of the tongue suggestive of confusion between self and the parent during the Adult Attachment Interview in Preoccupied parents; and tendencies in these same adults to lapse into the parent's voice in recounting past events (Main and Goldwyn in press). To date we have analyzed results for 15 pilot subjects: 9 secure with mother at 6 years, 3 insecure–avoidant, and 3 insecure–ambivalent.

All of the children who were secure or avoidant with mother gave reasonable answers to questions regarding the nature and privacy of thought. Most children gave adequate responses to the first question (what is a thought), and all located thoughts in their brains, mind, or heads. In answer to whether they had a thought they often found themselves thinking, most children gave cursory answers or said no. Avoidant children were restricted in their answers and apparently in their interest, while the secure children were more often thoughtful, fluid, and engaged. For example, asked for a thought she often found herself thinking, one secure child said '(Often) I think, what's the answer?'. Asked to what, she replied, 'Questions!'. Another secure child said that it wasn't possible for people to know the thoughts of other people, but that it remained a possibility for God.

In keeping with our hypothesis, we found that all three of the insecure–ambivalent children (and no others) stated that others knew what they were thinking when they could not see them ('my mom ... she's psychic ... she knows I'm thinking she wouldn't be so mean'), and that they themselves had the same powers ('I'm psychic too'). Table 8.1 provides an illustration of the responses of three 6-year-olds, all secure with father in infancy, but currently judged avoidant, secure, or ambivalent with mother.

Children's autobiographical memory at age 10 as related to early and concurrent security of attachment to the mother

Recently, we have been examining the spoken autobiographies of 10- to 11-year-old children in comparison to both first-year and concurrent child–mother attachment classifications (attachment organization at 10 is estimated from a brief laboratory reunion procedure, using the sixth-year classification system developed by Main and Cassidy (1988)). Children are first asked to speak an autobiography for 10 minutes, with as little prompting or interruption as possible. Afterwards, children are asked for spoken descriptions of their three earliest memories; for visualization of those memories; and whether they 'see' themselves within the visualization (an overview of our procedure is provided in Table 8.2).

Of the first 12 cases informally analyzed, 9 are stable in terms of appearing either secure (B) or insecure (non-B) with mother at both age periods. Our first analyses consist in a rough estimate of the overall coherence of the full transcript; the child's overall apparent access to completeness of memories; presence or absence of *early* (clearly preschool) memories of personal experience with accompanying feelings; and presence of apparent metacognitive monitoring of thinking or memory. For these first 9 subjects, coherence of transcript, access to memories, presence and quality of pre-school memories and metacognitive monitoring appear strongly related to security of attachment to the mother. At this point, only the stably secure and insecure children are being compared.

Considering coherence across the transcript as a whole, only 3 transcripts were markedly to highly coherent (all secure children), while 3 were

Table 8.1 Attachment to mother and metacognition at 6: excerpts from interviews regarding the nature and privacy of thought[a]

Insecure–avoidant with mother at 6 (A2)
What is a thought? I don't know. *Can you tell me what a thought is?* Something you think.
Where are thoughts? In your head.

Do you have a thought you often think? No. *(Repeat).* Yes, one. *What is that?* Uh, cartoons. *What one?* (Names cartoon character). *Do you often think about (cartoon character)?* Yeah. *Is there anything else that you often think about?* No. Well, sometimes. Sometimes I think about eating.

Do other people know what you are thinking when they can't see you? No. *No? They don't know what you're thinking if they can't see you?* Uh-huh. *Uh-huh what?* They might, if they couldn't see me, if I was lost, they might know that I was thinking that I wanted to go home.

Do you know what other people are thinking when you can't see them? No *(Repeat).* No.

Do you know what thoughts look like? I can't really describe them. *Are they like movies?* Yeah. *Movies, cartoons, TV?* Yeah. Cartoons.

Insecure–unclassified/ambivalent with mother at 6 (U/C2)
What is a thought? That's easy. Something you want, something you hope you get, something like that.
Where are thoughts? In the mind.

Do you have a thought that you often think? Mm hm. The thought is ... that I don't ever want to be alone. *That you don't want to be alone?* Ever, ever, ever! Or that I had something watching over me, and I'm watching over them. *Someone watching over you?* Something.

Do other people know what you're thinking when they can't see you? Mmhm. Yes. They know what I'm thinking. *Who?* Somebody. I promised I won't tell. You're gonna tell my mom. *How do they know?* Easy. I think of them and then they think of me. *Do you know what someone else is thinking when you can't see them?* Yes. *Who?* I can't tell.

Do you know what thoughts look like? YEAH. They're big and round (gestures).

Secure with Mother at 6 (B3)
What is a thought? You think like, uh, you think like something's gonna happen and you don't KNOW. You think but you don't know.
Where are thoughts? Thoughts are in your head.

Do you have a thought that you often think? I haven't thought so much. *(Repeat).* Yeah, um, sometimes I think what's happening with my cousins. Sometimes I think I'll ask my mom if I can go over to my friend's house maybe. But I don't KNOW if it's gonna happen.

Do other people know what you're thinking when they can't see you? No. *(Repeat).* No.

Do you know what other people are thinking when you can't see them? No. Maybe they aren't even thinking. *That's a possibility! (Laughs).* THAT's a thought (gestures, hand extended from elbow, palm up). That's what I THOUGHT. That they might not be thinking.

Do you know what thoughts look like? I don't know. *Like movies?* Maybe. *What else do thoughts look like?* Like teeny little things (gestures to show how tiny, closing thumb and forefinger), and there's all these teeny little things and like those are all the things in the whole, wide world. All those tiny things you can think of.

Note: [a] All three boys were secure with father in infancy.

Table 8.2 Berkeley Autobiographical Interview for 10–12-year-olds

1   Int. asks Ch. to 'tell the story of your life, whatever you think is most important to tell, starting from as early as you can and going right up to the present time. I'll keep quiet and just listen, and I'd like you to talk for ten minutes' (shows clock). (Prompts twice if needed for *begin as early as you can*, once for *remember, start at the beginning and go on forward*, 3 times for *keep going to ten minutes if you can.*)

2   'Now I'm going to ask you something that may take you a minute – tell me the first three things you can remember.' After Ch. describes all three, Int. asks Ch. 'to close your eyes and try to *see* the things you told me about – just try to look at that time you told me about, and tell me what you see'. After all memories have been described as seen, Int. names each memory and asks whether Ch. saw *herself* when she looked, or where she was.

3   'Now I'd like you to tell me (a) the most important thing that you ever *did* ... (b) the most important thing that ever *happened* to you. (c) What was your favorite thing that you ever did? (d) ... that ever happened to you? (e) What did you dislike most that you ever did? (f) ... that ever happened to you?'

4   (a) 'Can you tell me what Christmas is usually like – what would be typical over the years – for you and your family? (b) And now can you tell me what happened last Christmas? (c) Can you remember how you felt last Christmas?'

5   'I'm going to ask you to give me 5 words to describe yourself.' (Prompts help Ch. stay on track.) 'Now, could you tell me why you chose each of those words to describe yourself?' (If memories not spontaneously given as Ch. ends her attempt, Int. seeks supporting memories again before ending interview.)

Note: This interview follows an unstructured warm-up period. The Int. is friendly, thoughtful, quiet, and responsive. Int. makes few statements aside from the structured prompts, thanking Ch. for her participation, or answering her direct questions.

highly incoherent (all insecure children). With respect to the first question, 80 per cent (4 out of 5) of the secure children but only 25 per cent (1 of the 4) insecure children were able to offer a spoken autobiography, all but one[6] of the remaining children having no apparent spontaneous access to earlier memories. One insecure child described recent events only, after stating 'I don't remember much from third grade and second grade'. Another attempted to begin her autobiography (at age 6), but fell silent after seven largely incompleted sentences, her remaining efforts being unsuccessful and marked by long pauses. The third was unable to remember even events of the last month, responding 'I can't remember' to every query. The prompted memories she later briefly accessed appeared confused: for example, one event was first described as centrally concerned with her siblings, but when asked to visualize the same event, she said they were not there.

In response to our request for 'your three earliest memories', all 5 of the secure children produced at least one pre-school memory (100 per cent), but only 2 of the 4 insecure children did so (50 per cent). Only in the case of the secure children did these memories involve personal feelings and experience. One secure child, for example, remembered helping a new step-mother prepare dinner for the first time, a memory she recognized as being 'not very important' but which to her was 'real special'. Another recalled being afraid to enter the Zoo's 'pet snake' house with the rest of her nursery-school class, "'cause I was scared ... and I went, I went and started crying and stuff'. Later she got back in line with the rest of the class, and 'nobody seemed to notice'.

Spontaneous metacognitive monitoring of thinking and memory was observed in 3 out of the 5 secure children, but in none of the insecure children. For example, one secure child introduced his autobiography by stating that he didn't remember most of what had happened to him, but added that his parents had told him a number of things. Asked if he remembered his kindergarten room he said, 'Well, sort of, but that's because I've seen the kindergarten room again'. He became highly engaged on being asked whether he 'saw' himself as he closed his eyes and 'watched' scenes from his first memory:

Yeah. Wait − − wait. Sort of − − n − not really, not exactly my looks, but − − I *am* there.

Asked if he could visualize himself in a second memory (helping his new stepmother prepare dinner), he replied:

I don't really see − − like see the picture of myself, but I'm imagining myself entering the kitchen − − I'm feeling myself opening the door, but I'm not − − I'm not looking at myself. I'm just *being* myself.

Another secure child questioned the reliability of her memory at times ('I don't know if that's right, but that's the way I think of it'). She stated further that she might have been inaccurate "'cause I don't know if I'm sure or not, 'cause I *have* to think of something', implying early comprehension of the fact that memory can be constructive rather than re-constructive (Bartlett 1932), especially when an individual is being pressed.

CONCLUSIONS AND SUGGESTIONS FOR FURTHER STUDIES

This brief essay has had several aims. A first has been to introduce clinicians working with young children to a relatively new literature which may assist in explaining the young child's vulnerability to constructing conflicting and incompatible models of unfavorable relationships and events.

A second aim has been to review new studies linking a parent's narrative accounts of her own attachment history to the infant's behavioral response to her in a mildly stressful situation, i.e. to the infant's attachment classification. As I have indicated, the central feature of the narrative history produced by the parent of a secure infant is its apparent truthfulness, identified in terms of (1) its internal coherence and (2) its plausibility. In investigations still in progress, the life-narrative accounts offered by the parents of avoidant, ambivalent, and disorganized infants are emerged as featuring several distinct types of incoherence and/or implausibility.

These findings tie together the retrospective clinical interview (typically considered the province of psychiatry and clinical psychology), an emerging literature in discourse and cognitive psychology, and the direct observation of behavior. Because specific behavior observations are predicted to be tied to specific interview analyses, any particular hypothesis – e.g. that a particular incoherence of adult narrative will be predictive of a particular form of infant or adult behavior – can be invalidated. Retrospective accounts had previously been considered impermeable to scientific investigation, being in essence unfalsifiable.

Finally, our pilot studies with young children imply considerable concordance between security of attachment and (1) autobiographical memory, (2) recognition of the privacy of thought, and (3) the metacognitive monitoring of thinking, memory, and action. The links appearing between security of attachment and metacognitive functioning in our pilot studies are more wide-ranging than we had expected, and may ultimately increase our understanding of individual differences in the organization and structure of autobiographical memory.

SUGGESTIONS FOR FUTURE STUDIES

The work reviewed above suggests several future research directions. Some of the most compelling can be summarized as follows.

1. Studies linking individual differences in various aspects of the appearance–reality distinction with children's development in terms of attachment. Recent studies of children's understanding of appearance–reality distinctions indicate considerable variation in individual functioning, with some children fully grasping a given concept at 3, while others have not yet grasped it by 6 (Astington *et al.* 1988). This range is in fact a striking aspect of such studies. In Light's (1979) study of eight conceptual perspective-taking tasks in 4-year-olds, for example, scores within the sample of 56 children ranged from 9 to 37 (maximum = 40) with a mean of 22.[7]

At this early stage in the development of research in children's metacognitive abilities, relatively little attention has been paid to individual differences in functioning, e.g. to stability of functioning for individuals assigned a given task, or even to 'synchrony' (homogeneity of functioning) across tasks of several types (but see Flavell *et al.* 1986 and Gopnik and Astington 1988 for some encouraging evidence). In order to usefully connect children's attachment organization to children's understanding or appearance–reality distinctions, we would need to assure the sensitivity of the tests currently employed so as to result in a substantial range of scores (as did Light), and we would need to make some progress in assessing stability as well as range in individual differences.

Presuming that sufficiently sensitive tests for individual differences in metacognitive functioning had already been constructed, we would certainly want to conduct concurrent assessments of attachment status and aspects of metacognitive knowledge or metacognitive monitoring, as in our pilot studies. These are not, however, the most satisfying studies to conduct, because they do not permit us to determine whether security has positively influenced metacognitive functioning, or metacognitive functioning has positively influenced security. If *on the average* the young child's state of relative metacognitive deficit does make her more vulnerable to unfavorable attachment-related events, a child who is more advanced in metacognitive functioning at a given age will be less vulnerable to these events, and hence more likely to remain or even to become secure. To the extent that metacognitive functioning develops independently of early relationships, then, we may expect that relative advancement may enable one child to weather circumstances which would make a second child insecure.

One approach to this complex issue would be through longitudinal studies which test repeatedly for the child's security with respect to primary attachment figures (assessed at the behavioral level), the child's overall representational models of attachment (assessed through representational products such as drawings), and the child's metacognitive abilities and characteristics. Here we could test not only for any concurrent associations between attachment and metacognitive functioning, but also estimate the extent to which, e.g., insecure-to-secure change in attachment organization between 1 and 10^7 is related to earlier advancement with respect to metacognitive functioning.

2. Studies linking adult memory, reasoning, and epistemic workspace to adult attachment organization. As would be expected given the hypothesized connection between security of attachment and a relatively wide-ranging capacity for attentional monitoring (Main 1973), Mary Ainsworth has suggested that security in adulthood may be associated with the ability to simultaneously attend to several tasks (personal communication, November 1989).[8] In addition, a recent informal review of Adult Attachment Interview transcripts suggests to me that the parents of secure infants have adopted a more thoroughly constructivist view of their own knowledge-base than have less secure adults (see Chandler 1988 for a discussion of the appearance–reality distinction in its most complete or adult form).

These informal observations further underscore the possibility that, at least in some situations, there may be a somewhat greater processing capacity in working memory (or in short-term storage space, see Case 1985) in more secure individuals and that these same individuals may operate with somewhat more sophisticated theories of knowledge. These propositions could be directly tested, and the general relations among attachment, working memory capacity, and abstract reasoning[9] could be estimated. Finally – using, for example, Bartlett's schemas or Rumelhart's story grammars – it would seem interesting, if obvious, to conduct assessments of memory and reasoning in both standard and attachment-related forms.

© 1991 Mary Main

ACKNOWLEDGEMENTS

Nancy Kaplan directed the pilot studies described here. Melinda Travis conducted most of the child interviews, and Esther Chou assessed child–parent reunions. I am grateful to Inge Bretherton and Robbie Case for introducing me to parts of the literature reviewed here, to Wanda Bronson and Mary Ainsworth for criticism of earlier editions of this manuscript, and to Erik Hesse for several contributions to its content.

NOTES

1   Conceivably, obtaining contradictory information regarding an event (observed/ heard) at very early ages *could* lead to mutual cancelling of the items of information, so that only if 'what was heard (A)' and 'what was observed (B)' were again connected could either event be accessed (A can be activated only if B is activated, and vice versa). This kind of deadlock or 'malfunctioning loop' (Johnson-Laird 1983) may of course lead to mental pathologies and may be of special interest to clinicians.

Johnson-Laird suggests that consciousness may be needed to unlock such mental difficulties, but how could consciousness resurrect a deadlock such as this if stored in very early memory? Stern (1985) suggests that the patient's clinically discovered *narrative metaphor* may provide the key to troubled early memories which cannot be directly accessed. Note that metaphor could have a structurally correct relation to the original experiences, and in this sense serve as an accessing 'mental model'. Formal logic would be of little help in unlocking this kind of pathological loop.

2   In frequently writing as though attachment organization were stable, I presume that the reader is familiar with the principle that it is expected to be relatively stable only where an individual, dyad, or family does not undergo major changes in life circumstances (see Bretherton 1985 for a review).

3   The Adult Attachment Classification system is more complex than the infant system, and produces more sub-categories. Here I necessarily overlook a number of complexities. The parents of A infants occasionally have, e.g., good memories for childhood and are not idealizing but rather derogating and dismissing of parents, a strategy which may function equally well to keep attachment-related memories and intentions at a distance.

4   A third, less-traditional theory – the *pragmatic* theory of truth usually associated with the work of C.S. Pierce and William James – is not discussed here.

5   In the studies reviewed in this section, the reader will note that attachment security has been assessed in relation to the mother rather than the father. This is because fathers in both the Bay Area and South German samples typically

worked fulltime throughout the infant's first year while mothers spent at most only 24 hours per week away from the infant. The infant therefore presumably interacted more with the mother than the father, and is presumed likely to have taken the mother as its primary attachment figure.

Two studies to date have endeavored to compare the influence of infant–mother vs. infant–father attachment upon various aspects of functioning at 5 to 6 years of age; both have shown greater predictability from early infant–mother than from early infant–father attachment (Main *et al.* 1985; Suess, Grossmann, and Sroufe, submitted ms.). These outcomes would not necessarily be expected in samples in which father served as the primary caregiver. As it stands, they may be modified as the child develops towards puberty, and may ultimately differ by sex of child.

6   One secure child started an autobiography, but after raising the topic of missing her friends from early childhood she remained with current topics and was not prompted to begin again.
7   In Light's (1979) study, children's scores were related to the way the mother described herself as perceiving and treating her child, with mothers of high scorers appearing as much concerned with a child's feelings and intentions as his actual behavior.
8   In a recent self-report questionnaire administered to 174 college students (Main, Hesse, and Waters, unpublished data), self-reported difficulty with dividing attention among several simultaneous tasks was found associated with lack of memory for childhood, with descriptions of the subject's mother as unforgiving, and with uncertainty that the subject could turn to one or both parents in times of trouble.
9   Johnson-Laird (1983: 121) reports a substantial relation between a simple measure of the processing capacity of working memory devised with Jane Oakhill and accuracy in syllogistic reasoning. It would be relatively easy for researchers in adult attachment to employ these or similar assessments in conjunction with their own ongoing studies

REFERENCES

Ainsworth, M.D.S., Blehar, M., Waters, E., and Wall, S. (1978) *Patterns of Attachment*, Hillsdale, N.J: Erlbaum.

Ainsworth, M.D.S. and Eichberg, C.G. (this volume) 'Effects on infant–mother attachment of mother's unresolved loss of an attachment figure, or other traumatic experience'.

Anderson, J.R. (1983) *The Architecture of Cognition*, Cambridge, Mass.: Harvard University Press.

Astington, J.W. and Gopnik, A. (1988) 'Knowing you've changed your mind: children's understanding of representational change', in Astington, J.W., Harris, P.L., and Olson, D.R. (eds) *Developing Theories of Mind*, New York: Cambridge University Press.

Astington, J.W., Harris, P.L., and Olson, D.R. (eds) (1988) *Developing Theories of Mind*, New York: Cambridge University Press.

Bartlett, F.C. (1932) *Remembering: A Study in Experimental and Social Psychology*, Cambridge: Cambridge University Press.

Binet, A. (1909) *Les Idées Modernes Sur Les Enfants*, Paris: Ernest Flammarion.

Bowlby, J. (1969) *Attachment and Loss*, vol. 1: *Attachment* (also 1982, 2nd edn), New York: Basic Books.

—— (1973) *Attachment and Loss*, vol. 2: *Separation: Anxiety and Anger*, New York: Basic Books.

—— (1980) *Attachment and Loss*, vol. 3: *Loss: Sadness and Depression*, New York: Basic Books.

—— (1988) 'On knowing what you are not supposed to know and feeling what you are not supposed to feel', in J. Bowlby (ed.) *A Secure Base*, New York: Basic Books.

Bradley, F.H. (1955/1893) *Appearance and Reality: A Metaphysical Essay*, Oxford: Oxford University Press.

Braine, M.D.S. and Shanks, B.L. (1965) 'The development of conservation of size', *Journal of Verbal Learning and Verbal Behavior* 4: 227–42.

Bretherton, I. (1984) 'Representing the social world in symbolic play: reality and fantasy', in I. Bretherton (ed.) *Symbolic Play: The Development of Social Understanding* (pp. 3–41), New York: Academic Press.

—— (1985) 'Attachment Theory: retrospect and prospect', in I. Bretherton and E. Waters (eds) Growing Points in Attachment Theory and Research, *Monographs of the Society for Research in Child Development* 50 (1–2), Serial No. 209.

Bretherton, I. Ridgeway, D., and Cassidy, J. (in press) 'The role of internal working models in the attachment relationship: can it be assessed in 3-year-olds?', in M. Greenberg, D. Cicchetti, and E.M. Cummings (eds) *Attachment during the Preschool Years*, Chicago: University of Chicago Press.

Brown, A.L., Bransford, J.D., Ferrara, R.A., and Campione, J.C. (1983) 'Learning, remembering and understanding', in J.H. Flavell and E.M. Markman (eds), P.H. Mussen (Series ed.) *Handbook of Child Psychology*, vol. 3: *Cognitive Development* (pp. 77–166), New York: Wiley.

Cain, A.C. and Fast, I. (1972) 'Children's disturbed reactions to parent suicide', in A.C. Cain (ed.) *Survivors of Suicide*, Springfield, Ill.: C.C. Thomas.

Case, R. (1985) *Intellectual Development: A Systematic Reinterpretation*, New York: Academic Press.

Chandler, M. (1988) 'Doubt and developing theories of mind', in Astington, J.W., Harris, P.L., and Olson, D.R. (eds) *Developing Theories of Mind*, New York: Cambridge University Press.

Clark, E.V. (1987) 'The principle of contrast: a constraint on language acquisition', in B. MacWhinney (ed.) *Mechanisms of Language Acquisition: Proceedings of the 20th Annual Carnegie Symposium on Cognition, 1985* (pp. 1–33), Hillsdale, N.J.: Erlbaum.

Craik, K. (1943) *The Nature of Explanation*, Cambridge: Cambridge University Press.

Crowell, J. and Feldman, S. (1988) 'The effects of mothers' internal models of relations and children's developmental and behavioral status on mother–child interactions', *Child Development* 59: 1273–85.

Dennett, D.C. (1978) *Brainstorms: Philosophical Essays on Mind and Psychology*, Cambridge, Mass.: MIT/Bradford Books.

Fischer, K.W. (1980) 'A theory of cognitive development: the control and construction of hierarchies of skills', *Psychological Review* 87: 477–531.

Flavell, J.H. (1979) 'Metacognition and cognitive monitoring: a new area of cognitive-developmental inquiry', *American Psychologist* 34: 906–11.

Flavell, J.H., Flavell, E.R., and Green, F.L. (1983) 'Development of the appearance-reality distinction', *Cognitive Psychology* 15: 95–120.

Flavell, J.H., Green, F.L., and Flavell, E.R. (1986) 'Development of knowledge about the appearance–reality distinction', *Monographs of the Society for Research in Child Development* 51 (1), Serial No. 212.

Fodor, J. (1978) 'Propositional attitudes', *The Monist* 61.
—— (1987) *Psychosemantics: The Problem of Meaning in the Philosophy of Mind,* Cambridge, Mass.: Bradford Books/MIT Press.
Forguson, L. and Gopnik, A. (1988) 'The ontogeny of common sense', in Astington, J.W., Harris, P.L., and Olson, D.R. (eds) *Developing Theories of Mind,* New York: Cambridge Press.
George, C., Kaplan, N., and Main, M. (1985) 'An Adult Attachment Interview: Interview Protocol', Unpublished manuscript, University of California, Berkeley, Department of Psychology.
Gopnik, A. and Astington, J.W. (1988) 'Children's understanding of representational change and its relation to the understanding of false beliefs and the appearance–reality distinction', *Child Development* 59: 26–37.
Gopnik, A. and Graf, P. (1988) 'Knowing how you know: young children's ability to identify and remember the sources of their beliefs', *Child Development* 59: 1366–71.
Grice, H.P. (1975) 'Logic and conversation', in P. Cole and J.L. Moran (eds) *Syntax and Semantics III: Speech Acts* (pp. 41–58), New York: Academic Press.
Grossmann, K., Fremmer-Bombik, E., Rudolph, J., and Grossmann, K.E. (1988) 'Maternal attachment representations as related to patterns of child–mother attachment patterns and maternal sensitivity and acceptance of her infant', in R.A. Hinde and J. Stevenson-Hinde (eds) *Relations within Families,* Oxford: Oxford University Press.
Harris, P.L, Donnelly, K., Guz, G.R., and Pitt-Watson, R. (1986) 'Children's understanding of the distinction between real and apparent emotion', *Child Development* 57: 895–909.
Harter, S. and Buddin, B.J. (1987) 'Children's understanding of the simultaneity of two emotions: a five-stage developmental acquisition sequence', *Developmental Psychology* 23: 388–99.
Inhelder, B., Sinclair, H., and Bovet, M. (1974) *Learning and the Development of Cognition,* Cambridge, Mass.: Harvard Press.
Johnson-Laird, P.N. (1988) *Mental Models: Towards a Cognitive Science of Language, Inference and Consciousness,* Cambridge, Mass.: Harvard University Press.
Johnson-Laird, P.N., Legrenzi, P., and Legrenzi, M.S. (1972) 'Reasoning and a sense of reality', *British Journal of Psychology* 63: 395–400.
Kahneman, D. and Tversky, A. (1982) 'The psychology of preferences', *Scientific American* 246: 160–74.
Kaplan, N. (1987) 'Individual differences in 6-year-old's thoughts about separation: predicted from attachment to mother at age 1', Unpublished doctoral dissertation, University of California, Berkeley, Department of Psychology.
Kaplan, N. and Main, M. (1989) 'A system for the analysis of family drawings', Unpublished manuscript, Department of Psychology, University of California, Berkeley.
Karmiloff-Smith, A. (1979) 'Micro- and macro-developmental changes in language acquisition and other representational systems', *Cognitive Science* 3: 91–118.
Kosslyn, S. (1983) *Ghosts in the Mind's Machine: Creating and Using Images in the Brain,* New York: W.W. Norton.
Leslie, A.M. (1987) 'Pretense and representation: the origins of a "theory of mind"', *Psychological Review* 94: 412–26.
Light, P. (1979) *Development of a Child's Sensitivity to People,* London: Cambridge University Press.
Main, M. (1973) 'Exploration, play and cognitive functioning as related to child–

mother attachment', Unpublished doctoral dissertation, Johns Hopkins University.
—— (1983) 'Exploration, play and cognitive functioning as related to infant-mother attachment', *Infant Behavior and Development* 6: 167–74.
Main, M. and Cassidy, J. (1988) 'Categories of response to reunion with the parent at age 6: Predictable from infant attachment classifications and stable over a 1-month period', *Developmental Psychology* 24(3): 415–26.
Main, M. and Goldwyn, R. (1984) 'Predicting rejection of her infants from mother's representation of her own experience: implications for the abused–abusing intergenerational cycle', *International Journal of Child Abuse and Neglect* 8: 203–17.
—— (in press). 'Interview-based adult attachment classifications: related to infant–mother and infant–father attachment', *Developmental Psychology*.
—— (1989) 'Adult Attachment Rating and Classification System', Unpublished scoring manual, Department of Psychology, University of California, Berkeley.
Main, M., Kaplan, N., and Cassidy, J. (1985) 'Security in infancy, childhood and adulthood: a move to the level of representation', in I. Bretherton and E. Waters (eds) Growing Points of Attachment Theory and Research, *Monographs of the Society for Research in Child Development* 50 (1–2), Serial No. 209.
Main, M. and Hesse, E. (submitted manuscript, 1989) 'Interview-based assessments of a parent's unresolved trauma are related to infant "D" attachment status: linking parental states of mind to infant behavior observed in a stressful situation'.
—— (in press) 'Parents' unresolved traumatic experiences are related to infant disorganized attachment status: is frightened and/or frightening parental behavior the linking mechanism?', in M. Greenberg, D. Cicchetti, and M. Cummings (eds) *Attachment in the Preschool Years: Theory, Research and Intervention*, Chicago: University of Chicago Press.
Main, M. and Solomon, J. (in press) 'Procedures for identifying infants as disorganized/disoriented during the Ainsworth Strange Situation', in M. Greenberg, D. Cicchetti, and M. Cummings (eds) *Attachment in the Preschool Years: Theory, Research and Intervention*, Chicago: University of Chicago Press.
Main, M. and Weston, D. (1982) 'Avoidance of the attachment figure in infancy: descriptions and interpretations', in C.M. Parkes and J. Stevenson-Hinde (eds) *The Place of Attachment in Human Behavior* (pp. 31–59), New York: Basic Books.
Mandler, J.M. (1983) 'Representation', in J.H. Flavell and E.M. Markman (eds), P.H. Mussen (Series ed.) *Handbook of Child Psychology*, vol. 3: *Cognitive Development* (pp. 420–94), New York: Wiley.
Markman, E.M. (1984) 'The acquisition and hierarchical organization of categories by children', in C. Sophian (ed.) *Origins of Cognitive Skills* (pp. 371–406), Hillsdale, N.J.: Erlbaum.
Marshall, J.C. and Morton, J. (1978) 'On the mechanics of EMMA', in A. Sinclair, R.J. Javella, and W.J.M. Levelt (eds) *The Child's Conception of Language*, Berlin: Springer-Verlag.
Mura, S.S. (1983) 'Licensing violations: legitimate violations of Grice's conversational principle', in R.T. Craig and Karen Tracy (eds) *Conversational Coherence: Form, Structure and Strategy*, Beverly Hills: Sage Publications.
Paivo, A. (1971) *Imagery and Verbal Processes*, New York: Holt, Rinehart and Winston.
Perner, J., Leekman, S., and Wimmer, H. (1987) 'Three-year-olds' difficulty with false beliefs: the case for a conceptual deficit', *British Journal of Development Psychology* 5: 125–37.

Peterfreund, E. (1971) 'Information, systems and psychoanalysis', *Psychological Issues*, Vol. VII, Monogr, 25–26, New York: International Universities Press.

Pylyshyn, Z.W. (1984) *Computation and Cognition: Towards a Foundation for Cognitive Science*, Cambridge, Mass.: MIT Press.

Robinson, E.J., Goelman, H., and Olson, D.R. (1983) 'Children's understanding of the relation between expressions (what was said) and intentions (what was meant)', *British Journal of Developmental Psychology* 1: 75–86.

Rozin, P., Millman, L., and Nemeroff, C. (1986) 'Operation of the laws of sympathetic magic in disgust and other domains', *Journal of Personality and Social Psychology* 50: 703–12.

Russell, B. (1948) *Human Knowledge: Its Scope and Limits*, New York: Simon & Schuster.

Stern, D.N. (1985) *The Interpersonal World of the Infant: A View from Psychoanalysis and Developmental Psychology*, New York: Basic Books.

Suess, G., Grossmann, K.E., and Sroufe, L.A. (submitted manuscript, 1989) 'Effects of infant attachment to mother and father on quality of adaptation in preschool: from dyadic to individual organization of self'.

Vygotsky, L.S. (1966) 'Play and its role in the mental development of the child', *Voposy Psykhologi* 12: 62–76.

Ward, M., Carlson, B., Altman, S.C., Greenberg, R.H., and Kessler, D.B. (1989) 'Predicting infant–mother attachment from adolescents' working models of relationships', Unpublished manuscript, The New York Hospital, New York.

Wason, P.C. and Johnson-Laird, P.N. (1972) *The Psychology of Reasoning: Structure in Content*, Cambridge, Mass.: Harvard University Press.

Watson, M.W. (1984) 'Development of social role understanding', *Developmental Review* 4: 192–213.

Wimmer, H., Gruber, S., and Perner, J. (1984) 'Young children's conception of lying: Lexical realism–moral subjectivism', *Journal of Experimental Child Psychology* 37: 1–30.

Wimmer, H. and Perner, J. (1983) 'Beliefs about beliefs: representation and constraining function of wrong beliefs in young children's understanding of deception', *Cognition* 13: 103–128.

Wittgenstein, L. (1961) *Tractatus Logico-Philosophicus*, trans. D.F. Pears and B.F. McGuiness, London: Routledge & Kegan Paul. Original work published 1921.

Yanomoto, J., Okonogi, K., Iwasaki, T., and Yoshimura, S. (1969) 'Mourning in Japan', *American Journal of Psychiatry* 125: 1660–5.

Chapter 9

Effects on infant–mother attachment of mother's unresolved loss of an attachment figure, or other traumatic experience

Mary D. Salter Ainsworth and Carolyn Eichberg

This chapter stems from recent advances in attachment research by Mary Main and her associates, which began in a search to understand infants whose strange-situation behavior with either mother or father was 'unclassifiable', that is, it did not fit any of the A, B, and C patterns identified by Ainsworth (e.g. Ainsworth *et al.* 1978). These infants constituted 13 per cent of Main's Berkeley sample. A follow-up in the children's sixth year was undertaken to learn more about them and how they differed from secure infants and from other insecure infants, (1) in their strange-situation behavior with each parent at 1 year of age, and the strategies these reflect, (2) in the nature of their attachment to parents in their sixth year, and (3) in their parents' attachment histories.

1   Main and Solomon (in press) re-examined the strange-situation behavior of the unclassifiable infants in great detail. They found no one clear-cut fourth pattern of behavior, but a variety of behaviors that had in common that they signified disorganization and/or disorientation. They categorized infants displaying such behavior as 'D'.

2   Several procedures were developed for the assessment of child–parent attachment in the sixth year that differentiated significantly among those who had been classified, as A, B, C, or D in infancy, and which implied an impressive degree of continuity in the inner organization and behavioral strategies associated with each category. An initial report by Main *et al.* (1985) is being succeeded by more detailed separate reports, which are reviewed by Main and Hesse (1989, in press) in so far as they are specifically related to Ds.

3   The Berkeley Adult Attachment Interview (AAI) was devised by George *et al.* (1985) and used with each parent separately in order to elicit his/her attachment history. Main and Goldwyn (1988, 1989) developed a classification procedure, which identified three chief patterns indicating the adult's current state of mind regarding attachment: secure–autonomous, dismissing of attachment, or preoccupied with early attachments. Excluding that proportion of the sample which

had been used in the development of these procedures, Main found that there was a predicted match of 75 per cent between the mother's AAI classification and the A/B/C attachment classification of the infant in relation to the mother, and a 69 per cent match in the case of the father, thus demonstrating an impressive degree of cross-generational similarity and influence. In regard to the D infants, it was ascertained that in this sample they tended to belong to mothers who had experienced unresolved mourning for the death of a close family member before they had reached adulthood.

The research reported in this present chapter represents part of a collaborative study directed by Julia Green at the University of Virginia, which focused on a sample of 50 white, middle-class infants and their mothers, in an attempt to gain further knowledge of antecedent and concurrent factors correlated with quality of attachment of the infants to their mothers, especially factors pertaining to the parents, including those involved in marital relations and maternal attachments.

Eichberg, one of the collaborating students in the project, focused her dissertation research especially on the relationship between infant quality of attachment (as assessed in the strange situation) and maternal state of mind regarding attachments (as assessed by the Berkeley Adult Attachment Interview procedure). This chapter is based on that part of her research that concerns infant disorganization–disorientation and its relation to maternal lack of resolution of loss of an attachment figure through death or, indeed, lack of resolution of some other significant traumatic experience. As such it constitutes a replication of relevant aspects of the Berkeley follow-up project, which have been presented and discussed by Main and Hesse (1989, in press).

THE MAIN–HESSE FINDINGS AND HYPOTHESES

Let us review specific points made by Main and Hesse that are particularly relevant to our replication.

1 Main and Hesse (in press) characterize the strange-situation behavior of D infants as indicating failure to mobilize a strategy to deal with attachment-related stress, whereas infants otherwise classified have clear-cut strategies. Under stress, babies who are securely attached (B) tend to abandon exploratory behavior and seek proximity to the attachment figure, confident of her accessibility and responsiveness. Those who are insecure–avoidant (A), expecting the caregiver to reject intense attachment behavior, have adopted defensive strategies of reducing their reactivity to threatening cues that would otherwise elicit both fear and attachment behavior and diverting their attention to other objects in the environment. Those who are insecure–resistant/

ambivalent (C), being uncertain of the accessibility and responsiveness of the attachment figure, focus on her, and greatly heighten the intensity of their attachment behavior, wanting to ensure that she will be accessible and responsive.

On the other hand, the insecure–disorganized (D) infant acts as though it is not only the environmental threat that is fear-eliciting, but also the attachment figure. Thus to increase attachment behavior would result in closer proximity to one of the sources of fear. This results in a conflict between two quite incompatible behaviors – to seek proximity to the attachment figure and to also avoid proximity to her. Indeed most of the anomalous behavioral markers of disorganization/ disorientation are compatible with this explanation – appearing as contradiction or inhibition of action as it is undertaken, or freezing as though there is no alternative solution, or other more direct markers of fear. Consequently, Main and Hesse hypothesize that in the D baby's experience that attachment figure either has behaved in a threatening way, or has behaved as though frightened – and it is frightening to the infant to have his haven of security frightened.

2   In regard to parental experiences associated with infant disorganiza- tion, we have already mentioned their association in the Berkeley sample with early loss of an attachment figure through death. Main and Hesse (in press) reported that 15 of the mothers in the sample had lost a parent through death before having completed high school. Of these, 9 (60 per cent) had D infants. Among the 38 mothers who had not experienced early loss only 8 (21 per cent) had D infants ($p = 0.009$).

Early loss in itself does not seem inevitably to lead to the kind of parental behavior that is responsible for disorganization in the infant. Main and Hesse (1989, in press) suggest that the critical issue is whether the loss has been resolved or not. The Adult Attachment Interview inquires about the relationships of the person with figures significant in his/her life, and, if one of these has been lost through death, there is an inquiry into the circumstances of the death, the person's reaction to it at the time, and what influence it had on subsequent development.

Among the several rating scales that had been developed to supplement the AAI classification system (Main and Goldwyn 1988), there is a Lack of Resolution of Mourning (LRM) scale, which was based on Bowlby's (1980) discussion of normal and pathological outcomes of mourning a lost attachment figure. This scale was used for all parents who reported the death of a figure significant enough to be identified as an attachment figure. Main and Hesse reported that the mean LRM score of the 9 early-loss mothers whose infants were disorganized in their attachment to them was 7.2 on the 9-point scale, whereas that of the 6 whose infants were not disorganized was 3.9.

'Thus, mother's early loss of an older family member did not itself lead to infant D attachment status, *unless the mother had experienced lack of resolution of mourning as a consequence*' (Main and Hesse in press). (Note: A revised version of the LRM scale by Main and DeMoss was used by Main and Hesse, and is included in a revision of the Adult Classification System manual (Main and Goldwyn 1989).)

3   Main and Hesse also touched on the state of mind regarding attachments of parents who were most likely to fail to resolve mourning for an attachment figure lost through death. They inferred an association between parental failure to resolve mourning and the adult pattern of preoccupation with early attachments.

4   Finally, Main and Hesse (1989) discussed the various experiences antecedent to infant disorganization other than unresolved parental mourning for loss of an attachment figure through death. In the Berkeley sample the behavior of one or two infants toward the parent in the strange situation appeared to be sexualized, which suggested the possibility of early sexual abuse, although there was no hint of this in the parental interview. Furthermore, they cited findings of studies of maltreated infants and infants of psychotic parents in which it was reasonable to suppose that disorganized behavior could be linked to frightening or frightened behavior on the part of the parent.

THE CHARLOTTESVILLE STUDY

Aims of the study

The aims of the present study are drawn from the Main–Hesse findings and hypotheses relevant to the cross-generational influence of parental (in this case maternal) state of mind regarding attachments on the quality of attachment of the infant, with special focus on disorganized infants. Specifically, we are interested in the following.

1   The extent to which infant disorganization is associated with mother's loss of an attachment figure through death, considering the whole range of lost figure and the mother's age at which the loss occurred. Especially, we are interested in the extent to which infant disorganization is associated with mother's *unresolved* mourning for a lost attachment figure in comparison with mourning that has been resolved.

2   The factors in the mother's experience that are associated with resolved mourning in comparison with mourning which is unresolved.

3   Maternal experiences other than unresolved mourning that are associated with infant disorganization. Also we are concerned as to whether the three basic patterns of state of mind regarding attachment differ in the likelihood that loss or other trauma will be resolved or unresolved.

4   Evidence relevant to the Main–Hesse hypothesis that disorganized infant behavior under mild stress is attributable to maternal behavior that is directly or indirecty frightening to the infant.

Procedures

Fifty white, middle-class infants were assessed in the strange situation when aged somewhere between 12 and 18 months. Within 2 to 6 months after this assessment the mothers were interviewed by one of us (CGE), using the Adult Attachment Interview procedure. Four of the families had moved out of state, so only 46 mothers were interviewed. Only 45 mother–infant dyads were used in the present study, however, for the illness of one infant at the time of the strange situation was judged to invalidate the assessment.

Three judges were trained in interview analysis – the two authors and a graduate student.[1] We assessed transcripts of the interviews independently of one another, and many of these were also independently assessed by Mary Main. We also 'predicted' what the infant's attachment classification would be on the basis of the assessment of the mother, including the LRM (Lack of Resolution of Mourning) rating. Upon Mary Main's advice we used 6 on the LRM scale (rather than 5) as our marker minimum for unresolved mourning (cf. Main 1985). We resolved in conference any differences in our assessments of the mother or our predictions about the baby. However, since only one of us (MDSA) who had classified and rated all the mothers was also entirely blind to the assessments that had been made of the infants, her ratings, classifications, and predictions were used in this study. (Substantially later, when a revised version of the LRM scale[2] appeared, MDSA reviewed and revised her ratings. She found that two women who had previously been judged to have resolved their mourning should have been identified as unresolved. Each had manifested extreme behavioral reactions at the time of the loss – a behavioral marker of unresolved mourning made more explicit in the revised LRM scale than in the earlier version. She made *post hoc* corrections, which are acknowledged in the relevant tables and text.)

We could not usefully check these against the attachment classifications previously made by Julia Green's team, since they antedated the Main/Solomon system for identification of D infants. Therefore, two expert judges,[3] blind to all other assessments, reclassified the infants.

Since we wanted to gain more understanding of how the mothers manifested their resolution or lack of resolution of mourning in their interviews, and why it seemed that some could successfully resolve mourning for a lost attachment figure, we abstracted from the transcripts a series of case study vignettes. Our report includes some of these vignettes as illustrative cases, together with our inferences from the whole series.

First, we consider those who lost an attachment figure through death, and who were judged to have resolved their mourning. Second, we consider those whose mourning for a lost attachment figure was unresolved. Third, we consider those who had suffered no loss. Finally, throughout all three groups we identify those who could be judged to have suffered severe trauma other than loss which they had not yet resolved.

As an assistance to the reader, Table 9.1 is provided, which lists for each case the chief kinds of information highlighted in the data analysis: the serial number identifying the case, with the serial numbers in italics of those specifically discussed in the text; identification of the figure lost through death; the age of the woman when the death occurred; her Lack of Resolution of Mourning (LRM) score, as originally rated; her attachment classification judged on the basis of the Adult Attachment interview (AAI); the classification of her baby's attachment to her, judged on the basis of his or her behavior in the strange situation, whether A, B, C, or D, and, if D, also the 'forced' A/B/C classification;[4] and comments regarding the infant's strange-situation classification, i.e., if A, B, or C, whether it is a match to the mother's classification, or, if D, whether it was predicted from the LRM score.

Findings

Loss of attachment figure: mourning resolved

Of the 30 women in the sample who had experienced loss of an attachment figure through death, 20 were judged to have resolved their mourning. Eight of the 20 had lost a parent, 10 had lost a relative other than a parent, and two had lost an attachment figure who was entirely unrelated to them. In 11 cases the loss had occurred in childhood (i.e. before the woman had finished high school, according to Main's criterion), whereas in 9 it had occurred in adulthood.

Resolved mourning for loss of parent. We searched for similarities among those who had been successful in resolving the loss of a parent that differentiated them from those who had been unsuccessful. Two characteristic themes were identified: (1) feeling supported by a strong sense of family solidarity, with mutual comforting, expression of feelings, and sharing of grief, and/or (2) taking responsibility for others in the family during the mourning period.

Let us consider some illustrative cases, beginning with two illustrating *a sense of family solidarity.* Our first illustrative case (*No. 137*) was 32 when her father died of cancer. Although she had not been really attached to her father until she was about 12, when he stopped working evening shifts, she came to know him as companionable and supportive, and in many ways more understanding than her very strict and controlling mother. At the

Table 9.1 The relationship between maternal loss status and mother's and baby's attachment classifications

Lost figure	Age at loss	LRM[a] Rtg.	M's AAI[b] Classification	Baby's[c] S/S Cl.	Comments re S/S Cl.
Loss of Attachment Figure: Resolved					
118 F	10	3.0	Autonomous	B	Match to AAI
132 F	12	3.0	Dismissing	A	Match to AAI
137 F	Adult	3.0	Autonomous	B	Match to AAI
140 M	9	3.0	Autonomous	B	Match to AAI
128 F	5	5.0	Autonomous	B	Match to AAI
131 F	11	3.0	Autonomous	B	Match to AAI
107 F	Adult	3.0	Autonomous	B	Match to AAI
146 M	Adult	3.0	Autonomous	B	Match to AAI
117 MGM	HS	3.5	Autonomous	D/B	D not predicted[d]
129 Aunt	HS	3.0	Autonomous	D/B	D not predicted
106 MGM	7?	3.0	Autonomous	B	Match to AAI
113 GMs	Adult	3.0	Autonomous	B	Match to AAI
138 GPs	HS	3.0	Autonomous	B	Match to AAI
147 MGM	Adult	3.0	Autonomous	B	Match to AAI
105 MGM	Adult	5.0	Autonomous	B	Match to AAI
110 PGM	Adult	3.0	Dismissing	A	Match to AAI
149 PGM	Adult	3.0	Autonomous	B	Match to AAI
151 MGM	Adult	5.0	Autonomous	B	Match to AAI
114 Maid	13	5.0	Autonomous	B	Match to AAI
109 Friend	18	4.0	Autonomous	B	Match to AAI
148 F	Adult	6.5	Dismissing	D/B	Predicted from LRM
124 F	Adult	4.0	Autonomous	D/B	Not predicted/LRM wrong
102 Aunt	Adult	7.0	Preoccupied	D/C	Predicted from LRM
127 MGM	HS	7.0	Preoccupied	D/C	Predicted from LRM
142 MGM	13	7.0	Dismissing	D/A	Predicted from LRM
143 PGPs	Adult	7.0	Preoccupied	D/C	Predicted from LRM
120 Sister	Adult	6.0	Preoccupied	D/B	Predicted from LRM
112 Brother	Adult	6.0	Dismissing	D/B	Predicted from LRM
115 Old man	8	8.0	Preoccupied	D/A	Predicted from LRM
119 Boyfriend	HS	3.0	Autonomous	D/B	Not predicted/LRM wrong
No loss					
141			Preoccupied	D/B	D predicted/M abused
139			Autonomous	D/C	D predicted[e]
125			Preoccupied	D/C	D not predicted
101			Autonomous	B	Match to AAI
104			Dismissing	A	Match to AAI
105			Autonomous	B	Match to AAI
121			Autonomous	A	No match to AAI
126			Dismissing	B	No match to AAI
130			Dismissing	A	Match to AAI
134			Autonomous	B	Match to AAI
135			Autonomous	B	Match to AAI
136			Autonomous	C	No match to AAI
144			Autonomous	B	Match to AAI
145			Autonomous	B	Match to AAI
150			Dismissing	A	Match to AAI

Notes: [a] Mother's rating on Lack of Resolution of Mourning Scale.
  [b] Mother's classification on the basis of the Adult Attachment Interview.

Table 9.1 (continued)

The categories are: Autonomous/secure in regard to attachment
                     Dismissing of attachment
                     Preoccupied with early attachment
- [c] Baby's classification of attachment to mother on the basis of behavior in the strange situation. The categories are:
  A   Attachment is insecure–avoidant
  B   Attachment is secure
  C   Attachment is insecure–resistant (or insecure–ambivalent)
  D   Attachment is insecure–disorganized (or insecure–disoriented)
  Note: In the case of Ds a 'forced' A, B, or C classification is also given to indicate the attachment pattern underlying the disorganization.
- [d] Disorganization in the infant could not be predicted from the mother's rating, but she seems not to have resolved her anxiety associated with her husband's drug addiction.
- [e] Disorganization in the infant was predicted because the mother clearly had not resolved the anxiety occasioned by a recent illness from which she very nearly died.

time her father became ill, she and her siblings were all living away from home but gradually they all returned home to be there for the last month of his life. The long terminal period was hard on all of them but there was nevertheless, she said, 'a great coming together of all of us at that time, and I think finally a lightening toward the end, because it was such a burden for all of us, and I think my father finally accepted it and resolved that this was what was happening. He even lightened and was very humorous the last couple of weeks before he died – and then after that my brother and my sister and myself and my mother really pulled together.' After the death they all stayed home to help out with things on the farm and made sure that their mother was 'okay' before they went back to what they were doing and where they were living. 'After that, even though we're not in close touch with each other, there's a closeness that never was there before.'

Family solidarity helped in another way with a child reared in upper-class circumstances whose mother died suddenly of a heart attack when she was 9 years old (*No. 140*). Despite the fact that the neurotic, alcoholic father took no responsibility for the family of five children either before or after his wife died, a sense of family solidarity was provided by the siblings themselves and by an extended family of highly supportive adults, who indeed had been 'close' throughout. During the summer after the mother's death, our subject, visiting relatives, spent much time alone thinking things over, and by the end of this she felt she had come to terms with her mother's death, and indeed she did seem to have resolved her mourning reasonably well.

As an example of *taking responsibility* let us tell you about a woman (*No. 118*) who had an obviously secure childhood in which she was given much freedom to explore her country environs. Her mother was very busy with a large household and garden to look after, but was caring and consistent. Our subject dearly loved her father, to whom she felt closer than to her mother.

The father died when our subject was 10 years old, after a number of long hospitalizations. The cause of death was cancer, but no one explained to the child what was wrong, or that he finally was dying. This she heard from a classmate, and was 'thrown into outer space' by the news. Her mother was very distressed, and was given valium and barbiturates to calm her. The mother went back to school to train to be a counsellor, while our subject did a great deal to care for her younger brothers. Mother worked for a while as a counsellor, then 'burned out', her health having become impaired by the prescription drugs she was still taking. She remarried, but her new husband turned out to be an alcoholic, and she herself became addicted to alcohol as well as to the drugs. Our subject gave her young brothers their breakfast, saw them off to school, and then at night saw that they were fed and gotten to bed. Indeed often enough she had to put her mother to bed too.

When the time came for her to go off to college, she left the family to cope. Then the step-father was found to have cancer. Mother stopped drinking and took responsibility for his care – but when he died finally after a long illness, she again turned to alcohol. Our subject returned home to deal with the situation. She got her mother and indeed the whole family into family therapy, then supported hospitalization for mother in a rehabilitation program. And it worked.

Another illustrative case is *No. 132*, a woman who had been identified as dismissing of attachment, and who seemed to have resolved her mourning. She apparently coped with her father's death when she was 12 by assuming responsibility. It was a very sudden death and her mother was devastated. Our subject reacted to the death by 'pushing it aside'. However, her mother was so obviously distraught that our subject took over much responsibility in order to ease her burden. Later her mother said she did not know how she could have managed had her daughter not pitched in.

One could easily hypothesize that taking responsibility under such circumstances might well be a defensive kind of role reversal or compulsive caregiving that did little or nothing to resolve mourning. However, it might function – and perhaps did in these cases – as a way of facing up to the reality of the loss, accepting it, and going on from there.

It is understandable that a sense of family solidarity – being able to acknowledge feelings and to share them with others – and the ability to face the reality of loss and to take responsibility for comforting and supporting others and carrying on could all help a bereaved person to resolve his or her own mourning. It is worthy of notice, however, that the great majority of the women who had resolved their mourning for a lost parent (18 of 20) were judged to have achieved a secure and autonomous state of mind in regard to attachment by the time of their interview, whether because of secure attachment to at least one parent throughout childhood, or because of successful revision of the working models of troubled early attachments. Is it that the autonomous and secure view of attachment enables the person to experience the sense of family solidarity and/or responsibility that facilitates resolution of mourning? Or is it that the experience of solidarity and/or responsibility and the ensuing ability to resolve mourning foster the development of a secure and autonomous state of mind about attachment? Obviously, an answer to these questions might well differ in the case of loss experienced in childhood from the case of loss experienced in adulthood, as well as with individual circumstances. In any event these cases suggest that successful resolution of mourning somehow tends to be linked to secure attachment.

Resolved mourning for loss of an attachment figure other than a parent. Although it had not been always easy to judge whether a relative (let alone an unrelated figure) had played a significant enough role in a person's life to have become an attachment figure, and therefore for his or her death to cause true mourning rather than transient regret and sadness, it would not seem that this group of women whose mourning was resolved were simply less fond of the figures for whom they mourned. On the other hand, the very fact that in most cases attachments to parents were essentially secure throughout childhood must have made it less urgent to establish closeness with other attachment figures, especially those who acted as parent surrogates. At the same time, mourning for the loss of one of these secondary figures might be expected to be eased by sharing the feelings of grief with primary attachment figures. Consequently, loss of one of these secondary attachment figures could be expected to be less devastating and thus easier to mourn successfully. In any event, successful resolution of mourning is clearly linked to an autonomous and secure state of mind in regard to attachment.

Match of mother's and infant's attachment classifications. In 18 of the 20 cases of resolved mourning the mother's and infant's attachment classifications match. Thus in 16 cases mothers who have an autonomous and secure state of mind in regard to attachment have infants who are securely attached to them, and the two mothers who were dismissing of attachment have infants who are insecure and defensively avoidant in their attachment.

However, there are two infants in which the infant's attachment to mother was classified as disorganized/disoriented (D), despite the fact that mother's mourning for the loss of an attachment figure had been resolved. In one case (*No. 117*) the mother seemed to have coped with early difficulties fairly well and was considered to be autonomous and secure in regard to her state of mind regarding attachment, with mourning of the death of her maternal grandmother successfully resolved. However, her husband was addicted to drugs and alcohol. Although she had tried to be constructive in her efforts to help him to overcome these addictions, it is plausible that the extreme anxiety inherent in the situation adversely affected her interactions with her baby – consistent with the Main–Hesse hypothesis that when a mother herself is frightened, this frightens the baby and tends to make him disorganized and/or disoriented in his attachment to her.

The other case (*No. 129*) was of a mother who had been judged to be autonomous and secure as an adult, despite evidence of earlier insecurity. She had lost an aunt for whom she cared, and had seemed to have resolved her mourning for her. Her infant thus was expected to emerge as securely attached, but instead he was identified as a 'D' and therefore clearly insecure. We do not know why this should be, but hypothesize that the mother had suffered some other severe trauma – perhaps abuse as a child – which she did not disclose in the interview.

Loss of attachment figure: mourning unresolved

Of the 30 women who had lost an attachment figure, 10 failed to resolve their mourning. In 2 cases the lost figure was the father, in 4 a close adult relative, in 2 a sibling, and in 2 a totally unrelated person to whom an attachment had been formed. In 4 cases the loss occurred while the woman was still a child, whereas in 6 it occurred in adulthood.

Unresolved loss of parent. Let us first consider the two who had lost their fathers. The first case (*No. 148*) was one of a very bright, highly defended woman, who had become fanatically religious while attending college, much to the dismay of her father, who thought she 'was losing her balance'. Much of the detail she remembers about her childhood suggests a high degree of insecurity in her attachments to her parents. However, she has defensively revised her working models of her parents so that she now views even her worst experiences as having been for the best. For example, she had a life-threatening illness during infancy and early childhood, from which she did not recover until she was 6 years old. Between the ages of 1 and 2, particularly, she had repeated long periods of hospitalization, and was subject to intravenous feeding for severe dehydration. For at least two weeks during one of these periods her parents were forbidden to visit. She remembers this, but does not recall her feelings, which must have included intense distress and fearfulness. She now believes that the experience was strengthening, and that it evoked from her parents 'special doses of love and affection'.

She admired her father as a role model, but described him as a workaholic, who neglected his family in preoccupation with his distinguished career. She characterized her mother as an alcoholic, beginning before the time our subject entered school. When she was 7 years old, and just before the birth of the youngest child in the family, the father attempted suicide. He was subsequently absent for a long period of rehabilitation, but when he returned he asked our subject to spy on her mother for him. When the mother found out, she accused the child of siding with father and 'telling' on her. When mother was drunk she sometimes got quite out of control, and our subject was scared of her. However, now she idealizes her parents and says: 'Mother is basically a superb Mom – she is wonderfully supportive', and 'I can never say that Father was not a good father to me'.

Four years prior to the interview, our subject's father died. She was away at law school and had not realized that his health had seriously deteriorated. He died under anaesthetic for a biopsy, and on autopsy was discovered to have had bone cancer. The mother was first informed that he had a heart attack and that they were trying to revive him. She immediately telephoned her daughter, who screamed 'No! no! it can't be! No!' refusing to accept the prospect of his death. When the mother phoned again, confirming that he had indeed died, our subject again screamed in the same way. In interview she said: 'I just didn't want to hear it – there was real beating of the breast and wailing'. She went on to say that all of this happened during her final law school exams, and that she was glad she had had her hardest exam before he died. She did not want to miss graduation, so did not attend the memorial service for her father, although she said it was the saddest day of her life when neither of her parents was present to see her receive her diploma. She had a week between this and her bar examination, and spent it at the beach with a girlfriend, having what she described as a 'scheduled grieving'. She said that she had not wanted her father to die because she was concerned about the state of his soul – and then went on coolly to discuss her religious beliefs.

She said that now she was still grieving, but at the end of active grieving. Nonetheless, we cannot believe that she had really resolved her mourning. She is so massively defended, so restricted in feeling, that she was identified as dismissing of attachment. At the end of the interview she talked of her life as having been 'an unbroken chain of love and acceptance'. Quite in addition to the unresolved mourning in this case, it is worthy of note that as a child this woman was frightened of her mother – a traumatic influence that may also be inferred as unresolved.

The second case (*No. 124*) is of a woman who has won through to a reasonably secure and autonomous view of attachment, despite the fact that she still is somewhat conflicted and angry in relationship to her mother, and still unresolved in her mourning for her father. Although she said that she had been very close to her mother as a child, it was clear that the attachment to her was insecure. Her mother was very perfectionistic, and critical to the point of quite undermining the child's feelings of trust and self-esteem. Although she said that her mother was always there for all the basic things, she remembers no comforting when she was upset and no physical closeness.

Relations with her father were quite different. When he came home from work he devoted himself to her and to her younger brother. He sat with them while they played, gave them their baths, and our subject said that at bedtime she always fell asleep on his lap. He was the one who took them to the circus, to the fair, and weekly to the library.

Our subject went away to college, but in her second year, when she was 19, her father suddenly died of a stroke. She happened to be at home when this occurred, and helped rush him to the hospital. In interview she said: 'It was just real bizarre. I couldn't really handle what was going on. I cried like everybody does, I know but ...' and her voice trailed off. 'We were all just in shock. It was a real bad thing ... my mother ... she was just ... it was just so incredibly bizarre for it to happen. We were not expecting it at all. See! that was it!' She began to cry. 'We were never the same again. It was like ... now that I think about it ... the nucleus just exploded ... the whole situation ... and we were never the same again. It took a long time for my mother to pull herself together, and I was an idiot.' She moved away from home and lived with her boyfriend, 'which was just an effort to find someone to hold on to'.

At the time that we assessed this woman's current state of mind regarding attachment we were impressed with the way she had worked through the traumatic events of her earlier years. She seemed to be happy in her marriage, and trying to work out her relationship with her mother. This led us to minimize the indications that her mourning for her father was still unresolved. In a *post hoc* review we had access to a revised version of the LRM scale which made it clearer that extreme responses at the time of the death and for sometime afterward is a marker for mourning that is likely to be unresolved.

Unresolved loss of other relative. There were 6 who failed to resolve loss of a relative other than a parent. In 2 cases the lost figure was a sibling; in 4 cases it was an adult relative who served as a supplementary parent figure. First let us consider two of the latter.

Number 102 is a woman who failed to resolve her mourning for her maternal aunt, who died when she was 21. She had very confused and ambivalent feelings about both mother and father – and indeed has never been able to integrate a coherent working model of either. She identified the aunt 'as a very important parent figure for me'. The aunt lived with the family for much of the time during our subject's childhood, and after marrying she lived nearby. The mother worked full-time in an important job, and when she came home she absorbed herself in her newspaper. Our subject said: 'She just wasn't there when I needed her'. There was a full-time housekeeper, whom she found uncongenial. After school she went to the aunt's house rather than going home. It was the aunt who made the Hallowe'en costumes, worked in the cooperative nursery-school in lieu of the mother, and shopped for the children's clothes. Our subject felt very close to this aunt, even after having gone away to college, and subsequently when living with one or other boyfriend. At one point the aunt talked about putting her down in her will as guardian of her two young daughters. Our subject was touched by this, and even made alterations in her job and living arrangements so she could remain closer to her aunt and little cousins.

The circumstances of the aunt's death were very traumatic. Accompanied by our subject's mother, the aunt, holding one of her daughters in her arms, was standing on a curb when a drunken taxi driver ran up over the curb. She was able to throw the child to safety in her sister's arms, but she herself was killed.

Our subject said she had a severe emotional collapse following this loss. 'I didn't feel good about myself at this point in my life. I didn't feel in touch with what was going on. I didn't have any tools to communicate with people in my life about what was going on. I was really out of it.' She continued: 'The death sparked off a lot of stuff – a lot of pain and confusion – and growth'. And: 'I still dream about her. Occasionally I dream she's not really dead, she's just hiding somewhere and just doesn't want to come to see me – which is pretty classic, isn't it?'

Nor did it help to find out that the aunt had changed her mind about her daughters' guardianship – because she didn't like the man that our subject was currently living with. Nevertheless, our subject felt 'very tied in with those kids'.

It seems likely that the maternal aunt would not have played such a significant role as parent surrogate in this woman's life had her attachments to her own parents not been so insecure and ambivalent. Similarly, it seems likely that these same factors made it difficult for her to face the realities of her loss sufficiently well to resolve her mourning.

Number 142 presented a different picture. She was classified as dismissing of attachment, and there was unresolved mourning for the maternal grandmother, who died of a heart attack when our subject was 13. The death occurred only three days after our subject had been visiting her for a week. She said: 'I remember feeling very, very guilty that I had seen her last, that my mother had not even had a chance to talk to her on the phone'. And that was all she said about the matter. This, in the context of her massive defenses, seems to have remained an encapsulated and irrational feeling of guilty fear.

In the case of the two women who failed to resolve their mourning for the loss of siblings, there had been no indication in either case that the sibling had been a parent surrogate, and indeed no evidence that the relationship had been particularly close. However, in each case it was clear that the attachments to parents were very insecure. We shall consider one of these (*No. 120*) as an example. As a child this woman remembered her mother as very cold, harsh, cruel, and angry. She was afraid of her mother and thought she would like to be rid of her. In contrast she remembered her father as warm, loving, and affectionate. However, he was alcoholic, and this grew worse over time. She feared that he would leave, and eventually he did, when she was 15. She cried for days after he went, and was angry with him for abandoning his family.

The parents had not gotten along even while the father was at home. Our subject resented her mother's feelings toward the treatment of him, and had tried vainly to play the peacemaker in their quarrels. She felt very criticized by her mother, and described herself as very lacking in feelings of self-worth. 'Often,' she said, she 'just hated' her mother, but 'on another level I think we're close'.

Our subject studied at a school of nursing, and during her last year of training she began dating the man she later married, while he was in his final year at medical school. Both stayed on in the same hospital, she working in the intensive care unit and he continuing as intern, then resident. While he was an intern they became engaged, and at the end of that year they married.

Six months before the marriage, our subject's younger sister was killed in an automobile crash. She said that she was 'very, very depressed and did not function well' after this. 'I felt numb when I was getting married.' After the wedding they moved to the country, and she got a new and better job, but one that involved a night shift. At that time, she would sit all day long in the kitchen in a rocking chair. 'It was the change in shifts, it was my sister's death, it was being married, and all of a sudden being in a new world. It was very, very hard, and really, I think, in some ways I'm still trying to sort it all out.'

Not until the very end of the interview did it emerge that she had had two abortions before being married. The first was before she graduated from nursing school, and the second was soon after her sister's death. She still feels guilty about them.

There is little doubt that she still has not resolved her mourning for her sister – but the death came when she was ill-prepared to cope with it, on top of a very disturbed childhood that left her anxious in her attachment to both parents – and her mourning was certainly complicated by the anxiety and guilt she felt about the abortions. Furthermore, that anxiety and guilt must have interfered with the security she might otherwise have found in her relationship with her husband. It seems that in this case, as well as in the other case of unresolved mourning of a sibling, it was not so much the loss of the sibling that was significant as the overwhelmingly insecure and unresolved status of attachment in the woman's life.

Unresolved mourning for unrelated figures. There were two women who manifested unresolved mourning for an attachment figure totally unrelated to them. In the first of these the lack of resolution was more extreme and more pathological than in any other case in the sample.

Number 115 is a woman whose parents were both physicians, practicing in various localities in Africa. Her mother was rejecting and our subject was very hurt by this. Mother had wanted a blonde, blue-eyed child, like the older sister in the family, but our subject was dark-haired and brown-eyed. Often throughout the years, the mother had commented on how ugly she was, such that she (the mother) had hidden her face beneath a blanket when she was little. Mother was also interferingly perfectionistic, pressing the child toward high achievement and perfection in all areas. Our subject also described her mother as very nervous, and said that she and her sister had been taking care of her over the years, implying role reversal. At the same time our subject has always been frightened of her mother, although she does not know why.

The parents were divorced when she was in her fifth year, and thenceforward she spent only vacations with her father. Her relationship with him was no better than with her mother, for he was both neglecting and rejecting – although the extent to which he left her free to do as she pleased was a comfortable change from her mother's constant interference. But she tells a dreadful story of an episode that happened when she was about 6 years of age. They were in a meadow gathering snails for his ducks, when suddenly he got in his car and drove away, abandoning her. She ran after the car screaming 'Papa, papa!' but he kept on going. She said: 'It was horrible … there was no one around, just this big, big field and the car looked so very small'. Eventually he stopped the car, and she caught up, very upset indeed. Her father said it was a joke.

When asked in the interview about surrogate parent figures she said: 'Yes, there was a little man', and began to cry. Apparently when she started school this old man had been hired to take her to school, and pick her up after school. He often took her to the harbor, where he did odd jobs – and she enjoyed his companionship. She said: 'I don't remember his face – I remember his clothes, his smell, the essence of the person, I think'. And she cried some more. He cannot have been an ideal 'baby-sitter' for she recounted with pleasure an episode in which he was drunk, and hung the shelves he had been constructing crookedly, which she remembered as very funny. She said: 'Yeah! he was a good man. That was the man in my life'.

He died of a brain hemorrhage when she was 8 years old. One day shortly before this he had asked her whether she would marry him when she grew older, and she replied: 'No, you'd be dead'. So when he died she felt as though she had killed him – 'with one sentence', she added. She went on to say that she believed in reincarnation in a way. 'As long as you think of people, so you can carry them with you, there's no death; it's here!' – pointing to her heart, and beginning to cry again. 'I've felt him in me for a long time.'

It is indeed tragic to think that her parents gave her so little security that this relatively brief relationship with an inappropriate caregiver should be felt to be the most significant in her life. Also this case illustrates the way in which damaging misconceptions can arise when the significant loss takes place in childhood – something not so clearly illustrated by any other case in this sample. On the basis of the interview we judged this woman highly insecure and still very preoccupied with her relationships with parents, especially her mother, to the extent that she seemed not to have discovered an identity for herself, despite her undoubted scholarly achievements.

Finally, *No. 119* is a woman whose childhood attachment to her mother seemed essentially secure, although not especially close. Her attachment to her father, however, was insecure; his standards for achievement were too high, and this sapped her self-confidence and self-esteem. When she went away to college she did much working through of these relationships, thanks to a close friend and confidante and her own study of child psychology – and later she found security in her relationship with her husband. We judged her to be secure and autonomous.

She had experienced a very traumatic loss during her last year in high school. Her boyfriend, whom she had been dating for over two years, was killed in a factory explosion – blown to bits. 'That was without a doubt the most devastating experience of my life. I freaked out. I was pretty much a basket case.... We were talking of getting married.... A real tragedy ... a bizarre occurrence.... At first I reacted with total disbelief ... after that I sank into a sort of nothingness ... walking around like a zombie for a month.... I lost 20 pounds. I couldn't eat ... I cried all the time. I talked to him a lot. I thought he was watching me ... so if I showed any interest in another guy ... he would have thought I didn't really love him.' Four pages of the transcript were devoted to this loss and her reactions to it. Although it took a long time for her to get over this loss, she convinced us that she had indeed resolved her mourning. In retrospect, we were clearly in error when we initially assigned her a rating of 3.0 on the LRM scale. It should have been at least 7.0 because of her very extreme and long-lasting reaction to this sudden, catastrophic loss of a figure so central to her life at that time – as the revised LRM scale now available to us makes quite clear.

Match of mother and infant attachment patterns. It was predicted that mothers whose mourning was unresolved would have babies whose attachment to them was disorganized/disoriented. This prediction was entirely confirmed in this sample; *all* of those whose mourning was judged to be unresolved had D babies. This was irrespective of the mother's general state of mind in regard to attachments. Five of the mothers were judged to be preoccupied with early attachments, 3 as dismissing of attachment, and 2 as autonomous and secure. This is in contrast with those who had resolved their mourning, of whom 90 per cent were classified as autonomous and secure, and *none* as preoccupied.

The forced A/B/C classifications of the babies were in less striking agreement with hypotheses, although 3 of the 5 preoccupied mothers had babies whose forced classification was C, both of the autonomous mothers had babies who were forced B, and 1 of the 3 dismissing mothers had babies who were forced A, as expected. However, in 4 of the 10 cases the baby's forced classification did not match the mother's basic AAI classification.

No loss

There were 15 women in the sample who had suffered no loss of any figure significant enough to have been judged an attachment figure. Of these, 9 were classified as autonomous and secure, 4 as dismissing of attachment, and 2 as preoccupied with early attachments. Six of those classified as autonomous had infants who were classified as secure (i.e. B) as predicted, but one each of the other infants were classified as A, C, and D. Three of those classified as dismissing of attachment had infants who were judged to be insecure–avoidant (A) as predicted, but one was classified as B. Both of those classified as preoccupied with early attachments had infants classified as insecure–disorganized, rather than as insecure–ambivalent as predicted.

Unresolved trauma other than loss

There were 15 cases of D infants, 10 of whose mothers had failed to resolve their mourning for an attachment figure lost through death. The other 5 mothers of Ds are also of interest. Let us consider them in turn.

In one case (*No. 139*) the mother had herself had a very close brush with death – a traumatic experience which she clearly had not resolved by the time of the interview. Death had nearly resulted from peritonitis for which she was hospitalized, and which of course involved separation from her 1-year-old son. For the child the 2-week separation may well have been especially traumatic, because his father was likely to have been much too concerned about his wife's illness to be an adequately responsive caregiver. Furthermore, the mother undoubtedly behaved differently toward him after the separation, upset as she was about her own recent frightening experience, and this different behavior may well have been frightening to him. It was on the basis of these considerations that we predicted that the baby would be classified as a D. On the other hand, we classified her as autonomous and basically secure in her state of mind regarding attachment, and therefore it seems likely that she will resolve her recent upsetting experience and that therefore her child's disorganization will prove to be transient.

A second similar case (*No. 117*) was discussed earlier, in which mourning for a lost attachment figure was judged to have been resolved, but in which the father's drug addiction was believed to be causing the mother anxiety, which was believed to account for the infant's disorganization.

In a third case (*No. 141*) the mother had experienced physical abuse by her father when she was an adolescent – severe enough that she was placed in a foster home at her own instigation. We thought it likely that she had not yet resolved the trauma of the abuse, and had predicted that her baby would be classified as D.

In a fourth case (*No. 125*) the mother had been classified as pre-occupied with early attachments, and was quite disorganized and incoherent. Since she had suffered no loss and since no other traumatic experience was reported in her interview, her baby was predicted to be insecure–ambivalent (C), rather than insecure–disorganized (D). It is suggested that she had experienced some other trauma which was unresolved, and which was not disclosed in the interview.

In this she resembles the fifth case (*No. 129*) who was mentioned earlier – a woman classified as autonomous and secure, who had resolved her mourning for a maternal aunt, but had a disorganized baby despite the fact that the interview gave no indication of any unresolved trauma.

Summary of findings

(1) The first aim of the study was to examine the association of infant disorganization with mother's failure to resolve the loss of an attachment figure through death. In examining this we included those who were identified *post hoc* as unresolved, as well those who had initially been so identified because of an LRM score of 6 or more.

Table 9.2 shows that all 10 of the mothers who had been identified as unresolved mourners had D babies, in comparison with only 2 among 20 who had resolved their mourning, and only 3 of the 15 who had experienced no loss. This distribution of cases shows a highly significant association of infant disorganization with mother's unresolved mourning for the loss of an attachment figure through death. This central finding clearly supports Main and Hesse's (in press) conclusion that it is *unresolved* loss of an attachment figure that is associated with infant disorganization of attachment behavior and not the death as such.

Table 9.2 Infant disorganization as related to mother's loss status

	Mourning resolved	Mourning unresolved	No loss	Totals
Infant Ds	2	10	3	15
Infant Non-Ds	18	0	12	30
Totals	20	10	15	45

Note: Chi-square = 25.43 $p < 0.001$

(2) From the findings for our sample we cannot confirm Main and Hesse's (in press) findings that infant disorganization is especially associated with early loss of a close family figure through death. As reported earlier, 60 per cent of mothers who had experienced such early loss had infants classified as disorganized, whereas only 21 per cent of those who had *not* experienced early loss had D infants. In contrast, in the Charlottesville sample 33 per cent of both mothers who had and those who had *not* experienced comparable early loss had D infants. Furthermore, only 2 of the 15 (13 per cent) of our Charlottesville parents of D infants had experienced loss of a parent at any age, and *none* of them had lost a parent in childhood.

(3) In the Charlottesville sample 18 of 20 women who resolved their mourning for a lost attachment figure were judged to be secure and autonomous in their state of mind in regard to attachment, 2 were dismissing of attachment, and none was preoccupied. (See Table 9.3.) In contrast, 5 of 10 women who failed to resolve their mourning were classed as preoccupied with early attachments, 2 as autonomous, and 3 as dismissing of attachment. On the other hand, the distribution of the three attachment patterns in the whole sample was closely approximated by the distribution among the 15 women who suffered no loss. (Chi square is significant at the 0.01 level.) This result is in line with Main and Hesse's inference that, if loss has occurred, a preoccupied state of mind in regard to early attachments is particularly likely to be associated with unresolved mourning and a secure and autonomous state of mind with resolution.

(4) It is perhaps appropriate to refer here to the degree of match between the mother's attachment classification and that of her infant found by Eichberg (1987), since the requisite data are included in Table 9.1. For the 30 non-D infants there was a match between mother's and baby's classifications in 27 cases (90 per cent), that is, with autonomous/secure mothers having secure babies, dismissing mothers having insecure–avoidant babies, and preoccupied mothers having insecure–ambivalent babies. In the total sample, that is, including the D babies and using their forced

Table 9.3 Relationship between AAI classification and loss status

AAI classification	Loss status			
	Resolved	Unresolved	No loss	Total
Autonomous	18	2	9	29
Dismissing	2	3	4	9
Preoccupied	0	5	2	7
Totals	20	10	15	45

Note: Chi-square = 18.1523 $p < 0.01$

A/B/C classifications, there was a match in 36 of the 45 cases (80 per cent). This represents a very strong cross-generational effect – even stronger than that reported by Main and her associates.

(5) We found that parental failure to resolve mourning for an attachment figure did not account for all cases of infant disorganization. Indeed 5 of our 15 Ds were not associated with unresolved mourning on the part of the mother. In 3 of these 5 cases we identified other sources of unresolved traumatic experiences severe enough to account for the disorganization of the baby, although in the remaining 2 cases the interview yielded no evidence of what the trauma might have been. However, unlike Main and Hesse, we identified no case in which sexual abuse seemed to be involved.

(6) This leads us to the Main–Hesse hypothesis that what causes the infant to behave in a disorganized way under attachment-related stress is that the parent behaves in a directly threatening way which frightens the baby, or behaves in such a way that he or she indirectly frightens the baby. Our study, which was mainly focused on information yielded by the Adult Attachment Interview, can offer but little confirmation of this hypothesis. There were several cases in which a mother of a D infant said that she had often found the behavior of one of her own parents frightening. Particularly in the case of a mother who is preoccupied with early attachments, it is reasonable to suppose that the memory of her fear of the parent might sometimes intrude into everyday life, and re-evoke the anxiety; at such times the infant might find his mother's behavior especially frightening since there was no apparent occasion for it. We noted no instance in which the fear of a parent was reported by the mother of a non-D infant. We are thus led to give credence to the Main–Hesse hypothesis, despite our scanty evidence.

Discussion

Most of the findings of this study require no further discussion. The study provided strong confirmation of the findings of Main and her associates in regard to a significant cross-generational effect of mother's state of mind in regard to attachment on the quality of the infant's attachment to her. More specifically, it confirmed the Main–Hesse conclusion that a parent's failure to resolve mourning for the loss of an attachment figure through death is associated with disorganization and/or disorientation in infant attachment behavior. However, we need to discuss those findings which are not in line with those reported by Main and Hesse.

Main and Hesse's findings pertinent to the adverse effect of a parent's early loss of a close family figure on the security of a child's attachment to the parent are in line with the literature on loss that suggests the death of a parent experienced in early childhood may well have more adverse effect on subsequent development and mental health than such loss experienced later on. We found that 4 of the 5 mothers in our sample who had experienced loss of a parent in childhood were themselves secure–autonomous in regard to attachments, and none of them had D babies. Indeed, of 10 mothers who had experienced loss of a parent at any age, 8 were themselves secure–autonomous, and only 2 had D babies.

We do not believe that our finding weakens the case made in the literature on loss (reviewed by Bowlby 1980) that the death of a parent experienced in childhood, especially the death of a mother, may well have adverse effects on subsequent mental health, or that such loss is over-represented in the histories of adults with severe depression. Bowlby reviewed some of the circumstances under which childhood loss may be particularly difficult to resolve. Our emphasis on *unresolved* mourning regardless of the figure that is mourned or the age at which the loss took place in no way minimizes the importance of favorable circumstances if loss of a parent in childhood is to be successfully resolved.

In presenting our findings regarding women whose mourning had been resolved, we searched for factors in their experience that characterized their response to the loss, and which seemed to assist them to resolve it – a feature of our study that had not been addressed by Main and Hesse. We identified two factors: a sense of family solidarity, and the ability to take responsibility for the care of other members of the family. It is easy to understand that ability to express one's feelings, to share one's grief, and to engage in mutual comforting with other surviving family members both leads to feeling secure in a sense of family solidarity, and facilitates the resolution of mourning. It also seems likely that freedom to express feelings of grief and anxiety and to receive and accept comfort would be helpful in overcoming misconceptions such as unrealistic fears or feelings of guilt that may make loss, especially childhood loss, difficult to resolve.

Parkes (1972) and Bowlby (1980) both have emphasized that in the final phase of mourning in which resolution takes place the mourner comes to accept the loss as permanent, and to realize that life must be undertaken anew and that representational models must be reshaped in line with changed circumstances. It seems likely that such acceptance and reshaping would be facilitated by shouldering responsibility for the care of other surviving family members. To be sure, this may be part of a mutual sense of family solidarity mentioned earlier, but it sometimes seems to occur unilaterally and still to be helpful.

Furthermore, and usually interacting with family solidarity and ability to take responsibility for others, a history of secure attachment surely facilitates the successful resolution of mourning the loss of an attachment figure. For a child, the loss of a parent to whom he had been securely attached may be assumed to be easier to resolve if he is also securely attached to the surviving parent, and for an adult a generally secure and autonomous state of mind may be expected to be associated with resolution of mourning – as indeed was borne out by our findings as well as those of the Berkeley study.

© 1991 Mary D. Salter Ainsworth and Carolyn Eichberg

NOTES

1   We thank Sarah Borrero for her assistance in this project.
2   This revised scale may be requested from Mary Main, Department of Psychology, Tolman Hall, University of California, Berkeley, CA 94720.
3   We are grateful to Nancy Kaplan and Donna Weston for their expert help in reclassifying the strange-situation behavior of the infants in this sample so that 'D' infants could be accurately identified, together with their appropriate 'forced' A, B, or C classifications
4   According to Main and Solomon (in press), the forced classification reflects the infant's basic strategy that underlies the disorganization or disorientation, and which may be inferred from behavior in the strange situation despite the occurrence of behavioral indices leading to a classification of D. This sometimes leads to the seemingly paradoxical finding that an infant classified as D and thus insecure has an underlying B or secure strategy.

REFERENCES

Ainsworth, M.D.S., Blehar, M.C., Waters, E., and Wall, S. (1978) *Patterns of Attachment: A Psychological Study of the Strange Situation*, Hillsdale, N.J.: Erlbaum.
Bowlby, J. (1980) *Attachment and Loss*, vol. 3: *Loss: Sadness and Depression*, London: Hogarth, and New York: Basic Books.
Eichberg, C.G. (1987) 'Quality of infant–parent attachment: related to mother's representation of her own relationship history and child care attitudes', Unpublished doctoral dissertation, University of Virginia.
George, C., Kaplan, N., and Main, M. (1985) 'The Berkeley Adult Attachment Interview', Unpublished protocol, Department of Psychology, University of California, Berkeley.
Main, M. (1985) 'An adult attachment classification system', Paper presented at the biennial meeting of the Society for Research in Child Development, Toronto, April 1985.
Main, M. and Goldwyn, R. (1988) 'Adult Attachment Classification System', Unpublished manual, Department of Psychology, University of California, Berkeley. (Revised version, 1989.)
Main, M. and Hesse, E. (1989) 'Discovery of a second-generation effect of unresolved trauma: lapses in a parent's reasoning or discourse in discussing traumatic experiences predict Disorganized infant Strange-Situation behavior', Unpublished monograph, submitted for publication.
Main, M. and Hesse, E. (in press) 'Lack of resolution of mourning in adulthood and its relationship to infant disorganization: some speculations regarding causal mechanisms', in M. Greenberg, D. Cicchetti, and M. Cummings (eds) *Attachment in the Preschool Years*, Chicago: University of Chicago Press.
Main, M., Kaplan, N., and Cassidy, J. (1985) 'Security in infancy, childhood and adulthood: a move to the level of representation', in I. Bretherton and E. Waters

(eds) Growing Points of Attachment Theory and Research, *Monographs of the Society for Research in Child Development*, Serial No. 209, 50 (1–2): 66–104.

Main, M. and Solomon, J. (in press) 'Procedures for identifying insecure-disorganized/disoriented infants within the Ainsworth strange situation', in M. Greenberg, D. Cicchetti, and M. Cummings (eds) *Attachment in the Preschool Years*, Chicago: University of Chicago Press.

Parkes, C.M. (1972) *Bereavement: Studies of Grief in Adult Life*, London: Tavistock Publications and New York: International Universities Press.

Part III

Clinical Applications

Chapter 10

Failure of the holding relationship

Some effects of physical rejection on the child's attachment and inner experience

Juliet Hopkins

INTRODUCTION

Bowlby's immense contribution to our awareness of the importance of holding in the early mother–child relationship was acknowledged by Winnicott in his last public lecture (1970). 'John Bowlby has done more than one man's share of drawing the world's attention to the sacredness of the early holding situation and the extreme difficulties that belong to the work of those that try to mend it.'

In this paper I shall participate in Bowlby's work of drawing attention to the early holding situation, in order to consider some implications for the child psychotherapist in trying both to understand and to mend it.

Winnicott's term, 'the holding situation', was used by him to cover many aspects of the early mother–child relationship besides the actual physical holding of the baby. But here I intend to restrict myself to that aspect alone: that is, to the mother's provision of physical holding and body contact for her young child. I intend to illustrate its significance by reference to the response of children whose mothers, though present, are physically rejecting of their infacts. I shall bring together contributions from attachment research and clinical work, and finally consider some implications for psychotherapy.

When Ainsworth initiated her research on infant attachment she expected to find that different mothers would prefer different modes of communication with their infants, some stressing physical contact, for example, others relying more on vocalization or eye-to-eye contact. However, she discovered that desirable forms of maternal behaviour tended to occur together (Ainsworth 1982). Mothers who were sensitive to their infants' signals tended to respond with all the modes available to them, and when distal modes of contact failed to soothe their infants, they picked them up and cuddled them. However, mothers whose babies developed an avoidant attachment all manifested what Ainsworth called 'the rejection syndrome', characterized primarily by deep aversion to bodily contact which led them to rebuff their infants' attempts to initiate physical contact. In addition these mothers were liable to be rough or threatening with their infants and to perceive their infants' demands as conflicting with their own activities. They were noticeably restricted in their range of emotional expression, conveying detachment or stiffness, which could be interpreted as an effort to control expression of their resentment. These findings mean that babies whose mothers are physically aversive have mothers who are also liable to be emotionally out of touch. The effect of physical rejection cannot be considered in isolation from the effect of lack of emotional rapport.

Ainsworth has used the term 'rejecting mothers' to describe the mothers of avoidant infants. Some may find the term unduly harsh. Since the percentage of babies with an avoidant attachment, assessed at a year old, is in the region of 20 per cent in middle-class samples (e.g. Ainsworth *et al.* 1978), clearly the term does not apply simply to the tiny minority of mothers who seriously abuse, neglect, or abandon their infants. Perhaps the label may seem more acceptable if it is emphasized that these mothers are in no way to blame. Both clinical and research evidence indicate that they themselves were victims of similar treatment in their own childhoods.

It might be supposed that infants who have developed an avoidant attachment by a year were more difficult or less cuddly than other babies in their earliest months, but research has shown that this is not so. However, by the age of 9 months these babies do not respond positively to their mothers' initiation of contact; they neither cuddle nor cling but are carried like a sack of potatoes. At this age they still initiate as many contacts to their mothers as other babies, though often mainly to mother's distal parts, like her feet.

In the second year, babies with an avoidant attachment show no anger with mother after the short stressful separation, although secure babies do. However, they show a high incidence of angry behaviour towards the mother in stress-free settings. This anger is often out of context and seems entirely inexplicable, for example, suddenly hitting the mother's legs while smiling. Other problems manifest by avoidant babies are a high incidence of disobedience, hitting and banging of toys, and a variety of odd and stereotyped behaviours, such as hand-flapping, inexplicable fears, rocking, and inaccessible trance-like states. Avoidant babies appear to be psychiatrically at risk. Bowlby (1988) has described how the avoidant child's attempts to be self-sufficient in order to avoid rebuff may lead to personality organization which is later diagnosed as narcissistic or as a false self, of the type described by Winnicott (1960).

Main (1986) postulates that the avoidant infant is the victim of an irresolvable and self-perpetuating conflict, caused by his mother's aversion to physical contact. 'The situation is *irresolvable* because rejection by an established attachment figure activates simultaneous and contradictory impulses both to withdraw and to approach. The infant cannot approach because of the parent's rejection, and cannot withdraw because of its own attachment. The situation is *self-perpetuating* because rebuff heightens alarm and hence heightens attachment, leading to increased rebuff, increased alarm and increased heightening of attachment ... In other words, by repelling the infant the mother simultaneously attracts him.'

At first sight this conflict might be thought to have much in common with Bateson's double-bind (Bateson *et al.* 1956), which he considered to be an environmental contribution to the development of schizophrenia. But Main and Stadtman (1981) point out that it differs from the double-bind in three respects. First, it is entirely non-verbal. Second, it is the infant's own attachment which creates the competing tendency to approach the mother, rather than the mother's conflicting signals. Thirdly, the conflict is self-perpetuating and does not end with the immediate interaction. An infant can only escape from it by turning to another attachment figure, if available, or by avoidance through a shift of attention away from the mother, often at first to a neutral object, but eventually away from the situation and events which have the potential for activating attachment.

A PSYCHOLOGICAL CONSTELLATION ASSOCIATED WITH PHYSICAL REJECTION

Reading Main's work made me wonder how often this irresolvable and self-perpetuating conflict of infancy is at the root of later psychopathology. I turned to the records of children I have seen in psychotherapy in search of evidence of the effects of physical rejection on their inner experience.

In the clinical material that follows I present material from three children whose mothers provided convincing evidence that they had avoided physical contact with them as far as possible in their infancy. All three children came from intact families with well-intentioned parents; there were no hints of physical abuse. I have omitted further mention of the fathers who in each case played a minimal part in their children's care and were often absent for long periods.

Material from these patients enabled me to distinguish a psychological constellation which I believe to be associated with the experience of repeated physical rejection in infancy. This constellation consists of the conflict which Main has described, associated with a terror of physical rejection and an almost equal dread of physical acceptance lest physical contact results in mutual aggression. In addition there are feelings of intense pain and a self-representation of being in some way untouchable and repellent.

CLINICAL MATERIAL

Clare was referred for psychotherapy at the age of 6 years on account of nightmares. Her mother reported that she had resented the child's arrival and found her physically repellent as a baby, though she had gradually come to enjoy talking and playing with her. She had always propped Clare's bottle and kept her in a playpen all day until she started nursery school. She thought that Clare had always resisted being cuddled. As soon as Clare could walk she walked away from her mother and was liable to get lost. She had always been stoically independent, never asking for help except when she had hurt herself. Her mother described her as 'accident prone' and felt that she had accidents to gain the attention which she had no other means of seeking. Even when she had hurt herself she did not cry.

The psychiatrist who assessed Clare described her as having a false personality (Winnicott 1960). She was strongly identified with her mother whose phrases and gestures she accurately reproduced. It seemed that she did not need her mother because she had become her. Similarly, in therapy, Clare took over my capacity to make interpretations and gave them to herself so that she would not need to depend on me. Once, when I spoke to her of her hidden wish to cry, Clare explained, 'I never cry because if I started I would never stop.' I understood this to mean that she feared there would never be anyone to comfort her.

Clare often spoke of her worry about lepers which gave her bad dreams. She explained that lepers were contagious which meant that 'if they touch someone they die'. She thought they could be cured by the laying on of hands. As therapy proceeded Clare became aware that she felt herself to be a leper whom no-one wanted to touch because she would kill them, and she also became aware of her longing to cry and to be comforted. In her sessions she was tortured by the longing to touch and be touched by me which conflicted with her terror of it, and by her longing to cry which she fiercely resisted because it was 'so silly and only babies do it'.

After nearly a year of therapy Clare allowed an accident to happen which enabled her to translate some of her longings into action. She fell heavily from my desk onto the floor. As she lay there she raised her arms beseechingly towards me and burst into tears. I picked her up and she sobbed for some minutes on my lap, though keeping her head averted from me.

Clare's mother reported that the day after this event Clare came to her to be comforted in distress for the first time. Mother, who had been greatly helped by her own therapist, was ready to respond to Clare and thereafter Clare continued to turn to her mother when upset and began for the first time to confide her worries to her. She became cuddly and, before long, very clinging and demanding, and no longer accident prone.

Laura, 16 years, suffered from depression and compulsive eating. In therapy she recounted a recurrent nightmare of finding herself alone in a desert, covered with a revolting skin disease. In association to this dream she mentioned that she had a collecting box for Hindu 'untouchables'. No-one in Laura's family had ever suffered from a skin disease, but Laura's mother, like Clare's, could not tolerate physical contact with her throughout her infancy. However, she had been able to enjoy cuddling Laura's younger sister when she was a baby. In therapy Laura represented herself as a tortoise and her sister as a cuddly rabbit.

I have found it common for physically rejected children to dramatize or draw themselves as physically repellent or unstrokeable creatures, like tortoises, toads, crocodiles, and hedgehogs. They feel themselves at depth to be unattractive, though this is something over-compensated for with pretty clothes.

In a session in the second year of her therapy in which she suffered great distress, Laura became obsessed with the image of the moth's fatal fascination for the candle flame. She wept as she expressed her horror at the moth's repeated return to the flame that burned it, and said that she experienced the pain of the burning acutely in her own skin.

This image of the moth and the candle flame is a dramatic reminder of Main's finding that, by repelling the infant the mother simultaneously attracts him. For Laura it expressed the conflict between her burning desire to be loved by her alluring mother and the burning pain and rage associated with the continued rejections which she had experienced.

Before Laura's preoccupation with the image of the moth and the candle flame she had been concerned with being frozen rather than being burned. Her images had been of icebergs, snow, and refrigerators.

Children's images of being frozen are familiar to psychotherapists. The burnt child dreads the fire and the frozen withdrawal of the avoidant child prevents any further risk of being burned. Laura's shift from freezing to burning imagery was accompanied by intense awareness of her longing for physical love and of her hatred of her mother for her rejection of her.

After getting in touch with the feelings represented by the moth and the candle flame, Laura lost her urge to eat compulsively. This would not surprise Bowlby who has expressed the view (1982) that oral symptoms can develop in response to the frustration of a child's attachment to his mother. However, I think that Laura's compulsive eating was not an arbitrary displacement activity. The way in which she had felt compulsively drawn to the desired but hated food mirrored the moth's addiction to the candle flame. This parallel has made me wonder whether the compelling lure of the physically rejecting mother may contribute to other compulsive or even addictive practices.

Both Laura and Clare suffered acute pain, verbalized as 'burning' and 'torture' as they faced the issues inherent in their experience of physical rejection and their desire for and dread of physical contact. Winnicott (1963b) has described how the toddler's need for his mother becomes 'fierce and truly terrible'. When this need is frustrated by a physically aversive mother then I believe that the pain which is aroused is also fierce and truly terrible, like burning or torture, stabbing or biting. It seems to me that the infant experiences the pain as a physical assault, not as a psychological rejection.

In their book on psychotherapy with severely deprived children, Boston and Szur (1983) write of the long struggle through which deprived children must come to terms with pain and loss. 'Central to this struggle seems to be the transformation of pain from something which has the character of an overwhelming physical attack into something which can be considered in the mind as an experience.'

Clare and Laura were both intelligent and articulate; they had been able to translate the pain of their physical rejection into symbols which could be understood. My third clinical example concerns the therapy of a 3-year-old, Paddy, who was incapable of symbolic expression when his therapy began. I present his material in some detail in order to illustrate how the conflict which Main described could first be deduced from his behaviour, before it emerged in symbolic form in the context of the constellation which I have come to associate with a history of physical rejection. Paddy's therapy, like Clare's, also touches on the issue of the role of physical contact between therapist and child patient, a topic to which I shall return.

Paddy was the only child of Irish parents. He was referred for psychiatric assessment at the age of 3 years by a paediatrician who wondered whether he was mentally defective or psychotic. He had no speech and was not toilet-trained. His parents reported that he had never shown signs of preferring them to anyone else; he had never greeted them on arrival or protested at their departure. He showed no awareness of danger and would wander off and get lost unless kept locked indoors. When he injured himself, even severely, he appeared to feel no pain. He regularly ate dirt and rubbish, and even occasionally his own faeces. He rejected being cuddled and was a constant thumb-sucker. He did not play but wandered about 'getting into things'. Although he never cried, he was upset if other children did, and was also upset by the sight of mess spilled on the floor. In spite of the many worrying features of his development, Paddy presented at the clinic as a jolly little boy who usually made good eye contact, though there were times when his eyes glazed over and he became inaccessible.

What sort of history lies behind such an extreme example of avoidant attachment? Paddy's mother was a chronically depressed and very anxious woman who had made several attempts at suicide in her teens. She suffered from severe eczema and explained that although she loved

Paddy she had always avoided touching and cuddling him for fear that his germs would infect her skin. She reported that Paddy's birth had been normal and he was a healthy baby, but she lost all her confidence as a mother when he was a month old and a paediatrician suggested that he might have Down's Syndrome. At this time breast-feeding failed and mother employed a series of au-pairs to help with Paddy's care; however, none of them stayed longer than a month because conditions in the home were so chaotic. The marriage was unstable and father did not help.

Paddy showed no sign of anxiety at meeting me, a complete stranger in a strange room. I was surprised to find that he was immediately interested and pleased by the way that I verbalized his activities and reflected his feelings. Although he usually seemed vastly cheerful his anxiety suddenly became very acute at any moment that there was a loud noise or a threatened loss of control, like spilling water. At such times he attempted to bolt from the room, and when I held the door shut he turned his back to me and indulged in a variety of tense nervous mannerisms such as pulling his ears and rocking. At times when he was especially pleased and happy he also avoided eye contact, by closing his eyes while grasping his nose and mouth and seeming acutely abashed.

Attachment theory (e.g. Main and Weston 1982) explains how, by turning his back, closing his eyes or attending to an inanimate object, the avoidant child reduces the rejecting mother's power to elicit flight or aggression, and is thus enabled to stay safely in her proximity. By deduction, Paddy avoided eye contact at moments when he most wanted physical contact and so feared both my rejection and the expression of his own hostility. At times when he had no particular desire to be held he easily made eye contact while being perfectly comfortable for me to touch him, for example, by helping him undo his coat.

One of the clues to Paddy's fear of bodily contact was manifest in what became the central activity of his therapy sessions. With enormous effort he erected piles of wobbly furniture. He aimed to put a cushion on the top, climb up and sit on it. However, the furniture was always stacked too insecurely to make this possible, and I had to intervene to prevent him from falling. I thought Paddy's building represented both his wish for a mother with an available lap, and his fear, based on experience, that she would never prove strong enough to hold him.

Paddy took great pleasure in having or doing the same as me. He would be thrilled, for example, to discover that we both had hankies and that we could draw circles together. This need for sameness has been described as mutual identification (Winnicott, personal communication) or imitative fusion (Tustin 1986). It is used as a means of denying a separate identity and therefore denying the possibility of separation. Paddy not only sought refuge from his approach–avoidance conflict in this way, but also by hiding inside safe places. He would lie for long periods under the couch or sit wrapped in a blanket with his head inside a cushion cover. Such behaviour has traditionally been understood as an expression of the wish to be safe inside mother. More poignantly, it might also be considered as an attempt to create a secure base when there is no mother available, a nest or a den instead of a lap.

As the first term of therapy progressed Paddy sometimes risked coming close enough to touch me when distressed. On the first occasion he bumped into me backwards and then sat down and held my shoe. This new ability to touch my extremities was accompanied by occasionally thumping me hard for no apparent reason. As he grew bolder and began to approach me from in front, he clutched his mouth very tightly. From observation of his movements I interpreted his longing to use his mouth to cry, to kiss and to bite, and his fears of doing so.

During the first term of therapy Paddy blossomed into speech and also toilet-trained himself. These developments were of immense reassurance to his parents who no longer feared that he was mentally defective. They attended the clinic for regular weekly casework themselves; their marriage stabilized, they showed increasing interest in Paddy, and mother's eczema healed.

In his second term of therapy Paddy risked more direct physical contact with me by jumping off the window-sill into my arms. He did this with clenched teeth and fisted hands, not snuggling into me but wildly thrashing the air as though fending off an assault. Soon after he had trusted me to catch him he began to greet me in the waiting room and to resist leaving me at the end of sessions. This was an extremely painful period for his parents who had to observe their son manifesting an affectionate attachment to his therapist which he had never shown to them. I wondered whether I had been too explicit about Paddy's wish to be close to me and too accepting of his advances. I tried making myself less physically available and I emphasized his wish for physical contact with his parents. Paddy felt crushed. He withdrew from me, and various of his mannerisms, which had almost disappeared, returned. In the third term of treatment I again made myself more available and spoke directly of his longing to be held and comforted by me when distressed, while also fully acknowledging his negative feelings.

At the time of his referral Paddy had seemed oblivious to pain. His reckless climbing led to many bruises which he completely ignored. I verbalized his need not to know that he was hurt because he feared that there would be no-one to comfort him. Bowlby (1988) has emphasized the link between emotion and action. 'Failure to express emotion is due very largely to unconscious fears lest the action of which the emotion is a part will lead to a dreaded outcome.' This close link between emotion and action has also been demonstrated in the work of Fraiberg (1982).

She found that toddlers who had seemed oblivious to pain became able to respond to their injuries with cries or screams once they had established a relationship with their mother in which they could expect consolation. The same proved true of Paddy with me. In his third term of therapy he began to whimper when he hurt himself, and eventually one day when he had injured his thumb, he climbed into my lap, crying loudly. After this he not only sought my lap when he hurt himself, he took better care to avoid injury. However, when Paddy climbed on my lap for consolation, traces of his anxiety about physical contact remained. Like Clare, he kept his head averted from me.

When the first year of therapy ended I was worried that I had seduced Paddy away from his parents whom he still ignored and rejected, in spite of many positive changes in their attitude to him. However, during the long summer holiday Paddy caught measles, and it was while his mother nursed him through this illness that he first sought refuge and comfort in her arms. After his illness he became affectionate and sometimes clinging to both his parents.

Paddy's acute approach–avoidance conflict had been apparent in his behaviour from the start of therapy. It was only in the second year of his treatment that he achieved the capacity to express it symbolically and to convey accompanying fears of being both physically repellent and contaminating.

When Paddy first began to speak one of his most repeated phrases was 'dirty boy'. He gradually brought increasing associations to his sense of being disgustingly dirty and identified with 'smelly poos', only fit to be flushed down the toilet. It seemed that behind his habit of eating rubbish and faeces were fears that his mother had rejected him on account of his dirtiness, and that this dirtiness was also the cause of her eczema. Like Clare with her fears of leprosy and Laura with her skin disease, Paddy felt repellent and dangerous to others. Like them he feared the physical acceptance which he also longed for, because he might cause harm. This fear of hurting was exacerbated by powerful wishes to hurt which Paddy began to express in endless fantasy fights between crocodiles. In these fights, which were enacted with great urgency, Paddy and I were both crocodiles who intended to eat each other up while protecting ourselves by biting and scratching each other. Paddy often described our sore and bleeding wounds and he found it very meaningful when I likened these wounds to his mother's sore and scaly skin. The crocodile fights seemed to represent the acute approach–avoidance conflict of Paddy's infancy and the agony he suffered when longing to be close enough to eat his mother up while dreading rejection and mutual assaults.

Paddy ended therapy at the age of $5\frac{1}{2}$ years when he entered his local primary school. He settled well and made progress. His parents' only remaining worry about him was that he was indiscriminately friendly to strangers.

IMPLICATIONS FOR PSYCHOTHERAPY

Physical contact between therapist and child patient

Paddy's and Clare's use of my lap for comfort may be considered a controversial technique. When Freud advocated abstinence throughout the course of treatment (1915), he intended that language and interpretation should suffice. However, Winnicott (1963b) wrote that in the course of therapy, 'Occasionally holding must take a physical form, but I think that is only because there is a delay in the analyst's understanding which he can use for verbalizing what is afoot'. With regard to children, it could be added that there may also be a delay in the *child's* understanding which needs to be bridged by physical holding. I doubt whether for Paddy or Clare there could have been a satisfactory alternative to the availability of my lap at a critical time in their therapy.

Main (1986) concluded that what has most meaning to an infant is not the *amount* of physical contact which he receives from his mother: it is her physical *accessibility* in response to *his* initative that matters. Where the treatment of young avoidant children is concerned it is probably essential to respond with more than words to their first initiatives for physical consolation when distressed. Not to do so would be to repeat the history of rejection which they endured from their parents, and so could nip a new beginning in the bud.

Once a new beginning has been made with the therapist, the question remains of how it can be transferred to the parents. This happened immediately and spontaneously for Clare, whose mother was eagerly awaiting the opportunity to comfort her. Clare only needed my physical comfort once, before she turned to her mother to meet this need in future. From then on in her therapy, in the manner of older children like Laura, she was able to use the cushions for comfort while feeling herself symbolically held by my capacity to be verbally 'in touch' with her feelings. Paddy is the only child I have worked with who preferred initimacy with me to closeness with his own parents for an extended period. I am left not knowing how I could have managed this better.

Another area of technique about which I am uncertain is the degree of intimacy which it is helpful to develop in therapy with very young children. Even after accepting comfort on my lap both Clare and Paddy continued to show their fears of a more intimate relationship by averting their faces. I did not comment on this behaviour for fear of seeming to want to draw them into a more intimate contact which I felt belonged to their relationship with their parents. However, although their parents described both children as becoming 'cuddly', I never learned how intimate they became, and it seems possible that further exploration of these issues in therapy could have been valuable.

Parent–infant psychotherapy

One way of obviating the difficulties which can arise if a young child becomes more attached to his therapist than to his parents is by the use of parent–infant psychotherapy. In this method, developed by Fraiberg (1980), parent and child are seen together. I have found it very effective in helping parents and children with attachment problems, although I have no experience of using this approach with families as severely disturbed as that of Paddy and his parents. However, whatever therapeutic approach is used, it is clearly essential to include the parents, so that they can become responsively available when their child becomes able to initiate contact with them.

Untouchability

A final implication for our work concerns the understanding of the avoidant child's feelings of being untouchable, repellent, or contaminated. These feelings need to be traced to their origin in the parents' treatment of their child, and not ascribed only to the hatred and guilt which the child inevitably feels. Failure to do this may increase the child's tendency towards self-blame, depression, and low self-esteem.

Freud discovered that what has been remembered and understood need not be repeated. Further research by Main (Main and Goldwyn 1984) provides some evidence that when early rejection is understood and recognized as a function of the parent, not of the self, then the risk of repetition is reduced. Children who know that their parents rejected them are less likely to reject their own children.

CONCLUSION

This paper has brought together research and clinical evidence to demonstrate the central significance for healthy development of the mother's physical availability at times of her infant's need. In doing so it has described some adverse effects on development when she fails to provide this secure base. Bowlby and his coworkers have enabled us to recognize that the reliable availability of a responsive and sensitive mother is more fundamental to satisfactory personality development than conventional issues concerning feeding, weaning, and toilet training. We can now explore in detail the psychopathology associated with the various deviations in maternal care which attachment workers have shown to be significant.

© 1991 Juliet Hopkins

REFERENCES

Ainsworth, M.D.S. (1982) 'Attachment: retrospect and prospect', in C.M. Parkes and J. Stevenson-Hinde (eds) *The Place of Attachment in Human Behaviour*, London: Tavistock.

Ainsworth, M.D.S., Blehar, M.C., Waters, E., and Wall, S. (1978) *Patterns of Attachment: A Psychological Study of the Strange Situation*, Hillsdale, N.J.: Lawrence Erlbaum.

Bateson, G., Jackson, D., Haley, J., and Weakland, J. (1956) 'Towards a theory of schizophrenia', *Behavioural Science* 1: 251–64.

Boston, M. and Szur, R. (1983) *Psychotherapy with Severely Deprived Children*, London: Routledge & Kegan Paul.

Bowlby, J. (1982) *Attachment and Loss*, vol. 1: *Attachment*, (2nd ed.), London: Hogarth.

—— (1988) 'Attachment, communication and the therapeutic process', in J. Bowlby *A Secure Base: Clinical Applications of Attachment Theory* (pp. 137–57), London: Routledge, and New York: Basic Books.

Fraiberg, S. (ed.) (1980) *Clinical Studies in Infant Mental Health: The First Year of Life*, London: Tavistock.

—— (1982) 'Pathological defences in infancy', *Psychoanalytic Quarterly* LI: 612–35.

Freud, S. (1915) 'Observations on transference-love', *S.E. 12*, London: Hogarth.

Main, M. (in press) 'Parental aversion to physical contact with the infant: stability, consequences and reasons', in T.B. Brazelton (ed.) *Touch*, New York: International Universities Press.

Main, M. and Goldwyn, R. (1984) 'Predicting rejection of her infant from mother's representation of her own experiences: a preliminary report', *Child Abuse & Neglect, 8*.

Main, M. and Stadtman, J. (1981) 'Infant response to rejection of physical contact by the mother: aggression, avoidance and conflict', *Journal of Child Psychiatry* 20: 292–307.

Main, M. and Weston, D. (1982) 'Avoidance of the attachment figure in infancy: descriptions and interpretations', in C.M. Parkes and J. Stevenson-Hinde (eds) *The Place of Attachment in Human Behaviour*, London: Tavistock.

Tustin, F. (1986) *Autistic Barriers in Neurotic Patients*, London: Karnac.

Winnicott, D.W. (1960) 'Ego distortion in terms of true and false self', in *The Maturational Processes and the Facilitating Environment*, London: Hogarth.

—— (1963a) 'Psychiatric disorder in terms of infantile maturational processes', in *The Maturational Processes and the Facilitating Environment*, London: Hogarth. 1965.

—— (1963b) 'From dependence towards independence in the development of the individual', in *The Maturational Processes and the Facilitating Environment*, London: Hogarth.

—— (1970) 'Residential care as therapy', in C. Winnicott, R. Shepherd, M. Davis (eds) *Deprivation and Deliquency*, London: Tavistock.

Chapter 11

The application of attachment theory to understanding and treatment in family therapy

John Byng-Hall

A father describes his open heart surgery, and states 'I am not frightened of dying'. The therapist exclaims 'I would be!', and, turning towards Simon (aged 8), who is sitting next to his father, says, 'Your father is brave! Do you think he always feels so brave inside?' Simon looks up admiringly at his father and slowly shakes his head with a knowing smile. Father says 'Well, it is not very nice coming round in that operating theatre'. He remembers how upset he was that his wife had not been there when he regained consciousness. She had told him that she had to be with the children; but he has never forgiven her for deserting him in his hour of need. He leans over and gives Simon a cuddle – or was it Simon who was cuddling his father. It is hard to tell. Simon is sitting next to his older brother Jeremy, who is 13. The two sit separating their parents. Mrs X says 'I wonder if it's all this talk of death that is upsetting Jeremy?' Jeremy is so paralysed by obsessional rituals that he cannot get to school, or go to bed at night; he now sits slouching back in his chair, head and shoulders turned away from his father, but looking at the floor – and so also avoiding his mother's gaze. She is hovering over him. He glances up at the therapist to give him a fleeting look of beseeching despair, but says nothing and returns his gaze to a point on the floor.

(The X family: twenty minutes into their first family therapy session.)

INTRODUCTION

John Bowlby had an early influence on family therapy. He wrote one of the first family therapy papers (Bowlby 1949). It is still well worth reading; it captures all the excitement of having discovered a potent new method of helping families. Bowlby saw whole families together when the individual therapy became stuck. He describes how this reduced the tension in the family, and freed the therapy to continue. He had discovered the power of working directly on relationships as they unfold in the room. However, at that time he decided not to develop this form of therapy. Instead he concentrated on the mother–child dyad as this represented a more manageable unit of investigation (Bowlby, personal communication). But he always kept in mind that once the intricacies of a dyadic relationship have been adequately researched the full range of family relationships could, and should, be explored.

The first direct influence that Bowlby had on the origins of family therapy came through John Bell (1961), one of the original pioneers of family therapy, who had heard that Bowlby worked with whole families. Bell then devised a way of doing all the therapy with the whole family present, believing that this was what Bowlby was doing, and not realizing that Bowlby was using it as an adjunct to other approaches.

In practice, family therapists themselves have not, as yet, specifically used attachment theory extensively. Perhaps this is because of their need to think and act beyond the dyadic patterns of interaction which have been the main units of study in attachment theory. For instance, how would the therapist think about the X family's conflicting attachment needs? There is now, however, a growing potential for collaboration between attachment theorists and family therapists. General systems theory (Bertalanffy 1968), which is used by most family therapists, provides a framework for thinking about how dyadic relationships are themselves affected by, and in turn affect, all the other relationships in the family – in short the effect of relationships on relationships. Developmental research is yielding useful results in this area (Emde 1988). Patricia Minuchin (1985) suggests that attachment theory, with its emphasis on the reciprocal nature of relation-ships, represents the theory of child development most compatible with systems theory. She goes on (Minuchin, P. 1988) to elaborate what is required in order to put child development research within a systems theory perspective. Marvin and Stewart (in press) have outlined those aspects of the general systems theory framework within which attachment theory might be studied.

FAMILY SCRIPTS: A MULTI-PERSON CONCEPT

Family therapists need a concept formulation which readily encompasses all the members of the family, beyond dyads or triads. Heard (1982) formulated the concept of an attachment dynamic, with its biological evolutionary roots, which influences all relationships within the family. The concept of family script (Byng-Hall 1985b, 1986, 1988) can also be used. Family scripts are manifest in interaction patterns which are evoked in particular contexts. In this way, family roles appropriate to the context are brought into play, including those of caregiver and careseeker in those situations which activate attachment behaviour, such as potential danger or illness. If the whole family is involved in these situations it will reveal how competing attachment needs are either met or thwarted. Can everyone's attachment needs be met or are some left out, and, if so, what are their responses to that? Is there an appropriate priority given to the younger children, or those in particular need? Mr X's need for his wife in hospital competed with his children's needs, creating a further rift in the marriage by confirming his suspicion that she only loved them, and not him. Or does a parent seek care inappropriately from a child? Simon was his father's comforter, Jeremy was his mother's constant companion. Do other people mediate in an attachment relationship, either facilitating it like a father supporting his wife, or do they hinder? Did the two sons' alliances with each parent undermine the marriage? Family therapy provides an almost unique setting in which to study all these questions. All members of the family are brought together, in the strange situation of a clinic at a point of crisis. Every member's attachment behaviour is likely to be activated by this situation. The therapist is, in addition, given the role of carer and has a brief to explore the significance of what is going on.

Bretherton (1985) suggested that the concept of an event script might be used to understand the mental representation of attachment behaviour. She describes (p. 32) event scripts (or schemas) as dynamic frameworks containing information on the who, what, when, where, why, and how of events such as daily separations and reunions. Such scripts are usually constructed through repeated experience of similar scenarios, and so can then be used to predict the next step in the usual sequence of interactions. Of course all events which are part of attachment behaviour are observed by other members of the family. Thus everyone in the family, depending on their developmental phase, constructs scripts for all the family attachments, even those in which they are not centrally involved. These attachment scripts will also include rules about when, and how, other people get involved at points of stress in a relationship – say, when there is tension in the marriage.

Although each person's script for the family attachments will differ in some ways, especially in the significance each gives to the shared scenarios, there will be a measure of agreement about the way they unfold. It is the overlapping reciprocal nature of each person's script that enables family members to co-ordinate their behaviour. A shared script provides a mutually held working model of how all the various attachments operate; this allows for members to move into roles vacated by absentees – say, when elder siblings take over looking after younger children if their parents are away.

As we know from the research, the pattern of attachment often differs from relationship to relationship, some being secure and others insecure. Large numbers of individuals must know from experience, or observation, about more than one attachment pattern; but, despite this knowledge of the whole pattern, each particular relationship seems to remain remarkably stable over time (Main *et al.* 1985; Grossmann and Grossmann this volume), and it seems to be the child–mother (or main attachment figure) pattern which determines the child's mental representation of attachments at age 6 (Main *et al.* 1985). But can there be any transfer of patterns from one relationship to another, or learning of patterns that are new to the family, and, if so, in what circumstances, and what will ensure that a new pattern is maintained? These are the key questions for family therapists.

Clinical experience, in contrast to the research evidence for the continuity of pattern in non-clinic families (Main *et al.* 1985), suggests that quite dramatic switches can occur, during therapy anyway: say, a peripheral father may become close to his child, apparently for the first time, while the child's relationship with his mother is modified from a clinging insecure–resistant to a more secure, relaxed style – which seems to be more likely to occur if mother's relationship with someone else, say her mother or husband, also changes. Systems theory states that every relationship has some influence on every other relationship. Indeed, this is one of the main reasons for including all the family in the family therapy sessions. Simultaneous changes in the whole pattern seem to be easier to achieve and to maintain than changing one at a time.

Family therapists nevertheless do encounter resistance to their attempts to get families to relate differently. Many concepts, such as homeostasis, are used to explain this. Attachment theory may offer further explanations. After a shift in the pattern of relationships no-one should feel left out, or end up with less, or no, access to an attachment figure. If that happens he or she may escalate attachment behaviour and pull the whole system back to the status quo. Therapeutic moves that are successful in altering the whole pattern of relationships are often those that make sure that everyone, including 'well' siblings, benefit from the changes.

If a normal family transition, such as a child growing up and leaving home, threatens to reduce the availability of attachment figures for those still in need of them, it may halt the process and jeopardize the developmental steps that would have taken place. This is especially likely to happen if a parent's, or grandparent's, or even a sibling's, attachment needs have been overly met by the child who has grown up. This situation is frequently encountered by family therapists, who call this form of role reversal 'parentification'. The families themselves often perceive the child as being unable to leave, rather than recognizing that the parents also find it difficult to let their child go. The therapist's role is to unravel the reciprocal nature of the bond, and to help the potentially bereft person find alternative ways of dealing with his or her attachment needs.

Family scripts can be likened to a play in which every member of the cast has a copy of the script and plays a particular role, while the plot illustrates how and why the various relationships intertwine during the performance. Knowledge about scripts then can be gained from either observing the interaction and making inferences about its underlying models, or by interviewing individual members. How script theory can be related to attachment behaviour is illustrated by Main and her coworkers. Main *et al.* (1985) have devised an Adult Interview with a parent which measures the parent's mental representation of attachments and their emotional significance. This is analogous to a personal script for attachments. The pattern of interaction which results from activation of both a parent's and child's attachment behavioral systems is analogous to the enactment of the attachment script for that dyad, and allocates caregiving and careseeking roles. A family attachment script includes the interplay between all attachment relationships, which includes the way caregiving and careseeking roles are shared around, as well as each person's mental representation of how that works in practice.

SCRIPTS AS GOAL-CORRECTED SYSTEMS – IMPLICATIONS FOR BASIC GOALS OF THERAPY

Clinicians find conceptual models that are simple enough to use during a complicated family session very useful, even if they cannot do justice to all the complex research data. The concept of a goal-corrected system helps to bring meaning to much behaviour which otherwise may seem fragmented and purposeless. Both attachment theory (Bowlby 1969) and script theory (Schank and Abelson 1977) use the concept of goal-corrected control systems. A script has a particular goal and plans to achieve that goal. It also has subgoals, each with its own subplan, *en route* to achieving that plan. Using script theory the attachment and exploratory behavioural system can be described as operating in the following way.

The overall goal of the attachment system is to attain as secure a base as possible from which exploration can be undertaken (Ainsworth 1967; Ainsworth *et al.* 1978). The pair of interacting systems can then be seen as working with two subgoals, the first of which has to be reached before the second can be achieved. The first subgoal is safety in the presence of potential danger. The plan is to gain proximity rapidly so that any potential danger can be assessed and tackled in the presence of someone perceived as stronger and wiser. Danger can come either from outside or inside the family – say, when anger flares. In each case seeking or maintaining proximity while tackling the danger is potentially an adaptive response. Emergency action can be taken to remove the danger, either by moving away from an outside threat or cooling tempers inside the family.

When any danger has been tackled, and if routes to proximity have been reliably established, the second subgoal – that of exploration – can be brought into action. Exploration can occur when members of the family are either together or apart. When together it takes place both in improvising fresh ways of relating – including exploring ways that do not create dangerous tensions – and through the exchange of ideas. Secure attachments are thus potentially self-maintaining, in that difficulties and dangers within the relationship itself are constantly being tackled and new solutions explored.

Of course, dangers or difficulties emanating from within the family are more likely than outside dangers to disrupt this problem-solving mechanism. Family members may develop mutually-protective scripts which include both safety and defensive scripts. Safety scripts include those developed to prevent violence – in which the protagonists are either withdrawn from each other, or other members intervene – or those scripts which prevent over-intimate intrusive behaviour by distancing the participants from each other. Defensive scripts act to reduce intolerable emotion, or memories, from being evoked.

Mutually protective scripts may, when appropriately applied, make the family a safer place. On the other hand the form that protective scripts take, or the vigour with which they are applied, may hinder resolution of conflict or create additional difficulties, especially for particular members of the family. This renders the family no longer capable of providing a safe base for exploration for all its members.

One value to the clinician of this much-simplified conceptual framework is that it provides some goals for family therapy. It follows that the therapist's overall aim is to help the family to establish their own sufficiently secure attachment pattern so that they can resolve problems for themselves when they arise. Part of the therapeutic plan will be to help the family adjust its mutually protective mechanisms to facilitate this process. This is intended to be a recipe for future, as well as current, mental health.

Those aspects of the therapy with the X family that are relevant to attachment theory will be used to illustrate some of the steps taken to reach this goal. A detailed case study of this family, illustrating the whole family script, has been published elsewhere (Byng-Hall 1986).

START OF THERAPY

At first the therapist uses the fact that the family has sought him or her out as someone perceived as stronger (emotionally) and wiser (i.e. a temporary attachment figure) who might provide a secure enough base from which they can explore their own attachments. I try to see families as soon as possible. I ring the family to make the first appointment, making at least 20 minutes available to establish contact if that is needed. This telephone call is really the first session and can make it more likely that the family will all come to the first session, since a relationship has already begun to be established. If one can find out how each member of the family is involved with the symptom, and convey that understanding to the person with whom one is in conversation, it is then easier to persuade him or her that all of them should come.

In the case of the X family, Mr X rang me about Jeremy's obsessional symptoms. He said that he was terrified that he would get so angry with Jeremy that it would kill him (the father), explaining that he had had heart surgery a year ago following a coronary. An appointment was offered for a week later. Mr X rang in a state of anxiety several times before the session. He had already established something of a relationship with me by the time they arrived.

I try to make warm contact with each member of the family in the first few minutes of the first session, and try to make sure that each has felt that his or her predicament has been appreciated by the end of the session. I make the first session long enough – $1^{1}/_{2}$ to 2 hours – to get in touch with the pain of the family. This is the most important part of the formation of a therapeutic attachment. The distress arouses attachment behaviour and also opens up the possibility of new forms of caring being fostered within the family itself.

Within the first few minutes of the first session Mr X told me that when Jeremy would refuse to go to bed, he himself would insist and would get very angry with Jeremy when he would not do as he was told, but his wife would then give in to Jeremy's entreaties to continue his rituals a little longer. He and his wife would then have a row about it; finally, in exasperation, he would be violent to Jeremy, only to regret it soon afterwards. This account indicated the way the family script was enacted.

The therapist must help the family to define what the real dangers are and take appropriate action. An early exploration of the family's worst fears can be fruitful. It is often a revelation to all concerned to discover what other member's terrors are. Some, of course, may be well founded; other anxieties may be allayed when their true roots are discovered. In the X family, exploring each person's fears served a double purpose since I could establish a link with each member and empathize with his or her own particular worries.

I said that the family was probably used to father's losing his temper, but what were their very worst fears? What catastrophes did they imagine? A number of these were elicited. I knew already that they feared that father might die if he got angry; but I also discovered that they feared that he might kill his wife, or kill Jeremy; or send Jeremy, or both Jeremy and his 8-year-old brother Simon, into care; he might also divorce his wife, and he might leave. All of these fears had been voiced in threats made by Mr X. Although Mrs X said that she did not think he would carry out his threats, it took time to help the family assess their meaning and the degree of risk involved. I asked Mr X's cardiologist how serious his heart condition was, but my reporting back in the next session that neither anger nor anxiety were dangerous emotions for him did not reduce the family panic about his getting upset.

The therapist has to be clearly in charge and respond rapidly and appropriately if the situation is indeed potentially dangerous. This entails that in the case of out-of-control behaviour, a very common situation at the beginning of therapy, the therapist has to help the family to regain control. As we know from attachment theory it is only when the situation feels sufficiently safe that it will be possible to start fully exploring the reasons behind the problem. A great deal of time is wasted if this aspect of attachment theory is not appreciated. Indeed, many families or patients drop out of therapy because they do not feel secure. A clever interpretation may help the family to feel that the therapist knows what he is doing, but it soon loses its magic if frightening escalations persist. Family therapy has a number of techniques available which can help to restore control (e.g. structural family therapy – see Minuchin, S. (1974)) and for reducing symptoms. It was only possible for the X family to take in and use the good news about father's heart when their interactions were less explosive. The threat of father's dying, real enough in itself, had in addition been used as one way of trying to halt frightening escalations. The use of a threat that a child's behaviour will lead to the death of a parent as a method of controlling children's behaviour has been discussed by Bowlby (1973).

INSECURE ATTACHMENT SCRIPTS – PAST AND PRESENT – WHICH CREATE DISTANCE CONFLICTS

Clinicians know the complicated way in which closeness in one relationship may affect the distance in other relationships. Jeremy's rituals kept his mother by his side. He was at home all day and she often slept on Jeremy's bed at night as it seemed the only way to get him to sleep. Part of Mr X's fury arose from his wife's not coming to bed with him. This story can be told another way; the marriage had many difficulties, made much worse by the fear that sex might kill Mr X, so mother's staying the night with Jeremy reduced everyone's anxiety and also met Mrs X's attachment needs. Clearly, all these relationships are interdependent, as systems theory would predict. To start from one point – either the anxious child or the rocky marriage – is to address only half the story, and is called linear thinking in systems theory terminology. Linear thinking leads to therapeutic endeavours aimed at one point in what in fact is a circular, recursive causal chain. This thinking is likely to suggest only half a solution: fix either the child or the marriage. A far more fruitful approach is to intervene in the whole circular process. The concept of family distance regulation (Kantor and Lehr 1977; Byng-Hall and Campbell 1981) allows the distance pattern to be considered.

To illustrate the complexities of distance regulation let us consider the situation in which attachment behaviour is aroused when the available attachment figure is also a source of anxiety. For instance, Mrs X was highly unpredictable in her responses to Jeremy, switched from protective, to highly intrusive, to rejecting – she was once heard to mutter that she also felt like killing him. In this situation the goals of the two distance scripts – one to get close to, the other to withdraw from, the attachment figure – are at odds. This creates a classical approach/avoidance conflict. Exploratory behaviour is restricted because proximity does not provide a sufficiently safe base, and when separated the child is constantly worrying about whether his mother will desert or not. If this becomes a long-standing state of affairs it is reminiscent of Ainsworth's category of the insecure–ambivalent attachment pattern (C). Movements towards and movements away from mother can both be observed in the reunion of mother and child after a brief separation in the Strange Situation test. Both withdrawal and attachment scripts are activated simultaneously and elements of each activity appear at different moments. These scripts are shared as mother, as well as her child, will at times withdraw, and push her child away, but use her child as an attachment figure at other times.

Another strategy for reducing the intensity of the approach/avoidance conflict is for the individuals to inhibit attachment behaviour in inter-personal contexts in which it should be highly activated, for example on reunion of child and parent in the Strange Situation test when the child turns away from the mother on reunion, often towards an object. This is typical of an insecure–avoidant pattern of attachment (Ainsworth's A classification). Thus one component of the behaviour which is likely to lead to a rebound is reduced: i.e. clinging, which in the past has been found to lead to an angry withdrawal on the part of the caregiver. Main and Weston (1982) postulate that this strategy, although maladaptive in most ways, may have the advantage for the child of not alienating a potentially rejecting parent when being collected by her. If this is correct, it represents a 'safety' script.

Avoidant patterns of behaviour (Category A) can also be conceptual-ized as being 'defensive' scripts because unpleasant affect is avoided. Bowlby (1980) discusses the mechanism of defensive exclusion in which cues that might evoke unpleasant memories and emotions are excluded from consciousness. Main et al. (1985) showed that parents who have either lost touch with the memories of painful attachment experiences in their childhood, or, if they have retained the memory, have detached the appropriate affect from those memories, have children who have de-veloped insecure attachments to them. Defensive exclusion renders the parent insensitive to his or her child's painful attachment experiences, and both participants come to avoid closeness which exposes them to the possibility of painful rejections.

In clinical practice those parents whose own parents were unsatisfactory show either a heightened vigilant awareness, in which they try desperately to prevent what happened to them as children from happening to their children when they reach a similar age (what can be called a corrective trans-generational script), or their memories are blunted and sensitivity to what is going on is reduced, but their behaviour is, nevertheless, based on the assumption that the same thing is about to happen. This often works as a self-fulfilling prophecy (a so-called replicative trans-generational script). When any of these memories are about traumatic separations they are likely to affect current attachment patterns, as attachment research has shown (Main *et al.* 1985).

Mr X described how his father had had a stroke when Mr X was 8 years old, and how he had been like a vegetable for many years. His older brother took over the role of father, but, when Mr X was 14, his brother died suddenly of a coronary, and Mr X found himself, as the only surviving son, having to look after the family (a tradition in his Arabic culture). His panic about his health (he thought at first that he had had a stroke when he had his coronary) was now understandable, especially as he had one son aged 8 and another rising 14. But his desperate efforts to turn Jeremy into an adult, which included making out his will to him, in preparation to his taking over, were rebounding; Jeremy was acting younger than his age.

Mrs X described, without any affect, how her father had left home and she and her twin brother had been put into a children's home when they were 3. Both were adopted aged 6, but she was 'thrown out' of home when she was a teenager while her brother was kept in the family, much, she said, to her fury. So all the nightmares of her past were now being echoed in her husband's threats: break-up of the marriage, both children going to a children's home, or one child being rejected. Also, there had almost certainly been some violence in her own childhood, of which she has no memory. Why otherwise would she and her brother have been put into care? If so, this was now being re-enacted in the violence towards Jeremy. The mechanisms by which she had played a part in recreating her own worst nightmares are fascinating and complex. Suffice it to say that it was an enormous relief to the whole family to discover why there was such an intense reaction to what was going on.

One of the advantages of the concept of a family script is that it allows for the idea that each individual could theoretically have a script that includes all of the following: avoidant withdrawal, resistant pushing away, clinging attachment, and secure attachment, enacting each aspect of it with particular members of the family. Also, if one style of attachment is manifest in one relationship then it may reduce its intensity in another. Jeremy had a distant relationship with his father and a clinging relationship with his mother. At one point in the therapy this seemed to reverse, Jeremy becoming closer to father and distant to mother, and towards the end of therapy he was much more securely attached to both, indicating that each style was latent in both relationships once the scripting from the past had lost its power, and a new developmental experience had been provided.

Distance regulation in 'too close / too far' systems

In terms of distance regulation an approach/avoidance conflict can be called a 'too far/too close' system (Byng-Hall 1980) which is potentially unstable in a dyad in which each sees the other as being as powerful as, or more powerful than, the self. Each then feels compelled to take very active measures to prevent the other from either approaching too close, or deserting altogether. If this does not seem to work then even-greater efforts, on each participant's part, are felt to be needed to prevent the other from forcing an intolerable situation on an unwilling victim. There is then the possibility of a symmetrically escalating conflict, in which each move away from, or towards, is resisted with increasing force. This is in contrast to a complementary system in which, say, a caregiver can see herself as the stronger one needing to accommodate to the more vulnerable careseeker's needs for proximity or distance, even if those demands are unwelcome at the time. In this conflict of interests one person is likely to give way to the other in a de-escalating cycle.

The most obvious examples of symmetrical escalations are to be found in dyads of the same generation, spouses or siblings. But not infrequently, a child is scripted as an adult figure in the parent's script. Indeed the child may be seen as a parent of the parent, i.e. his or her own grandparent: a 'parental child' in family therapy terminology. This role reversal is very common and highly damaging to a child's emotional development. It is also highly dangerous in a symmetrically escalating distance conflict. A young isolated mother, perhaps battered herself as a child, and who hopes finally to get some decent mothering herself from her baby, i.e. has cast the baby as her mother, then may see her own screaming child as a monstrous nightmare 'mother' out to attack her. She cannot escape and the violence rapidly escalates. This quite common scenario illustrates how a script is more likely to be acted out if a number of factors are present at a time – in this case a replicative script of her mother's battering, role reversal, and isolation. Bowlby (1985) discusses the role of attachment behaviour in family violence.

Despite the multiple factors involved it is worth considering the detailed mechanism of a symmetrical escalation. Any move – either towards or away from each other – only makes matters even worse. The withdrawal and attachment scripts each become increasingly activated by the other. In cybernetic terms this is called a mutually positive feedback system which, if unchecked, can lead to escalating activity – known, appropriately, as 'runaways' – which potentially leads to the destruction of the system; in the present case it could end in violence or separation or both. Hoffman

(1971) calls these escalations 'irresistible runs', but also notes that in practice they are almost always aborted before the final potential catastrophe befalls the relationship. How are they aborted? There are many mechanisms which may be involved but the impact of other people on what is going on will be explored here.

At the point of a potential escalation of an approach/avoidance conflict a third person, or group of people, may try to stop it. A third person is particularly likely to intervene as a 'go-between' if either, or both, of the protagonists are important figures for him or her – say, a child responding to difficulties in an executive dyad in the family. An executive dyad is that couple which is central to the running of the family – say, parents or cohabitees, but not infrequently a mother and grandmother, or mother and eldest child, etc. Whether or not this is appropriate, each member of the dyad is on a par in terms of potential power, and thus they are subject to symmetrical escalations. If this 'management' dyad breaks down the children fear that it may be disastrous. An escalating conflict is often also extremely frightening to the protagonists, who find that every effort each of them makes only exacerbates the situation. Both are likely to welcome the intervention which calms things down. Everyone then gains something from a halt in the destructive escalations.

The go-between or distance regulator may then be repeatedly recruited into the re-enactment of a mutually protective script in which, whenever the tension between two people rises, he or she will intervene, perhaps by creating a distraction, or drawing the anger onto him(/her)self. The script may then generalize. The content and details of the re-enactment may differ, family members may change roles, and new recruits to the role of go-between may be found such as another child, an in-law, lover, or therapist, but the basic plot of the script for handling approach/avoidance conflicts is made available to be replayed whenever and wherever it appears in the family. Jeremy intervened in his parents' tensions, as did Simon and Mr X's 90-year-old mother. Mr X and Jeremy also had symmetrical battles when Mr X treated him as an adult – Mrs X then intervened, etc.

Children as distance regulators in their parents' marriages

In clinical practice there are many ways in which a 'too close / too far' system is manifest: for instance, in a marital couple who are afraid of intimacy, but who are also afraid of losing each other, which is a rather common marital situation (Byng-Hall 1985a). The Xs' marriage could be described in this way. First, Mr X felt abandoned after his operation, while his wife feared losing him – their relationship was threatened. A child such as Jeremy, who in such a situation develops a symptom, may provoke caregiving responses from both parents which bring them together to look after him, but in a non-intimate – and hence safe – way. But it was also too close – they were frightened of sex and violence when together. Jeremy's symptoms, however, not only brought them together but also drove a wedge between them. He had become the distance regulator to both the too-close and the too-distant aspects of his parents' relationship.

Most children carry a degree of ambivalence for their parents' marriage which makes them ideal recruits to the role of go-between; they want parents to stay together but also enjoy occasions when they can get one parent to themselves. The child's ambivalent behaviour may receive positive feedback from parents who feel some relief at finding that it decreases their own escalating conflicts. No wonder these children develop symptoms as they become torn apart, pulled this way and that by their parents' toing and froing. A further development of this scenario is an ever-closer coalition between a child and one parent, say the parent of the opposite sex, as in the case of Jeremy and his mother. This of course lies behind the concept of the Oedipal triangle in psychoanalytic theorizing, the extreme form of which leads to child sexual abuse. A daughter's sexual relationship with her father, or step-father, may be what keeps him in the family but it also threatens to oust the father, especially if she discloses what is going on.

The form of the symptoms may symbolize the nature of the distance regulator's dilemmas. I said that the symptoms were Jeremy's way of making him feel safe. One of his rituals was to run up stairs for a specific number of steps, and then down again. This, I said, showed his difficulty in deciding whether to obey his father and grow up, or his mother, and stay a child. Another ritual involved stepping from foot to foot. This I said represented the same dilemma, should he move towards his mother or his father? Performing each ritual helped him to avoid taking sides and thus being disloyal to one or the other. Having defined them as having some good understandable purpose I was able to say that he should go on doing it, except that he should pick a time before bedtime and do it in an even more vigorous way. I also said that he needed his parents' support and so both his mother and father should spend time afterwards with Jeremy. This enabled Jeremy to stop his symptoms almost completely.

I had noticed that Jeremy's symptoms increased if his father told him to stop them, in a symmetrical escalation. In the above intervention I interrupted the escalation by reversing the direction of the usual injunctions, a technique known as paradoxical injunction. And I had made sense of his rituals; up till then they were seen as evidence of madness. Finally, I had put his parents on the same side, in which they both supported Jeremy, and could not start up their perennial row precipitated by father telling Jeremy to stop; the official line was now that he should continue them.

Another frequent finding is that siblings can take on different roles in each aspect of the distance regulations: one keeping the peace, the other splitting the parents. This almost always leads to conflict between the siblings. Jeremy did more of the dividing of his parents; Simon had a warmer relationship with each, and they could come together over him more easily. The sibling fights were monumental, especially when Jeremy felt that his brother was being favoured. Many other people may also become involved: therapists, lovers, groups of workers, etc., all lining themselves up on one side or another and disagreeing. Mr X's mother, aged 90, as well as Simon, used to intervene on Mr X's side, while Jeremy went to his mother's rescue whenever the couple came into conflict. In all these cases the intensity of the original couple's split loses some of its immediacy and the conflict is played out by proxy in other relationships as well. Work to help the brothers to stop fighting or acting, along with Mrs X senior, as go-betweens was needed, before work with the marriage was felt to be necessary by the parents.

SOME USES OF SPACE AND TIME IN THERAPY

Seating arrangements can provide important cues about closeness and distance. In the first session the children sat dividing their parents. This had to be altered. In structural family therapy (Minuchin, S. 1974) seating arrangements are used to facilitate changes in the family structure. At one time I moved the children out from sitting between their parents, and, arranging for the parents to sit facing each other, I asked them to decide what to do about Jeremy. I blocked all the children's attempts to interrupt their discussion. In short I took over the role of distance regulator from the children, who, observing that I could be trusted with this job and that I did not allow any violence to erupt, went off to play. This placed a boundary around the marital subsystem.

I further strengthened this boundary by seeing the couple together on their own, and working on ways for them to de-escalate their own distance conflicts. I used space to explore their different distance thresholds by asking them to stand up and walk towards each other, indicating at what point they felt uncomfortable. I helped them to see that when either of them pushed away it was not necessarily the first sign of a rejection but could be an automatic adjustment to make the correct space for their particular cultural and family background.

I start by seeing the family every week if possible, but after four to six sessions reduce the frequency to once a month and then once every 3 months or so. The average number of sessions is between eight and fourteen, spread out eventually to cover 2 to 3 years. This early intensity allows for the attachment to be made and important issues to be opened up, the decrease thereafter helps to ensure that the family turns to itself to find support and to solve problems. At the end of therapy I tell the family that I am available at the clinic, suggesting that they give me a ring if anyone wants to talk about something. The Xs kept me in touch with Jeremy's excellent progress by sending cards.

In the latter part of therapy, and after termination, I become like a non-intrusive grandparent or extended family member, available if needed. I think the 'grandparent' role is enormously important in what it can do to either support, or undermine, attachments of parents to their children. For this reason I try to involve grandparents whenever possible in the work at some point. The extended family is also part of the 'safe base'.

CONCLUSION

Clinical experience suggests that attachment patterns can become more secure. How does this happen? Research shows that good parent–child communication is the hallmark of secure attachments. If the parent can perceive and respond to the attachment cues of his or her children then an appropriate response is made possible. If for some reason these communications are excluded, contradicted, or misdirected by maladaptive protective scripts the secure base is undermined. Family therapists have an opportunity to work on the communications about attachment needs as they occur in the room. He or she can provide a base in which it is safe enough for the members of the family to reconnect with old memories that are resonating with current themes. It is then possible to provide a new experience of being understood and responded to, both by the therapist and other members of the family. The family therapist strives, not only for changes in behaviour, but also for interactional awareness (Byng-Hall 1986). Interactional awareness involves each member's being aware of the nature and significance of the interaction, including attachment behaviour, and how it is affecting everyone; it also includes some insight into one's own contribution to what is going on, and some sense that that input can be changed. Members of the family then have the possibility of creating new forms, and hence new working models, of attachment/exploratory behaviour. This is different to a pure insight approach. Family attachments are both understood and enacted in a more secure way.

© 1991 John Byng-Hall

REFERENCES

Ainsworth, M.D.S. (1967) *Infancy in Uganda: Infant Care and Growth of Love*, Baltimore: The Johns Hopkins Press.

Ainsworth, M.D.A., Blehar, R.M.C., Waters, E., and Wall, S. (1978) *Patterns of Attachment: A Psychological Study of the Strange Situation*, Hillsdale, N.J.: Erlbaum.

Bell, J.E. (1961) *Family Group Therapy*, Public Health Monograph No. 64, US Dept. of Health, Education and Welfare.

Bertalanffy, L. von (1968) *General Systems Theory*, New York: George Braziller.

Bowlby, J. (1949) 'The study and reduction of group tension in the family', *Human Relations* 2: 123.

—— (1969) *Attachment and Loss*, vol. 1: *Attachment* (2nd edn 1982) London: Hogarth, and New York: Basic Books.

—— (1973) *Attachment and Loss*, vol. 2: *Separation: Anxiety and Anger*, London: Hogarth, and New York: Basic Books.

—— (1980) *Attachment and Loss*, vol. 3: *Loss: Sadness and Depression*, London: Hogarth, and New York: Basic Books.

—— (1985) 'Violence in the family', *American Journal of Psychoanalysis*, 44: 9–27. Reprinted in Bowlby, J. (1988) *A Secure Base*, London: Routledge; 2nd edn New York: Basic Books.

Bretherton, I. (1985) 'Attachment Theory: retrospect and prospect', in *Monographs of the Society for Research in Child Development*, Serial No. 209, 50 (1–2), The University of Chicago Press.

Byng-Hall, J. (1980) 'The symptom bearer as marital distance regulator: clinical implications', *Family Process* 19: 355–65.

—— (1985a) 'Resolving distance conflicts', in A. Gurman (ed.) *Casebook of Marital Therapy*, New York: Guilford Press.

—— (1985b) 'The family script: a useful bridge between theory and practice', *Journal of Family Therapy* 7: 301–5.

—— (1986) 'Family scripts: a concept which can bridge child psychotherapy and family therapy thinking', *Journal of Child Psychotherapy* 12 (2): 3–13.

—— (1988) 'Scripts and legends in families and family therapy', *Family Process* 27: 167–79.

Byng-Hall, J. and Campbell, D.S. (1981) 'Resolving conflicts in distance regulation: an integrative approach', *Journal of Marital and Family Therapy* 7: 321–30.

Emde, R.N. (1988) 'The effects of relationships on relationships: a developmental approach to clinical intervention', in R.A. Hinde and J. Stevenson-Hinde (eds) *Relationships within Families*, Oxford Science Publications.

Heard, D. (1982) 'Family systems and the attachment dynamic', *Journal of Family Therapy* 4 (2): 99–116.

Hoffman, L. (1971) 'Deviation amplifying processes in natural groups', in J. Haley (ed.) *Changing Families: A Family Therapy Reader*, New York: Grune & Stratton.

Kantor, D. and Lehr, W. (1977) *Inside the Family*, San Francisco: Jossey-Bass.

Main, M., Kaplan, N., and Cassidy, J. (1985) 'Security in infancy, childhood, and adulthood: a move to the level of representation', in *Monographs of the Society for Research in Child Development*, Serial No. 209, 50 (1–2), The University of Chicago Press.

Main, M. and Weston, D.R. (1982) 'Avoidance of the attachment figure in infancy: description and interpretations', in C.M. Parkes and J. Stevenson-Hinde (eds) *The Place of Attachment in Human Behaviour*, London: Tavistock Publications.

Marvin, R.S. and Stewart, R.B. (in press) 'A family systems framework for the study of attachment', in M. Greenberg, D.Cicchetti, and E.M. Cummings (eds) *Attachment in the Preschool Years: Research and Intervention*, University of Chicago Press.

Minuchin, P. (1985) 'Families and individual development: provocations from the field of family therapy', *Child Development* 56: 289–302.

—— (1988) 'Relationships within the family: a systems perspective on development', in R.A. Hinde and J. Stevenson-Hinde (eds) *Relationships within Families*, Oxford Science Publications.

Minuchin, S. (1974) *Families and Family Therapy*, Boston: Harvard Press, and London: Tavistock.
Schank, R.S. and Abelson, R.P. (1977) *Scripts, Plans, Goals and Understanding*, Hillsdale, N.J.: Erlbaum.

Chapter 12

Insecure attachment and agoraphobia

Giovanni Liotti

In this paper I set out to explain cognitive and behavioral aspects of agoraphobia in terms of attachment, and to examine the developmental history of agoraphobic patients in the light of attachment theory. I hope to shed light upon the etiology of a common disorder (agoraphobia is estimated to afflict between 1 and 6 per cent of the adult population (Reich 1986; Robins *et al.* 1984)) and to help clinicians dealing with agoraphobic patients to devise effective therapeutic strategies.

The generalizations concerning agoraphobics' behavior, cognition, and developmental history which the reader will find in this paper come when not otherwise indicated in the text, from a pool of data provided by 31 agoraphobic patients personally interviewed or whose treatment has been supervised by this writer in the course of 15 years of clinical work. Age ranged from 21 to 54 years, and 20 patients were female. This sample overlaps partially with a wider one (over one hundred patients) treated by six cognitive psychotherapists interested in the clinical applications of attachment theory. The composition and demographic features of this wider sample are described in a book on the cognitive and developmental aspects of emotional disorders (Guidano and Liotti 1983: 204–42 and 321–2).

ABNORMAL ATTACHMENT BEHAVIOR IN AGORAPHOBIA

Agoraphobics seem to have lost the ability to tolerate temporary and explicable separations from attachment figures – an ability that distinguishes adult attachment from attachment in childhood (Weiss 1982: 173). These patients typically avoid, or tend to avoid, staying alone, either in public places or in their own home. In moderately severe cases, the patient will stay alone at home only when a trusted member of the family can be called back easily. In more severe cases, the partial availability of a protective figure is insufficient, and nothing less than having a familiar person within immediate reach assuages the patient's anxiety.

Agoraphobics are usually distressed when they find themselves in daily situations which are objectively safe but where a quick escape to a familiar place is difficult or impossible. Thus, they become anxious when they join a queue in a store or in a public office, find themselves trapped in a traffic jam, sit in a barber's or a beautician's chair, or travel on a motorway where it is impossible to turn around (see e.g., Guidano and Liotti 1983: 205). The distress experienced by the patients in these situations is terminated only when they regain the possibility of freely moving toward a nearby place of safety, such as their own home, a friend's house, or their doctor's office.

These clinical features of agoraphobia are the main targets of any explanation of the syndrome based on attachment theory (see, e.g., Bowlby 1973: 292–312). There is, however, another and more subtle feature of agoraphobia that may be usefully approached from the point of view of attachment theory: agoraphobics find it difficult to attribute meaning to emotions related to threatened separation from a significant other. This feature, that may not be immediately apparent as the result of standard clinical interviews, can be assessed by confronting two kinds of information: that concerning the state of the patient's interpersonal relationships at the onset of the syndrome, and that related to the causal attributions of their symptoms which agoraphobics typically provide in the course of any accurate clinical interview.

THE ONSET OF AGORAPHOBIA

It is a widely diffused impression, among psychotherapists and researchers, that the onset of agoraphobia may be related to life events that imply changes or expected changes in the network of the patient's affectional bonds (Guidano and Liotti 1983; Tearnan *et al.* 1984). Wolpe, for instance, stated that, among the agoraphobics he had treated, the commonest antecedent of the first fear reactions to brief situations of physical loneliness was the presence of unfulfilled fantasies of liberation from an unhappy marriage. These fantasies remained unfulfilled precisely because they evoked great fear of loneliness (Wolpe 1976: 161). Other interpersonal problems that appear to be temporally and, very likely, also causally related to the onset of panic attacks and/or of agoraphobic avoidance behavior are threats of loss or of separation from parents or spouse, marital quarrels, and perceived rejection from a beloved person (Bowen and Kohout 1979; Chambless and Goldstein 1981; Hafner 1977, 1979; Liotti and Guidano 1976; Roberts 1964; Shafar 1976).

Many agoraphobics do not acknowledge the possibility of a relationship between these changes or prospective changes in their life and the appearance of their phobic disturbance, and insist that their distress is the result of some morbid process that could not possibly be related to their interpersonal life. Even those who do acknowledge that their interpersonal difficulties may be related to their phobic anxieties, are unable consistently to deal with this anxiety as one may be expected to deal with a meaningful personal emotion. Most agoraphobics, in other words, attribute their painful feelings to an impending illness – either a somatic or a mental illness, but in any case an *illness*, that is, a process utterly alien to their experience of the Self (see, e.g., Guidano and Liotti 1983).

The following clinical vignette illustrates a typical interpersonal context in which many cases of agoraphobia take their onset, and the meaning that patients attribute to their emotional experience in such a context.

Mary B., after three years of marriage, accepted the courtship of a colleague of hers. She felt that a brief relationship with her suitor could be pleasant, and unthreatening to her solid, happy marriage. She kept the affair secret for a while, but then felt the need to be sincere to her husband, together with the fear that a confession could bring her marriage to an end. When Mrs B. eventually decided to inform her husband of her extramarital relationship, she was at first pleasantly affected by his understanding and his willingness to save their marriage, but shortly thereafter experienced a panic attack while coming home from work. For the next few days she awoke with uncanny feelings of depersonalization. She interpreted the panic attack and the frightening feelings of depersonalization as the signs of a mental illness. She quickly developed full-blown agoraphobic behavior. Mrs B., after her husband had declared his wish to save their relationship and before her first panic attack, had for the first time doubted which relationship was more important to her, and had also vaguely considered the possibility of taking the initiative to break her marriage. She, however, found it impossible to relate her vague idea of deserting her husband to the panic attack, the experience of depersonalization, or to the phobic behavior that was now making her require the constant companionship of her husband and compelling her to stay home from work.

The above clinical example illustrates a phenomenon that, according to my experience (Guidano and Liotti 1983, 1985; Liotti 1981, 1986), may be observed in every agoraphobic patient: a blindness to the meaning of a certain class of one's own emotions, so that these emotions, in a certain sense, cease to deserve their psychological status and are transformed into the symptoms of a disease. Emotional experience is reduced to autonomic arousal if we do not make sense of it, and an unexplained autonomic arousal is usually appraised in a negatively biased way (Marshall and Zimbardo 1979; Maslach 1979).

Of course, the blindness to the meaning of one's feelings and actions has been a classic problem of psychopathology and psychotherapy since Freud discovered the possibility of exploring the unconscious meaning of psychiatric symptoms. Attachment theory provides us with a new, elegant, and economic way of approaching this classic problem (Bowlby 1977, 1979, 1980).

MEANING STRUCTURES AND THE EMOTIONS OF ATTACHMENT

According to attachment theory, the behavioral system controlling attachment behavior is operating before we, as children, develop the verbal and cognitive skills that are needed in order to perceive and label emotions as meaningfully related to our own and to other people's behavior. In the early period of life when a child is unable to give verbal labels and to attribute causal relationships to emotions, powerful affects related to the functioning of the attachment system are experienced and encoded into memory schemata. We may conceive of these early memory structures as episodic memories (Tulving 1972), event schemata (Mandler 1983), or emotional schemata. Emotional schemata are the structures of a relatively concrete type of memory processing, and are made up of key perceptual features representing (1) the situations eliciting the emotion, (2) the expressive motor patterns, and (3) the visceral reactions consequent upon these situations (Leventhal 1982). With cognitive growth and the development of language, the early emotional schemata may evolve into more complex meaning structures concerning Self and other people. These semantic structures imply abstraction, generalization, and explicit, verbalizable attribution of causality to feelings and of purpose to behavior.

The cognitive development of the early emotional schemata is regulated by information provided to the child by the caregivers (Lane and Schwartz 1987: 137; Rosen 1985: 62). Children begin acquiring explicit, propositional models of Self and others (Self-schemata: see, e.g., Markus 1977; Markus and Sentis 1982) by *talking* about their emotional experience to their caretakers (Bretherton and Beeghly 1982), who may react with either confirmatory or disconfirming responses. Because of the social influences on the cognitive development of the early emotional schemata, this development can be variously deviated, hindered, or blocked (cf. Bretherton 1985: 33). If, for instance, the caretakers consistently refuse to listen to the child's statements about his/her emotional experience, or force the child to accept interpretations of its meaning and cause that radically to diverge from his/her first-hand experience, a dissocation will ensue in the child's memory. The episodic memories of the emotional experience the child is not allowed to talk about will not be associated with the explicit semantic structures developed through communication with the caregivers. In this case, the early emotional schemata will be segregated in those domains of episodic memory that cannot be easily associated with the verbalizable aspects of self-knowledge. Instances of such a dissociation between episodic memories of the interaction with the caregivers and generalized descriptions of the Self and the attachment figures are being collected by researchers using the Adult Attachment Interview (Main and Goldwyn in press). The parents of many insecurely attached children provide idealized descriptions (semantic memories) of their own parents and/or of their attachment relationships that are in striking contrast with those episodes of their actual interaction with the attachment figures which they are able to recollect (Main *et al.* 1985). These parents do not acknowledge the discrepancy between the idealized descriptions and the painful episodic memories. Their behavior with their children tends to reproduce the painful episodes of their own attachment relationships more than it reflects their idealized version of that relationship. The dissociated episodic memories (or, as we can alternatively name them, the segregated emotional schemata) seem, then, to operate in an automatic and un-conscious way, related to the processing of specific affective stimuli, but unrelated to the attributional processes of causality and meaning that involve semantic structures of a more abstract type.

This writer believes that there is indirect but substantial evidence that agoraphobics have developed, during infancy or preschool years, emotional schemata related to the interpersonal processes of insecure–anxious attachment (Bowlby 1973; Gittelman and Klein 1984; Liotti 1984; Parker 1979; Tearnan *et al.* 1984) and that these schemata have remained disconnected from the propositional structures of Self-knowledge (Guidano and Liotti 1983; Liotti 1981, 1986). If this is the case, it becomes important to assess, during the psychotherapy of agoraphobic patients, the influences that may have brought over the dissociation between the emotional schemata related to an insecure attachment and the meaning structures of adult Self-knowledge.

This disconnection may be the outcome of pressures exerted by the caregivers who, as has been stated above, can regulate the cognitive development of the child's emotional schemata because they have the power of deciding whether or not the child can talk about his or her internal states (feelings, thoughts, memories). Parents, for instance, can easily exert this power by diverting their child's attention from the painful implications of unhappy family relationships in an attempt to make the child unaware of aspects of their life they wish their child to ignore (Bowlby 1979, 1985). This is more likely to happen inside insecure attachment relationships. When the child begins to talk about emotional experiences related to his or her insecure attachments, he or she is likely to do it in a sad, aggressive, or anxious mood (sadness, anxiety, and anger are emotions easily elicited in insecure attachments): the parent to whom the child is so talking is likely to feel guilty, hostile, or otherwise annoyed, and therefore to be motivated to divert the child's attention from the topic.

The disconnection between Self-schemata and emotional schemata related to attachment may also be the by-product of the solutions the patients themselves may have found to the problems posed by a difficult attachment relationship (Liotti 1981, 1986, 1989). In order to avoid the painful rehearsal of the memories of an unpleasant interaction with a parent, or in order to avoid the repetition of this type of interaction, children may learn to avoid situations that will elicit the parent's untoward behavior or will evoke the memory of it. Children, thus, may learn to control their behavior and their thoughts so as to avoid painful situations that are represented in some of their emotional schemata, thereby excluding the information contained in these schemata from further conscious processing. This information, therefore, will not enter into the ongoing development of propositional self-knowledge.

THE PSYCHOTHERAPY OF AGORAPHOBIA ACCORDING TO ATTACHMENT THEORY

Attachment theory, thus, implies that we should explore the agoraphobic's history of attachment, having in mind that the patient may have become blind to the meaning of the corresponding emotions. The aim of this exploration is to assist the patient in developing the knowledge of his/her own emotions and in regaining the ability of understanding their meaning.

Of course, this is not the only goal of the therapeutic intervention. Other important goals are to foster the patient's ability to tolerate temporary separations from the attachment figures, to help him or her conquer freedom of moving about alone, and to assist him or her in clarifying and solving the interpersonal problems that have marked the onset of the syndrome.

In order to reach these goals of treatment, attachment theory suggests that the therapeutic relationship may be so shaped as to function as a secure base for the exploration both of 'inner' and of 'outer' realities (Bowlby 1977). If the therapeutic relationship is perceived as a secure base, the patient may more easily be fostered to explore both the memories of his/her past relationships with the attachment figures (memories that may be very painful), and the aspects of the 'outer world' that have become frightening – for instance, a road in one's town that is at a distance from one's places of security.

The value of the patient's graded self-exposure to feared real-life situations in the treatment of agoraphobia is well established (see, e.g., Cohen *et al.* 1984; Mathews *et al.* 1981: 85–97). For this reason I systematically encourage my agoraphobic patients to expose themselves to the situations they have learned to avoid after the onset of the syndrome. However, I regard 'exploration', rather than 'self-exposure', as a more suitable term to denote the activity I encourage my patients to engage in, since I ask them not only to move about in previously avoided situations, but also to take accurate note of what happens around them, of what they feel, and of their thoughts during the 'exposure'.

The patterns of thought and feeling that are identified during this process of exploratory self-exposure and self-observation are used as raw material, during the therapeutic sessions, for working out a better understanding of the patient's emotions, and of the relationship between his/her emotions and his/her internal dialogue. General representational models of the Self and of other people (Self-schemata) may be thereupon safely inferred. The subsequent therapeutic work is mainly aimed at the recall of reconstruction of the past experiences that have prompted the patient to build up the inferred Self-schemata, and the ways of this construction. Once this reconstruction has been completed, it is usually easy to understand why certain emotions, such as the emotions of attachment, cannot be assimilated to the Self-schemata operating at the onset of the syndrome.

The therapeutic relationship, once shaped according to the idea of the 'secure base', is likely to bring about the activation of the patient's attachment system. Therefore, the therapeutic relationship may provide many occasions for assessing the patients' responses to expected separations from the attachment figure (e.g. before a holiday) and for evaluating their biased perceptions of the therapist's behavior according to the expectations about the attachment figure's behavior deriving from earlier experiences (e.g. the patients may easily construe an innocent piece of the therapist's behavior as a sign of insensitivity, emotional unavailability, proneness to overcontrol their decisions, or intention of abandoning them). Thanks to this direct assessment, the disowned emotions of attachment may be more easily acknowledged by patients, Also, the representations of the attachment figures, provided by early emotional schemata and now tacitly biasing the construing of actual relationships implying attachment (such as the therapeutic one), may be made explicit and become the target of direct corrective interventions.

During the strategic process of psychotherapy, guided by the above-mentioned principles of attachment theory, much information concerning the developmental psychopathology (Bowlby 1988; Cicchetti 1984) of agoraphobia may be collected.

SELF-SCHEMATA IN AGORAPHOBIA

When, encouraged by the therapist, agoraphobics expose themselves to the situations they are afraid of, and observe the thoughts that accompany their anxiety during this exposure, it becomes evident that the threatening self-representations have at their core the possibility of *losing control* of one's behavior. This observation (cf. Guidano and Liotti 1983; Liotti 1981, 1986) allows for the inference that the Self-schemata characterizing the cognitive organization of agoraphobics before the onset of the syndrome stemmed from an overcontrolling attitude toward one's own emotions and behavior. It is not difficult to validate this inference through clinical observations and inquiries (Guidano and Liotti 1983; Liotti 1986).

Self-schemata that are constructed through a premature or excessive exercise of the ability to control the expressions of one's emotions have a disadvantage. The urge to exert control as soon as possible over a given phenomenon, in order to suppress it or modify its course, is largely incompatible with the possibility of carefully exploring that phenomenon. Such schemata, therefore, cannot be instrumental in assimilating the meaning of emotions. Self-control, if it comes before proper self-observation, tends both to become ineffective and to hamper the development of self-knowledge.

Here we find the first level of a possible explanation of the agoraphobics' blindness to the meaning of their phobic anxiety. Self-schemata stemming from an overcontrolling attitude toward one's early emotions of attachment could be responsible for such a blindness. Since these schemata exclude the emotional information related to attachment from conscious processing, they cannot be instrumental in attributing meaning to one's reactions to threats to meaningful relationships – threats that imply the activation of the attachment system.

EARLY PATTERNS OF ATTACHMENT AND THE DEVELOPMENT OF AGORAPHOBIA

What are the conditions for acquiring such an overcontrolling attitude toward one's own emotions of attachment, as to become blind to their meaning once they are evoked by specific life events like those marking the onset of agoraphobia?

I shall approach one possible answer to this question through the study of Mary B.'s case, where I had the opportunity of interviewing her mother at length. I had treated the mother, who suffered from dissociative hysteria (depersonalization disorder, according to the DSM III), several years before she had referred her only daughter to me.

Mary B. was 28 years old when I saw her for the first time. In the course of psychotherapy, I encouraged her to recollect her past experiences of maintaining control over the fear of losing the protection of an attachment figure. In response, she reported three sets of memories. The first theme concerned her mother forcing her to walk in the street alone, when she was 6 years old and was very afraid of doing so. She accepted her mother's argument, that one should overcome one's childish fears, learn to control oneself and be independent. Therefore, the little girl walked in the street alone whenever her mother prompted her to do so. While wandering in the street, she strived to divert her attention from the fear she was experiencing, and found it possible 'to forget her fear' by immersing herself in daydreams. The second set of memories was related to the mother's hysterical disorder. When Mary's mother screamed, dramatically expressed her feelings of depersonalization, threatened to kill herself or stated that she was going mad, Mary was frightened but controlled her fear both because she could not, obviously, expect any attention from her parents (her father was either at work or busy calming his wife) and because she wished to spare her ill mother any trouble. The third, related theme of Mary's recollections concerned the period when her mother went through an exacerbation of her 'strange illness' and was hospitalized. Mary was then 14 years old, and was afraid her mother would never come back again, even when the family doctor assured her that her mother's stay in the hospital would last only 3 weeks. She could not find comfort from her father on this occasion, because he, as usual, was very busy with his work, and devoted his scarce free time to caring for her sick mother: therefore, she had to resort, again, to her skill of 'forgetting her fear' through the immersion in pleasant daydreaming.

I started treating Mary's mother three years after her hospitalization, and got a complementary picture of the relationship with her daughter. She saw her daughter as overdependent on her, frail, and unable to cope with many situations (cf. the description of the early interaction of agoraphobics with their parents provided by Chambless and Goldstein (1981)). For this reason, and in order to help her acquire 'independence', she had frequently forced her to 'cope' with her fears. I had the impression that Mary's mother found her little daughter a burden that she was both unable and unwilling to bear, but did not obtain confirmatory evidence for this impression from the patient. It was certain, that when Mary was in her preschool years her mother had frequently been emotionally unavailable to her, because of the recurring fits of her 'strange illness' that had been exacerbated for a few years after childbirth.

By combining the information I obtained from Mrs B. and from her mother, it is possible to reconstruct the following line of development. During infancy and preschool years, Mary developed a pattern of insecure, anxious attachment to her mother (Ainsworth 1982; Bowlby 1973; Bretherton 1985). Due to the looking-glass effect in the development of Self-schemata (see Bretherton 1985; Cooley 1902; Mead 1934; Guidano and Liotti 1983), she started identifying with her mother's view of herself not as reacting normally to a too difficult relationship with an insensitive caregiver, but as basically incompetent, unable to cope with many daily situations and to practice 'independent' behaviors. The emotions of attachment were deprived of their proper meaning by this view of the self. Then, as a consequence of her mother's pressures, she developed the ability to 'forget her fear' by absorbing herself in daydreams while separating herself from her mother in order to practice the prescribed 'independent' behaviors. Thus, she learned to mislabel her fears as abnormal emotions and to exclude them from conscious processing. In this way, Mary set the ground for constructing a false or at least partial image of herself as an 'independent' and self-confident person. This image of 'independence' was reinforced by her parents' approval; finally, by modeling on her mother's attitude of labeling disowned emotions as symptoms of an illness (depersonalization), Mary completed the work of excluding the painful emotions of anxious attachment from conscious scrutiny. Then she developed another bond of attachment with her husband, and when this bond was threatened by her fantasy of deserting him for another man she was ill-equipped to attribute meaning to the ensuing emotions. She started dealing with these emotions as if they were the symptoms of an illness extraneous to the happenings of her affectional life, and also tried automatically to 'forget' them by absorbing herself as usual in daydreams, this time concerning her suitor. It is not unlikely that the feelings of depersonalization (a trance-like state) she experienced after her first attack of panic were the consequence of the state of consciousness created by this kind of compulsive daydreaming, and of the elicited memory of her mother's depersonalization.

Of course, this account of Mrs B.'s case is far from being exhaustive. It does not do justice to the complexity of her feelings, and of her representational models of Self and the attachment figure. These feelings and models comprised frequent states of emotional detachment, guilt, shame, sexual problems, difficulty in perceiving and respecting the point of view of the partner when it diverged from her own (egocentrism), views of herself as 'weak' and 'unable to cope with problems', idealization but also denigration of her partner. This sketchy account of Mrs B.'s developmental history does, however, convey the idea of the essential steps in the development of agoraphobia: an anxious attachment, a mislabeling of the corresponding emotions due to the caregivers' attitude toward them, a representation of the Self as incompetent and frail, a way to cope with this alleged frailty through the premature and excessive development of control over one's emotions, and the consequent disconnection of the emotional schemata of anxious attachment from the semantic processes of propositional self-knowledge. To this set of vulnerability factors, one may sometimes add the effects of modeling an anxious, depressed, hysterical or sometimes frankly agoraphobic parent (Bowlby 1973; Guidano and Liotti 1983; Tearnan *et al.* 1984). The interpersonal problems, implying the strong activation of the attachment system, that usually mark the onset of the syndrome cannot be coped with properly by the cognitive–emotional–behavioral organization deriving from these developmental steps.

According to my experience (Guidano and Liotti 1983, 1985; Liotti 1981, 1984, 1986), these developmental steps may be reconstructed during the psychotherapy of every agoraphobic patient. It is, of course, often difficult to obtain substantial evidence of *early* patterns of anxious attachment if one does not have the opportunity of interviewing the patient's parents, but the patients' recollections of childhood episodes of interaction with the caregivers consistently support the hypothesis that early patterns of insecure–anxious attachment were the starting point of the development of agoraphobia.[1]

Sometimes, in my reconstruction of an agoraphobic patient's developmental history, it has been impossible to identify pressures from the caregivers aimed at directly inducing the child to control the emotions of an anxious attachment. In these cases, it seems, according to the patient's recollections, that he has discovered that, through distracting his attention from his fears and/or through concealing his emotions from an over-controlling parent, he could solve the problem posed by the conflict between an anxious pattern of attachment and the need to explore the extra-familiar environment (Guidano and Liotti 1983; Liotti 1986). The result of this strategy of problem-solving is, of course, the same as that described in Mrs B.'s case: important emotional information related to attachment is excluded from conscious scrutiny and from the process of constructing models of Self and others.

Eric E., an agoraphobic patient, 37 years old, was able during psycho-therapy to provide the following recollection of his relationship with his mother when he was a child and was eager to go out and play with his mates: Eric's mother (who had divorced her husband when Eric was 4 years old) was frightened when her child showed any sign of physical discomfort, even when the cause of it was an obviously minor illness such as, for instance, a cold. For at least one week after having *completely* recovered from *any* illness, the child was forced to stay at home. If Eric complained of a quarrel with a playmate, or of a bruise he had got while playing out of doors, he was not allowed to go out and play until his mother had forgotten the incident, which might take many days. Cold weather was another reason for Eric's mother to keep her only son at home, allegedly because he was a sickly child prone to catch chest colds. In the context of such a relationship, Eric soon learned that he had to conceal his feelings of vulnerability (e.g. when he was feverish, when he was afraid of the hostility of a playmate, etc.) if he wished to be free from his mother's control. Since, as stated above, a child's knowledge of his own emotions is contingent upon his talking about them with his caregivers (Bretherton and Beeghly 1982), the development of Eric's understanding of his own feelings of vulnerability was seriously hindered. In therapeutic conversations, Eric's limited understanding of his own emotional vulnerability was all too evident whenever he spoke of his agoraphobic fear and of its antecedents (misunderstandings with his wife, doubting whether or not to divorce her). Eric's decision to cut off his feelings of vulnerability had also another side-effect: he avoided reflecting on why his mother took such an over-contolling attitude toward him. It required much therapeutic effort to help him entertain the hypothesis that his mother may have somehow reversed roles in the parent–child relationship – tacitly asking her child for company and protection from her own fear of loneliness, and taking advantage of any incident in her son's life to keep him close to her for as long as possible. When Eric was finally able to dwell on this hypothesis, he realized that he had been blind not only to his mother's but also to his *wife's* need for company and feelings of affective loneliness. Many misunderstandings in his marriage stemmed from his misinterpreting his wife's requests for emotional closeness. Having, since he was a child, shut off feelings of loneliness and vulnerability (as they may be perceived both in the Self and in others) from conversation and from conscious scrutiny, he eventually found himself unable to understand both his wife's and his own needs for company and comfort.

The model of agoraphobic development outlined here does not exclude the intervention of other factors in the etiology of agoraphobia. Genetic, constitutional, or other acquired factors, for instance, modulating the behavioral systems that mediate attachment and exploration of novelty (e.g. readiness of their activation, intensity of the corresponding emotions, etc.), can easily fit into the model. It is not impossible that hypothetical temperamental characteristics of female children such as a more ready activation of the attachment system (or an easier 'behavioural inhibition to the unfamiliar' – see Rosenbaum *et al.* 1988) may explain the higher incidence of agoraphobia among women.

NOTES ON THE RESPONSE TO TREATMENT

Since the crucial point in the development of agoraphobia, according to the model I have outlined here, is the exclusion of emotional information related to anxious attachment, and the mistaken labeling of the corresponding feelings and needs as abnormal (childish, morbid, etc.), it is interesting to note the consequences of therapeutic maneuvers aimed at helping patients to attribute an acceptable personal meaning to their phobic anxiety. Among the therapeutic procedures useful to this effect, I would recommend that self-observation be practiced during each episode of anxiety – phobic or otherwise – and especially during graded self-exposure to the feared situations. I encourage my patients to keep a diary of the results of these observations, as a homework assignment between therapeutic sessions. Each entry in the diary should show in outline form: (a) the environmental events preceding the emotional–behavioral episode; (b) the evaluative thoughts concurrent with those events; (c) the emotions (including perceived bodily changes) experienced; and (d) the plans of action subsequently envisaged by the patient (Liotti 1986: 111). These records are discussed during the therapeutic sessions, the therapist's aim being mainly to develop 'linking hypotheses' (cf. Goldberg *et al.* 1984; Margison and Shapiro 1986) connecting different areas of the patient's experience, and to encourage the patient to focus attention on the meaning of the perceived emotions. Comments on the feelings experienced during the therapeutic relationship may be instrumental in increasing the patient's knowledge of his or her own emotions, and may be linked to recollections of similar reactions in other present and past relationships. Particular care should be taken by the therapist not to confirm, during this kind of therapeutic work, the negative view the patient usually has of attachment emotions such as fear, anger, and sadness.

As a rule, when these maneuvers are successful in making the patient understand the emotional meaning of what he or she experienced as an illness, a lessening of anxiety and avoidance behavior quickly follows. The new Self-schemata, constructed in the course of treatment and able to assimilate the emotional information related to attachment, however, frequently displace but do not replace the old ones. The cohabiting of the new and old Self-schemata is well illustrated by the following clinical vignette.

John C., 31 years old, had been suffering from agoraphobia and claustrophobia for about 7 years. His phobias started a few months before his marriage, and worsened during a long conjugal crisis which ended with a divorce. After about 6 months of treatment (gradual self-exposure, self-observation, development of the first 'linking hypotheses') he managed to go skiing with his girlfriend and, remembering the conversations with his therapist, found the courage to take the cable-car. The cable-car stopped halfway. John panicked, but was soon able to cope with his feelings by saying to himself: 'This is only my fear, there is no impending tragedy, it is not madness'. He calmed down, and noticed that he was even calmer than other people around him. Then the cable-car moved off, and John thought: 'This time I have been able *to control this phobic attack.* ... Shall I be able to control a bigger one?' What had been justly evaluated as a personal emotion was again, after a few minutes, regarded as the sign of an illness (phobia, to him a synonym of 'madness') alien to the Self and therefore to be controlled rather than understood.

The resistance to change of the agoraphobic Self-schemata, that are so unfit for the proper assimilation of emotional information, is, at least in the clinical sample I have treated, quite considerable. They may persist unmodified even for a long time after the patient has regained, thanks to the effects of graded self-exposure to the feared situations, his or her freedom of going out alone.

Ann D. had been treated for agoraphobia 12 years before her coming back to me, because of a sudden and extremely intense recurrence of her 'symptoms'. The outcome of the first treatment had been, apparently, very good. The main ingredients of the therapy had been gradual self-exposure, self-observation, and the exploration of a few hypotheses linking the development of her painful emotions of fear to the uncertain outcome of an important sentimental relationship. A rational criticism of her self-description as a potentially weak person, who could only save her self-esteem by fighting the temptation of 'dependency', was also performed. Ann, however, refused to explore her past history of attachment, the full implications of the interpersonal problems with her partner and the reasons for having not grieved over the death of her first husband 2 years before the onset of her agoraphobia. When I suggested that these could be areas of experience deserving accurate scrutiny, she stated that she was now feeling much better, thanks to the discovering of the emotional meaning of her phobic distress, the newly developed ability to cope with her fear of going out alone, and the understanding that her self-worth was not dependent on her self-control. Her psychotherapy had lasted more than one year, she considered it to be quite successful, and felt 'ready to walk on her own two feet'.

When she referred again to me 12 years later, the relationship with her partner was breaking off. He had fallen in love with another woman, and shortly after having suspected that this could indeed be the case, she had experienced frightening feelings (like being on the verge of fainting) while she was far from home alone. Her linking these two events was extremely uncertain: she believed that she was developing a cardio-vascular illness, and came back to me only after her cardiologist had repeatedly assured her that this was certainly not true. She was also despising herself for not being able to leave her partner, and justified her 'dependency' only on account of her 'illness'. The Self-schemata developed during her first psychotherapy, implying a different view of emotions, dependency, and self-worth, seemed to have disappeared, or become dormant. They were, however, quickly reactivated in the course of the following treatment, and this reactivation brought with it a sharp reduction (although not a full disappearance) of the phobic fears. During the 12 years that had elapsed between the two treatments, Ann D. had been completely free from phobic or other emotional distur-bances.

There are at least two reasons why cognitive structures related to the

Self are resistant to change in the treatment of agoraphobic patients. The first reason is related to the general resistance to change of Self-schemata in every human being – a resistance that, in turn, is rooted in the equilibrium between assimilative and accommodative processes (Flavell 1963). In the process of assimilation, the new incoming information is actively modified to make it as similar as possible to the already stored one, while in the process of accommodation the existing cognitive structures change to adapt themselves to the new incoming information. When information related to the Self is involved in cognitive processing, assimilation seems usually to prevail over accommodation (Liotti 1987, 1989; Swann and Hill 1982), so that the potential correction of Self-schemata as a function of new information is minimized.

The second reason for the resistance to change of the agoraphobic Self-schemata is characteristic of many abnormal cognitive structures, and is related to the dissociation between semantic (abstract, propositional) and episodic (concrete, emotional) aspects of self-knowledge. Fragments of episodic knowledge, that may ally with information provided by psychotherapy for a better understanding of one's attachment emotions (and therefore for a change of propositional self-knowledge), are usually shut off from conscious examination either because they are painful or because influential others have prohibited one from reflecting on them since childhood (Bowlby 1979, 1980, 1985). In order to overcome this second aspect of the resistance to change of the agoraphobic Self-schemata, a careful reconstruction of the past history of attachment seems very advisable (Bowlby 1977; Guidano and Liotti 1983; Liotti 1987, 1989). The clinical examples of John C. and Ann D. show how self-exposure to feared situations, and rational disputing of the logical fallacies implied by one's self-descriptions (Beck 1976; Beck and Emery 1985; Ellis 1962), may be sufficient to bring about an improvement of the phobic disturbances, but do not sufficiently change the cognitive causes of vulnerability, so that relapses are to be expected.

I do not possess follow-up information concerning the different rates of relapses in patients that have paid, during psychotherapy, different degrees of attention to their history of attachment – other therapeutic ingredients (self-exposure, self-observation, development of 'linking hypotheses', etc.) being equal. The anecdotal evidence that I can draw from my sample, however, supports the hypothesis that those who have understood their phobic anxiety as a meaningful emotion, thanks to the reconstruction of their childhood history of attachment, are better equipped than those who have not yet performed such a reconstruction to cope with the recurrence of painful life events such as losses or expected losses without relapsing into phobia.

NOTE

1   Controlled studies concerning the differentiation of agoraphobics from other anxious patients along such dimensions as recalled parental overprotection, low parental care, and parental loss before age 15, have yielded contradictory results (Arrindell *et al.* 1983; Parker 1979). The questionnaires that have been used in these studies lack some of the key questions needed to pinpoint the rearing practices that most clinicians consider as factors of vulnerability in the development of agoraphobia. For instance, in these questionnaires there are no questions related to the parent's habit of threatening to leave the child alone in order to discipline him. Notwithstanding this limit of the method of the researches, their results support the general hypothesis that agoraphobics have been subjected to untoward rearing practices (parental overcontrol, over-protection, lack of parental support during autonomous exploration of the environment, etc.: see also Tearnan *et al.* 1984).

REFERENCES

Ainsworth, M.D.S. (1982) 'Attachment: retrospect and prospect', in C.M. Parkes and J. Stevenson-Hinde (eds) *The Place of Attachment in Human Behaviour* (pp. 3–30), London: Tavistock.

Arrindell, W.A., Emmelkamp, P.M., Monsma, A., and Brilman, E. (1983) 'The role of perceived parental rearing practices in the aetiology of phobic disorders', *British Journal of Psychiatry* 143: 183–7.

Beck, A.T. (1976) *Cognitive Therapy and Emotional Disorders*, New York: International Universities Press.

Beck, A.T. and Emery, G. (1985) *Anxiety Disorders and Phobias: A Cognitive Perspective*, New York: Basic Books.

Bowen, R.C. and Kohout, J. (1979) 'The relationship between agoraphobia and primary affective disorders', *Canadian Journal of Psychiatry* 24: 317–22.

Bower, T. (1981) 'Competent newborns', in L.D. Stenberg (ed.) *The Life Cycle* (pp. 3–12), New York: Columbia University Press.

Bowlby, J. (1973) *Attachment and Loss*, vol. 2: *Separation*, London: Hogarth Press.

—— (1977) 'The making and breaking of affectional bonds: II, Some principles of psychotherapy', *British Journal of Psychiatry* 130: 421–31.

—— (1979) 'On knowing what you are not supposed to know and on feeling what you are not supposed to feel', *Canadian Journal of Psychiatry* 24: 403–8.

—— (1980) *Attachment and Loss*, vol. 3: *Loss: Sadness and Depression*, London: Hogarth Press.

—— (1982) *Attachment and Loss*, vol 1: *Attachment* (2nd edn), London: Hogarth Press.

—— (1985) 'The role of childhood experience in cognitive disturbance', in M.J. Mahoney and A. Freeman (eds) *Cognition and Psychotherapy*, New York: Plenum Press.

—— (1988) 'Developmental psychiatry comes of age', *American Journal of Psychiatry* 145: 1–10.

Bretherton, I. (1985) 'Attachment theory: retrospect and prospect', in I. Bretherton and E. Waters (eds) Growing Points of Attachment Theory and Research, *Monographs of the Society for Research in Child Development* 50: 3–35.

Bretherton, I. and Beeghly, M. (1982) 'Talking about internal states: the acquisition of an explicit theory of mind', *Developmental Psychology* 18: 906–21.

Chambless, D.L. and Goldstein, A.J. (1981) 'Clinical treatment of agoraphobia', in M. Mavissakalian and D.H. Barlow (eds) *Phobia: Psychological and Pharmacological Treatment* (pp. 105–27), New York: Guilford.

Cicchetti, D. (1984) 'The emergence of developmental psychopathology', *Child Development* 52: 44–52.

Cohen, S.D., Monteiro, W., and Marks, I.M. (1984) 'Two-year follow-up of agoraphobics after exposure and Imipramine', *British Journal of Psychiatry* 144: 276–81.

Cooley, C.H. (1902) *Human Nature and the Social Order*, New York: Scribner's.

Ellis, A. (1962) *Reason and Emotion in Psychotherapy*, New York: Lyle Stuart.

Flavell, J.H. (1963) *The Developmental Psychology of Jean Piaget*, New York: Van Nostrand.

Gittelman, R. and Klein, D.F. (1984) 'Relationship between separation anxiety and panic and agoraphobia disorders', *Psychopathology* 17 (supp. 1): 56–65.

Goldberg, D.P., Hobson, R.F., and Maguire, G.P. (1984) 'The clarification and assessment of a method of psychotherapy', *British Journal of Psychiatry* 144: 567–75.

Guidano, V.F. and Liotti, G. (1983) *Cognitive Processes and Emotional Disorders*, New York: Guilford.

—— (1985) 'A constructivistic foundation for cognitive therapy', in M.J. Mahoney and A. Freeman (eds) *Cognition and Psychotherapy* (pp. 101–42), New York: Plenum.

Hafner, J.R. (1977) 'The husbands of agoraphobic women: assortative mating or pathogenic interaction?' *British Journal of Psychiatry* 130: 233–9.

—— (1979) 'Agoraphobic women married to abnormally jealous men', *British Journal of Medical Psychology* 52: 99–104.

Lane, R.D. and Schwartz, G.E. (1987) 'Levels of emotional awareness: a cognitive-developmental theory and its application to psychopathology', *American Journal of Psychiatry* 144: 133–43.

Leventhal, H. (1982) 'The integration of emotion and cognition: a view from the perceptual-motor theory of emotion', in M.S. Clark and S.T. Fiske (eds) *Affect and Cognition* (pp. 121–56), Hillsdale, N.J.: Erlbaum.

Liotti, G. (1981) 'Un modello cognitivo-comportamentale dell'agorafobia', in V. Guidano and M. Reda (eds) *Cognitivismo e Psicoterapia*, Milano: Angeli.

—— (1984) 'Cognitive therapy, attachment theory, and psychiatric nosology', in M. Reda and M.J. Mahoney (eds) *Cognitive Psychotherapies*, Cambridge, Mass.: Ballinger.

—— (1986) 'Structural cognitive therapy', in W. Dryden and W. Golden (eds) *Cognitive–Behavioral Approaches to Psychotherapy* (pp. 92–128), London: Harper & Row.

—— (1987) 'The resistance to change of cognitive structures: a counterproposal to psychoanalytic metapsychology', *Journal of Cognitive Psychotherapy* 1: 87–104.

—— (1989) 'Attachment and cognition', in C. Perris, I. Blackburn, and H. Perris (eds) *The Theory and Practice of Cognitive Psychotherapy*, New York: Springer.

Liotti, G. and Guidano, V.F. (1976) 'Behavioral analysis of marital interaction in agoraphobic male patients', *Behaviour Research and Therapy* 14: 161–2.

Main, M. and Goldwyn, R. (in press), 'Interview-based adult attachment classifications', *Developmental Psychology*.

Main, M., Kaplan, N., and Cassidy, J. (1985) 'Security in infancy, childhood and adulthood: a move to the level of representation', in I. Bretherton and E. Waters (eds) Growing Points of Attachment Theory and Research, *Monographs of the Society for Research in Child Development* 50: 66–104.

Mandler, J.H. (1983) 'Representation', in J. Flavell and E. Markman (eds) *Handbook of Child Psychology*, vol. 3: *Cognitive Development* (pp. 420–94), New York: Wiley.

Margison, F. and Shapiro, D.A. (1986) 'Hobson's conversational model of psychotherapy', *Journal of the Royal Society of Medicine* 79: 468–472.

Markus, H. (1977) 'Self-schemata and processing information about the Self', *Journal of Personality and Social Psychology* 35: 63–78.

Markus, H. and Sentis, K. (1982) 'The self in social information processing', in J. Suls (ed.) *Psychological Perspectives on the Self*, vol. 1 (pp. 41–70), London: Erlbaum.

Marshall, G.D. and Zimbardo, P.G. (1979) 'Affective consequences of inadequately explained physiological arousal', *Journal of Personality and Social Psychology* 36: 970–88.

Maslach, C. (1979) 'Negative emotional biasing of unexplained arousal', *Journal of Personality and Social Psychology* 36: 953–69.

Mathews, A.M., Gelder, M.G., and Johnston, D.W. (1981) *Agoraphobia: Nature and Treatment*, New York: Guilford.

Mead, G.H. (1934) *Mind, Self and Society*, Chicago: University of Chicago Press.

Parker, G. (1979) 'Reported parental characteristics of agoraphobics and social phobics', *British Journal of Psychiatry* 135: 555–60.

Reich, J. (1986) 'The epidemiology of anxiety', *Journal of Nervous and Mental Diseases* 174: 129–36.

Roberts, A.H. (1964) 'Housebound housewives: a follow-up study of a phobic anxiety state', *British Journal of Psychiatry* 110: 191–7.

Robins, H., Helzer, J., Weissman, M., Orvaschel, H., Gruenberg, E., Burke, J., and Regier, D. (1984) 'Lifetime prevalence of specific psychiatric disorders in three sites', *Archives of General Psychiatry* 41: 949–58.

Rosen, H. (1985) *Piagetian Dimensions of Clinical Relevance*, New York: Columbia University Press.

Rosenbaum, J., Biedermann, J., Gersten, M., Hirshfeld, D., Memiger, S., Herman, J., Kagan, J., and Reznick, S. (1988) 'Behavioral inhibition in children of parents with panic disorder and agoraphobia', *Archives of General Psychiatry* 45: 463–70.

Shafar, S. (1976) 'Aspects of phobic illness: a study of 90 personal cases', *British Journal of Medical Psychology* 49: 221–36.

Swann, W.B. and Hill, C.A. (1982) 'When our identities are mistaken: reaffirming self-conceptions through social interactions', *Journal of Personality and Social Psychology* 43: 59–66.

Tearnan, B.H., Telch, M.J. and Keefe, P. (1984) 'Etiology and onset of agoraphobia: a critical review', *Comprehensive Psychiatry* 25: 51–62.

Tulving, E. (1972) 'Episodic and semantic memory', in E. Tulving and W. Donaldson (eds) *Organization of Memory* (pp. 382–483), New York: Academic Press.

Weiss, R.S. (1982) 'Attachment in adult life', in C.M. Parkes and J. Stevenson-Hinde (eds) *The Place of Attachment in Human Behaviour*, London: Tavistock Publications.

Wolpe, J. (1976) *Theme and Variations: A Behavior Therapy Casebook*, New York: Pergamon Press.

Chapter 13

Loss of parent in childhood, attachment style, and depression in adulthood

Tirril Harris and Antonia Bifulco

... an unloved orphan, which is how she experienced herself, must be clever and amusing in order to ensure survival in this world. Therefore behaviours ordinarily frowned upon might very well be excused or considered virtuous if a person happened to be an orphan ... Even though she looked wan and still felt weak from crying, she greeted her Round Table friends with a cheerful grin and a barrage of four-letter words. Had she been candid about her despair, they might have been forced to acknowledge the depth of her suffering and probably would have responded in a manner more suitable to the occasion.

(Marion Meade 1988: 21, 101, *Dorothy Parker: What Fresh Hell is This? A Biography*)

With the advent of the 1990s, attachment theory can fairly be said to have come of age. No longer is it looked upon as primarily a variant of psychoanalysis and thus automatically suspect in scientific terms because unamenable to empirical disconfirmation. Its tenets have begun to inform 'hard-nosed' projects involving not only experimental designs but also biochemical variables. Many, for example, are following the lead of Hinde and his team (Hinde and Davies 1972; Hinde and Spencer-Booth 1971): McKinney and colleagues have utilized separation in nonhuman primates as a model for human depression (McKinney *et al.* 1984), and rat pups isolated at a critical stage of development have been shown to exhibit increased activity during wakefulness (Smith and Anderson 1984) and disorganized EEG sleep patterns (Hofer 1976). Furthermore, even in what might be considered the 'softer' areas of human studies utilizing verbal interviews, methods have become stricter and more elaborate: Parkes and Weiss's discussion of recovery from bereavement in 1983 contains a wealth of statistical analyses which complement their sensitive reporting of qualitative material, whereas 9 years earlier their description of the first year of bereavement lacked the statistical cutting edge likely to convince a sceptic (Glick *et al.* 1974). In addition, Ainsworth and colleagues' classic initial insights with children (Ainsworth and Wittig 1969; Ainsworth *et al.*

1971) have been subtly refined (Main and Weston 1982; Main and Solomon 1986), and extended beyond the Anglo-Saxon world (Grossmann and Grossmann 1981; Sagi *et al.* 1985; Miyake *et al.* 1985).

Other authors have celebrated these developments far better than we could hope to do, taking a broad perspective to review the development of the theoretical framework in general (Bretherton and Waters 1985; Bretherton 1987; Bowlby 1988). However, it seemed there was one contribution we could make: a study which had been conceived in the mid-1970s against the general background of early attachment theory could now be used for further exploration of the more detailed hypotheses required by its subsequent elaboration. One of us (AB) suggested that our style of data collection made it possible to reanalyse material gathered before the publication of John Bowlby's third volume on *Attachment and Loss* in 1980, but approximating the categories he outlined there to describe personalities especially vulnerable to loss experiences. By raking over the ground again we might produce some confirmation and perhaps new insights.

THE WALTHAMSTOW STUDY

Background to the study and its aims

The study in question formed part of an ongoing series investigating the role of psychosocial factors in the onset of depression among women. The first study, in Camberwell, London, of psychiatric patients and two successive general population samples, outlined an aetiological model of depression (Brown and Harris 1978). This identified certain recent severe loss experiences as 'provoking agents' which interacted in a statistical sense with background demographic 'vulnerability factors' to produce onset. Among the four vulnerability factors were two of key importance in attachment theory: current absence of a confiding relationship with a partner, and loss of mother before age 11, either by death or by a separation of at least 1 year. The other two vulnerability factors involved the women's roles, the presence at home of three or more children under age 15, and the lack of outside employment. In order to understand their contribution to depression the concept of 'role-identity' was invoked (McCall and Simmons 1966): that women with various role-identities outside the home would have that much more opportunity to restore in one role area, such as their job, a general sense of hope which might have been threatened by a loss experience in another domain, such as the marital relationship, under threat by a husband's arrest by the police. Thus the model identified the generalization of hopelessness as a central core of the depressive experience (following Beck 1967), and suggested that such generalization was more likely among women with a poor self-image. It was argued that lack of supportive relationships, either with a partner in adulthood or in the childhood family, could be expected to raise the chance of low self-esteem which would promote this generalization after a severe loss event, and so depression. In focusing upon the sense of self-worth the model appeared consonant with a perspective of volume 2 of *Attachment and Loss* where the concept of self-reliance seemed to play a similar role, originating in a 'good-enough environment' and promoting psychological resilience.

The Walthamstow study was designed to explore this last idea by focusing on the processes by which childhood loss of mother might link with depression in adulthood (Brown 1982; Brown *et al.* 1986a). Broadly, two aetiological strands were conceived which, although inextricably linked, could be conceptually separated. The first involved factors external to the individual (strand 1), such as being sent to an institution after the mother's death or being kept home from school to help look after younger siblings. The second strand involved intra-psychic factors such as tendencies to be open or mistrustful, resentful and assertive, and, of course, the level of self-esteem. As intimated in Fig. 13.1, factors from one strand might influence those in the other at any stage in life, not only in the formative childhood years, and the influence might go in either direction. While it was clear that a small retrospective study could never completely chart all the processes in the diagram, it was hoped that it could throw light on some and thereby provide material of relevance for attachment theory.

Although an exploratory project, the study did include certain specific hypotheses. Some involved no more than an attempt to replicate earlier findings – for example, a higher prevalence of depression among those with loss of parent. Some involved testing predictions of attachment theory – for example, that both the nature of caregiving in childhood, and adequacy of mourning, would determine later personality development and psychopathology. Some involved testing the speculations arising from the Camberwell model concerning the interrelationship of demographic and psychological vulnerability.

Sample and measures

The sample and method have been described elsewhere (Harris *et al.* 1986, 1987). All women aged between 18 and 65 registered with certain general practitioners were asked in a brief postal questionnaire about childhood loss of parent. When account was taken of the numbers who had left the surgery the response rate was found to be acceptable, providing a sample of 225 women. Of the total of 180, 139 had lost a mother before age 17 (78 by death and 61 by separation of at least 1 year, with 91 of these also losing a father). A further 41 had lost only a father. In addition, 45 women with broadly similar demographic characteristics without loss of either

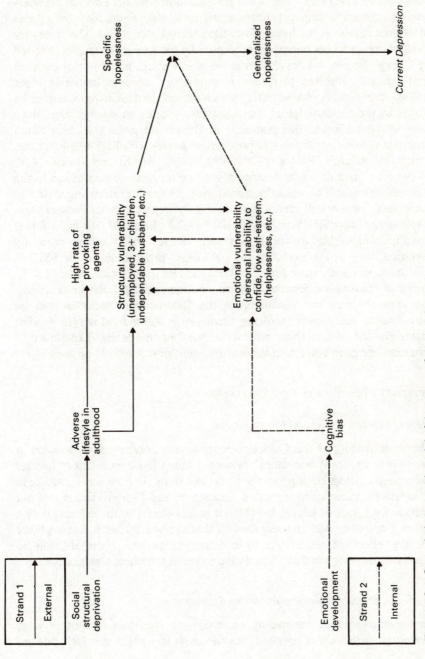

Figure 13.1 Speculative causal model of the onset of depression

parent were selected to act as a comparison group.

Data collection involved semi-structured tape-recorded interviews which encouraged the women to tell their own story, but with additional probing questions to ensure all items were covered. Interviewers (who had undergone an extensive training) subsequently rated the respondents on a series of ordinal scales on the basis of the tape-recorded material. The scales for most of the variables were devised especially for a series of studies, headed by George Brown, on depression in women. Ratings made in this research tradition are subjected to review in consensus meetings involving other trained interviewers, whose rating standards on particular items cannot be biased by their knowledge of the respondent's status on another item, since they are kept blind to this information. Details are given elsewhere about how this general approach can produce measures with high reliability and acceptable validity (Brown 1974, 1981, 1988; Brown and Harris 1978, 1979). The main dependent variable was the measure of depression in the year of interview. This used the same threshold for discriminating 'cases' as the earlier Camberwell survey, based on a shortened form of Present State Examination or PSE (Wing *et al.* 1974). This threshold has been found broadly comparable to (or if anything stricter than) others currently favoured, such as ID level 5 of the CATEGO programme of the PSE, or 'major depression' according to RDC criteria (see Dean *et al.* 1983). Previous episodes of depression were also measured (Harris *et al.* 1986). To avoid tedium the measures of the independent variables will be described as the results involving them are presented. Most are 4-point scales divided so that those with a 'marked' or 'moderate' experience of that item are contrasted with those with only 'some' or 'little or none'.

Summary of previously reported results

Depression and childhood loss of parent

The basic finding of the Camberwell study was confirmed: depression in the year of the study was more prevalent among those with loss of mother before age 11 than among those with no loss of mother. However, unlike in Camberwell, those losing a mother between 11 and 17 had a raised, but not quite as high, rate of depression (Harris *et al.* 1986). For those losing only a father, depression was no more likely if that loss was by death, but evidence for the effect of separation from father alone was more difficult to interpret, showing a trend which failed to reach statistical significance.

Lack of adequate replacement care and depression

Several measures of the quality of caregiving after loss of mother were associated with such depression, but the most important involved marked or moderate indifference or lax control on the part of a surrogate parent for a minimum of at least 1 year (Harris *et al.* 1986). When these were used to form an index of 'lack of care' it became clear that such neglect was common among those with loss of mother, less frequent among those with only loss of father, and rare among those without loss of parent; in sum, lack of care underlay the different rates of depression between the loss groups. While other childrearing measures (such as 'rejection') were weakly associated with depression, others such as 'warmth' and 'punitiveness' were unrelated.

The launching period and depression

Having established that lack of care, rather than loss of mother as such, underlay the association of early loss and depression, the first causal strand in Fig. 13.1 was explored to see if a chain of environmental adversity did indeed stem from lack of care. Premarital pregnancy turned out to be highly associated with later depression, whether or not it was followed by marriage or a live birth (Harris *et al.* 1987). Many of the associations between depression and other variables involved in this launching period were related in one way or another to such a pregnancy.

The adult environment and depression

Following the women into adulthood it became clear that both lack of care and these premarital pregnancies were associated with strand-1-type experiences identified as risk factors for depression in Camberwell. In particular they were associated with having an undependable partner, lack of intimate confiding stemming from this undependability, and a high rate of provoking agents (Harris *et al.* 1987).

The cognitive set of situational helplessness

A different picture emerged, however, when a cognitive factor, helplessness, was examined. As with other strand-2 measures, the period used to rate helplessness was the 'proximal' one (just before onset for those depressed in the year of interview, but currently for those not depressed). By avoiding using a rating of helplessness of those depressed at the time of interview it was hoped to deal with the problem faced by any retrospective study: namely, that cognitive sets such as helplessness may be a consequence of, rather than antecedent to, depression. Inquiring about the proximal period before onset for those currently depressed is designed to reduce this confusion, but, of course, the fact that the ratings are retrospective needs to be borne in mind. Both in childhood and in this proximal period, helplessness related to depression in the year before interview (see Harris *et al.* (1990a, b), where the measure and its justi-fication are described in detail). Childhood and adult helplessness were correlated, suggesting a continuing disposition along strand 2. Although adult helplessness was closely associated with the key strand-1 environ-mental factors identified as increasing risk of depression – such as lack of care, poor support, and premarital pregnancy – such helplessness made a contribution to depression over and above these strand-1 factors (Harris *et al.* 1990b). Particularly interesting was the association between *childhood* helplessness and both the experiencing of a premarital pregnancy and coping ineffectively with it. On the other hand the associations of strand-1 factors with *adult* helplessness were greater, suggesting that dispositions continue to be shaped by the adult environment, sometimes reinforcing and sometimes counteracting the earlier cognitive sets. In summary then, there is a suggestion that a lack of mastery, stemming both from a lack of mastery in childhood and even more clearly from environmental experi-ences throughout the life span, was linked with current depression.

Age at loss of mother and depression

In terms of the first 10 years of life, for those with a loss of mother by death, depression was more common among those with a loss before age 6, whereas there was no such trend among those losing her by separation (Bifulco *et al.* 1989). Re-examination of two other samples in the series (Camberwell and Islington) essentially repeated this pattern (Bifulco 1985). Since loss at under 6 was not associated in either the death or the separation group with any strand-1 (environmental) factor, it seemed that a strand-2 (intra-psychic) factor might be involved in the result for those with death of mother. The most obvious first line of inquiry was a hypothesis suggested by Bowlby – that failure to mourn a mother lost by death was involved, given such failure is generally considered more likely at a very young age (Bowlby 1980, especially chapters 1, 12, 23, and 25).

Aspects of loss and failure to mourn: the problem of recall

There were 85 items coded in the mourning section of the interview given to all who lost a parent. These fell into three broad groupings. One aimed to capture objective features of the loss itself – whether there was an element of trauma (for example seeing a disfigured corpse) or relief (for example a death after a painful illness), age of the parent, the presence of other relatives at the time of the death. A second group of items dealt with the child's reactions, both after the loss, and in the longer term, in terms of sadness, anxiety, dreams, preoccupational thoughts, willingness to discuss the lost parent, understanding of the cause of loss, comfort derived from religion, and so on. A third grouping dealt with the reactions of others –

the amount and character of the emotion expressed, and the willingness to talk about the lost person (for a full account see Bifulco *et al.* 1989). Despite the large number of items, none of the many correlations that might have been expected with depression emerged. However, some associations were found between lack of care and practices generally considered likely to impede healthy mourning, and it is thus quite possible that the widespread impression among clinicians that failure to mourn goes with later pathology may be due to the impact of the accompanying lack of care which has brought people into treatment. The picture is complicated by the fact that an earlier age at loss was related to an inability to remember relevant experiences, with consequent missing data. However, it is of some interest that a straightforward protective role for the observance of mourning ritual was not confirmed.

The cognitive set of situational hostility

The different impacts of loss by death and by separation are of special interest for another cognitive factor – situational hostility (the tendency to react aggressively or exhibit a high degree of criticism of others) both publicly and privately. Although such hostility related to depression, it was also closely associated with helplessness and it did not make a contribution to depression once helplessness had been taken into account. However, hostility had been included in the study in order to explore a quite difficult hypothesis concerning symptom-formation *after* onset (as opposed to initial vulnerability to experiencing an episode). On the basis of results for the patient series in Camberwell it was speculated that a meaningful connection existed between type of 'past loss'[1] and the current symptom morphology: a past experience of death, being more final, would induce more hopelessness and thus more symptoms of retardation and giving-up. By contrast a past experience of separation might have left more hope that some dramatic gesture could in the end retrieve the deserting attachment figure. A separation might also, more often than a death, be experienced as a rejection which would provoke resentment, or at least some form of Bowlbyan protest (Bowlby 1973). It was therefore suggested that a long-term continuing disposition of some type of resentment/protest/hostility might link manipulative suicide gestures with past separation.

In Walthamstow hostility was measured in situations very similar to those utilized in the estimation of helplessness (for details see Harris *et al.* 1990c). In deliberately contrasting deaths with separations we had to face a problem which in general was not an issue – namely, that some had been separated from their mothers for 6 months or longer before they died and it was by no means obvious which experience would have most affected them. For this reason the 11 women with such a separation were examined separately in a further subgroup. The prediction of more proximal hostility among those separated than those with only a loss by death was confirmed when this subgroup was treated as a separation grouping. In terms of the person's life as a whole there had been more suicide attempts – particularly gestures rather than serious attempts – among those separated rather than bereaved (especially those separated only from a father). The degree of hostility was much higher among those who had made suicidal gestures, whereas those whose serious attempts had been fortuitously forestalled turned out to be less 'hostile'. The Walthamstow sample, therefore, appeared to confirm the causal chain:

past separation (i.e. not death) → hostility → suicidal gesture

Further results

Hitherto we have been summarizing previously-reported findings, but we now turn to new results.

The cognitive sets dependency, nurturance, and overall ability to relate to others

The publication of the third volume of *Attachment and Loss* suggested that those measures concerning relationships could be used to pursue a more detailed analysis of ideas concerning vulnerability to depression. In that volume Bowlby describes three categories of personality especially prone to disordered mourning: those disposed to make anxious or ambivalent relationships, those disposed to compulsive caregiving, and those disposed to assert independence of affectional ties (Bowlby 1980: 202–13). Since a proneness to depression could be considered a variant of proneness to disordered mourning, it might be possible to offer some confirmation or otherwise of Bowlby's ideas.

The cognitive sets described so far will have given some impression of the information we gathered concerning a woman's helplessness and hostility with a wide range of people; information was also provided about other personal styles such as dependency and the propensity to protect and care for others (or nurturance). For 'adult relationships' most attention was focused on partner, children, and 'main friend'. The information available about helplessness and hostility was supplemented by additional ratings concerning confiding and active emotional support (both by and to the respondent), joint activity or companionship, warmth, considerateness, dependency, praise, criticism, approval and disapproval. Questions were asked about attachment figures such as godmothers or former school teachers, who might be seen only infrequently but whose continued existence might still provide a sense of security (O'Connor 1987).

Following previous work on depression and so called *'dependency'*

(Hirschfield *et al.* 1977; Birtchnell 1974; see also Navran 1954), we have adopted the same term to describe interpersonal behaviour involving a high degree of 'clinging' or 'insecurity of attachment' at one extreme and a high degree of self-sufficiency, or even detachment, at the other. Because of the assumptions of attachment theory concerning relationships which allow optimal psychological functioning, the word 'dependency' has been avoided by workers in that field in order to distance arguments from the notion that *any* degree of dependence is pathogenic. Because we wished to look again at Birtchnell's finding we kept the term, but did adjust its definition to bring it more in line with a Bowlbyan perspective by assuming that the standard ('normal') pattern involved a 'moderate' amount of interpersonal dependency rather than 'little or none'. Anyone with a global score of high (the top 2 points, 'marked' or 'very marked', on the 5-point scale) was considered more 'dependent' than would be expected of a standard adult, that is more insecure or clinging, and anyone rated only 'some' or 'little or none' (the lowest 2 points) was considered more 'independent' than the standard. It is important to clarify these terminological issues at the outset in order to make it explicit that, despite the vocabulary of the Walthamstow study, its perspective does not render its findings irrelevant for attachment theory. For simplicity of presentation, results will merely be summarily described in the text, with most of the detailed figures and statistical analyses provided in the tables. For reasons already outlined, only ratings for the proximal period will be reported. High dependency was associated with depression, but only slightly with loss of mother (Table 13.1).

The global rating of *nurturance* was designed to reflect the respondent's concern to relate to others in a particularly protective or altruistic way, together with her enjoyment in giving and seeking to forgive rather than to blame – for example, the dedicated nurse and foster mother, the helpful member of the bus queue who is not resentful of queue-barging old age pensioners. It was only the 8 women with a 'very high' score who had a higher rate of depression, and all 8 had lost a mother, though the overall association is not statistically significant.

Overall *ability to relate to others* was a judgement based on the respondent's overall skills in making and keeping good friendships and absence of significant dissatisfaction in her relationships. A poor ability was associated with depression in the sample as a whole. However, this inability was not associated with loss of mother as such and was closely linked with both childhood and adult helplessness.

Attachment style

Although the Walthamstow data were largely collected by the time Bowlby's third volume had outlined three vulnerable attachment styles, it

Table 13.1 Depression in the year of interview among women in Walthamstow by loss of mother and certain interpersonal styles

	Proportion depressed							
	× Dependency							
	High ('very marked' or 'marked')		Standard		Independent ('some' or 'little/none')		Proportion highly dependent	
	%	n	%	n	%	n	%	n
Loss of mother[a]	39	(11/28)	18	(14/80)	13	(4/30)	20	(28/138)
No loss of mother	10	(1/10)	7	(4/59)	6	(1/17)	12	(10/86)
Total	32	(12/38)	13	(18/139)	11	(5/47)	$p < 0.02$	

	Proportion depressed							
	× Nurturance						Proportion whose nurturance was very high	
	Very high		High		Moderate		Low	
	%	n	%	n	%	n	%	n
Loss of mother[a]	50	(4/8)	15	(5/33)	23	(18/77)	10	(2/20)	6	(8/138)
No loss of mother	–		0	(0/17)	6	(3/54)	20	(3/15)	0	(0/86)
Total	50	(4/8)	10	(5/50)	16	(21/131)	14	(5/35)	$p < 0.07$	

	Proportion depressed				
	× Ability to relate to others			Proportion with poor ability	
	Poor ability		Others		
	%	n	%	n	%	n
Loss of mother	45	(10/22)	17	(20/117)	16	(22/139)
No loss of mother	17	(2/12)	5	(4/74)	14	(12/86)
Total	35	(12/34)	14	(24/191)	n.s.	

Note: [a] 1 case is missing due to incomplete interview.

seemed possible that by combining the measures so far outlined we might be able to approximate these three. Further, given the modest correlations with depression obtained so far with the relationship measures, it seemed likely that results might not emerge clearly until we had isolated *all* women with *any* vulnerable attachment style. The argument here is that with small numbers in each vulnerable group, comparing each group with *all* other women (including those in the other vulnerable groups) will be likely to mask what are genuine effects. While we believe the logic of this is impeccable, it leaves us open to capitalizing on chance associations – a type one error. We have judged this an acceptable risk in what is, after all, only an exploratory exercise. In what follows we first describe the development of a set of more complex categories, and how six rather than the three suggested by Bowlby were required for statistically significant relationships to emerge. Thus, although we will provide statistical information in the course of outlining the six categories of attachment style, we will not consider each individually as constituting a critical test since some in the overall group without one particular characteristic (say, without ambivalence) might fall in another high-risk category (say, compulsive caregiving). For a final judgement of the exercise it is necessary to wait until all six categories are considered together.

Highly dependent attachment styles. A total of 38 women were highly dependent and, as already noted, they had a higher rate of depression. Such dependency would be expected to play a key role in two of Bowlby's attachment styles – compulsive caregiving and ambivalent attachment. In order to create a category of *compulsive caregiving*, both dependency and nurturance were considered. Table 13.2 shows that they are modestly, but by no means highly, associated. The table also indicates that those with both 'high' dependency and 'very high' nurturance might be more susceptible to depression than those with either alone, although numbers are far too small for anything definitive to be concluded. However, on the basis

Table 13.2 Depression in the year of interview among women in Walthamstow – degrees of nurturance and dependency[a]

Total sample

	Proportion depressed				
	Nurturance				
Dependency	Very high	High	Moderate	Low	Total
	% n	% n	% n	% n	% n
High	60 (3/5)	20 (2/10)	32 (6/19)	25 (1/4)	32 (12/38)
Standard	33 (1/3)	10 (3/31)	12 (11/90)	20 (3/15)	13 (18/139)
Independent	nil	0 (0/9)	18 (4/22)	6 (1/16)	11 (5/47)
Total	50 (4/8)	10 (5/50)	16 (21/131)	14 (5/35)	16 (35/224)

Note: Gamma = 0.35 $p < 0.001$

Those with loss of mother

	Nurturance				
Dependency	Very high	High	Moderate	Low	Total
	% n	% n	% n	% n	% n
High	60 (3/5)	29 (2/7)	38 (5/13)	33 (1/3)	39 (11/28)
Standard	33 (1/3)	16 (3/19)	18 (9/51)	14 (1/7)	18 (14/80)
Independent	nil	0 (0/7)	31 (4/13)	0 (0/10)	13 (4/30)
Total	50 (4/8)	15 (5/33)	23 (18/77)	10 (2/20)	21 (29/138)

Notes: Gamma = 0.34 $p < 0.002$
    Gammas show the association between nurturance and dependency.
    [a] 1 case missing due to incomplete interview.

of this result, compulsive caregiving was defined as 'very high' (not merely 'high') nurturance along with 'high' dependency.

In a similar way a combination of higher than average 'hostility' (see above) and 'dependency' might succeed in capturing the flavour of Bowlby's *ambivalent attachment.* While Table 13.3 shows a higher rate of depression among those with both characteristics (top left cell) than among those with neither (bottom right), it is no higher than the rates among those with either high 'dependency' without 'hostility' (top right cell) or with high 'hostility' but without high 'dependency' (bottom left cell). As mentioned earlier, this did not discourage us from pursuing the exercise further as those cells with a higher than expected rate of depression may contain examples of other vulnerable attachment styles. Meanwhile, it is interesting to notice that the two dimensions in Table 13.3 show some association.[2]

At this point we made the decision to include high dependency as a third 'attachment style' irrespective of a woman's score on nurturance or hostility. It seemed possible that a disposition to make anxious relationships, even without the ambivalence cited by Bowlby, might play an aetiological role. We therefore added simple *high dependency* to the

Table 13.3 Depression by degrees of hostility and dependency[a]

Total sample

Dependency	Proportion depressed				
	Hostility				
	High (1, 2)		Moderate (3)		Average/Low (4, 5)		Total	
	%	n	%	n	%	n	%	n
High	29	(2/7)	33	(4/12)	32	(6/19)	32	(12/38)
Standard	33	(2/6)	5	(1/19)	13	(15/113)	13	(18/138)
Independent	100	(2/2)	11	(1/9)	5	(2/37)	10	(5/48)
Total	40	(6/15)	15	(6/40)	14	(23/169)	16	(35/224)

Note: Gamma = 0.32 $p < 0.001$

Those with loss of mother

Dependency	Hostility				
	High		Moderate		Average/Low		Total	
	%	n	%	n	%	n	%	n
High	33	(2/6)	40	(4/10)	42	(5/12)	39	(11/28)
Standard	50	(2/4)	10	(1/10)	17	(11/66)	18	(14/80)
Independent	100	(2/2)	14	(1/7)	5	(1/21)	13	(4/30)
Total	50	(6/12)	22	(6/27)	17	(17/99)	21	(29/138)

Notes: Gamma = 0.31 $p < 0.002$
Gammas show the association between hostility and dependency.
[a] 1 case missing due to incomplete interview.

attachment styles of compulsive caregiving and ambivalent attachment.

Independent attachment styles. So far we have concentrated on high dependency. But since this scale also deals with *lack of dependency,* it is relevant for Bowlby's third category of attachment – the compulsively self-reliant. However, those low on dependency do not have a raised rate of depression – 10 per cent (5/48) compared with 13 per cent (18/138) for those neither high nor low on 'dependency' (the 'standard' group) – see Tables 13.1, 13.2, and 13.3.

A second approach to Bowlby's compulsively self-reliant group is to combine 'independence' and 'hostility'. If 'independence' is combined with higher than average 'hostility', a higher rate of depression is obtained (Table 13.3). Nonetheless, there must be some doubt as to whether 'hostility' quite captures the flavour of Bowlby's notion of compulsive self-reliance. Table 13.4 shows a third approach that combines 'independence' with another cognitive set, 'defendedness'. This global rating sought to capture the overall degree to which the respondent 'defended' herself against knowing things at any period of her life, either by poor memory, or by reluctance to stay with a topic, especially if it is painful. The latter may be shown by increasing tension or 'prickliness' in the face of the inter-viewer's probing (although not all such resistance to the interviewer is evidence of defendedness – some is straightforward irritation). This disposition might be considered a better representative than hostility of the

Table 13.4 Depression by independence in relation to others and by defendedness, by loss of mother[a]

Total sample

Independence in relationships	Proportion depressed					
	Defendedness					
	Yes		No		Total	
	%	n	%	n	%	n
Yes	67	(2/3)	7	(3/44)	11	(5/47)
No	24	(4/17)	16	(26/160)	17	(30/177)
Total	30	(6/20)	14	(29/204)	16	(35/224)

Those with loss of mother

Independence in relationships	Defendedness					
	Yes		No		Total	
	%	n	%	n	%	n
Yes	50	(1/2)	11	(3/28)	13	(4/30)
No	27	(4/15)	23	(21/93)	23	(25/108)
Total	29	(5/17)	20	(24/121)	21	(29/138)

Note: [a] 1 case missing due to incomplete interview.

reserve implied by the notion of 'asserting independence of emotional ties'. The combination of the two dimensions in Table 13.4 again raises the rate of depression over that in either category singly, but numbers are, as in Table 13.2, far too small for a conclusion to be drawn. Moreover, the small number of cases of depression involved had also been rated on another cognitive set related to depression – poor ability to make relationships – and it seemed that this, rather than the 'defendedness', might be the contributing factor.

In the light of this exploration, we decided to present results separately for three further attachment styles which might be said to have some relevance for Bowlby's category of compulsive self-reliance. But each probably diverges in some important way from his original concept. Those 16 not classed in the the earlier three groups (ambivalent, compulsive caregiver, and simple dependent), but with poor overall ability to make relationships, were separated out into a fourth group of 'poor relaters'. (Five of these 16 were also 'independent' – that is, low scorers on dependency.) Then the others rated 'independent' on the dependency scale were divided into first those with high or moderate 'hostility', giving an *independent hostile* group,[3] and second, those with average or low 'hostility', giving a fifth, *detached,* group. By giving special attention to those whose poor ability in relationships did not involve high dependency we hoped to learn something more about attachment styles than we could glean from the more obvious dimensions.

Table 13.5 summarizes results using this six-fold categorization along with rates of depression. The low rate of depression in the detached group is especially striking. When the other five non-standard attachment styles are combined they have a three times higher rate than the standard group, and eleven times the rate of the detached. There is therefore a case to be made for simplifying subsequent analyses by combining standard and detached attachment styles, in so far as both have low rates of depression, and contrasting them with the other (vulnerable) attachment styles. On the other hand there is a case to be made for looking at the attachment styles in a different set of combinations, along the lines of Table 13.6, where there is a clear trend for the three styles most closely approximating the Bowlbyan categories to have the highest rate of loss of mother, the other vulnerable and detached styles to have an intermediate rate, and the standard the lowest rate. This is in contrast to the last row of Table 13.5 where the differences between the three loss groups (i.e. no loss of mother, death of mother, and separation from mother) in the proportions with 'vulnerable' styles fail to reach statistical significance. This is because the detached group, while showing a relatively high rate of loss of mother, is not vulnerable to depression. Lack of care shows a similar tendency to be more common in the Bowlbyan than in the other vulnerable attachment groups (Table 13.6), but interestingly is *less* common among the detached even

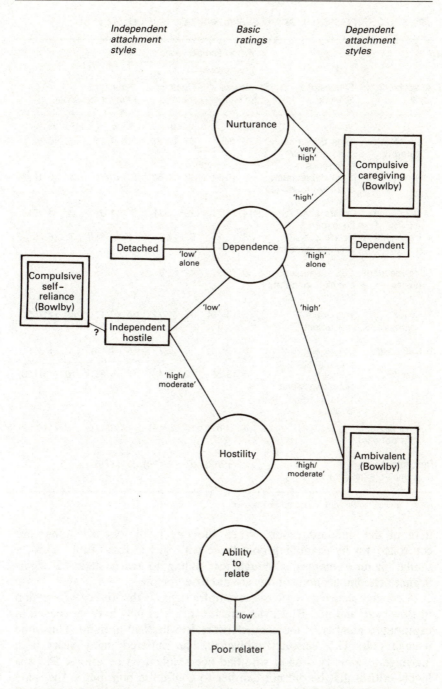

Figure 13.2 The relationship between Walthamstow measures (circles) and different attachment styles (squares)

Table 13.5 Depression, proximal attachment style and loss of mother

Attachment style	Dimensions involved	Proportion depressed			
		Loss group			
		No loss of mother	Death of mother	Separation[a] from mother	Total
		% n	% n	% n	% n
1 Compulsive caregiver	'High' dependency and 'very high' nurturance	nil	67 (2/3)	50 (1/2)	60 (3/5)
2 Ambivalent	'High' dependency and 'high/moderate' hostility	0 (0/3)	17 (1/6)	57 (4/7)	31 (5/16)
3 Dependent	Others with 'high' dependency	14 (1/7)	29 (2/7)	33 (1/3)	24 (4/17)
4 Poor relaters	'Low' scorers on ability to relate to others	28 (2/7)	67 (4/6)	0 (0/3)	38 (6/16)
5 Independent hostile	'Low' dependency and high/moderate hostility	0 (0/2)	42 (3/7)	0 (0/2)	27 (3/11)
Total for groups 1–5	Vulnerable attachment	16 (3/19)	41 (12/29)	35 (6/17)	32 (21/65)
6 Detached	Others with 'low' dependency	0 (0/11)	0 (0/7)	8 (1/13)	3 (1/31)
7 Standard	'Average' dependency and 'good/average' ability to relate	5 (3/56)	12 (5/42)	17 (5/30)	10 (13/128)
Total detached and standard		4 (3/67)	10 (5/49)	14 (6/43)	9 (14/159)
Percentage with vulnerable attachment		22 (19/86)	37 (29/78)	28 (17/60)	

Note [a] 1 case missing due to incomplete interview.

than in the standard group. When the effects of loss of mother are controlled for by examining only those with such a loss (Table 13.6), a similar picture emerges, although just failing to reach statistical significance. The implications of this are discussed below.

A cursory glance at some case examples suggests that this categorization of Bowlbyan and non-Bowlbyan attachment styles may have succeeded in capturing a number of the characteristics Bowlby had in mind. Thus, one woman (Mrs G.), classed *ambivalent*, had suffered many years in a marriage to a heavy drinker who had been violent on occasions. She was highly critical that he did not like her to confide in him, but at the same time she did not want him to confide in her since she felt that she had enough problems to cope with on her own. But when he left her for

Table 13.6 Attachment style by loss of mother and lack of care

(a) Total sample (*n* = 225)

	Attachment style					
	Bowlbyan	Other vulnerable	Detached	Standard	Total	
	(n = 32)	(n = 33)	(n = 31)	(n = 128)	(n = 225)	
Percentage with loss of mother	84	61	65	44	62	*p* < 0.001, 3 d.f.
Percentage with lack of care	66	45	23	33	36	*p* < 0.01, 3 d.f.

(b) Loss of mother group (*n* = 138)

	(n = 27)	(n = 19)	(n = 20)	(n = 92)	(n = 138)	
Percentage with lack of care	70	47	35	46	51	*p* < 0.10, 3 d.f.

another woman she confronted the other woman and demanded that her husband return. This was against the advice of her sister and friends who thought her well rid of him. This then created a rift with them. Mrs G.'s sister was also part of our sample, and, on both their accounts, had always been supportive – for example, taken Mrs G. and the children round to her house when the husband was violent. Nevertheless, Mrs G. told us 'She's [the sister] in a much better position than me financially and she just didn't want to know. I didn't find her any support. I let go then all that I've bottled up for years. I said what I thought, and she just sat there and cried.' On the one hand her resentment and on the other her vacillation over whether to continue in a dependent relationship seemed a satisfactory example of Bowlby's ambivalent disposition.

By contrast Mrs H., with highly *dependent* (or clinging) attachment style, reacted more with fear than with anger in somewhat similar circumstances. Her husband, also a drinker, was extremely possessive. He, for example, did not allow her to go out or wear short-sleeved dresses because other men would see her arms, and he would always draw the curtains early to prevent people looking at her through the window. In spite of this apparent jealousy, he would say to her 'You'll never leave me because who would take you looking like that?' She felt unable to mix with neighbours: her only friend was her husband's sister without whom she would have been totally alone. Mrs H.'s anxiety thus meant that she was unable to expand her social network, with the result that she was highly dependent on her sister-in-law. This, and her inability to end her dependence on her husband, underlay the global rating of high dependency.

It was possible to see how Mrs G. and Mrs H.'s attachment styles were liable to promote depression by trapping them in relationships which were likely to give rise to particularly severe experiences of loss and hopelessness. But this was not so obvious among those classified as *compulsive caregivers*. Mrs F. had always wanted to be a nurse, and was involved in numerous charities and was an active member of an organization for the mentally handicapped, regularly babysitting for a couple with a Down's syndrome child, and frequently visiting an old man down the street who needed help: 'If somebody personally asked for my help I would stop everything to do so – I would never say no', she told us. She had faced depression three times in her life. The first time was when, aged 18, a couple of years after her stepmother had left her to look after her alcoholic father on her own, she returned to her grandmother's. (She and her older sister had lived there for 7 years after their mother's death and before the father's remarriage.) The second time was when her fourth child was born mentally handicapped, and her current episode she attributed to her 20-year-old daughter's having been defrauded of a large sum of money by her boyfriend. Interestingly enough, when her husband had died, leaving her a widow at the early age of 41, she had kept going with no more than nominal grief: 'there was so much to do', she explained. Although it could be argued that the situations she faced on these three occasions could have given rise to depression whatever the attachment style, it is also possible to see how they might affect a 'compulsive' caregiver just that much more profoundly, given that each involved persons who could be seen as her dependants and to whose wellbeing she would therefore be even more committed than someone with a different attachment style. When events threatened their wellbeing this commitment would render her more vulnerable to depression than a 'non-caregiver'. There is good reason to believe that Mrs F. had such extreme commitments: for example, 10 years after the first depression she dedicated herself to nursing her father for months before he died.

Although *poor relating* is not explicitly a Bowlbyan category, it contributes one quarter of the cases of depression among the vulnerable attachment styles and is especially important among those without loss of mother. The distinguishing feature of these 16 was their inability to make friends. Many had one or two good relationships – with a husband, sister, or even one non-kin friend – but all talked of their difficulties in approaching new potential friends, most with regret, although some sought to make virtue of their relative isolation. Thus Mrs M., a widow, commented 'Well, I've not made a lot of friends. I never did. Girls were always jealous of me ... and then I would get shoved into the background'. She told us 'I do feel guilty sometimes just sitting at home ... but I'm not lonely you know. I always keep myself busy'. She had recently been on holiday in a camp where her son was employed and recounted proudly how she had not needed to get to know any of the other holiday makers. Almost the first thing she told us, when we inquired as to her marital status, was that she 'had never been coddled' and again at the end of the interview she summarized 'It's my early upbringing – I have to be self-reliant'. (Her father had left when she was 5, and her grandparents had drilled her to believe that he was no longer a member of the family.) Mrs M. had never been depressed. Most of the poor relaters were less proud than Mrs M., and about half were quite open that their loneliness stemmed from a basic anxiety about people. Others talked as if they had earlier drifted away from social life as a result of family commitments and now felt they could never get back. Yet others described a sense of long-term alienation, long predating any depressive episode they might currently be experiencing: Mrs T explained 'I either could not talk to people or I told them so much they weren't interested'. While Mrs M. might resemble one of Bowlby's compulsively self-reliant personalities, most of the poor relaters were more retiring, the type of women who might have received a rating of high dependency if only there were more people in their lives on whom they would have the opportunity to depend.

This last comment provokes a query. Is it the style of attachment or the absence of supportive figures that gives rise to the vulnerability to depression among the poor relaters? Using an index of poor support in the proximal period, based on the availability at least weekly of a partner (or friend for those without partners or boyfriends) rated 1 or 2 on the active emotional support measure, the poor relaters had no higher an experience of poor support than the ambivalent and the independent hostile groups (44, 47, and 45 per cent respectively), although these proportions are twice as high as in the dependent group (21 per cent), with the remaining three styles ('compulsive caregivers', 'standard', and 'detached') falling some-where between, but nearer the dependent group (25, 27, and 29 per cent). This is a reminder that the next step must be to relate these six attachment styles to the environmental variables identified along strand 1 as important for depression. A series of linear logistic regression analyses had pin-pointed lack of adequate care in childhood (for a minimum of 1 year) and recent poor support as the two most critical of these environmental factors (Harris *et al.* 1989b). Table 13.7 presents results showing how depression relates both to these background factors and to attachment style. In order to simplify matters the five vulnerable attachment styles which related to depression in Table 13.5 (that is all excluding the detached and, of course, the standard) are presented together. The table is also simplified in another way: only those with childhood loss of mother have been included. This is to guard against possible confounding by other factors which have been found to influence depression and which were more frequent in the mother-loss group (for example premarital pregnancy; see Harris *et al.* 1987). The bottom row (total) shows how depression increases with the two environmental factors, but the third row shows how the identified attachment styles add over and above these two variables.

Finally, it is necessary to ask whether the results in Table 13.7 could not

Table 13.7 Depression by lack of care after loss in childhood, recent poor support, and proximal attachment style among women with loss of mother before age 17 ($n = 139$)

	Proportion depressed				
	Lack of care				
	Yes		No		
	Recent poor support		Recent poor support		
Attachment style	Yes	No	Yes	No	Total
	% n	% n	% n	% n	% n
Detached	33 (1/3)	0 (0/4)	0 (0/3)	0 (0/10)	5 (1/20)
Standard	45 (5/11)	8 (2/24)	0 (0/6)	10 (3/31)	14 (10/72)
Vulnerable attachment styles	79 (11/14)	40 (6/15)	17 (1/6)	8 (1/12)	40 (19/47)
Total	61 (17/28)	19 (8/43)	7 (1/15)	8 (4/53)	22 (30/139)

arise from some other process which happens to be connected with these attachment styles. An obvious candidate is helplessness, which has already been described as playing a key role in the intra-psychic strand, and which we have seen is associated with poor ability to make relationships. Table 13.8 shows not only how the identified attachment styles are modestly associated with high helplessness, but also how the detached have an especially high proportion with the lowest helplessness score. In other words the detached are particularly masterful, and this could explain their notably low rate of depression. (Much the same degree of association emerges when cases are excluded from the table suggesting that this link cannot be explained as merely the result of a tendency by *depressed* women to report both a helpless and an unusual attachment style.) Nonetheless, when the results from Table 13.7 involving attachment style, lack of care, and poor support are looked at again in Table 13.9 – in terms of higher than average helplessness as well as the other three variables – it seems that attachment style is still contributing something beyond helplessness (in column 2, compare row 3 with row 5 and row 4 with row 6), although the effect is at best modest. In Table 13.10 this is put to statistical test using a dichotomous variable for attachment style, where the standard and the detached are combined in one category and all other variants of attachment style kept in the vulnerable category. The linear logistic regression shows that the best model (15) requires all four independent variables to predict depression. Neither helplessness nor vulnerable attachment style on their own is enough to capture the full cognitive emotional predisposition to depression.

At this point it might be objected that to follow our previous work and

Table 13.8 Proximal attachment style and helplessness in adulthood in the total sample

Attachment style	Score on adult helplessness								Total	
	High (1–3)		Moderate (4)		Average (5)		Very low (6)			
	%	n	%	n	%	n	%	n	%	n
Detached	10	(3)	13	(4)	39	(12)	39	(12)	100	(31)
Standard	12	(15)	22	(28)	45	(58)	21	(27)	100	(128)
Vulnerable attachment styles	44	(29)	24	(16)	23	(15)	10	(6)	100	(66)

Notes: Chi-square 31.32, d.f. 6, $p < 0.001$
Gamma 0.30

Table 13.9 Depression by lack of care after loss of mother, poor support, proximal attachment style, and higher than average adult helplessness among women with loss of mother

Attachment style	Adult helplessness	Proportion depressed								Total	
		Lack of care									
		Yes				No					
		Poor support									
		Yes		No		Yes		No			
		%	n	%	n	%	n	%	n	%	n
Detached	Yes	33	(1/3)	–		–		0	(0/1)	25	(1/4)
	No	–		0	(0/4)	0	(0/3)	0	(0/9)	0	(0/16)
Standard	Yes	80	(4/5)	22	(2/9)	0	(0/2)	14	(1/7)	30	(7/23)
	No	17	(1/6)	0	(0/15)	0	(0/4)	8	(2/24)	6	(3/49)
Vulnerable attachment styles	Yes	83	(10/12)	50	(4/8)	25	(1/4)	14	(1/7)	52	(16/31)
	No	50	(1/2)	29	(2/7)	0	(0/2)	0	(0/5)	19	(3/16)

dichotomize our 6-point helplessness scale between 'average' and 'higher than average' was to bias our conclusions, especially as Table 13.9 suggests the standard and vulnerable attachment styles have roughly similar proportions with moderate helplessness (22 and 24 per cent), but the latter have considerably more with high helplessness (12 and 44 per cent). The logistic regression was therefore re-run using a cut-point between high and moderate helplessness, but again the best model required attachment style as well as helplessness. This coalesced into a coherent picture when further examination showed that proportions with depression were barely different between those with high and those with moderate helplessness for the standard attachment styles (27 and 21 per cent), whereas for the vulnerable

Table 13.10 Linear logistic regression examining the impact on depression of (A) lack of care after loss of mother, (B) poor support, (C) proximal attachment style, and (D) adult helplessness

Model fitted	Scaled deviance	d.f.	p
Constant	55.06	15	<0.001
1 Lack of care (A)	37.91	14	<0.001
2 Poor support (B)	40.86	14	<0.001
3 Attachment style (C)	40.84	14	<0.001
4 Adult helplessness (D)	31.51	14	<0.01
5 A plus B	27.64	13	<0.02
6 A plus C	26.62	13	<0.02
7 A plus D	19.77	13	<0.01
8 B plus C	30.17	13	<0.01
9 B plus D	23.62	13	<0.05
10 C plus D	25.95	13	<0.02
11 A plus B plus C	18.57	12	n.s.
12 A plus B plus D	14.43	12	n.s.
13 A plus C plus D	14.47	12	n.s.
14 B plus C plus D	19.18	12	n.s.
15 A plus B plus C plus D[a]	9.85	11	n.s.

[a]Best fitting model is 15

Note: Detached attachment style has been combined with standard style and these compared as a dichotomy with one other grouping which includes all other categories of attachment style.

48 per cent with high and 25 per cent with moderate helplessness were depressed. In other words women with high helplessness are only more vulnerable to depression than those with moderate helplessness when they also have vulnerable attachment styles. What this probably means theoretically is that the tendency to generalize hopelessness postulated in Fig. 13.1 is more closely related to one aspect of high helplessness than to another – to the emotional tone of a woman's relationships, rather than to the more impersonal aspects of her competence in housework or at work. This speculation would be consistent with our perspective on the role of self-esteem as being of greater importance in depressive onset than helplessness: a major component in the measurement of self-esteem for women is the belief that other people think one a nice sympathetic person, or, in Bowlby's words, a belief that one is 'lovable', and this of course involves the interpersonal side of life rather than that more straightforward lack of mastery over material factors which can also be reflected in high helplessness.

INTEGRATION OF THE WALTHAMSTOW STUDY WITHIN ATTACHMENT THEORY

It must be reiterated that the findings presented here are exploratory. Accepting this, they offer some confirmation of, and if replicated later would offer considerable support for, the tenets of attachment theory which are relevant in accounting for adult depression. Many of the key variables identified in the different analyses as intervening between loss of mother and depression concern intimate relationships, and the impact these appear to have upon the women's cognitive sets and upon their subsequent life experiences. Lack of adequate parental care, more frequent after loss of mother, increased a young girl's chances of finding herself, as it were, on a conveyor belt to an unsupportive marriage in adulthood. A premarital pregnancy was one of the most notable ways of being trapped on such a trajectory: marriages stemming from such pregnancies seemed likely to be hampered first by the problems of a couple having to settle down before they are ready to start a family – with no savings yet for cots and prams, and probably without adequate housing for a baby – and second by the fact that many would not have chosen to marry each other if the pregnancy had not forced them to legitimize the child; the partnerships in such cases would likely fail to progress towards a true intimacy. For both these reasons such women would be more likely to find their lives beset with experiences of the type identified as 'provoking agents' for depression: the severe loss events and major difficulties involving money, housing, and marital neglect and infidelity. Although these provoking agents were unfortunately not documented in the Walthamstow study in the detail required to include them in model-fitting analyses, enough is known about their role from other studies to permit confidence in conclusions based on our less systematic records of them in the Walthamstow sample. It did seem that such provoking agents regularly occurred at the end of this causal chain (what has been called strand 1 in Fig. 1) and that they were several times more common before onset among those with depression than among the non-depressed in the year before interview. (Our most con-servative estimates suggested 90 per cent (27/30) of the depressed and 33 per cent (33/109) of the other women with loss of mother had undergone such an experience.) Moreover, a subsequent study in Islington has not only confirmed the series of links along strand 1, from lack of care via premarital pregnancy and marital disruption to provoking agent and depression, but also shown a link between lack of care and current negative evaluation of self (Bifulco *et al.* 1987).

The seemingly social nature of many such experiences should not mislead us into ignoring their relevance for attachment theory – when an eviction notice arrives it can carry with it not only the message of a society where housing can be uncaringly withdrawn, but also the further im-plication that for a long time the husband, who is supposed to look after his family, has been failing to do so by gambling or drinking away the rent money. In other words such events may reinforce the expectations of anyone whose early life has sensitized them to experiences of neglect. Furthermore, the additional role of poor support in coping with such provoking agents has consistently emerged in those studies which have examined depressive onset in detail in this way (Brown and Harris 1986). And the vulnerability conferred by poor support can be seen as typifying the central message of attachment theory (Bowlby 1980: 442). In addition, however, the findings which involve strand-2 factors are of even clearer relevance: the roles of helplessness and hostility, and their different aetiological roles when those losing mother by death are compared with those losing her by separation, were initially predicted on the basis of the conclusions of the second volume of *Attachment and Loss*. And the results reported here for the first time on style of attachment take the process of interpretation further: that strand-2 factors other than helplessness can make an additional contribution to depressive onset. Thus while linear logistic regression shows that, on its own, neither hostility nor dependency plays an extra causal role beyond helplessness, when such dimensions are used in combination to form categories along lines suggested by the third volume of *Attachment and Loss* an additional contribution for vulnerable attachment style does emerge, not only beyond helplessness but beyond the strand-1 factors of lack of care and poor support as well (see Table 13.9). On the other hand, these vulnerable attachment styles seem to be less clearly linked than helplessness to the childhood environment measures used in the study, and it will be important to explore their origins further.

Thus, on the one hand the important role of both childhood and adult helplessness, intervening between lack of adequate replacement care after loss of mother in childhood and depression in adulthood, echoes Bowlby's earlier arguments about the resilience of those whose self-reliance has been encouraged by secure attachments in early life (Bowlby 1973: 366–410). On the other hand the results involving attachment style support his later elaboration of the types of personalities whose manner of relating to others renders them more vulnerable to disordered mourning and to depression (Bowlby 1980); and here it is worth emphasizing that those vulnerable styles most resembling his descriptions (here called the Bowlbyan styles) showed a closer relationship to childhood loss and lack of care than the other vulnerable styles whose origins could not be identified in any of our range of variables. Detailed perusal of the information we did have about the particular women involved suggested these origins might lie in very early experience, if not be constitutional (see Table 13.6).

While some readers will find this concatenation of predictions unsurprising, some will focus especially on the one or two failures to confirm expected notions, and others, seeking a more precise delineation between various schools of thought, may consider that our conclusions blur many of the crucial distinctions. It may thus be necessary to expand in more detail. The findings which we have been unable to confirm straightforwardly concern the vulnerability of those whose disposition is to assert independence of affectional ties. Along with this goes our failure to find differences in vulnerability according to the actual mourning rituals and practices experienced. There are several possible explanations.

First, our measures may be inadequate indicators of the processes hypothesized. While the range of mourning items covered was extensive the retrospective nature of the data collection meant there were missing values, which may have masked a number of genuine associations that would have been obvious had we carried out a longitudinal study, observing whether the little girls, for example, did or did not see the mother's corpse which they have now completely forgotten as older women.

On the other hand this first explanation (imprecision of measurement) is of greater relevance to the other hypotheses we failed to confirm, involving compulsive self-reliance. Our measure of defendedness was not only exploratory but also global and impressionistic. It did not possess the more detailed content-analysis specifications of Main's 'disorganization' in her adult attachment interview (Main and Solomon 1986), or of the Grossmanns' defensiveness (Grossmann and Grossmann 1986). Moreover, our attempt to characterize those who were 'disposed to assert independence of affectional ties' was made on the basis of an already developed measure of independence which accounted as much for the amount of 'independence' *actually* exhibited as for a disposition (perhaps without success) to assert it. It would therefore be understandable if we were picking out the wrong women. Nevertheless, the degree to which we failed to support the hypothesis about compulsive self-reliance is so marked that it seems unlikely that it arose only from this discrepancy between actual exhibition and mere assertion of a tendency to 'independence'. According to the theory it would be expected that anyone keeping herself to herself must turn out to be vulnerable. Thus in Walthamstow an increased risk of depression would be expected among those rated more 'independent' than the standard pattern in their relationships. Of the 47 thus rated independent, it was possible to use other dimensions to pick out 16 'poor relaters' who might be at increased risk for other reasons (11 who were also hostile above a key threshold level and 5 who showed some further disability in their relationships), and indeed depression was more common among these women. This left the 31 who are here categorized as 'detached' and who emerged as the most resilient group (see Table 13.5). They also proved to have the highest proportion with scores of 'very low' (or 6) on adult helplessness (see Table 13.8). In other words they were the most self-reliant group and their self-reliance turned out to be protective rather than injurious. It seems, then, as if mere exhibition of 'independence' may not be the quality of attachment style which increases risk of depression. In the light of the figures in Table 13.6 it is tempting to relate this special resilience to a theory from a different tradition, namely that certain hardships in childhood can 'steel' a psyche to cope better with later adversity provided they are not accompanied by other more damaging childhood experiences. A comparison of the two rows in Table 13.6(a) suggests that the detached have a relatively greater experience of loss of mother and a relatively lower experience of lack of care than the standard group. However, numbers are small and this must remain highly speculative.

The second line of explanation for our failure to support the hypothesis about increased depression among the compulsively self-reliant is the nature of our sample. Table 13.4 suggests that there may be a very small group of such compulsively independent people where vulnerability *is* increased, a group identified by combining the measure of independence with that of moderate or marked defendedness. As with compulsive caregiving in Table 13.2 these dispositions may turn out to be extremely rare in community samples, although their greater frequency in clinical samples may allow adequate investigation of the hypothesis there in a case-control design. Another shortcoming of the Walthamstow sample is the absence of male respondents. Although not explicit in attachment theory, the notion of gender differences in styles of personal relationships has become a working hypothesis in social psychiatry, and men are now commonly thought of as more concerned to assert independence than women (see Cohen and Wills's (1985) discussion of gender differences in needs for social support). It may be therefore that a clinical sample including men would have given large enough numbers to come up with confirmations of these ideas.

While these explanations may satisfy some readers, others may reach for a third – namely, that those predictions involving mourning rituals and compulsive self-reliance have been definitely disconfirmed. Yet others may accept that judgement must still be reserved on these issues, yet consider the other Walthamstow findings confusing in the variety of causal chains supported.

Perhaps the culprit here is the term 'self-reliance', whose use to cover two rather different concepts may be causing confusion. One of these succeeds in blending elements from a diversity of the theoretical frameworks developed to explain clinical depression. Indeed, it could be argued that in this catholic appeal lies the true merit of the term, in that it can unite research workers from many disciplines. Thus it seems to summarize many of the concepts which have been proposed to account for the dimension of resilience versus susceptibility to depression; for example, 'self-esteem' (Rosenberg 1965; Ingham *et al.* 1986, 1987), 'self-efficacy' (Bandura 1977), 'mastery' (Caplan 1981), 'social competence' (Lewinsohn *et al.* 1980), and 'sense of coherence' (Antonovsky 1979), or at the other end of the dimension 'learned helplessness' (Seligman 1975), 'subjective incompetence' (De Figueiredo and Frank 1982), 'external locus of control' (Rotter 1966), 'negative evaluation of self' (Brown *et al.* 1986a), and 'dysfunctional attitudes' (Weissman and Beck 1978). Bowlby is renowned for just such an approach synthesizing findings from a wide spectrum of studies. His notion of 'internal working models' provides a theoretical framework ample enough to accommodate both conscious and unconscious 'schemas', and to span the broad developmental sequence linking childhood with adult experience; it would encompass not only the depressogenic behavioural dispositions listed above but also the other more cognitive tendencies proposed by attribution theory in its various forms (Abramson *et al.* 1978; Krantz and Hammen 1979; Brewin and Shapiro 1984; Fennell and Campbell 1984). It is thus surprising that in his third volume the useful concept of self-reliance is rarely invoked without the prefix 'compulsive', and so the benefits of self-reliance are played down in comparison to its disadvantages when it is possessed to a compulsive degree. Yet the dimension still plays a crucial part in the theory, but under another name: for example, it carries the melody in that symphonic finale on the last page, but there it is referred to as 'strength' (Bowlby 1980: 442).

Meanwhile, 'compulsive self-reliance' has been introduced as a feature entailing only a pseudo-strength. Certainly, empirical data from studies informed by attachment theory suggest the value of contrasting an avoidant pattern with the other styles of relating. Using Ainsworth's 'strange situation' to classify infants there are consistent differences over time not only between secure (group B), anxious–ambivalent (group C), and disorganized (D) infants, but also between all these and the group A or avoidant ones (Ainsworth 1985; Main *et al.* 1985). At the other end of the life span, Parkes's categorization of reactions at the time of bereavement identifies a group who avoid the contact with others which could support them through the loss (Parkes this volume). His elegant classificatory scheme explicitly identifies mistrust of others as the feature underlying this avoidance, but it also identifies self-trust as the other key predictive dimension. In other words with this latter notion Parkes is implicitly acknowledging the predictive importance of a dimension resembling helplessness–mastery. It may be no accident that it is in his research rather than in the many studies of infants that this should arise: somehow the notion of rating a 12-month-old on mastery seems anomalous. In his sample, however, he finds many avoidant personalities who also mistrust themselves. Perhaps this brings us back to an earlier point about the nature of the Walthamstow sample. A large number of the 'independent' women had high mastery (i.e. self-trust, or self-reliance in its simple sense – see Table 13.7), and may therefore differ from the personalities seen in clinical samples, where those with low helplessness will tend to be selected out. Moreover, it is necessary to remind ourselves of the greater vulnerability of those 'independent' women who were also rated high or moderate on hostility, a rating capturing the mistrustful aspects of the avoidant style.

This extra dimension of self-mistrust points up the contrast with another type of 'independence', perhaps what we have here called detachment, which Winnicott saw as the end-product of the greatest personal security, the capacity to be alone (Winnicott 1958). Certainly, there seems evidence in our sample that the term 'autonomous' might have been a better description for the 31 detached women distinguished here. Whereas the notion of detachment implies a certain degree of withdrawal from people and activities, these 31 were often socially involved and committed to various projects, but without needing to depend on the support of others. In other words they had high levels of self-trust.

But whatever speculations the Walthamstow data may provoke about compulsive self-reliance, the bulk of evidence points to the increased risk of depression of those with the other attachment styles, regardless of the issue of their origin, and it is therefore appropriate to consider the implications. Here perhaps we need to remind ourselves that what was common to most of these styles was high dependency or, in the case of the poor relaters, a diffidence or anxiety about people which meant they had too few contacts for high dependency to be scored in practice, but had a similar feel to their personalities. Once again we are faced with the way in which the vulnerable attachment styles seem to represent a particularly acute form of interpersonal helplessness. As so often, and not only in retrospective studies, it is difficult to disentangle the roles of personality and life structure in perpetuating relationships where these attachment styles continue to manifest themselves. And here it is worth returning to the topic of the role of poor support in the proximal period. We saw how there were more women with poor support among the ambivalent, independent hostile, and the poor relaters than among the compulsive caregivers and the dependent. Further investigation suggests that higher than average hostility is likely to account for this: this characteristic, present by definition in the first two groups and absent in the last two, neatly divides those poor relaters according to degree of support: 75 per cent (3/4) with such hostility have poor support, compared with 33 per cent (4/12) of the other poor relaters. It is easy to see how a hostile wife, mother, or friend can alienate potential support figures, but it is also easy to see how certain failures to provide support on the part of these figures can give rise to the hostility. The citation at the beginning of this chapter is an example of just such a spiralling process in the life story of Dorothy Parker and reminds us once more how embedded in each other the two causal strands in Fig. 1 can become. In other words the pathway from vulnerable attachment styles to depression may lie as much through their impact upon the external world (for example, their ability to throw up provoking events such as rifts in relationships) as through an intra-psychic channel of personal susceptibility.

But when all is said and done perhaps the most important message of the Walthamstow study is that of a certain optimism: it did prove possible for some women to get off the conveyor belt from lack of care to depression if a secure attachment could be found in adulthood, typically in the form of a good marital partnership. One woman we saw at age 51 had remained well for the last 9 years, and was looking forward to her future with an optimism which belied her early history. Her father had died when she was 7, and her mother was unable to cope, sending her to an institution with her brother and sister until her teenage years when she had to return to take over helping her mother. Married young, she had children quickly, and faced her husband's infidelity. At this point she was divorced and suffered a breakdown. Some of her children were adopted away at this time. A second husband, while not unfaithful, drank and beat her regularly. After another depressive episode (her last) she was helped by the general practitioner and left this husband during another pregnancy, coming to London to set herself up alone with the new baby. Here she met a boyfriend of a different kind: 'He says he wishes he'd met me years ago. He's a very stabilizing person: I rely on him a lot. We talk and talk about everything, and sometimes we can't stop. He's so good for me – he's just like my Dad.' At the end of the interview she told us: 'I used to expect everything to go wrong and it did ... I used to be a terrible pessimist and I'm not any more'. The perspective of attachment theory not only gives us an account of how early relationships can set us on a downward spiral, but also gives us hope that secure attachments in later life can help us climb up once more.

ACKNOWLEDGEMENTS

The Walthamstow study was funded by the Medical Research Council. We would like to thank Brenda Freeman, Carol Greenberg, and Liz Smith for help with the interviewing, Laurie Letchford for help with the computing, Sue Ross and Eve Branston for help with the typing, and, above all, George Brown for help with the thinking and for providing a secure base.

NOTES

1   Past loss included not only childhood loss of parent but also of sibling, and, in addition, deaths in adulthood of husband or child (before the current 12 months), and separations of over 12 months from child (but not of husband).

2   However, nurturance and hostility were negatively related, despite each variable's showing a positive relationship with dependency. This probably reflects the scarcity of highly hostile and highly nurturant women as compared with highly dependent ones – a ratio of 5 or 6 to 1. It is therefore possible for the category 'highly dependent' to include many of the highly hostile and highly

nurturant women without overlap between these latter two groups.
3   The choice of a cut-point between moderate and average hostility to define the independent hostile group will be conservative. The bottom row of Table 13.3 only suggests more depression among the highly hostile independent women: those with moderate hostility do not have such an obviously raised rate.

REFERENCES

Abramson, L.Y., Seligman, M.E.P., and Teasdale, J. (1978) 'Learned helplessness in humans: critique and reformulation', *Journal of Abnormal Psychology* 87: 49–74.
Ainsworth, M.D. (1985) 'Patterns of infant–mother attachments: antecedents and effects on development', *Bulletin of New York Academic Medicine* 61: 771–91.
Ainsworth, M.D., Bell, S.M., and Stayton, D.J. (1971) 'Individual differences in strange situation behaviour of one-year-olds', in H.R. Schaffer (ed.) *The Origins of Human Social Relations*, London: Academic Press.
Ainsworth, M.D. and Wittig, B.A. (1969) 'Attachment and the exploratory behaviour of one-year-olds in a strange situation', in B.M. Foss (ed.) *Determinants of Infant Behaviour*, vol. 4, London: Methuen.
Antonovsky, A. (1979) *Health, Stress and Coping*, San Francisco: Jossey-Bass.
Bandura, A. (1977) 'Self-efficacy: toward a unifying theory of behavioural change', *Psychological Review* 84: 191–215.
Beck, A.T. (1967) *Depression: Clinical, Experimental and Theoretical Aspects*, London: Staples Press.
Bifulco, A.T. (1985) 'Death of mother in childhood and clinical depression in adult life: a biographical approach to aetiology', Doctoral dissertation, University of London, Department of Philosophy.
Bifulco, A.T., Brown, G.B., and Harris, T.O. (1987) 'Childhood loss of parent, lack of adequate parental care and adult depression: a replication', *Journal of Affective Disorders* 12: 115–28.
Bifulco, A.T., Harris, T.O., and Brown, G.W. (1989) 'Childhood mourning and depression', Ms.
Birtchnell, J. (1975) 'The personality characteristics of early-bereaved psychiatric patients', *Social Psychiatry* 10: 97–103.
Bowlby, J. (1969) *Attachment and Loss*, vol. 1: *Attachment*, New York: Basic Books.
—— (1973) *Attachment and Loss*, vol. 2: *Separation: Anxiety and Anger*, New York: Basic Books.
—— (1980) *Attachment and Loss*, vol. 3: *Loss: Sadness and Depression*, New York: Basic Books.
—— (1988) 'Developmental psychiatry comes of age', *American Journal of Psychiatry* 145: 1–10.
Bretherton, I. (1987) 'New perspectives on attachment relations: security, communication and internal working models', in J. Osofsky (ed.) *Handbook of Infant Development*, 2nd ed., New York: John Wiley and Sons.
Bretherton, I. and Waters, E. (1985) Growing Points of Attachment Theory and Research, *Monographs of the Society for Research in Child Development* 50 (1–2).
Brewin, C.R. and Shapiro, D.A. (1984) 'Beyond locus of control: attribution of responsibility for positive and negative outcomes', *British Journal of Psychology* 75: 43–9.
Brown, G.W. (1974) 'Meaning, measurement and stress of life events', in B.S.

Dohrenwend and B.P. Dohrenwend (eds) *Stressful Life Events: Their Nature and Effects*, New York: John Wiley.

—— (1981) 'Contextual measures of life events', in B.S. Dohrenwend and B.P. Dohrenwend (eds) *Stressful Life Events and Their Contexts*, New York: Neale Watson Academic Publications.

—— (1982) 'Early loss and depression', in Parkes, C.M. and Stevenson-Hinde, J. (eds) *The Place of Attachment in Human Behaviour*, New York: Basic Books, and London: Tavistock Publications.

—— (1988) 'Introduction: Life events and measurement', in G.W. Brown and T.O. Harris (eds) *Life Events and Illness*, New York: Guilford Press.

Brown, G.W., Andrews, B., Harris, T.O., Adler, Z., and Bridge, L. (1986) 'Social support, self-esteem and depression', *Psychological Medicine* 16: 813–31.

Brown, G.W. and Harris, T.O. (1978) *Social Origins of Depression: A Study of Psychiatric Disorder in Women*, London: Tavistock Publications, and New York: Free Press.

—— (1979) 'The sin of subjectivism: a reply to Shapiro', *Behavioural Research and Therapy* 17: 605–13.

—— (1986) 'Stressor, vulnerability and depression: a question of replication', *Psychological Medicine* 16: 739–44.

Brown, G.W., Harris, T.S., and Bifulco, A. (1986a) 'Long-term effect of early loss of parent', in M. Rutter, C. Izard, and P. Read (eds) *Depression in Childhood: Developmental Perspectives*, New York: Guilford Press.

Caplan, G. (1981) 'Mastery of stress: psychosocial aspects', *American Journal of Psychiatry* 138: 413–20.

Cohen, S. and Wills, T.A. (1985) 'Stress, social support and the buffering hypothesis', *Psychological Bulletin* 98: 310–57.

Coopersmith, S. (1967) *Antecedents of Self-esteem*, San Francisco: W.H. Freeman & Co.

Dean, C., Surtees, P.G., and Sashidharan, S.D. (1983) 'Comparison of research diagnostic systems in an Edinburgh community sample', *British Journal of Psychiatry* 142: 247–56.

De Figueiredo, J.M. and Frank, J.D. (1982) 'Subjective incompetence, the clinical hallmark of demoralisation', *Comprehensive Psychiatry* 23: 353–63.

Fennell, M.J.V. and Campbell, E.A. (1984) 'The cognitions questionnaire: specific thinking errors in depression', *British Journal of Clinical Psychology* 23: 81–92.

Glick, I.O., Weiss, R.S., and Parkes, C.M. (1974) *The First Year of Bereavement*, New York: John Wiley.

Grossmann, K.E. and Grossmann, K. (1981) 'Parent–infant attachment relationships in Bielefeld', in K. Immelmann, G. Barlow, L. Petrovich, and M. Main (eds) *Behavioural Development: The Bielefeld Interdisciplinary Project*, New York: Cambridge University Press.

Grossmann, K.E., Grossmann, K., and Schwan, A. (1986) 'Capturing the wider view of attachment: a reanalysis of Ainsworth's strange situation', in C.E. Izard and P.B. Read (eds) *Measuring Emotions in Infants and Children*, vol. 2, New York: Cambridge University Press.

Harris, T.O., Brown, G.W., and Bifulco, A. (1986) 'Loss of parent in childhood and adult psychiatric disorder: the role of lack of adequate parental care', *Psychological Medicine* 16: 641–59.

—— (1987) 'Loss of parent in childhood and adult psychiatric disorder: the role of social class position and premarital pregnancy', *Psychological Medicine* 17: 163–83.

—— (1990a) 'Depression and situational helplessness/mastery in a sample selected to study childhood parental loss', *Journal of Affective Disorders* (20) 1: 27–41.

—— (1990b) 'Loss of parent in childhood and psychiatric disorder in adulthood: a tentative overall model', *Development and Psychopathology.*

—— (1990c) 'Loss of parent in childhood and adult psychiatric disorder: the differential impact of death and separation, and the role of situational hostility', Ms.

Hinde, R.A. and Davies, L. (1972) 'Removing infant rhesus from mother for 13 days compared with removing mother from infant', *Journal of Child Psychology and Psychiatry* 13: 227–37.

Hinde, R.A. and Spencer-Booth, Y. (1971) 'Effects of brief separation from mother on rhesus monkeys', *Science* 173: 111–18.

Hirschfield, R.M.A., Klerman, G.L., Gough, H.G., Barrett, J., Korchin, S.J., and Chodoff, P. (1977) 'A measure of interpersonal dependency', *Journal of Personality Assessment* 41: 610–18.

Hofer, M.A. (1976) 'The organization of sleep and wakefulness after maternal separation in young rats', *Developmental Psychobiology* 9: 189–205.

Ingham, J.G., Kreitman, N.B., Miller, P. McC., Sashidharan, S.P., and Surtees, P. (1986) 'Self-esteem, vulnerability, and psychiatric disorder in the community', *British Journal of Psychiatry* 148: 375–85.

—— (1987) 'Self-appraisal, anxiety and depression in women – a prospective enquiry', *British Journal of Psychiatry* 151: 643–51.

Krantz, S. and Hammen, C.I. (1979) 'Assessment of cognitive bias in depression', *Journal of Abnormal Psychology* 88: 611–19.

Lewinsohn, P.M., Mischel, W., Chaplin, W., and Barton, R. (1980) 'Social competence and depression: the role of illusionary self-perception?' *Journal of Abnormal Psychology* 89: 203–12.

McCall, G.J. and Simmons, J.L. (1966) *Identities and Interactions,* New York: Free Press.

McKinney, W.T., Moran, E.C., and Kramer, G.W. (1984) 'Separation in nonhuman primates as a model for human depression: neurobiological implications', in R.M. Post and J.C. Ballenger (eds) *Neurobiology of Mood Disorders,* Baltimore, MD: Williams & Wilkins.

Main, M., Kaplan, N., and Cassidy, J. (1985) 'Security in infancy, childhood and adulthood: a move to the level of representation', in I. Bretherton and E. Waters (eds) Growing Points of Attachment Theory and Research, *Monographs of the Society for Research in Child Development* 50 (1–2).

Main, M. and Solomon, J. (1986) 'Discovery of an insecure–disorganised/ disoriented attachment pattern', in T.B. Brazelton and M. Yogman (eds) *Affective Development in Infancy,* Norwood, NJ: Ablex.

Main, M. and Weston, D. (1982) 'Avoidance of the attachment figure in infancy: descriptions and interpretations', in C.M. Parkes and J. Stevenson-Hinde (eds) *The Place of Attachment in Human Behaviour,* London: Tavistock; New York: Basic Books.

Meade, M. (1988) *Dorothy Parker: What Fresh Hell is This? A Biography,* London: Heinemann.

Miyake, K., Chen, S., and Campos, J. (1985) 'Infant temperament, mother's mode of interaction, and attachment in Japan: an interim report', in I. Bretherton and E. Waters (eds) Growing Points of Attachment Theory and Research, *Monographs of the Society for Research in Child Development* 50 (1–2).

Navran, L. (1954) 'A rationally derived M.M.P.I. scale to measure dependence', *J. Cons. Psychology* 18: 192.

O'Connor, P. (1987) 'Very close relationships', Doctoral dissertation, University of London.
Parkes, C.M. and Weiss, R.S. (1983) *Recovery from Bereavement*, New York: Basic Books.
Rosenberg, M. (1965) *Society and the Adolescent Self-Image*, Princeton: Princeton University Press.
Rotter, J.B. (1966) 'Generalised expectancies for internal vs external control of reinforcement', *Psychological Monographs* 80: 1–28.
Sagi, A., Lamb, M.E., Lewkowicz, K.S., Shoham, R., Dvir, R., and Estes, D. (1985) 'Security of infant–mother, –father, and –metapelet attachments among Kibbutz-reared Israeli children', in I. Bretherton and E. Waters (eds) Growing Points of Attachment Theory and Research, *Monographs of the Society for Research in Child Development* 50 (1–2).
Seligman, M.E. (1975) *Helplessness: On Depression, Development and Death*, San Francisco: W.H. Freeman.
Smith, G.K. and Anderson, V. (1984) 'Effects of maternal isolation on the development of activity rhythms in infant rats', *Physiology and Behaviour* 33: 751–6.
Weissman, M.M. and Beck, A.T. (1978) 'Development and validation of the DAS: a preliminary investigation', Paper presented at the Annual Meeting of the American Education Research Association, Toronto.
Wing, J.K., Cooper, J.E., and Sartorius, N. (1974) *The Measurement and Classification of Psychiatric Symptoms: an Instruction Manual for the Present State Examination and CATEGO Programme*, Cambridge: Cambridge University Press.
Winnicott, D.W. (1958) 'The capacity to be alone', *International Journal of Psychoanalysis* 39: 416–20.

Chapter 14

Attachment, bonding, and psychiatric problems after bereavement in adult life

Colin Murray Parkes

Since grief results from the severance of bonds it would be surprising if atypical or pathological grief were not sometimes the consequence of the severance of atypical bonds. And since atypical attachments in adult life are often thought to result from atypical parenting in childhood it would be surprising if there were not some causal connection between parenting and the pattern of grieving. Support for this claim comes from Sable's (1989) study of 81 widows who had lost their husbands 1–3 years previously. She found that 'those women who described more secure early attachment were handling bereavement better, they had less distress at the time of the loss and showed better adjustment for both outcome factors, depression and anxiety'.

Between the experience of parenting in childhood and the experience of bereavement in adult life comes a long series of events and influences which are also likely to influence the reaction to bereavement and may, indeed, outweigh the effects of parenting. The bereavement itself may influence the reaction according to the closeness and type of bond and way in which the loss occurs.

METHOD OF INVESTIGATION

It was with the object of exploring these interrelationships that a retrospective study has been carried out of the case notes of 54 adults who were referred to the writer for the treatment of psychiatric disorders which had come on following a bereavement by death and in which there was good evidence that the bereavement had been a substantial cause of the disorder. The study has all the disadvantages of retrospective data, hence it should be regarded as a preliminary rather than a hypothesis-testing study.

Even so, it is worth noting that much of the data was not collected by the writer at all but by the medical students who took the initial case history and who had only the most rudimentary knowledge of psychopathology and had few preconceptions likely to bias their reports.

Patients referred to the Department of Psychiatry at The London

Hospital are normally seen by a final-year medical student who asks questions covering a wide range of topics which include family history, childhood history, personality, and recent life events as well as a detailed account of onset and course of the current symptoms. The student will spend about $1^1/2$ hours obtaining and recording the case history. Other members of the patient's family are invited to attend, and additional information is sought from them. The student reports the findings to the consultant, who will then see the patient in order to ask further questions and develop a plan of management. In most instances (68 per cent in this study) the patient will be seen again and further information added. The result is a detailed case file which contains much information relevant to the issues under consideration.

In order to impose some order on this mass of data for the purposes of this research the writer prepared a check list of 120 variables thought likely to be relevant. The variables included 35 concerning parents and parenting, 30 about the patient's personality (with particular attention to factors reflecting basic trust in self and others), 28 concerning recent life circumstances and events, and 27 current symptoms and problems (with particular attention to pathological grief reactions). The full list of variables is given in the appendix at the end of this chapter.

Each case file was then scrutinized by the writer, who checked all the variables which were mentioned. It will at once be apparent that the quality of these data is very uneven. Some of them are concerned with factual issues (e.g. Qs 1–7, which record the presence or absence of parents at particular ages), but most of the remaining variables are 'soft' – they involved making generalizations from evidence that was often minimal about tendencies, feelings, and behaviour which could not be precisely defined because they were not precisely recorded. Even the broad symptom categories of 'anxiety' and 'depression' lack the precision that might be obtained from the use of systematic instruments such as the Beck Depression Inventory. In the end the measures are no more valid than the notes from which they derive. If we ask 'what does a particular measure actually mean?' the only answer possible is that it means that this particular psychiatrist thought there was evidence in the case notes that this rating was justified. No attempt was made to test the reliability of these measurements (e.g. by asking an independent assessor to inspect the ratings) and it seems likely that if this had been done the inter-rater reliability of many of the ratings would not have been high. Having said that, the fact that many of the findings do make logical sense does suggest that the ratings mean something. The reader will have to judge whether or not the tentative conclusions which are reached here are justified.

The data were analysed by postulating a series of hypotheses concerning the interrelationship of the four categories of variable and testing them out by examination of the data. In this paper we start by looking at the type of bereavement and ask whether or not, in certain circumstances, this may cause morbid grief irrespective of previous vulnerability. We then consider two types of vulnerability, 'learned fear' and 'learned helplessness', which have been proposed as parsimonious explanations for the two most prominent symptoms to follow bereavement: anxiety and depression. The findings suggest that different types of parenting can indeed influence vulnerability and symptom-formation. Attachment theory suggests that the security of early attachments can have an important influence on the development of self-trust and of trust in others. This study examines the relationship between these two aspects of basic trust and the two main patterns of pathological grieving ('excessive grief' and 'avoidance'). We then go on to look at two subtypes of morbid grief ('chronic grief' and 'delayed grief') which are found to reflect two types of bond ('dependence' and 'compulsive self-reliance').

Finally, we look at the special case of morbid grief arising after the death of a parent to whom the attachment in adult life is a continuation of the earlier bonding.

TYPES OF BEREAVEMENT

Table 14.1 Relationship of deceased person to patient and sex of patient

Relationship to patient	Male patient		Female patient		Both
	n	%[a]	n	%[a]	n
Spouse	3	(13)	21	(88)	24
Mother	1	(17)	5	(83)	6
Father	0	(0)	5	(100)	5
Son	0	(0)	2	(100)	2
Daughter	0	(0)	2	(100)	2
Stillbirth	0	(0)	1	(100)	1
Brother (no sister lost)	0	(0)	2	(100)	2
Other	0	(0)	5	(100)	5
Multiple	3	(43)	4	(57)	7
Total	7	(13)	47	(87)	54

Note: [a]Percentages are proportions of right hand column.

The sample comprised 49 women and 7 men with a mean age of 48.4 years (range 14–80). Forty-five per cent had lost a spouse, 20 per cent a parent, 13 per cent had multiple bereavements, and 9 per cent had lost a child (Table 14.1).

These findings are themselves interesting. The preponderance of women is partly a reflection of the fact that women tend to marry men older than themselves and men die at a younger age than women. Hence there are three times as many widows as widowers. But the sex difference is also found following other types of bereavement and this suggests that there may be something about the attachment patterns of women in this society (London, England) that makes them more vulnerable to bereavement.

Although the death of a parent is probably four times as common as the death of a spouse in the population as a whole it is less than half as common in the sample. Even so, it is the second commonest type of bereavement referred to the writer. Other types of death are more rare both in this sample and in the population as a whole.

The mode of death is a factor which, in other studies, has been shown to influence bereavement outcome. Thus sudden, unexpected, and untimely deaths can give rise to severe and protracted grief (Parkes and Weiss 1983; Lundin 1984). It was hypothesized that unexpected deaths together with multiple deaths can cause traumatic bereavements even in individuals who are not already vulnerable for other reasons. In other words the indicators of personal vulnerability (personality variables) mentioned above would be found less often in patients whose psychiatric disorder had followed an unexpected or multiple bereavement than in those whose bereavements were less traumatic. Table 14.2 shows mode of death for the sample studied.

As Bowlby (1973) has pointed out, secure attachments in early childhood can be expected to give rise to a reasonable degree of trust in oneself with a reasonable degree of trust in others. Out of these two components of basic trust arises the confidence with which we attempt to cope with all the stresses of life. It is reasonable to suppose, therefore, that 'self-trust' and 'other-trust' will be important determinants of a person's reaction to bereavement. Lack of either trait is likely to give rise to special problems at times of loss or change when a person's coping capacity is put to the test.

For the purposes of this study any patient with one or more of the personal traits listed under 51 to 57 of the check list (Appendix) was said to be low in 'self-trust', and any patient with one or more of the traits listed under 61 to 75 was said to be low in 'other-trust'.

In Fig. 14.1 the proportion in each of these trust groups who had experienced sudden and/or unexpected bereavements is shown. All of the

Table 14.2 Mode of death

	n	%
Sudden	28	(52)
Intermediate	1	(1.8)
Gradual	24	(44)
Complex	1	(1.8)

Note: In the case of multiple bereavements these figures refer to the most recent. The complex case refers to multiple losses of uncertain timing.

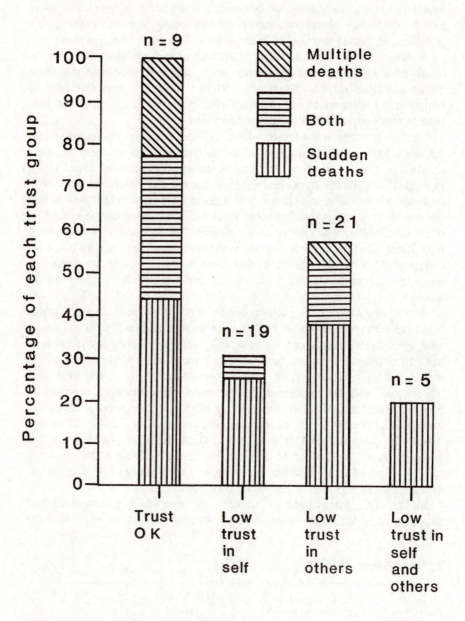

Figure 14.1 Mode of death × basic trust

9 patients who had none of these traits (i.e. who had a reasonable degree of 'self-trust' and 'other-trust') had suffered unexpected or multiple bereavements compared with 42 per cent of those who were lacking in either or both types of basic trust (Chi-squared = 7.85, 1 d.f., $p < 0.01$).

This finding was not anticipated. It not only confirms that unexpected and/or multiple bereavements can undermine people with a reasonable degree of basic trust but it also implies that the measures of trust which were employed in this study do have some validity.

VULNERABILITY AND PARENTING

The next general problem to be considered is the relationship between personal vulnerability and parenting. If these are related it seems likely that those patients who had the largest number of personality problems would also report the largest number of detrimental parental influences.

Figure 14.2 shows that this is, in fact, the case. Those patients who reported two or more negative parental influences had more negative

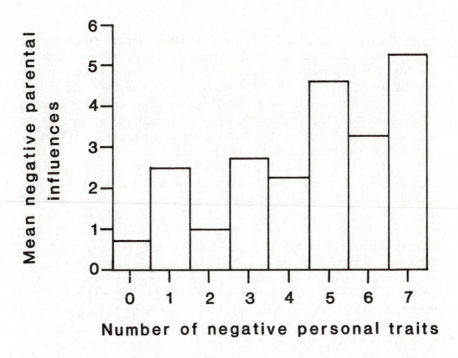

Figure 14.2 Mean negative parental influences (Q1–37) × number of negative personal traits (Q41–75)

personal traits or tendencies than those who had fewer negative influences. This suggests that the parental influences which we are studying do have some relevance but they tell us little about how they affect the pattern of personality development nor how personality affects the pattern of grieving.

ANTECEDENTS OF ANXIETY AND DEPRESSION

At the time of referral the two most prominent symptoms complained of were anxiety and depression. These were of sufficient magnitude to be regarded as symptomatic in 56 and 63 per cent of patients, respectively, with 30 per cent suffering both. (Note that, although strict research criteria for caseness could not be used on these case-note data, anxiety and depression were regarded as 'symptoms' if their intensity, duration, and associated features met the criteria commonly accepted by psychiatrists and formulated in the International Classification of Disease.) Examination of the data gave rise to two hypotheses regarding the origin of these two symptoms: (1) learned fear, (2) learned helplessness.

Learned fear

It was postulated that parents who are themselves worriers, perceiving the world as very dangerous and/or their children as frail, will have children who have similar perceptions of the world and of themselves. It is, after all, essential for survival that the child learn what to fear, and who else can we expect to learn from but our parents? The fact that survival is at stake places these issues high in the order of priorities and may account for the fact that strong emotions are involved and that, once learned, it is hard for these attitudes and expectations to be modified.

To test out this hypothesis a list (Table 14.3) was drawn up of the characteristics of parents thought likely to promote fear in the child. By adding together the number of items checked we can obtain a score of these early influences on the child. Another list (Table 14.4) was drawn up of the personal characteristics of the patient which were thought likely to indicate a tendency to fear as a personality trait. Table 14.5 shows the interaction of these two variables. All of the 10 patients who had experienced three or more of the parental influences listed in Table 14.3 had developed one or more of the personal traits listed in Table 14.4, and 6 of them had three or more of these 'fearful' traits. Among 25 patients whose parents had one or two of these characteristics, over a half had three or more 'fearful traits', compared with a quarter of those whose parents had *no* fear-promoting characteristics. Although these findings do not quite reach statistical significance it seems reasonable to conclude that Table 14.3 does tend to predict Table 14.4. Of particular interest is the finding

Table 14.3 Parental and other predictors of fear in childhood

Question		Number with feature
8	Mother anxious	10
18	Father anxious	5
10	Parental conflict	13
16	Parent alcohol or drug abuser	8
11	Child feared parent would die	6
28	Mother overprotected child	6
31	Parent repeatedly rebuffed or scoffed at child	6
32	Parent repeatedly physically abused child	5
14	Severe external threat (e.g. Nazi persecution)	4
15	Severe illness in child	3
24	Parent used threat of abandonment or suicide to control child	1
26	Parents fearful for child's health or strength	2
29	Parents cling to each other	1
30	Parents tease child	1

Table 14.4 Personality traits reflecting fear

Question		Number with feature
41	Insecure	37
46	Patient a 'worrier'	22
51	Low self-trust, lacked self-confidence, negative self image	22
54	Timid, reluctant to explore	11
52	Separation anxiety, grief-prone	7
53	Clinging, 'dependent'	7
55	Passive, high external locus of control	6
54	Under-achiever	2

Table 14.5 Parental predictors of fear (Table 14.3) × personality traits reflecting fear (Table 14.4)

Number of personality traits	Number of parental predictors		
	0	1–2	3+
0	9	5	0
1–2	6	7	4
3+	5	12	6

Note: Chi-squared = 8.09, 4 d.f., $p < 0.10$

that two-thirds of the 12 patients whose parents were described as 'anxious' described themselves as 'worriers'.

Table 14.6 shows that 82 per cent of those with three or more personal characteristics from Table 14.4 reflecting fear complained of anxiety symptoms after bereavement, whereas this was the case in only 21 per cent

Table 14.6 Personality traits reflecting fear (Table 14.4) × anxiety after
            bereavement

Number of personality traits	Anxiety	No anxiety
0	3	11
1–2	9	9
3+	18	4

Note: Chi-squared = 12.96, 2 d.f., $p < 0.01$

of those who had no such characteristics. In other words, the features of
Table 14.4 are a significant indicator of anxiety as a major symptom after
bereavement.

Finally, in Table 14.7, we can examine the relationships between the
parental influences in Table 14.3 and the complaint of severe anxiety after
bereavement. Despite the numerous other life events and influences which
might contribute to cause anxiety after bereavement, there is a significant
association, with no less than 8 out of the 9 patients who described three or
more parental influences promoting fear going on to complain of severe
anxiety after bereavement.

Learned helplessness

Seligman's theory of 'learned helplessness' found confirmation in this
study. He postulated (1975) that a crucial variable in the psychogenesis of
depression is the individual's belief that he or she cannot influence the
outcome of threatening events. A danger which may be averted will give
rise to anxiety not depression; but one which is believed to be beyond hope
of control will lead to depression and withdrawal.

Brown and Harris's studies (1978) indicate that losses by death in
childhood not only increase vulnerability to depression in later life but even
contribute to shape the kind of depressive symptoms which then ensue.
They conclude (p. 255): 'Loss by death may be related to psychotic-like
(depressive) symptoms because it tends to lead to a general attitude that
one's own efforts are useless; that loss of any kind becomes like death,
irreversible with nothing to be done'.

In the current study the death of a parent before the patient was 17
years old was included in a list of parental influences thought likely to
predispose a person to feelings of helplessness in the face of loss (Table
14.8). Other influences such as teasing (30) and physical abuse (32) have
not been included here since they can, at least in theory, be part of a
consistent system of rewards and punishments. As Seligman points out, it is
not punishment as such which evokes helplessness but lack of consistent
feedback. Likewise, separation as such (5 and 6) has not been seen as a

Table 14.7 Parental predictors of fear (Table 14.3) × anxiety after bereavement

Number of parental predictors	Anxiety	No anxiety
0	7	12
1–2	15	11
3+	8	1

Note: Chi-squared = 6.79, 2 d.f., $p < 0.05$

Table 14.8 Predictors of helplessness in childhood

Question		n
1–4	Death of parent before aged 17	12
21–22	Mother inconsistently available or responsive	9
31	Parent repeatedly rebuffed or scoffed at child	5
26	Parents fearful for child's health or strength	2
17	Parents unknown	2
	One or more of these	23

cause of helplessness, and neither have being unwanted (36) or unloved (37) since they may have the effect that children learn to stand on their own feet from an early age and to become anything but helpless. These speculations may, of course, be quite incorrect, but in the absence of clear evidence it has been thought better to omit them from the list of parental influences predicting helplessness.

Table 14.9 shows that people who developed depression after a bereavement were significantly more likely than others to have experienced the kinds of parental influence in childhood listed in Table 14.8. Because this finding had not been anticipated, only one question on 'helplessness' was included in the list of personality variables thought likely to predict bereavement outcome. In the event, only 2 patients were rated as 'helpless' personalities, and these are obviously too few to allow any conclusions to be drawn regarding the intervening variables between parenting and post-bereavement depression. Harris and Bifulco's research, reported in Chapter 13, provides further evidence for regarding learned helplessness as the intervening variable which predisposes to depression.

INFLUENCE OF BASIC TRUST ON PATTERN OF BEREAVEMENT

The simple designation of bereaved patients as 'depressed' or 'anxious' tells us little about the type of grief which they experienced. In clinical practice a variety of complications in the course of grieving have been recognized, and the more important types have been included among questions 91–

278   Clinical Applications

Table 14.9 Depression after bereavement × predictors of helplessness
(Table 14.8)

	Depression n	No depression n
One or more predictors of helplessness	15	8
None	10	21

Note: Chi-squared with Yates Correction = 5.8, 1 d.f., $p < 0.05$

115. They can be grouped into two main categories: those in which grief is unusually intense and/or prolonged (91–99), and those in which grief is avoided, denied, delayed, or in some other way minimized (101–115 excluding 111 and 114). This second group most often presented with symptoms of depression, alcoholism, and delayed grief. Clinical experience led the writer to expect to find that the types of 'self-trust' and 'other-trust' defined above would be associated with these two patterns of grieving, and this usually proved to be the case. People low on 'self-trust' were likely to cling to others and to develop chronic intense grief after bereavement, and people low on 'other-trust' were likely to withdraw and avoid situations which would evoke grief. Figure 14.3 demonstrates this. Here the proportion in each trust group with 'excessive grief' is shown along with the proportion with 'avoidance'. These overall categories have some value in designating overall tendencies, but they should not be assumed to be mutually exclusive.

It is possible for people to show both 'excessive grief' and 'avoidance' at different times just as it is possible for them to lack basic trust in themselves *and* others. Figure 14.3 shows that, in fact, those who lacked trust in self *and* others were likely to show 'excessive grief' *and* 'avoidance'. Conversely, patients who did not lack trust in themselves or others and who had all suffered traumatic bereavements often showed neither 'excessive grief' nor 'avoidance'. There were, however, 4 of the 9 in this last group who were thought to be 'avoidant'. They showed the numbness and disbelief which has previously been reported following traumatic bereavements (Parkes and Weiss 1983).

Confining attention to the 40 patients who lacked trust in themselves or others (but not both), there was a tendency for those who lacked trust in themselves to suffer excessive grief (not significant), and for those who lacked trust in others to avoid grieving (Chi-squared = 5.27, 1 d.f., $p < 0.05$).

Attempts to find a link between trust and parenting were only partially successful. Figure 14.4 shows that patients who lacked trust in themselves *and* others had more negative parental influences than those who lacked only one of these, and that those who *had* reasonable degrees of trust in

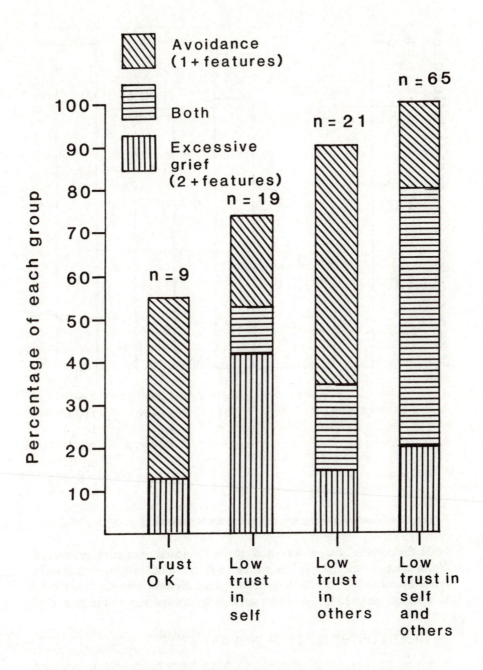

Figure 14.3 Reaction to bereavement × basic trust

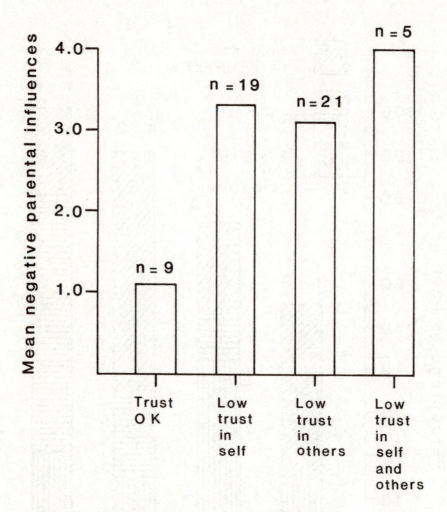

Figure 14.4 Mean negative parental influences × basic trust

both themselves *and* others had fewest negative parental influences. Unfortunately, attempts to link the two sub-types of basic trust to specific types of parenting were not successful, and further research is currently being undertaken to find more sensitive indicators of parental influence.

OTHER DETERMINANTS OF MORBID GRIEF

The patterns of morbid grief which have been prominent in previous studies – chronic grief and delayed grief – occurred in less than half of this sample of bereaved psychiatric patients. These two terms are used to describe subsets of the broader categories of 'excessive grief' and 'avoidance'. 'Chronic grief' was reserved for those patients whose main presenting problem was that of severe and protracted grief. 'Delayed grief', as the title implies, applied only to grief whose onset was delayed beyond the period of a few days which is the normal duration of the 'numbness' which is a part of the typical reaction to a major loss. There were 9 who were said to have developed *chronic grief*. Of these, 7 were people who had also suffered an unexpected or multiple bereavement, and 4 had been thought to have had a spouse who was unusually 'dependent' on them. It is interesting to note the direction of the 'dependency' in this study. There were 8 cases in which the patient was said to have been 'dependent' on the spouse who died, but only one of these had gone on to develop 'chronic grief'.

On the other hand, 4 of the 8 patients whose *spouse* was said to have been 'dependent' on them developed chronic grief. Two of these had experienced separation and severe external danger to their families during the war with subsequent feelings of insecurity and anxiety. The other two had suffered sudden, unexpected, and untimely bereavement. These figures confirm a finding of the writer's 1962 study in which 19 per cent of psychiatric patients with pathological grief were found to have had a spouse who was dependent on them (by comparison with 4 per cent of a group without pathological grief). They also support Bowlby's warning against simplistic thinking about 'dependency' (Bowlby 1982: 228–9). From these studies it would appear that 'dependency' can be a function of a dyad, with the 'weak' partner often contributing an important source of role identity and reassurance of strength to the 'strong' partner.

Although *delayed grief* was infrequent (diagnosed in 11 cases – 20 per cent) it was found in 4 of the 7 patients classed as 'compulsively self-reliant or pseudo-independent' (Q62); here again the link with attachment problems is obvious. The difference between these 'compulsively self-reliant' patients and the 'strong' partners of 'dependent' spouses lies in their apparent detachment. Following bereavement they initially showed little grief, maintaining an image of 'independence' – only with the passage of time did it become more and more difficult for them to maintain the assumption that their loss did not amount to much.

Three other delayed reactions occurred in people whose personalities had been classed as 'passive, high external locus of control' (i.e. half of those identified by Q55). These seem very different from the 'compulsively self-reliant' patients, but both of them can reasonably be regarded as insecure in their attachments.

Although not strictly a morbid grief reaction, *loneliness* can best be considered here. The term 'loneliness' is used in this study to mean a general dislike of being alone rather than a specific pining for a particular person. It is sometimes a cause of great distress and may be the presenting problem among bereaved patients. Loneliness was classed as a problem (Q98) in 18 patients, 12 of whom had either been left alone for the first time (Q130) or had nobody in whom they could confide (Q132). Their mean age was 56, 11 years older than that of the rest of the sample.

REACTIONS TO DEATH OF A PARENT

One group in whom the link between parenting and the pattern of grieving is likely to be particularly close is that of patients whose psychiatric disorder followed the death of a parent. In this study (see Table 14.10) there were 11 such patients, 6 of whom had lost a father and 5 a mother. Ten of them were women and there was only 1 man (who had lost a father). Only 2 were over the age of 50, and their mean age (36) was 15 years younger than that of the rest of the sample. This reflects the fact that parents can be expected to die when their children are still relatively young.

Nearly two-thirds (7) of these patients were said to have been lacking in self-trust prior to bereavement (cf. 39 per cent of the rest of the sample) and problems of clinging and dependency were commoner in this group than the rest. On the other hand, trust in others was seldom a problem, particularly in the 5 who had lost a mother. These results do not approach statistical significance and should, therefore, be interpreted with caution.

All who had lost a parent had experienced one or more of the negative parental influences listed (Q1–37) but in most respects these did not differ from the types of influence found in other patients. There was, however, a greater tendency for this group to report conflicts between their parents, and 4 of the 5 patients who did this (plus 1 other whose parent's marriage had not been reported as conflicted) had a form of grief following the death of the parent which was 'conflicted'.

The term 'conflicted grief' was used in the Harvard Bereavement Study

Table 14.10 Death of a parent × other deaths

| Question | Feature | Parent died | | Other | |
		n	%	n	%
145	Patient's sex male	1	9	6	14
146	Patient's age under 50	9	82	19	44
51–57	Low self-trust	7	64	17	39
53	Clinging/dependent	4	36	3	7
61–75	Low other-trust	4[a]	36	2	51
21–37	No negative parental influences	0	0	6	14
10	Parental conflict	5	45	8	19
103	Conflicted grief	5	45	2	4
120	Conflict in own marriage	5	45	10	23

Note: [a] All had lost a father.

(Parkes and Weiss 1983) to describe a syndrome which was found among bereaved spouses who admitted conflict with their spouses. In these widows and widowers, grief was often delayed but was then complicated by intense guilt and anger.

In the current study 7 patients were thought to have suffered grief reactions which had been complicated by their ambivalence towards the dead person (i.e. 'conflicted grief') but, as we have seen, the majority of these reactions followed the death of a parent (Chi-squared = 9.56, 1 d.f., $p < 0.01$).

One might have thought that an effect of marital conflicts between parents would be to evoke in the child distrust of others rather than distrust of the self, but this was not the case and those patients who had lost a mother were likely to have clung to her in an insecure way and to have lacked confidence in themselves rather than in others. Any ambivalence in the relationship seems to have been expressed as clinging, although some of it may have been projected. Thus, it is interesting to note that nearly a half (5) of the patients who had lost a parent had major conflicts in their own marriages.

Although no firm conclusions can be drawn from observations on so small a sample these figures do lend support to the contention that problems in relating to parents sometimes give rise to psychiatric problems after the death of that parent and that conflicts between parents, which may themselves be a consequence of insecure attachments, subsequently predispose their children, when adult, to make insecure bonds.

TREATMENT AND OUTCOME

In view of the large part which personality and childhood influences played in the psychiatric disorders of these patients, one might have expected that treatment would be difficult and the prognosis poor but, in fact, this was seldom the case. Table 14.11 shows that 72 per cent of these patients were seen less than six times, and over a half required only one or two interviews.

Estimates of outcome were not always easy to make, and in 24 patients,

Table 14.11 Number of interviews

	n	%
1	17	32
2	12	23
3–15	9	17
6–10	8	15
11+	7	13
Not recorded	1	–

Table 14.12 Outcome at conclusion of therapy

	n	%
Worse	0	0
Slightly worse	0	0
Unchanged	4	13
Better	18	60
Much better	8	27
Not known	24	–

17 of whom were seen only once, it is not possible to say whether or not the patient had benefited from therapy. Most of the remainder were thought to be better at the end of therapy and there was none who was worse.

In most cases a short-term form of psychotherapy was adopted. When it was a child who had died, both surviving parents were normally seen together but in most other cases individual therapy was undertaken. The aim was to establish a positive therapeutic alliance in which the patient would feel secure enough to face the painful implications of the death and to review his or her world model. Initial interviews were up to 2 hours in duration and were often of therapeutic value. The fact that nearly a third of patients did not return a second time is thought likely to indicate that they saw no need to.

Positive reassurance was given about the normality of grieving, and psychiatric diagnoses were seldom communicated to the patient. Emphasis was placed on the possibility of a positive outcome to grieving which was seen as a challenge rather than an illness or defeat. By encouraging the patient to talk about the worst aspects of the loss and accepting in an uncritical way the full range of negative affects which then arose an attempt was made to render the extraordinary ordinary and to create an expectation of recovery.

Proactive methods were used to increase self-trust and to overcome distrust of others. This involved a paternalistic approach in which the therapist deliberately acted as a surrogate 'parent', providing warmth, regard, confidence, and support to the bereaved patient as described by Bowlby (1977). The response was usually rapid and rewarding, with patients growing in confidence and trust despite the continuation of painful grieving.

Those patients who required more than a few interviews could be expected to find the ending of therapy difficult, and here it was important to plan this well in advance so that the patient had time to anticipate the loss of another parent figure, the therapist, and to grieve while support was still forthcoming. In most instances the therapist remained open to further consultation after the end of therapy. In this way the 'parent figure' remained available in much the same way that parents remain available to their children after childhood's end.

ILLUSTRATIVE EXAMPLE

Examples of the major findings described above are easily found, but the editing which would have been necessary to prevent them from breaking the flow of the argument if included in the main body of the text would have over-simplified and distorted clinical findings which are always complex.

To the writer one of the most interesting findings of the research is the overlap between categories which had previously been regarded as mutually exclusive. 'Clinging' and 'avoidance' overlap as do 'dependence' and 'independence' (or 'pseudo-independence' as some would call it). It follows that any attempt to force individual cases into the particular categories beloved by epidemiologists will probably prove unsatisfactory. On the other hand it is possible to illustrate, within one case history, many of the links which our research has demonstrated between parenting, personality development, and the outcome of bereavement.

Florence U. at the age of 41 lost her elderly father and mother within 8 months of each other. Following her mother's death she was overwhelmed with severe grief, and 2 days later she had the first of a series of epileptic fits which proved difficult to control. When seen by the writer 9 months later, she was still pining for her mother whom she would frequently 'see' among the elderly patients on the geriatric ward where she worked as a ward maid. She was finding it hard to express her grief although her parents were 'on my mind all of the time'. She had lost confidence in herself and was extremely anxious and tense, sleeping badly and inclined to panic. She had had no previous psychiatric problems.

As Owen *et al.* (1982) have pointed out, severe grief following the death of an 80-year-old parent is unusual, and requires explanation. In Florence's case there was no shortage of factors each of which seems to have contributed to her reaction to this double bereavement. The roots of her insecurity could be found in her childhood. She was the seventh of eight children of a warehouseman and his wife. Neither parent had been able to show affection or to hug or cuddle her, yet they did seem to care about her and she described them both as over-protective and inclined to worry excessively about her health and safety.

Her mother was insecure, worried, and inconsistent in her care of her child, sometimes responding and at other times ignoring her needs for affection and attention. Florence saw herself as 'very close' to her father but, although he was a placid man his relationship with his wife was unhappy and they eventually divorced when Florence was 8 years of age. She had remained with her mother thereafter.

In these circumstances it is hardly surprising that Florence grew up an insecure and anxious child who had little confidence in herself or others. She sees herself as having been a helpless, timid, and passive child who was easily upset by separation from her parents. People regarded her as delicate and fragile yet she was always looking after others.

In large families the younger children are often cared for by the older, yet in this family the children seem to have been in opposition, each competing with the others for the limited attention and affection that was available. Florence became a 'loner' and 'stubborn', avoiding others and finding it hard to ask for help despite her difficulty in coping with everyday problems. She was always near the bottom of her class at school and was regarded by her teachers as an under-achiever.

After her parents' divorce the patient resented having to live with mother, whom she saw as 'interfering' in her life. She was often in tears, particularly after visiting her father.

Leaving school at the age of 15 with no qualifications she worked in a factory until she married at 25 to manage a public house with her husband. This seems to have been the happiest period of her life. She describes her marital relationship as 'very close' and admits that she has always been 'dependent' on her husband and intolerant of any separation from him. One gets the impression of him as an extravert beside whom she appears as a 'mouse'. He is self-confident and came across to the writer as somewhat overwhelming. He admitted that he allows his wife to rely on him too much and seemed to enjoy being the 'superman' of the family.

This relationship, while superficially successful and meeting the needs of both partners, seems to have perpetuated Florence's image of herself as frail. They have three children ranging in age from 9 to 13. The eldest, a girl, is 'very bright' and doing well, but the two sons have problems: one resembles his mother in being 'highly strung' and, with several other members of his mother's family, suffers from epilepsy; the younger is uncontrolled and 'a tearaway'. Thus it would seem that the problems arising out of insecure attachments may well be affecting yet another generation.

In July 1986 her father died suddenly and unexpectedly of a 'heart attack'. This had occurred shortly after his 80th birthday when the children had given him a surprise party. Florence had not attended this, giving the excuse that she could not afford the fare, but in fact it was the tensions between her and several siblings whom she sees as hostile which caused her to avoid an occasion which she expected to be emotionally overwhelming. She subsequently felt very guilty that she had not taken this opportunity to express her appreciation of her father. She dealt with her grief by keeping busy, remained at work and devoted herself to her family.

Six months later another disagreement arose with her sisters who alleged that she was neglecting her part in the care of her mother who was suffering from the effects of several strokes. Two months after this her mother died. It would seem that this was the last straw which caused the defences which had enabled her to cope after her father's death to break down.

She was seen only twice. Initially she told the medical student who took her history that she could not remember her childhood and she was clearly attempting to avoid thinking about the distressing circumstances of her life. Before long, however, she was pouring out the story related above and expressing a great deal of ambivalence and guilt about both of her parents. Subsequently she felt very much better.

Her husband was inclined to blame her eldest sister for upsetting her, but it was important to point out to him that he did not need to over-protect her and the patient was surprised and proud to acknowledge that she is tougher than she seems.

As her confidence improved after the first visit her epilepsy was brought under control, and it was Florence who suggested at the end of her second visit that, since she had to travel a long way to visit the hospital, these visits could now be discontinued. She was now much less preoccupied with thoughts of her mother and was sleeping well.

This case illustrates well the interweaving of cause and effect which, taken together, provide an adequate explanation for the psychiatric problems which can follow bereavement. It also reminds us that in focusing on the influence of parenting on personality development we are omitting another dimension, that of the influence of siblings (who may themselves be influenced by parenting). The value of a study such as this which looks at statistical association as well as description is to obtain some idea of the magnitude of several influences, not a total, simplistic explanation of all of them.

SUMMARY AND CONCLUSION

It would seem, from the evidence presented in this chapter, that the majority of those who seek help from the writer after bereavement have some prior reason to be regarded as vulnerable. The exceptions had all suffered sudden and/or multiple losses.

Vulnerability factors included learned fear, learned helplessness, lack of trust in oneself, lack of trust in others, having a partner who is seen as 'dependent', being compulsively self-reliant, and being elderly and isolated. These factors seldom occur in isolation and they interact with each other to influence the pattern of reaction to bereavement. But the different types of influence can be teased out and there are indications from this study of distinct sequences from particular types of parenting to particular types of reaction to bereavement in adult life.

Although the potential number of such interactions is infinite the following have emerged as causal sequences worthy of further study.

1   Anxious and conflicted parents predispose their children to become insecure and very anxious after bereavement.
2   Absent or rejecting parents predispose their children to depression after bereavement in adult life.
3   Negative parental influences interfere with the development of trust in self and/or others. Low 'self-trust' predisposes to 'excessive grief' after bereavement and leaves the person unusually vulnerable to the death of a parent. Low 'other-trust' predisposes to a tendency to avoid others and to minimize grieving after bereavement.
4   Conflicts between parents in childhood increase the risk of marital conflicts when the children marry, and render them vulnerable to 'conflicted grief' when their parents die.

The following adult bonding patterns cannot, at this time, be tied to particular styles of parenting but each seems to give rise to a specific response to bereavement.

5   Relationships in which one partner relies on another for reassurance of independence and strength may give rise to 'chronic grief' when the overtly 'dependent' partner dies.
6   Persons who are 'compulsively' self-reliant are likely to suffer 'delayed grief' after bereavement.
7   Social isolation predisposes to loneliness after the loss of a partner.

Only the last of these factors is likely to be more frequent in women than in men, and this study has not explained the relative rarity of referrals of men to this clinic. Nor does it prove that this reflects a true difference between the sexes in their vulnerability to morbid grief. It may, rather, reflect the reluctance of bereaved men to accept the social implications of referral to a psychiatrist.

We have no way of knowing the extent to which these results may have been influenced by retrospective bias. This is, perhaps, most likely to be the case in anxious patients whose anxiety may prompt them to recall their parents or themselves in childhood as more anxious than they really were. Even so, the magnitude and diversity of the influences is such that this seems unlikely to explain the whole association between present state and previous influences. The findings of this study strongly suggest that the patterns of attachment formed in childhood colour the bonds of adult life and that these, in turn, influence the pattern of bereavement in distinctive and logically comprehensible ways.

Further research is being conducted to expand and confirm these findings and to eliminate the chance that they result from observer bias.

© Colin Murray Parkes

REFERENCES

Bowlby, J. (1973) 'Self-reliance and some conditions that promote it', in R.G. Gosling (ed.) *Support Innovation and Autonomy*, London: Tavistock.
—— (1977) 'The making and breaking of affectional bonds II: Some principles of psychotherapy', *British Journal of Psychiatry* 130: 421–31.
—— (1982) *Attachment and Loss*, vol. 1: *Attachment* (2nd ed), London: Hogarth.
Brown, G.W.S. and Harris, T. (1978) *Social Origins of Depression: A Study of Psychiatric Disorder in Women*, London: Tavistock.
Lundin T. (1984) 'Morbidity following sudden and unexpected bereavement', *British Journal of Psychiatry* 144: 848.
Owen, G., Fulton, R., and Markusen, E. (1982) 'Death at a distance: a study of family survivors', *Omega* 13: 191–225.
Parkes, C.M. (1962) 'Reactions to bereavement', MD Thesis, University of London.
Parkes, C.M. and Weiss, R.S. (1983) *Recovery from Bereavement*, New York: Basic Books, and London: Harper & Row.
Sable, P. (1989) 'Attachment, anxiety and loss of a husband', *American Journal of Orthopsychiatry* 59(4): 550–6.
Seligman, M.E.P. (1975) *Helplessness: On Depression, Development and Death*, San Francisco: Freeman.

APPENDIX: CHECK LIST

(A) Parental and other influences

		n	%
1	Mother died, patient aged 1–5	1	1.9
2	Mother died, patient aged 6–10	1	1.9
3	Mother died, patient aged 11–16	2	3.7
4	Father died, patient aged 0–16	8	15
5	Separated from mother > 1 month aged 0–5	4	7.4
6	Separated from mother > 1 month aged 6–16	9	17
7	Separated from father > 6 months aged 0–16	11	20
8	Mother excessively anxious	10	18
9	Mother excessively depressed	1	1.9
10	Parental conflict	13	24
11	Child feared parent would die or be killed	6	11
12	Only child for > 5 years	3	5.5
13	Low rank (4th or more) in large family	9	17
14	Severe external threat (e.g. Nazi persecution)	4	7.4

		n	%
15	Severe illness in child	3	5.7
16	Parent abused alcohol or drugs	8	15
17	Parents unknown	2	3.7
18	Father excessively anxious	5	9.2
21	Mother inconsistently available	6	11
22	Mother inconsistently responsive	7	13
23	Several brief separations	3	5.5
24	Parent(s) used threat of abandonment and/or suicide to control child	1	1.9
25	Parent(s) discouraged exploration/autonomy	0	0
26	Parent(s) fearful for child's health/strength	2	3.7
27	Parent(s) cling to child	5	9.3
28	Mother overprotective of child	6	11
29	Parents cling to each other	1	1.9
30	Parent(s) tease child	1	1.9
31	Parent(s) repeatedly rebuff or scoff at child	6	11
32	Parent(s) repeatedly physically abuse child	5	9.3
33	Parent(s) repeatedly sexually abuse child	0	0
34	Parent(s) perceives child as a powerful threat	0	0
35	Prolonged institutional care	3	5.5
36	Unwanted child	3	5.5
37	Parent(s) did not express affection	12	22

(B) Early personal traits

		n	%
41	Insecure	37	69
42	Depressive	3	5.5
43	Unhappy	12	22
44	Under-achiever	2	3.7
45	Ambivalent relationships	7	13
46	Patient a 'worrier'	22	41
47	Strong drive to be caregiver	5	93
51	Low self-trust, lacked confidence, negative self-image	22	41
52	Separation-anxiety high, grief prone	7	13
53	Clinging, dependent	7	13
54	Reluctant to explore, timid	11	20
55	Passive, high external locus of control	6	11
56	Helpless	2	3.7
57	Sweetly charming, appealing, childish	1	1.9
58	Deformity or other organ inferiority	3	5.5
61	Low trust of others	10	18
62	Compulsive self-reliance, pseudo-independent	7	13

		n	%
63	Loner self-isolating, avoids others	11	20
64	Unable or reluctant to seek help	3	5.5
65	Emotionally insulated, ungiving, unresponsive	7	13
66	Suspicious, paranoid, blaming others	1	1.9
67	Bad-tempered, hostile, rebellious	1	1.9
68	Treats others as things, uses people	0	0
69	Persistent delinquency, antisocial	2	3.7
70	High internal locus of control, controlling, 'bossy'	5	9.3
71	Serious suicidal risk	1	1.9
72	Absence of fantasy play about people	0	0
73	Intolerant of closeness to one or more others	6	11
74	Never cried	1	1.9
75	Stubborn	2	3.7

(C) Current symptoms and syndromes

		n	%
81	Depression	34	63
82	Anxiety	30	56
83	Physical concomitants of above	26	48
84	Uses drugs or alcohol to control distress	13	24
85	Recurrent horrific or panoramic memories or nightmares	3	5.5
91	Chronic grief	9	17
92	Panic state	12	22
93	Parasuicide, suicidal threat (non-serious)	4	7.4
94	Doubts own capacity to cope, low self-trust	22	41
95	Dependent, help-seeking	8	15
96	Clinging to familiar others	6	11
97	Seen as immature or childish	7	3.7
98	Loneliness a problem	18	33
99	Socially isolated (because of self-perception of inadequacy)	9	17
101	Delayed or avoided grief	11	20
102	Psychosomatic disorders (other than No. 83)	9	17
103	Conflicted grief	7	13
104	Resists help-seeking	2	3.7
105	Denies illness	2	3.7
106	Denies negative feelings	2	3.7
107	Unable to show affection	5	9.3
108	Quarrelsome, hostile, paranoid or aggressive personality	3	5.6
109	Unfeeling, shut-off, detached, schizoid	1	1.9
110	Bad-tempered	10	19

		n	%
111	Socially isolated (because of perceived inadequacy of others)	0	0
112	Fills life with activities/workaholic	3	5.6
113	Cannot cry	5	9.3
114	Serious suicide attempt or threat	0	0
115	Guilt at lack of love	3	5.6

(D) Recent life circumstances and events

		n	%
120	Marital conflict (or conflict with partner)	15	28
121	Over 40 and no children	5	9.3
122	Immigrant	7	13
123	Unexpected bereavement	24	44
124	Thought culpable for death or suffering of deceased	0	0
125	Bereavement by murder	0	0
126	Bereavement by suicide	1	1.9
127	More than one major loss	12	22
128	Illness threatening life	5	9.3
129	Close relative thought to have died of grief	1	1.9
130	Left alone for the first time	10	19
131	No occupation outside home	16	30
132	No confidante	11	20
133	Formerly dependent on deceased	8	15
134	Other unusual closeness to deceased	18	33
135	Family encourage florid expression of sentiment	0	0
136	Married 'parent' substitute	1	1.7
140	Never married and over 30	2	3.7
141	Loss of mobility	1	1.9
142	Other disability	2	3.7
143	Deceased dependent on patient	8	15
144	Pressure from family to repress feelings	3	5.4
145	Sex male	7	13
146	Age in years (Mean 48.4 years)		
147	Cause of death: Cancer	17	31
	Coronary thrombosis	8	15
	Accident	6	11
	Suicide	1	1.9
	Murder	0	0
	Stillbirth	1	1.9
	Other disease	16	30
	Not known	5	9.3

Postscript

John Bowlby

Nothing can give a scientist more lasting pleasure than to see his ideas utilized in well-executed and productive research. For that reason this collection of papers constitutes a wonderful present on my eightieth birthday, for which I am deeply grateful. Originating in a conference well-titled 'Fruits of Attachment Theory', it is testimony to the light that can be thrown on personality development and psychopathology when they are studied in an ethological perspective. Once we postulate the presence within the organism of an attachment behavioural system regarded as the product of evolution and as having protection as its biological function, many of the puzzles that have perplexed students of human relationships are found to be soluble. No longer are the desire for food or for sexual satisfaction regarded as the sole engines of personal intimacy. Instead, an urge to keep proximity or accessibility to someone seen as stronger or wiser, and who if responsive is deeply loved, comes to be recognized as an integral part of human nature and as having a vital role to play in life. Not only does its effective operation bring with it a strong feeling of security and contentment, but its temporary or long-term frustration causes acute or chronic anxiety and discontent. When seen in this light, the urge to keep proximity is to be respected, valued, and nurtured as making for potential strength, instead of being looked down upon, as so often hitherto, as a sign of inherent weakness. This radical shift in valuation, with its far-reaching influence on how we perceive and treat other people, especially those whose attachment needs have been and still are unmet, is, I believe, the single most important consequence of the change of conceptual framework.

During the course of time, the biologically given strategy of attachment in the young has evolved in parallel with the complementary parental strategy of responsive caregiving – the one presumes the other. For any systems to work together in harmony, efficient communication must exist between them, and for none more so than for the coupled systems of child and parent. It is therefore especially welcome that the field of communication has become a principal focus of attachment research. Already the findings are of the highest clinical interest.

It was a great misfortune for psychoanalysis that when Freud was for-mulating his ideas on metapsychology during the early years of this century, concepts of information and communication were unknown to science. Instead, therefore, of employing these eminently suitable concepts, he felt constrained to cast his theory in terms of energies and forces which, always ill-fitting, have ever since distorted and obstructed the progress of psychoanalytic theorizing and have, moreover, isolated it from other sciences. The fact, of course, is that, with defensive process as a central concept of psychoanalysis, the data requiring explanation are concerned almost entirely with information and its organization, and especially with the ways in which it is, or is not, communicated both within a person's own mind and between him and others. Indeed, the principal criterion of mental health and ill-health, inherent in all psychoanalytic thinking, is the extent to which communications within an individual personality are open or closed, and, if open, are clear and coherent or else opaque and contradictory.

One of the many unfortunate effects of the old theoretical model has been to obscure the fact that the principal function of emotion is one of communication – namely, the communication, both to the self and to others, of the current motivational state of the individual. Although, being non-verbal, emotional expression cannot refer to times past or times to come, as a system of communication about the present it has the ad-vantages of being instantly decoded and so of making immediate impact. Here again the concern of a psychoanalyst is not only with the extent to which a patient feels free to express his emotions openly, but with the prior questions of whether he knows what his feelings are and what has aroused them. These are issues of intra-psychic communication.

A well-known observation, which in the world of psychotherapy has perhaps been taken too much for granted without its theoretical impli-cations being given sufficient attention, is the constant interaction of, on the one hand, the patterns of communication, verbal and non-verbal, that are operating within an individual's mind and, on the other, the patterns of communication that obtain between him and those whom he feels he can trust. The more complete the information that a person is able to communicate to someone he trusts the more he himself becomes able to dwell on it, to understand it and to see its implications – a process well illustrated by the adage, 'How can I know what I think until I hear what I say?' Conversely, the more adequately a person can process information on his own the more capable will he be to communicate it to some other person. A key word here is trust. Without trust that the confidant will understand and respond helpfully, communication between self and other is blocked, with a corresponding blockage placed on intra-psychic com-munication.

Traditionally, psychoanalytic theory has tended to focus attention on these intra-psychic blockages, the array of defensive processes that result in a person's being unable to retrieve memories, to be unable to express emotion, to be unaware of how he is feeling and why, and that are responsible for his entertaining ideas about other people that are clearly mistaken. The reason, of course, is that the people who seek our help are, almost by definition, afflicted by such intra-psychic blockages, which, from the first, manifest themselves as blocks in communicating with the therapist; and it is towards helping a patient remove those blocks that our efforts are directed. Much less attention has been given to the circumstances which have led to the development of such intra-psychic blockages in the first place. The reason for that, of course, is that psychoanalytic theorizing has been built almost exclusively on data obtained during therapy and, until recently, has had no relevant normative data to draw upon.

It is here that the research tradition initiated by Mary Ainsworth is proving so immensely valuable. Very early in her work she was struck by the high degree of sensitivity to infant signals characteristic of mothers whose children at 12 months were securely attached, compared with the low degree of sensitivity of mothers of children showing anxious attachment. Mothers with secure children had from early days been attentive to the emotional signals of their infants and had responded to them in ways that reduced distress or discontent and increased happiness, in contrast to mothers of insecurely attached infants who were either not attentive to their infants' signals or did not respond with understanding. What subsequent work by the Grossmanns and other researchers has emphasized is that an infant's communication patterns develop, or fail to develop, in parallel with those of his mother. Whereas by 12 months a secure infant is in open two-way communication with his mother by means of gesture and expression which each partner interprets correctly, an insecure infant is not. Instead of turning to his mother to discover whether or not it is safe to approach and explore the toys and the visitor, and to indicate to her how he is feeling in the strange and changing situation, and how he would like her to respond, he tends to keep himself to himself, or else to give contradictory signals. Moreover, as the longitudinal studies conducted respectively by Mary Main in California and the Grossmanns in Bavaria show, these two-way patterns of communication tend to persist. Thus, at 6 years of age, mother–child pairs who were communicating freely and effectively at 12 months are continuing to do so, in contrast to the limited and inadequate communication patterns that are found to be still characteristic of pairs in which the child was earlier assessed as insecurely attached.

Thus what is happening during these early years is that the pattern of communication that a child adopts towards his mother comes to match the pattern of communication that she has been adopting towards him.

Furthermore, from the findings stemming from Mary Main's Adult Attachment Interview, it seems clear that the pattern of communication a mother adopts towards her infant and young child is modelled on the pattern characteristic of her own intra-psychic communications. Open and coherent intra-psychic communication in a mother is associated with open and coherent two-way communication with her child, and vice versa. The same holds in reverse, as is shown by the results of the Separation Anxiety Test at 6 years of age and by the interviewing of these children at the age of 10. A child who has experienced open and coherent communication with his mother develops a pattern of communication within his own mind which is equally open and coherent, and the same holds for faulty patterns.

Findings with far-reaching implications for psychopathology and psychotherapy are the very different ways in which secure and insecure children behave when frustrated, frightened or distressed. Thus, already at 12 months, whereas every infant classified as secure was observed by the Grossmanns to be in direct communication with his mother, not only when he was content but also when he was distressed, the infants classified as insecure–avoidant, when they did engage in direct communication, did so only when they were content. The more distressed they became the less they communicated. In a similar way, when during interview at the age of 10 these children were asked how they behaved when sad, afraid or angry, whereas the secure children said they were likely to turn to parents or to others for comfort and help, the insecure–avoidant children said they were more likely to keep their feelings to themselves – no doubt because they had learned from bitter experience that, were they to turn to a parent, they would receive, not sympathy, but a dusty answer.

The far-reaching implication of these findings for clinicians can hardly be exaggerated. For, as we know from the work of Colin Parkes and of George Brown and Tirril Harris, it is precisely in conditions of adversity, which evoke feelings of anger, fear and sadness, either overt and expressed or potential and unexpressed, that breakdowns of mental functioning are likely to occur. And it is precisely on these occasions that the ability or inability to express thoughts and feelings to others, and to seek their comfort and help, proves such a crucial variable. Those who during their childhood have met, when in conditions of adversity, with an under-standing response will hope for something similar in the present crisis, whereas those who have met with rebuff and contempt during childhood will expect the same when they are distressed during adult life. All too often these simple truths, long known to many a sensitive therapist, have been obscured by misleading theory.

Perhaps in conclusion I may be allowed to quote a passage in a chapter on infant–parent psychotherapy by Alicia Lieberman who, having been a student of Mary Ainsworth, went to San Francisco to work with Selma Fraiburg, and who has recently conducted a well-designed and successful project to test the efficacy of her therapeutic technique based explicitly on attachment theory. A major contribution of the theory, she reports, is that it provides 'a language in which the phenomenology of attachment experiences is given full legitimacy. This is often a new experience for a parent, who is accustomed to having her longing for protection and security ignored, dismissed or ridiculed as expressions of dependency or character-ological weakness. In raising attachment to the status of a primary moti-vational system with its own inner workings and its own interface with other motivational systems, attachment theory has enabled the clinician to attend to attachment experiences in their own right and not as displace-ments or derivatives of other motives. The language of feeling protected or unprotected, helpless or helped, valued or dismissed, anxious or secure in a variety of relationships and circumstances has powerful emotional reso-nances for the troubled parent of a troubled infant ... the concepts of attachment theory have provided the field with a unique magnifying glass for exploring and understanding early anxieties and fears as the legitimate responses of a young child to real experiences of emotional and physical maltreatment, separation and loss' (Lieberman in press).

© 1991 John Bowlby

EDITORS' NOTE

John Bowlby corrected the proofs of this Postscript in his summer retreat on the Isle of Skye. Shortly afterwards he died peacefully following the second of two strokes, which were a few days apart. He was buried in Skye on a hill overlooking the sea.

This book stands as a testimony to his life's work and as an expression of the regard in which he was held.

REFERENCE

Lieberman, A.F. (in press) 'Attachment theory and infant–parent psychotherapy: some conceptual, clinical and research considerations', in D. Cicchetti and S. Toth (eds) *Rochester Symposium on Developmental Psychopathology, vol. 3,* Hillsdale, N.J.: Erlbaum.

Name index

Ainsworth, Leonard 13, 21
Ainsworth, Mary D. Salter 1, 3, 9,
    12–17, 19, 21–7, 33–49, 52–3,
    59–60, 71, 94, 95–7, 117, 127, 141,
    145, 153, 160–82, 187–8, 207, 234,
    295
Alford, John 10
Ambrose, Tony 15
Appell, Genevieve 22

Bartlett, F.C. 154
Bateson, G. 189
Bell, John 200
Bell, S.M. 25, 234
Bifulco, Antonia 234, 277
Binet, A. 134
Bion, Wilfred 11
Birtchnell, J. 243
Blatz, William 12–13, 23
Blehar, M.C. 25, 117
Blood, R. 72
Boston, Mary 15, 192
Bowlby, John 1, 4, 5, 9–12, 14–26,
    27–8, 33, 36–8, 52–3, 56, 61–2, 66,
    77–9, 93–6, 100, 103–4, 110, 131–2,
    136–8, 162, 181, 187–8, 191, 194,
    197, 199–200, 206–7, 209, 235,
    240–53, 256, 258, 261, 271, 281,
    284, 293–7
Boyd, R. 55
Braine, M.D.S. 135
Bransford, J.D. 134
Bretherton, Inge 2, 9–28, 44, 60, 62,
    100, 131, 201
Brown, A.L. 134
Brown, G.W.S. 4, 82–3, 238, 276,
    296
Buddin, B.J. 136

Bundscherer, B. 103
Byng-Hall, John 4, 199–213
Byrne, D.G. 70

Cain, A.C. 137–8
Campione, J.C. 134
Caspi, A. 57
Cassidy, J. 94–5, 101–3, 107, 203
Craik, K. 130, 131
Crittenden, P.M. 40
Crowell, J. 141

David, Miriam 22
Deane, K.E. 26–7
DeMoss 163
Dicks, Henry 11
Duncan-Jones, P. 70
Durbin, Evan 11

Eichberg, Carolyn 3, 36, 46, 160–82
Elder, G.H. 57
Emde, R.N. 59

Fairbairn, W.R.D. 11, 25, 27
Fast, I. 137–8
Feldman, S. 141
Ferrara, R.A. 134
Fischer, K.W. 136
Flavell, E.R. 138
Flavell, J.H. 134–5, 138
Fraiberg, S. 194–5, 197, 296–7
Freud, Anna 14, 18, 20
Freud, Sigmund 12, 19, 196, 197, 294
Fulton, R. 285

George, C. 106, 141, 160
Gewirtz, Jack 22
Goldwyn, R. 160

Subject index

Note: Page references in italics indicate tables and figures.

abuse: sexual 163, 180, 211
accommodation 230
adolescence: and age peers 34;
loneliness in 71–2; and relinquishing
of attachment 2, 36, 68, 71
Adult Attachment Interview 26, 106–7,
141–5, 147, 153, 203; and
classification 95, 107, 128–9,
139–40, 160; and communication
295–6; and disoriented infant 160–2,
164–5, 180, 259; and emotional
schemata 220
adults: attachment between 27, 67;
attachment patterns 127–8, 153–4;
child–parent attachment 36–7,
67–75, 106–7, 127–9, 139, 141–5;
classification of attachment 26, 95,
107, 142–4, 154 n.3, 160–2; *see*
parents
affect, child 122–4
affect, maternal: and attachment
patterns 119–22; coding 117–18,
121–2; dysregulation 115, 121–2,
125
affection: inappropriate 120;
stress-related 120–1, 123, 124; *see
also* bonds, affectional
age: and difference in attachment 118;
and parental loss 163, 165, 170, 179,
180–1, 240–1
aggression 11, 20, 24, 101, 104
agoraphobia: abnormal attachment
behavior 4, 216–17; development
217–19, 223–7; and emotional
schemata 219–21; psychotherapy
220, 221–2, 227–30; self-schemata
219, 222–3, 224, 228–30
ambiguity, tolerance of 94–5, 103
ambivalence: and bereavement 83, 242,
283; and depression 245–7, 250–1,
262; and insecure attachment 102,
105, 108, 109, 127, 137, 141, 143–4,
179; and strange situation 24, 140,
162
anger 79; infant 24, 188; maternal
123–4; parental 205–6
anxiety: in agoraphobia 217–18, 222–3,
225–6, 227–8; and bereavement 270,
274–7, 288; in children of depressed
mothers 122, 125, 193; maternal
122–4, 192; *see also* separation
anxiety
appearance–reality conflict 127, 128–9,
134–5, 136, 138–9, 145, 152
approach–avoidance conflict 192–5,
207, 209–10
assertion: of child 79, 87
assessment: and cultural difference
59–61
assimilation 230
Attachment (Bowlby) 20, 52
attachment, individual differences 9, 22,
23–7, 34, 48, 93–4, 108–9; as
organizational construct 25, 93–110;
and specificity 66; withdrawal 2,
71–2
attachment, insecure: and adult
attachment 110, 127, 132, 143;
causes 3, 87, 137; and depressed
mothers 3, 118, 119–22, 125; effects